D1176043

In September 1666 the Great Fire destroyed four-fifths of the ancient City of London within three days. All that had been familiar, settled, *known*, was suddenly and entirely swept away. Londoners faced an emptiness that was not only physical but also historical, social, financial, and conceptual. *The Literary and Cultural Spaces of Restoration London* is the first study to situate the literature of Restoration and early Augustan England within the historical and cultural contexts of the rebuilding of London after the Great Fire. Cynthia Wall reads the marked topographical specificity of plays, poems, and novels as part of a wider cultural network of responses to changing perceptions of urban space, and she shows how the literatures of the period – along with the technologies of surveying, mapping, rebuilding, and official redescribing the city – attempt to reinvest the city with comprehensible meaning and create new spaces for new genres.

Cynthia Wall is Assistant Professor at the University of Virginia. She is editor of the Bedford Cultural Contexts edition of Alexander Pope's *The Rape of the Lock*, and has published essays on Defoe, Pope, and Lady Mary Wortley Montagu, and the gendering of architectural space in eighteenth-century literature.

THE LITERARY
AND CULTURAL SPACES OF
RESTORATION LONDON

Cynthia Wall

CAMBRIDGE
UNIVERSITY PRESS

PUBLISHED BY THE PRESS SYNDICATE OF THE UNIVERSITY OF CAMBRIDGE
The Pitt Building, Trumpington Street, Cambridge CB2 1RP, United Kingdom

CAMBRIDGE UNIVERSITY PRESS
The Edinburgh Building, Cambridge CB2 2RU, United Kingdom   http://www.cup.cam.ac.uk
40 West 20th Street, New York, NY 10011-4211, USA   http://www.cup.org
10 Stamford Road, Oakleigh, Melbourne 3166, Australia

First published 1998

Printed in the United Kingdom at the University Press, Cambridge

Typeset in Monotype Poliphilus 12/13.5pt using QuarkXPress [SE]

A catalogue record for this book is available from the British Library

Library of Congress cataloguing in publication data

Wall, Cynthia
The literary and cultural spaces of Restoration London / by
Cynthia Wall.
p.   cm.
Includes bibliographical references and index.
ISBN 0 521 63013 4 (hardback)
1. English literature – England – London – History and criticism.
2. English literature – Early modern, 1500–1700 – History and
criticism.   3. London (England) – Intellectual life – 17th century.
4. Great Britain – History – Restoration, 1660–1688.   5. Names,
Geographical, in literature.   6. Great Fire, London, England, 1666.
7. City and town life in literature.   8. Cities and towns in
literature.   9. Public spaces in literature.   1. Title.
PR8476.W35   1998
820.9'32421'09032 – dc21   98–13380 CIP

ISBN 0 521 63013 4 hardback

sben   512090IP

Contents

Illustrations

Preface

In September 1666, the Great Fire destroyed four-fifths of the ancient commercial and topographic center of London within three days. All that had been familiar, settled, phenomenologically *given* was suddenly and entirely swept away; Londoners faced an emptiness that was not only physical and structural but also historical, social, financial, *conceptual*. In the decades that followed, the demands of rebuilding the city generated an intense and widespread interest in urban redefinition that shaped a new set of technologies and a new set of literatures. This study situates the literature of Restoration and early Augustan England (roughly 1666 to 1730) within the historical and cultural contexts of the rebuilding of London after the Great Fire, reading the marked topographical specificity of the plays, poems, and novels as part of a wider cultural network of responses to changing perceptions of urban space. I want to argue that the literatures of this period share with the technologies of surveying, mapping, rebuilding, and officially redescribing the city an attempt to reinvest a city emptied of nominal topographic familiarity with comprehensible meaning, to reattach some sort of signification to the signs, both literal and figurative, of the city's streets and structures.

Part I, "Describing London," focuses primarily on the technical and cultural texts of the Fire and rebuilding to show in what different but conceptually related ways the changing, fluid boundaries of London came to shape a new kind of cultural self-consciousness that would in turn shape new kinds of literary self-representation. Part I reads the different disciplinary documents – political, journalistic, architectural, cartographic, and topographical – precisely for their common conceptual concerns. I assume that the disciplinary differences will remain obvious enough; I am interested in the ways their rhetorical features *correspond* in narrative structure, vocabulary, and even in imagery. I argue that such correspondence supplies evidence first, for shared cultural awareness – that is, that similarities across disciplinary strategies indicate similarities in disciplinary intent – and second, for the basic argument of part II, that the specific literary genres of the Restoration and early eighteenth century are equally grounded, conceptually and structurally, in the cultural strategies of remapping, rebuilding, and renegotiating the boundaries of urban space.

Chapter one, "The Great Fire and rhetorics of loss," describes how the narratives of the Fire, reiterated through various forms of public discourse such as royal proclamations, newspapers, sermons, and poems, on the one hand begin the cultural process of spatial self-awareness and on the other formulate patterns of narrative structure and emphasis that cross generic and diachronic boundaries. The contours of loss were publicized; the narratives of loss consistently structure themselves around litanies of street names, the sense of fragmentation, the inadequacy of traditional metaphors, the disruption of social space. The various forms of cultural texts combine, in reporting and renarrativizing the Fire, to create a consistent rhetorical pattern of response that literally as well as figuratively lays the ground for future, more "literary" representations of and in the city.

Chapter two, "*Londini Renascenti*: the spaces of rebuilding," argues how both the exigencies and the documents of rebuilding – the idealized plans by Wren, Evelyn, and Newcourt, the massive surveying by Mills and Oliver, the property disputes in the Fire Courts, and the publicization of the local and general concerns of rebuilding in the city's newspapers – contributed to an awareness of the contours and the implications of spatial boundaries across a wide swathe of citizenry, from distant landlords to social tiers of tenants within the same house, from members of Court to members of the guilds, from parish clerk to parish widow. Spatial debates became a matter of truly public concern. How the City was finally to look – what should be preserved and recovered, what should be changed and improved – was not in the end decided by King or Parliament or Men of Leisured Science (although lengthily debated by all those), but in fact by the cumulative pressures, desires, debates, and decisions of individual citizens, the tenants, the merchants, the shopkeepers, the tradespeople – the taverners and poulterers and brewers and chandlers, as much as the landlords and officials. Through such cultural reconstruction the contours of London both large and local became themselves possessive property, the conscious concern of virtually all Londoners. Thus, although most of my evidence and most of my argument have to do with texts, and therefore with those who wrote and read them, those texts also directly concerned, sometimes described, and always imply not just those whose historical responses, in the words of Pocock, "were verbalized, recorded, and presented," but also the "*mentalité* of the silent and inarticulate majority" (*Virtue, Commerce, History*, 18) whose voices appear (often verbatim) in the newspaper accounts, the Fire Courts, the trial minutes, the surveying records, the parish records, the many documents of cultural recovery.

Chapter three, "Redrawing London: maps and texts," charts the visual and verbal changes in spatial self-perception of the City. Both the strategies of cartography and the grammars of topography changed in response to the Fire and its demands for recovery, and reveal a perception of urban space that itself is changed, become abstract, modern, as much a product of social and economic practices and fluctuations as of physical structures and relations. Very few maps of

London before the Fire were drawn by Londoners, and such as existed (based primarily on Tudor map-stock) were largely bird's-eye-views, luxuriantly detailed elevations which privileged the viewer's sense of spatial comprehensibility over topographical accuracy. After the Fire, however, scores of new maps by London mapmakers appeared, and they unanimously favor the topographical comprehensiveness of the two-dimensional groundplan, which enables the accurate visual recovery of even the most obscure courts and alleys. The dense topographical anarchy of the medieval street patterns was thus stringently recovered rather than (as before) politely refigured. The textual topographies, on the other hand, mark a slightly different sense of change. As with the maps, before the Fire there were few published descriptions of London printed in London, and those few were based almost entirely on John Stow's 1598 *Survey of London*. Such topographies described the City as much in terms of history as in spatial structure, and their grammars were the grammars of stasis, built on forms of "to be" and resting on verbs of immotion and possession: "there sits," "there stands," "there lies"; "here have you," "here have we." Topographies after the Fire, however, are both more numerous and more "active," borrowing explicitly a technical vocabulary from new surveying strategies and, in response to the increasing anxieties about the expanding *new* building in the "out-parts," working out ever more comprehensive ways of capturing and containing the sense of the rapidly changing city for its own inhabitants.

The text which closes part I and leads directly into part II is Defoe's *A Tour thro' the Whole Island of Great Britain* (1724-26), because in the London section of the *Tour* Defoe comes closest to explicitly articulating what Henri Lefebvre calls "the production of space," the modern sense of space as abstract, shifting, culturally rather than simply physically produced. Defoe creates a surveyor's "Line" that *travels* with the energy and ingenuity of his novelistic characters around the contours of the city, creating as much as marking them, and offering a sense of spatial awareness that employs and celebrates elasticity, that replaces a view with a tour, and moves from description into narrative, into what Michel de Certeau calls a storied sense of space.

Defoe provides an apt transition into part II partly because he so explicitly connects cultural, disciplinary, and generic concerns from the 1660s to the 1730s. As Richard Helgerson has argued in *Forms of Nationhood*, "an atlas and a lengthy poem [can] be considered points on a single line – a line that also passes through an odd assortment of other texts, descriptive and antiquarian . . . [because] they are bound by a dense net of intertextual relations. Nor are the relations only between texts. They are also between people" (131). Throughout this book I make (and find) explicit and implicit connections between maps and poems, architectural treatises and comedies, topographies and novels, partly because the different genres share conceptual and rhetorical strategies, and partly because the mapsellers were also booksellers (Ogilby, Morden), the mapmakers were fablists (Hollar, Ogilby), the urban planners were Royal Society Fellows (Evelyn, Wren, Hooke), the architects and builders were writers (Wren, North, Pratt, Barbon), the playwrights were architects (Vanbrugh), the playwrights were Royal Society Fellows (Dryden), the playwrights satirized Royal Society Fellows (Shadwell, Behn, Centlivre), the poets satirized Royal Society Fellows (Swift), the novelists were spatial planners (Defoe), and above all, the most obvious: all were concerned with rebuilding or rewriting the city, and all were, in one way or another, at one end or the other, inhabitants of the city.

Defoe's works dominate the second part of the book, "Inhabiting London," because he does articulate so well and in so many generic forms the concerns and strategies of managing the many new forms of modern urban space in its various public and private forms. But I also look closely at how the urban poetry of Dryden, Pope, Gay, and Swift, and the formal and conceptual strategies of Restoration drama, participate in this larger literary reoccupation of London. Part II privileges literary texts and reads them as various generic manifestations of the same larger cultural attempt to reinvest place name with meaning, to remap social structures within spatial boundaries, to chart, contain, and inhabit the strange new spaces of the modern city. Defoe's urban novels and novelistic treatises most consistently employ the innovations in cultural and technical strategies within his narrative innovations. I take care to contextualize these works within and against the substantial body of preFire works that also center on London (the Jacobean city plays, the London tavern songs, the occasional poems, the conycatching manuals), illustrating the ways in which I see the postFire London literature as more specific, more concentrated, and more jointly involved not in negotiating within *given* space but in discovering and defining what had become a sort of *terra incognita*: some things could no longer be taken for granted; they needed to be *asserted*.

At one point I had considered making genre itself the chapterboundary: how do poems, plays, novels, *as* genres, separately represent and negotiate the urban space? But I decided finally to organize the literary material spatially, as I had in some ways ordered the cultural material generically, because of course different works often shape and imaginatively occupy the various spaces of London in a number of ways at once, and it became more interesting to me to study the ways that poems, plays, and novels approached the street spaces, the public buildings, the houses, and the dark corners of the city.

Chapter four, "The art of writing the streets of London," marks the most obvious and insistent connection with the other cultural material of the rebuilding in the nearly ubiquitous literary fascination with London streets. Street space in London before the Fire had been generally subordinate, liminal space designed for (or, at least "sustaining") transition, transportation – a physical configuration that either helped or hindered passage from one place to another, but which was literally and physically overshadowed by the combined domestic and commercial buildings of the City. But analogically like the cartographic changes – designed to recover the tiniest topographic corners of the vanished London – poems, plays, and novels from the 1670s to the 1720s not only recover and repeat the litanies of street names, they explore them as social and experiential territories, defining their cultural as well as physical implications. Dryden's *MacFlecknoe*, Pope's *Dunciad*, and Gay's *Trivia* trace the literary as well as social demographies of the city, as has been persuasively explored by Aubrey Williams and Pat Rogers, among others; but I emphasize their context of guidebooks and builders' manuals doing the same thing, and try to show that not only does Augustan poetic form work to contain contemporary urban content, it is also created by and lends new energies to the shifting meanings and ambiguous possibilities of the newly recovered streets. Prose fiction of the period offers a different avenue of approach. From Richard Head's *The English Rogue* (1667), Ned Ward's *The London Spy* (1698-1700), and Defoe's *Moll Flanders* (1722), we see that the streets of London, carefully named and almost literally mapped, become alternative habitations, sometimes safer than houses; the intimate knowledge of these streets means the difference between freedom and arrest. Their new fictional strategies repeople the streets, suggesting ways of navigation through the art of narration.

Chapter five looks at "New narratives of public spaces: parks and shops" as sites of social and economic exchange, and of psychological and phenomenological *change*. With the obvious institutional structures of St. Paul's and the Exchange destroyed and very publicly rebuilt (in both the practical and the conceptual sense), how had the sense of public space changed? Much of early Restoration drama spends most of its setting-time conspicuously *outside* the area of rebuilding, in the parks (St. James's, Hyde Park, the Mall) – in the public spaces of London which had *not* changed, which had no need of reinvestment, which offered a psychological refuge to an audience apparently interested in distancing itself from topographic unfamiliarity, particularly from that looming economic and social power of the City. The later plays spend more time in the rebuilt City, eventually contributing to rather than satirizing its growing gentrification. Meanwhile, in the City itself, trade was resettling and the shops opened for business. Defoe's *The Complete English Tradesman* (1725) creates a sort of how-to manual for the shopkeeper – who increasingly attends the theater – that in proto-novelistic moments stocks shops and warehouses with individualized characters and supplies a living realized context for those moments in Augustan poetry when, as in Swift's "Description of a City Shower" (1710), daggled females flee

from the rain to cheapen goods in shops. The mercantile world of the City is abandoned by drama but peopled by narrative.

With the rebuilding, and particularly with speculators like Nicholas Barbon
making affordable private houses that *look* like the new houses of the wealthy,
along with a wider European move from "civic community to bourgeois privacy"
(as Lawrence Manley argues in *Literature and Culture in Early Modern London*), the
perception of private space in the city also shifts. In chapter six, "Narratives of
private space: churches, houses, and novels," I look briefly at the rebuilt Anglican
churches and their role in Restoration drama as sites of *sexualized* space, and then
more closely at the Dissenting churches forced into concealment by religious persecution. Although Dissenting meeting-houses rarely appear in imaginative literature in this period (except as satiric targets in drama), Defoe's early experience
with their social and structural vulnerability and necessary architectural decep-
tions clearly shaped his fictional creations of private spaces in the domestic structures of *Robinson Crusoe* (1719) and *Roxana* (1724); all his works, from the *Tour*
and the *Tradesman* to his urban novels, are concerned with "an Inside answerable
to the Outside," or the other way around – with a private space that looks "nothing
like a Habitation."

Finally in this chapter I explore the relation between the changes in cultural
perceptions of urban space and the emergence of the novel as an extended narrative that visualizes and inhabits forms of public and more emphatically private
space. I argue that the early English novel is a particularly spatial exploration of
urban change, and that understanding its cultural contexts of destruction,
rebuilding, and redefinition recovers some of the contemporary power and resonance of street names, place lists, public places, private spaces, and the vast netting
of topographical allusion. The novel, like other new and newly adapted kinds of
texts at the time, both produced and was produced by the cultural reorganization
of space.

Any attempt at comprehensiveness naturally invites a search for what's left out,
and specialists in all the disciplines and genres that I'm trying to bring together
here will find significant gaps. Beyond the disciplinary categories of London's
cartography, architecture, and history in the late seventeenth and early eighteenth
centuries, all of which could be thickened by a book of their own, the issues of
gender, class, and race may seem to some be under-represented here. I have
addressed gender and class (and some ethnic and religious) considerations
throughout, but I have privileged space itself as a concept, partly because as a conceptual issue it has only recently begun to receive critical literary attention in
the wake of new theories in cultural geography, and partly because in its historical appearance in London in 1666 it began as a wider cultural moment of more

primitive *human* concern. My literary approach is largely phenomenological, trying to recover and understand what it might have meant to a tenant or a poet of London to suffer the loss of an experiential *given*, to confront the various abrupt intersections and transformations of physically and socially determined spaces. I hope what I have put together offers a persuasive structure within which to fit much of the period's more traditional literary patterns and idiosyncracies, and I hope as I have gone along that I have resisted the temptation to explain *everything* in terms of spatial reconstruction – that the more usual elements of explanation (political, religious, philosophical, social, technological) are in no danger of my hubristically displacing them. I want this book to add another dimension to our understanding of the shape, the concerns, the common ground, of Restoration and early Augustan literature, and to see them as part of yet another larger cultural network of assumptions and experiences in the historical production and experience and expression of a world.

Acknowledgments

It is a great honor to thank friends, colleagues, and institutions for the great pleasures of this project. The debts begin at the Newberry Library and I suspect will never end. Thanks most especially to John Aubrey, Paul Gehl, Diana Haskell, Bob Karrow, and Margaret Kulis – friends as well as former colleagues. This book bears a family resemblance to my dissertation, which developed under the keen and considered care of J. Paul Hunter, Bruce Redford, and Stuart Sherman, with shrewd comments along the way from James K. Chandler, Miriam Hansen, Gwin Kolb, Janel Mueller, Steven Pincus, Edward Rosenheim, Jay Schleusener, and Joshua Scodel; and from my former fellow students Janine Barchas, Vince Bertolini, Timothy Dykstal, Kevin Gilmartin, Laurie Lew, Mark Miller, John Morillo, John O'Brien, Shef Rogers, Carolyn Russell, Märi Schindele, and Tracy Weiner. I will always be grateful to Vassar College for twice nominating me (a Visiting Assistant Professor) – the second time successfully – for an NEH Summer Stipend. Thank you to Carolyn Cartier, Gabrielle Cody, Robert DeMaria, Don Foster, Gretchen Gerzina, Eamon Grennan, Donna Heiland, Barbara Page, Karen Robertson, and Anthony Wohl for steady encouragement and friendship. Perhaps the world's greatest NEH Summer Seminar was held at the University of California, Santa Barbara, in 1994, under the direction of Everett Zimmerman: most of us still keep in touch and read each other's work, and we all thank Everett, but I also thank Alan Chalmers, Lorna Clymer, Peter Cosgrove, Timothy Erwin, Carl Fisher, and Robert Mayer. The eighteenth-century reading group at the Folger Shakespeare Library has been a constant source of invaluable criticism and ideas over the past three years: I am particularly grateful to Vincent Carretta, Mary Fissell, Irene Fizer, Catherine Ingrassia, Deborah Kaplan, Ann Kelly, Kimberly Latta, Paula McDowell, John Radner, and Kathryn Temple. My list of happy debts to my colleagues at the University of Virginia is long and rich and reflects a most generous intellectual community: Steve Arata, Martin Battestin, Ruthe Battestin, Sara Blair, Gordon Braden, Paul Cantor, Libby Cohen, Ralph Cohen, Jessica Feldman, Jonathan Flatley, Alastair Fowler, Clare Kinney, Peter Metcalf, Tan Lin, Teju Olaniyan, Caroline Rody, Tom Scanlan, Patricia Meyer Spacks, Herbert Tucker, and David Vander Meulen. And graduate students: Caroline Breashears, Evelyn Ch'ien, Margaret Croskery, June Griffin, Tom Lukas, Anna Patchias, Megan

Raymond, Joshua Rutsky, Joseph Walsh. Thanks also to various academic and intellectual friends along the way: David Benson, David Blewett, Tom Bonnell, Kevin Cope, Paul Courtright, Peggy Courtright, Robert Erickson, Robert Folkenflik, Teresa LaMaster, Robert MacCubbin, Allen Wall, and Howard Weinbrot.

For various grants and the privilege of working with wonderful collections and courteous, competent staff I thank the British Academy, the British Library, the Guildhall Library (especially Lynne MacNab, John Fisher, and Jeremy Smith), the Clark Library, the Houghton Library, the Huntington Library, Alderman Library at the University of Virginia, the New York Public Library, the National Endowment for the Humanities, and the American Society for Eighteenth-Century Studies. Thanks are due too, to Josie Dixon for promoting the project, Linda Bree for overseeing it, and Hilary Stock for beautifully correct-ing it.

Finally, to my parents – Steven, Nancy, Richard, and Jill – for being really good ones; and to Carolyn Russell, Clare Kinney, Peter Metcalf, Kathy Temple, Jim Slevin, and Paul Hunter, for being such good friends.

Part of chapter 3 first appered in *Philological Quarterly* (1998); part of chapter 4 in *Studies in the Novel* (1998); and part of chapter 6 in *Eighteenth-Century Fiction* (1992). Permission to reprint is gratefully acknowledged.

PART I
DESCRIBING LONDON

CHAPTER ONE

THE GREAT FIRE AND
RHETORICS OF LOSS

[T]he vast yron Chaines of the Cittie streetes . . . were many of them mealted, & reduc'd to cinders by the vehement heats: nor was I yet able to passe through any of the narrower streets, but kept the widest . . . The bielanes & narrower streetes were quite fill'd up with rubbish, nor could one have possibly knowne where he was, but by the ruine of some church, or hall, that had some remark-able towre or pinacle remaining.   John Evelyn, *Diary*, September 7, 1666[1]

Entring the *City* once *exactly known,*
Thalia found her *marks* were *gone.*   [Simon Ford], *Londons Remains*, 1667[2]

Tis changd, without a Metaphor, I may say
From *Terr'del foego* to *Incognita.*
      Elkanah Settle, *An Elegie On the late Fire And Ruines of London*, 1667[3]

From his walk through the hot ruins of London, John Evelyn marked in his diary the conditions of fundamental change, of terrifying difference: the ancient, famil-iar, topographically stable city had become inaccessible and unknowable within the space of four days. The streets were filled with rubbish but emptied of meaning; the city once exactly known was signless. The intricate, irregular webbing of narrow medieval streets had always had at least the epistemological advantage of historically denotative place names, as Stow had patiently pointed out in 1598:[4] "Iuie lane, so called of Iuie growing on the walles of the Prebend almes houses" (*Survey*, 277); "Loue lane, so called of wantons" (*Survey*, 236); the Fire began in the place "from *empty'd Tripes* call'd *Pudding-Lane*" (Ford, *Londons Remains*, 10). J. Hillis Miller has recently explored the power of topography in the psychological and cultural coextension of place name with place meaning: "Place names seem to be intrinsic to the places they name. The names are moti-vated. By a species of Cratylism they tell what the places are like. The place is carried into the name and becomes available to us there. You can get to the place by way of its name."[5] But in medieval London, "seeming" *was* being: place names were functionally intrinsic to — not just traditionally associated with — the places they named.[6] What happens to a city, to a culture, when its oldest, most reliable signs suddenly and completely lose their referents? When the defensive chains of the streets are quite literally as well as figuratively melted, when alien new space must be navigated by deformed spatial referents, by architectural ruins, by the dreadful contingency of a *piece* of public edifice remaining, and remaining identifiable?

The answer is, in part, a cultural reconception of space. What had been taken for granted, as obvious everyday background both private and public, social and commercial — as more or less static, assumed, phenomenologically *given* — was suddenly foregrounded, its impact in shaping daily life made apparent by absence, its power by loss. Merleau-Ponty defines space not as "the setting (real or logical) in which things are arranged, but the means whereby the position of things becomes possible."[7] The aftermath of the Fire produced a shift in the cultural perception of space from that of setting to that of enabling context; when the city was destroyed, its whole abstract network of associative meaning disappeared and a new relational context for living had to be constructed. Edward Soja, among others,[8] has argued for a necessarily dialectical relationship between physical and experiential space, between where we live and how we live in it. Both material and ideational space are socially produced, and conversely, spatiality can never fully be separated from physical and psychological spaces; "Social life is never entirely free of such restrictive impingements or the physical friction of distance."[9] The rhetorics of loss generated by the Fire, in official narratives, sermons, diaries, and poems, all share to some degree a heightened spatial consciousness in imagery and expression, an awareness of a new kind of conceptual emptiness in the ruined physical spaces, of boundaries previously invisible and now transgressed, of structures previously assumed and now collapsed, of spaces once fixed and stable, now shifting and treacherous.

Perspective is everything, of course; to the Elizabethans, London was already growing too fast for fancy, too unwieldy for commerce or aesthetics, and laws were passed repeatedly and unsuccessfully to keep boundaries fixed and populations stable. Spiro Kostof notes that any city, "however perfect its initial shape, is never complete, never at rest. Thousands of witting and unwitting acts every day alter its lines in ways that are perceptible only over a certain stretch of time. City walls are pulled down and filled in; once rational grids are slowly obscured; a slashing diagonal is run through close-grained residential neighborhoods."[10] But: perspective is everything. London, though never topographically rational and no more than others at rest, had seemed — at least in nostalgic retrospect to post-Fire writers — by virtue of its age, size, history, and even its idiosyncratic configurations, in some sense known, open, available, part of the psychological and cultural horizon. The narratives of the Fire and the rebuilding generically and conceptually grope for new ways to express loss, to define emptiness, to articulate need, to recover and define an old London in the process of defining and constructing a new one — to find "the means whereby the position of things becomes [once again] possible" – and the possibility whereby the position of things becomes meaningful.

"Londoners," of course, is a problematic term. On a very basic level I do mean virtually all the inhabitants of London, regardless of class or trade or gender; one of the central interests of this study is precisely the common concep-tual and rhetorical ground that is immediately and then selectively shared by widely different genres and even disciplines. But I will take care not to over-simplify, and to distinguish social difference when it becomes relevant. The different genres often speak to different audiences, of course; a broadside ballad describing the Fire spells things out differently from a Latin poem, and a survey-ing manual and a topographic guide address widely different needs. But the Fire was perhaps distinctive in its levelling properties, at least for crucial moments – experiential and rhetorical.

The Fire literally and figuratively levelled London at a crucially important historical and cultural moment in the mid-seventeenth century. England, lagging behind the Continent, had been poised on the edge of political, economic, social, aesthetic, and urban change: the monarchy had been restored and Charles II was encouraging new forms of arts and sciences; trading power and therefore mer-chants' power was increasing; Inigo Jones had earlier begun to open up his baroque piazzas in the west and to open up or at least prepare popular as well as aristocratic appreciation for architectural change; and London was becoming what Kostof defines as an industrial rather than pre-industrial city, with urban ownership divorced from urban land use, and that land use increasingly special-ized and segregated, both commercially and socially.[11] By destroying four-fifths of the historical, commercial, topographic, and imaginative center of London within four days, the Fire threw existing and potential changes into calcined relief, bringing to a culturally universal level the history and meaning and shape of London to Londoners.

But the Fire also specifically heightened a larger sense of cultural, religious, and political insecurity. Many writers of London before the Fire had already remarked on the changes or depredations to the urban landscape made by the Commonwealth, such as the pulling down of the Cross in Cheapside in 1644. The Restoration of the monarchy in 1660 seemed to promise vast social and cul-tural changes for the City, not the least of which would be a tense return of the Church of England as the state religion, battling and then persecuting the Dissenters on the one hand, and the Roman Catholics on the other. England was also fighting the Dutch for trade supremacy, and in the spring of 1665 the Dutch ships sailed into the Thames (as Neander and his friends watch in Dryden's *Essay of Dramatick Poesy*) – to be defeated, but with the price of the *sense* of invasion. And then the plague: over 97,000 killed, and all the city dislocated as people attempted to escape from or hide in their houses. The whole context of city life in London in the years immediately before the Fire was mined with anxiety, disruption, instability, indeterminacy. The Fire completed the job with a devastating literalness, laying bare the psychological as well as the physical structures that needed to be rebuilt.

The shape and structure of the old City will emerge cumulatively and comparatively throughout this study. This work will be archaeological to some extent in Foucault's sense, concerned with "discourse in its own volume" and attempting "to define discourses in their specificity,"[12] sifting through contemporary and synchronic responses to the Fire and reconstructing the London of the past through the eyes of the late seventeenth and early eighteenth centuries. The mass of published and private narratives of the Fire records a moment of widespread spatial and cultural self-analysis, re-articulations of urban self-definition, not only by courtiers and administrators, but also by gentlemen and clergy, Anglicans and Nonconformists, poets "high" and "low," and, through various legal and civic documents, by those often silenced by or in literary texts. J. G. A. Pocock has defined as one of the jobs of the historian to "study the processes by which humans acquire new means of verbalization and new ways of using those they already possess."[13] He argues that "the perception of the new is carried out over time, and in the form of a debate about time; the historical animal deals with experience by discussing old ways of perceiving it, as a necessary preliminary to erecting new ways, which then serve as means of perceiving both the new experience and the old modes of perception" (*Virtue, Commerce, History*, 29). The Great Fire, according to the nineteenth-century Laureate Robert Southey, "inspired more bad poetry than was happily destroyed by it"[14] – but another way of putting it, perhaps, is that the Great Fire reworked old and generated new rhetorics and vocabularies of loss, and in the demands of the rebuilding, produced yet another level of conceptualizing and shaping space, and of articulating spatial discourse within the contexts of political, economic, social, religious, and aesthetic assumptions, expectations, and changes.

For Londoners in 1666, the perception of the new was indeed carried out over time, but that "new" and those "perceptions" were historically and psychologically gargantuan, far too uncontainable in their first instances for either individual or institution. Too many distinctions seemed to collapse: the streets were closed, emptied of buildings and refilled with rubble, their defensive chains melted; the privacy of houses, the sanctuaries of churches, the institutionalized spaces of the Company Halls, all alike were blown open and lost; rich and poor spilled homeless into Moorfields; the very fabric of urban and social meaning was undone into topographic incoherence.

This chapter will look at the earliest accounts of the Fire – in newspapers, proclamations, sermons, and poems – and explore how these different genres combine to produce a common ground of rhetorical response in narrative structure, descriptive vocabulary, and imagery. Although I will note relevant generic differences in the various narratives of the Fire, I am more concerned in part I to set out cultural and rhetorical similarities, leaving more explicit generic examinations for part II. I will look first at the different genres of loss – official narratives in the *London Gazette*, royal proclamations, sermons, and poems, analyzing their rhetorical patterns as they represent the city first as a whole collapsed and then as fragments to be interpreted. In place etymologies, in lists, and in literalized metaphors, the stories of the Fire find ways to recover and reassert boundaries, to reinvest traditional imagery with local relevance, to lay foundations for refamiliarization – common images of loss become common narratives of loss. I will then look at three spatial categories of loss – public space, private space, and their mediators, the streets – to set up the cultural and conceptual contexts for the literary rebuilding of the city explored in part II. Like the newspapers, proclamations, and sermons, the poems, plays, and novels of the Restoration will often focus intensely on defining what was lost; yet in the very process of recovering the old, the rhetorics of loss (and later, rebuilding) found themselves in new spaces of their own making.

Genres of loss: official narratives, sermons, and poems

The history of the Fire includes all the narratives of itself; all its retellings by definition reshape the events.[15] I want to emphasize the literalness of that "reshaping." The "official" narratives – the account of the Fire in the *London Gazette*, the structures of response in the royal proclamations, and the local voices captured in the court proceedings – set up formal and conceptual patterns of spatial emphasis that will come to be repeated and refined throughout other genres in terms of the loss and reconfiguration of public spaces, private spaces, and those peculiar intermediaries, the streets. The different forms and demands of various genres shaped their common conceptual ground of spatial anxiety, variously voicing and imaging an apocalypse of division, of shattering, of dismembering, of a city seen suddenly in parts, and simultaneously articulating the human struggle to deal with the new, to make things conceptually, physically, linguistically whole.

Official accounts of the Fire emerge both from the *London Gazette* of that week (Number 85, September 3–10, 1666), and from Charles's assorted proclamations to deal with the Fire. The *London Gazette*, the earliest regular "newspaper" in England, was at that time one of only two news sheets permitted to be published since Cromwell had suppressed all newspapers in 1655, and was basically the mouthpiece of the government.[16] The *Gazette* offers a "factual" account in the sense of the day, which includes a gesture to God for theoretical considerations (determining whether the Fire was an "unhappy chance" or "the heavy hand of God upon us for our sins") and to the King for practical ones ("His Majesties care was most signal in this occasion"). But the *Gazette* also gives a succinct and conceptually telling account that moves in and out of impersonal documentary prose about the temporal and spatial progress of the Fire.

The *Gazette*'s narrative begins with an interruption: "The ordinary course of this Paper having been interrupted by a sad and lamentable accident of Fire lately hapned in the City of *London*." That sense of narrative as well as experiential interruption underlies various forms of perceived physical, social, and spatial disruption. I will quote extensively from the account because it sets up what will become three dominant rhetorical emphases in narrative accounts of the Fire in (1) assigning spatial significance (2) locating spatial consequences, and (3) fastening on spatial boundaries:

> On the second instant at one of the clock in the Morning there hapned to break out a sad deplorable Fire, in *Pudding-lane*, neer *New Fishstreet*, which falling out at that hour of the night, and in a quarter of the town so close built with wooden pitched houses, spread itself so far before day, and with such distraction to the inhabitants and Neighbours, that . . . this lamentable Fire in a short time became too big to be mastred by any Engines or working neer it . . . spreading itself up to *Grace-church street*, and downwards from *Cannon-street* to the Water-side as far as the *Three Cranes* in the *Vintrey*.
>
> The people in all parts about it distracted by the vastness of it, and their particular care to carry away their Goods, many attempts were made to prevent the spreading of it by pulling down Houses, and making great Intervals, but all in vain, the Fire seising upon the Timber and Rubbish and so continuing itself, even through those spaces, and raging in a bright flame all Monday and Tuesday . . . By the favour of God the Wind slackned a little on Tuesday night & the Flames meeting with Brick-buildings at the Temple, by little and little it was observed to lose its force on that side, so that on Wednesday morning we began to hope well . . . [A] stop was put to it at the *Temple-church*, neer *Holborn-bridge*, *Pie-corner*, *Aldersgate*, *Cripplegate*, neer the lower end of *Coleman-street*, at the end of *Basing-hall-street*, by the *Postern*, at the *Standard* in *Cornhill*, at the Church in *Fanchurch-street*, neer *Clothworkers Hall* in *Mincing-lane*, at the middle of *Mark-lane*, and at the *Tower-dock*.

First, the physical impact of the Fire is assigned a causal relation to particular urban spaces, emphasizing the significant details of local space ("a quarter of the town so close built"); second, that collapse of physical space prefigures, causes, and contains a temporary social and psychological collapse ("distracted by the vastness"); third, street names emerge as talismanic, simultaneously defining boundaries and charting boundlessness.

Place becomes premise (in both senses) of the Fire, functioning as a source for its physical, moral, and political explanations. The *London Gazette* notes that "this Fire happened in a part of the Town where tho the Commodities were not very rich, yet they were so bulky that they could not well be removed, so that the inhabitants of that part where it first began have sustained very great loss." Pudding Lane, where the Fire started, east towards the Tower and close to the river, was an area of closely built wooden houses and warehouses stuffed with oil, flax, wines, and other highly combustible materials, as Simon Ford's poem notes: "what was the *Nurse* of *Trade*, becomes its *Fate*."[17] The overhanging roofs nearly met over the narrow, twisting streets. The area had very little visible or open public space; the close commercial fabric literally did provide the fuel that sustained the vast power of the fire. Edward Waterhouse (1619–1670), a Royal Society Fellow (though described by Anthony Wood as "a cock-brain'd man" and by the *Dictionary of National Biography* as a "fantastical preacher"), centers his *Short Narrative Of the late Dreadful Fire in London* (1667) on the particulars of that commercial space:

> This little pittyful [Pudding] Lane, crowded in behind little *East-cheap* on the West St. *Buttolph's-lane* on the East, and *Thames-street* on the South of it, was the place where the Fire originated, and that forwarded by a Bakers stack of wood in the house, and by all the neighbouring houses, which were as so many matches to kindle and carry it on to its havock; there the Fire meeting with the Star Inn on *Fish-street-hill* on the back of it, and that Inn full of Hay, and other combustibles, and with the houses opposite to it, and closed with it at the top, burned three ways at once, into *Thames-street*, (the lodge of all combustibles, Oyl, Hemp, Flax, Pitch, Tar, Cordage, Hops, Wines, Brandies, and other materials favourable to Fire; all heavy goods being in ware-houses there neer the waterside, and all the wharfs for Coale, Timber, Wood, &c. being in a line consumed by it unto *Fish-street-hill*.   (45–47)

Waterhouse's narrative, like so many Fire narratives, underscores the fact that place is a condition of story; that both the pattern and the narration of the Fire's destruction depend intimately on the topographical contours of the city, themselves shaped historically into social, political, and physical idiosyncracies.

Most narratives look for providential or political – moral or conspiratorial – causes for the Fire. Yet these too are usually topographically located and defined. A number of the sermons (most but not all by Anglican ministers) are fond of attaching blame to Moorfields in particular; Robert Elborough ("Minister of the Parish that was lately St. *Laurence Pountney*") thinks the Fire was brought on by the

breaking of Sabbath by walking in Moorfields and Hyde Park;[18] so does Thomas
Brooks ("late Preacher of the Word at S. *Margarets*"), who apostrophizes:

> Ah, *London! London!* were there none within nor without thy Walls that made
> light of this Institution of God and that did offer violence to the Queen of
> days by their looseness and prophaneness, by their sitting at their doors, by
> their walking in *Moor-fields*, by their sportings and wrestlings there.[19]

Moorfields itself lay just north of London Wall, a popular pleasure ground from
the sixteenth century, in which, according to Stow's version of Fitzstephen, "the
youths are exercised in leaping, dancing, shooting, wrastling, casting the stone, and
practising their shields" (Stow, *Survey*, 85). The "suburb without the walls" had
long had an uneasy status and lay in easy moral as well as physical proximity to the
cause of the Fire. Politically, on the other hand, the area where the Fire began was
heavily populated with French and Dutch tradespeople, a number of whom were
Roman Catholic, and so place seemed ideologically as well as physically
inflammable. Catholics, along with Quakers and Nonconformists, had been pre-
dicting a fiery wrath of God on the Sodom-and-Gomorrah that was London in the
years before the Fire; the ground was prepared for the public presumption of a *plot*.[20]
In a not uncommon response to panic, natives viewed foreigners more than ever as
intruders, as aliens intent on changing and even destroying familiar, lived, English
space, as a (perhaps apocryphal) contemporary Dutch account notes: "All foreigners alike were held to be guilty ... A poor woman walking in Moorfields, who had
chickens in her apron, was seized by the mob, who declared that she carried fire-
balls, and not only did they violently abuse her, but they beat her with sticks and cut
off her breasts."[21] Although Charles quickly issued proclamations denying
foreign sabotage, going in person to calm the crowds, and the later trials initiated to
discover any treasonous human agency found nothing of substance, the under-
currents of fear and suspicion increasingly exacerbated one bitter xenophobic division in the moment of – and presumably because of – other traditional collapses.

The *Gazette*'s narrative outlines the consequences of spatial disruption in
terms of at least temporary social and psychological collapse within and without
the walls of London. The emphasis on disruption and distraction, for example,
even within the structure of the narrative itself, in its various repetitions, gives a
public voice to the stunned confusion of individuals and of the populace as a
whole: by the end of the second paragraph quoted above, the objective "people"
have slid into the subjective "we" (who "began to hope"). The account emphasizes – indeed, distractingly repeats – the distraction of the inhabitants and the
jumble made of the city not only by the Fire but also by the efforts to escape and
quench it ("with such distraction to the inhabitants" and "the people in all parts
about it distracted by the vastness of it"). Sense of time, sense of identity, were

notoriously shaken by the loss of spatial address: the most famous marker of time himself, Samuel Pepys, who circumscribed his day within rhythms bounded by watch and routine, wonders: "it is a strange thing to see how long this time did look since Sunday, having been alway full of variety of actions, and little sleep, that it looked like a week or more. And I had forgot almost the day of the week."[22] And away in Oxford, the antiquary Anthony Wood recorded:

> The fire. Soe suddenly did it come and therby caused such distraction and severall forgat their names when they with their money or goods under their armes were examined by the watch that then immediatly was appointed. Others that had occasion to write letters a day or 2 after it ended, forgat the day of the mounth and the mounth of the year.[23]

Familiar social boundaries were momentarily swept away with the physical and psychological ones. Those "people" who turn into "we" in the *Gazette* account, of various ranks and conditions, "were necessitated to remove them-selves and goods into the open fields, where they were forced to continue some time." The temporary spatial collapse of social divisions remarked in this official narrative is continually pointed to in letters, diaries, poems, and sermons; Evelyn notes, for example: "I then went towards Islington, & high-gate, where one might have seene two hundred thousand people of all ranks & degrees, dispersed, & laying along by their heapes of what they could save from the *Incendium*, deploring their losse" (Evelyn, *Diary*, 111:461). The spectre of such visible social disintegra-tion persistently haunts all immediate genres of the narrative accounts of the Fire, and according to those accounts, all levels of London consciousness. Part of the (unsuccessful) rebuilding rhetoric would become the spatial resorting of class, stabilizing these collapsed social boundaries through redefining place.

The identification and recovery of boundaries in all forms of reconstruction – narrative, social, architectural – always begins and often ends with the topograph-ical. Streets constitute boundaries, and on one level the *Gazette*'s litany of streets at the end of the quoted excerpt marks the containment of the Fire. But at the same time the streets now measured the extent of the uncontained, and the perception of that extent. What had for centuries sorted out the known now marked the pre-liminary boundaries of a temporal and spatial unknown. On September 4, Evelyn writes: "The burning still rages; I went now on horse back, & it was now gotten as far as the Inner Temple; all *Fleetstreete*, old baily, Ludgate hill, Warwick Lane, Newgate, Paules Chaine, Wattling-streete now flaming & most of it reduc'd to ashes" (Evelyn, *Diary*, 111:454). One London citizen, Henry Griffith, described the Fire to his kinsman with a list large enough to contain both the *Gazette*'s and Evelyn's – large enough to contain all the sense of the unknown in the vast detail of the previously known:

> It has burnt all from the Towre to the Temple, and part of that too along the Thames side, carrying before itt the Custome House, Billingsgate, London Bridge, Coleharbour, Queenehith, Baynard's Castle, Black and White Fryers, from east to west. Northwards itt burnt to Cripple and Mooregate, and something further to Moor Fields, carrying before itt Cannon and Lumbart Street, Cornehill, Exchange, Bartholomew Lane, Lothbury, and most of the Buildings towards Moor Fields, Guildhall, Aldermanbury, Basinghall, and Colman-street. North-westward it burnt the Poultry, Cheapside, Bread and Friday streets, Fishstreet, Doctors' Commons, Paul's Church-yard, Newgate Market, Catteaton street, Wood and Milk streets, Frost [Foster] Lane, St. Martens to and from Aldersgate, Pye Corner to Smithfield, Holborn to the bridge, Ludgate-hill, Old Bailey, the Fleet and Fleet street to the Church, all Shooe and part of Fetter lanes. Northeastward, Threadneedle street, Augustine Fryers, part of Bishopsgate streete, Gratia [Gracechurch] street, Eastcheape, Fenchurch street, almost to Marke Lane End a good way past the Church, part of Lime street, Minsing Lane, Tower street, and most of Marke Lane, together with all lanes, alleys, streets, and parish churches within this compasse.[24]

Over the next sixty years "all lanes, alleys, streets," along with yards, closes, greens, squares, markets, courts, rows, rents, "or any other Place, by what Name soever call'd,"[25] will increasingly dominate the vocabulary of topographic as well as literary efforts to reclaim and remap the lost city, from the guides of Edward Hatton and William Stow to the satires of Ned Ward and the novels of Daniel Defoe.

Charles II's proclamations and declarations essentially recapitulate the categories of concern and expression of the newspaper, although with some interesting generic differences. Declarations and proclamations by their very form work differently from (but may include) narrative reports. The monarch declares or proclaims what is; or rather, the act of monarchical declaration creates truth. There's an idealism of fixity in that authority. For example, one of Charles's first proclamations, *A proclamation for restoring goods imbezzll'd during the late fire and since* (September 19, 1666), marks the confusion of persons and property and *commands* restoration. But at this point in time Charles's declarations and proclamations are doubly destabilized, partly by the magnitude of what needs pronouncing upon, and partly because the monarchy had been so newly reestablished, and on such different, ideologically unsettled ground. A proclamation in such a case shifts sideways in power and weight, becoming more a representation of things past or things redesired or things reconstituted, but itself only the form of the familiar, the form of authority, a signifier not quite firmly reattached to its signified, and all the seams showing – as the offer of a reward in this proclamation to bolster the royal decree seems to suggest.[26] Yet various forms of evidence have persuaded historians of the Fire that Charles, whatever his daily habits and aptitudes as a ruler might be, acted promptly, efficiently, and responsibly in organizing the efforts to put out the Fire and to rebuild the City. His recorded voice is thus granted a practical and moral if not an ideological or phenomenological authority. A month after the Fire, when he calls for a commemorative fast throughout the country, he offers the nation a narrative that in retelling the story of the Fire re-marks the boundaries of spatial collapse:

> Whereas it hath pleased Almighty God by a most lamentable and devouring Fire . . . to lay waste the greatest part of the City of *London* within the Walls, and some part of the Suburbs, whereof more then fourscore Parishes, and all the Houses, Churches, Chappels, Hospitals, and other the great and Magnificent Buildings of pious or publique use which were within that Circuit, are now brought into Ashes and become one ruinous Heap: A Visitation so dreadful, that scarce any Age or Nation hath ever seen or felt the like . . . [A]ll men ought to look upon it as a Judgment upon the whole Nation, and to humble themselves accordingly.[27]

His interpretive structure parallels many of the didactic declarations of the sermons and poems, and is intended among other things to transform spatial collapse into social unity and spiritual integrity: what levels London into one ruinous heap ought figuratively to collapse national pride; what literally levels houses, churches, chapels, and hospitals simultaneously levels former social distinctions: "Many Persons and Families, who were formerly able to give great relief to others, are now become great objects of Charity themselves." The king posits a conceptually *whole* moral to make narrative sense of these shattered parts.

The *London Gazette* offers a public voice of authority; Charles presumably speaks for himself in his declarations; the records of the court proceedings in which Catholics were tried for starting the Fire, on the other hand, record not so much a witch-hunt as a chorus of local, confused, and indeterminate voices. The documents in the *True and Faithful Account*,[28] which comprises "Informations touching the Insolency of Popish Priests and Jesuites; and the Increase of Popery, brought to the Honourable Committee appointed by the Parliament for that purpose," have been systematically dismissed as a source of significant historical evidence – Bell calls them "the statements of chatterboxes" (*Great Fire*, xii). Yet the legal narratives give local (if secondhand) voice to people besides the educated and the literary. The committee's accounts offer a series of internal miniature fire-narratives, the individual human experiences of particular houses and streets set within the larger physical and narrative spaces of the city. We hear with a sense of realism if not with a guarantee of accuracy the voices of different people caught in particular local dramas.

The committee appointed to investigate the origins of the Fire opens its account with its own exploratory narrative – *A True and Faithful Account of the Several Informations . . . [concerning] the late Dreadful Burning of the City of London* (1667) that supplies a different local perspective on space, using units of measurement rather than names of streets to compute limits and to reinforce the importance of the spatial references in its contents:

> Upon the second of *September* 1666, the Fire began in *London*, at one *Farryners* House, a Baker in *Pudding-Lane*, between the hours of one and two in the morning, and continued burning until the sixth of *September* following; consuming, as by the Surveyors appears in print, three hundred seventy three Acres within the Walls of the City of *London*, and sixty three Acres three Roods without the Walls. There remains seventy five Acres three Roods yet standing within the Walls unburnt. Eighty nine Parish Churches, besides Chappels, burnt. Eleven Parishes within the Walls left standing. Houses burnt, thirteen thousand two hundred. Per *Jonas Moore, Ralph Gatrix* Surveyors.

The opening Fire narrative is followed by dozens of "eyewitness" accounts of Catholic "confessions," either in wish or in deed. Each of these accounts is firmly located topographically, as, for example, "That near *West-Smithfield* in *Cheek-Lane*, there was a man taken in the very Act of Firing a House" (*Faithful Account*, 19), or "Mr. *Oakes*, a Physician dwelling in *Shadwell*, Informed, That a little after the Burning of *London*, one Mr. *Carpenter* a Minister, came to his house on *Tower-Wharf*, and spake to him to this purpose" (*Faithful Account*, 29). The topographical details grant a plausible authority to the individual account, locate the witness and the hearer or reader within the familiar pattern of London streets, and implicitly or explicitly underline the loss of that familiarity. In one account we get a version of Fire rhetoric which might be called a catechism, employing the repeated patterns of topography and suspicion but, like most of the narratives, its open-endedness and ambiguity transform it into a narrative of uncertain human experience rather than a document of pure xenophobia:

> A Citizen being Fired out of his House, had hyred a Lodging in Queens street in *Covent-Garden*; and going up *Holborn* (there being a Crowd of people) steps in amongst them, and hears a woman say, That she had a hand in Firing the City. The people askt her, whether she were an Anabaptist? She said No: Are you an Independent? She said No: Are you a Presbyterian? She said No? [sic] Are you a *Roman Catholic*? to which she would give no answer. The Citizen asked her, But Mrs. had you a hand in Burning the City? She answered, what will you have me to say? I have confessed it already, and do deserve to Dye for it; This she said with great trembling, and seemed to be

much troubled. The Citizen inquires for a Constable, the people reply, There
was one gone for. But a Gallant comes, and takes her by the Arm, and leads
her away, saying, he would have her examined, and forthwith another
Gallant closeth with him, and they both carryed her to the *Griffin* Tavern in
Holborn.   *(Faithful Account,* 17*)*

This is both a peculiar and a typical narrative; the voice of the central figure, the
woman confessing, is embedded in the Citizen's account, which itself is reported
by the Committee. Its levels of abstraction would seem to remove immediacy, yet
the dialogue is vividly vernacular and some sort of plot, if not a simply "papist"
one, seems present if submerged. The woman's account seems not to be believed
(but at least this particular crowd of people isn't rushing to cut off her breasts), and
it's not at all clear whether she's rescued or flung out of the frying pan into the fire
(so to speak) with the arrival of the two "gallants." The account ends with what
tends to be the result of most of the reports: the citizen, after tracking her to the
public house and reporting her to some officers, "leaves his name with the captain,
and where he might be found, but was never called for to justify the words spoken
by her." Most accounts end with the witness admitting that the apprehended
suspect was "heard of no more," or the witness "could never hear nor learn" of his
or her tale producing verifiable results. In fact, although these accounts are presented as authoritatively grounded both in specificity of streets and of eyewit-
nessed dialogue, the inconclusivity of narrative here prefigures the result of the
committee's findings as a whole: the Roman Catholics were established not to
have designed nor started the Fire nor systematically hindered the efforts to stop
it.[29] The Great Fire certainly fuelled religious and political fears, but even in these
official Fire narratives the larger psychic consequences seem at least for the moment
to rhetorically consume them.

For the genres of sermons and poems – providential as well as political – a whole
biblical as well as classical vocabulary and set of images waited empty as it were to
express the devastation of the London Fire. Job, Isaiah, Matthew, Proverbs,
Lamentations, Ezekiel, Nebuchadnezzar; Homer and Virgil and Tacitus; even
the previous recorded memories of fires, all give voice to the early responses to the
Fire, yet seem suddenly inadequate to their burden. The familiar vocabulary, capacious as it is, gets consistently distorted partly because its historical familiarity
cannot express the enormity of the new – its perceptual value and power are precisely disqualified by its well-worn shape, its different contexts of comfort – it
simply no longer fits. As with Manley's account of the "dynamics of Tudor complaint," the traditional models "were not simply backward-looking in their
appeal to long-established social myths and models, but, in their response to social
crisis, generative of new ones" (Manley, *Literature and Culture,* 75). The images of

the sermonic analyses, the metaphorical properties of the vocabulary, are destabilized precisely because they are literalized. The power of a metaphor lies partly in its distance from its referent; as Karsten Harries says, "Metaphors speak of what remains absent."[30] "She has roses in her cheeks" loses its particular descriptive appeal if the flower actually sprouts out of the skin. After the Fire a number of sermons and poems begin to shudder away from the existing but disconcertingly inadequate imagery of loss and begin to reconstruct new rhetorics to locate and articulate the spaces emptied, the contours to be redrawn.

Most genres of Fire narratives generally construct some sort of Foucauldian heterotopias in both their extremes, offering on the one hand an ultimately unsuccessful rhetoric of spatial "illusion" (or otherness) that tries to expose each real space as illusory – that is, contrasting the real, suffering, ruined London with its eternally, fundamentally reliable biblical counterpart; or on the other hand a rhetoric of "compensation," creating an ideal future space that transcends this one, that supplies the promise of a better London, the old city purified, refined, restored.[31] It is largely and perhaps not surprisingly the sermons that self-consciously offer a dismally ill-fitting cliché of the House of God, and the poems that figure the equally mis-sized phoenix of rebuilding.

For the sermons, I quote mostly from Anglican divines and from some Nonconformist ministers, and will note their particular backgrounds and interests as I go,[32] but I am interested here in marking the common rhetorical ground that the Fire sermons display. Although these years were deeply troubled with regulations and persecutions, the texts after the Fire, much like Defoe's representation of the different clergy during the plague in *A Journal of the Plague Year,* are striking in their (if temporary) *common* voice of loss: "*nor did the Church Ministers… make any Difficulty of accepting their Assistance, so that many of those who they called silenced Ministers, had their Mouths open'd on this Occasion, and preach'd publickly to the people.*"[33] Other explanations for momentary religious unity or a particular flourish of rhetoric may also apply in each case, of course; Nonconformists may well have been broadcasting their loyalty by widely distributing the moral blame over the metropolis as a whole, rather than pointing directly to the wicked sinful Court. Defoe's agenda in the *Journal* is still promoting mutual tolerance between Anglicans and Dissenters in applauding the nonsectarian courage of the silenced ministers. And many of the Anglican priests might have had their eye on their patron in his pew as they shaped their ringing discourses. But none of these angles alone can account for the uniformity of rhetorical response that begins with the obvious – what shall we do with this unspeakable disaster, this shocking ruin, this shattered whole – and moves into variously odd ways of fitting traditional metaphors to brutally concrete particulars. Many of these ministers were speaking in a sense from the ruins of their own churches, to the homeless of their own parish.

The first sweeping image of London in the sermons is that the whole vanishes – London was, but is no more – or that it is transformed, its wholeness of structure and order (however optimistically remembered) flung into antithesis, most usually an Isaiahan heap, as Robert Elborough, minister of St. Laurence Pountney (and schoolmate of Pepys, who thought him a fool) points out: "My beloved, our eyes have seen, our goods and estates have found, and our persons have experienced the greatness of Gods Judgment, when he hath made a *City an heap, and a ruine of a defenced City, Isa.25.2*" (*London's Calamity*). (On the tenth of September Evelyn notes: "I went again to the ruines, for it was now no longer a Citty" [Evelyn, 111:462]). The Puritan Thomas Brooks (1608–1680), ejected in 1662 from St. Margaret's, New Fish Street Hill and then preacher in Moorfields, printed a sort of extended sermon that in its title alone twice reduces London to a ruinous heap:

> *LONDON'S LAMENTATIONS: or, A serious Discourse concerning that late fiery Dispensation that turned our (once renowned) City into a ruinous Heap. Also the several lessons that are incumbent upon those whose Houses have escaped the consuming Flames.* By *THOMAS BROOKS, late Preacher of the Word at S.* Margarets, *New-Fish-street*, where that Fatal Fire first began that turned *London* into a ruinous Heap.

Within the discourse the theme is repeated; what had been structured, placed, properly and functionally differentiated – "Houses, Churches, Chappels, Hospitals, and other the great and magnificent buildings of Pious or Publick use, which were within that Circuit" (*London's Lamentations*, 26) – are now "one ruinous heap," "a common ruine," "a heap of Rubbish" (*London's Lamentations*, 26, 38). The *Counsel to the Afflicted* retells the fury of the fire such that "none was able to quench it, until it had consumed the greatest part of that renowned City, and had made of a City an Heap, of a defenced City a ruine."[34] William Gearing (fl. 1659–1679, rector of Christ Church, Surrey) also lingers on the details of the city "made ruinous heaps."[35] Over and over again, the city is called a "heap," shapeless, prostrate, its *indistinguishability* its distinguishing mark.

Language itself seems collapsed, the familiar discourse inadequate to express the cultural and spiritual horror. Lawrence Manley notes the general earlier "inarticulateness of the image of the city" (*Literature and Culture*, 75); the immediate post-Fire literatures become experiments in articulation. Robert Elborough declaims that the Fire is kindled "not within the usual Lines of Communication, but in the Center whence those Lines are drawn" (*London's Calamity*, 3). London-born Nathaniel Hardy (1618–1670), Dean of Rochester and Rector of St. Dionis, Backchurch, in Fenchurch Street, apologizes for his language in his epistle dedicatory to *Lamentation, Mourning and Woe*, claiming it is the effect and emblem of his experience and that "broken Language" is the "best Rhetorick":

> I *First* preached, *and have now* published *this Discourse as a* Testimony *of my* sorrow *for* Londons Ruines. *If the* phrase *and* composure *be (as I am* conscious *they are) very* defective, *my* Apology *is, That it was a time of* Distraction; *besides,* broken *Language is the best* Rhetorick *upon a* mournful *occasion: And considering those manifold* Relations *and* Obligations *I have to that once illustrious* City, *it will not (I hope) be looked upon as a* presumption, *that I have thus* publickly *expressed my* sorrow; *for that* cloud *of* smoke *which hath* covered her, *or rather that* flame *of* fire *which hath* laid her honour in the dust.[36]

Even in a time when printers made inconsistently free use of italics, Hardy's epistle dedicatory is particularly fraught; whether intentional or otherwise (on the part of Hardy or the printer), the visual (not to mention transcribal) effect is of passionate disorder. It's not just the nouns that get their typographical emphasis – the empha-sized words tell enough of the thumping narrative on their own: "broken," "mournful," "publickly," "covered her," "laid her honour in the dust."

A primary rhetorical response of the sermons to the sense of cultural shatter-ing is to rebuild the idea of the House of God. The function of sermons is gener-ally to instruct and either to comfort or to disconcert as needed. Sermons *explain*; they open texts, interpret events, offer answers. They close the spiritual and tempo-ral distance between the Bible and this world, applying the vocabulary and imagery of scripture to local everyday life. Sermons in general after the Fire remain more allegorical, less locally, topographically explicit, than the poetry or private narratives do – and not surprisingly, as their psychological or spiritual success is predicated on the translation to another world, a Foucauldian heterotopia of illu-sion (or Elsewhere) – thus in William Gearing's dismal *No Abiding City* we are adjured to remember that, even if our greatest cities don't hold up ("your continual repairing them sheweth them to be of no long continuance" [191]), there is a heav-enly city "too high for any Adversary to approach" (227), which "hath founda-tions in the Plural number; it hath many foundations, firm and immoveable, foundations that cannot be shaken" (228). (Yet even in his pessimism is a rhetoric of assurance: "*Foundations* in the plural" – foundations, foundations, foundations – hammering solidity home, so to speak.) And in Gearing's even more dismal and punishing *God's Soveraignty Displayed*, after reminding us that "Death is neer, Death is in your streets, Death is creeping in at your houses, and entring in at your windows" (11), and that God "hath cast you out of your pleasant habitations" (120), there is the assurance that "he, who is the keeper of *Israel*, is your home and habitation."[37] William Thomas (1593–1667), an ejected Puritan minister writing from Oxford as a "well-wisher to the City," consoles the Londoners:

But O, How great a comfort is it, that a Mans outward Estate is never so lost, ruined, and laid in the rubbish, but God can renew it, and make it as good as ever it was ... And though (as here it is said, *verse* 14) all young mens musick be gone, yet (as it is, *Zech.* 8.5.) *the streets of the City* (if it be a City of *truth and holiness*, verse 3) *shall be full of Boyes and Girles playing in the streets thereof*, which to God is very feasible and familiar.[38]

The ministers offer the comfort of the house of God, of the foundations of heaven, as security for the loss of these. The fact that those images lay in waiting, that the house of God was a familiar structure that withstood the Fire and remained available, must have had a certain comfort in its very historical as well as religious sanction.

On the other hand, shifts in sermonic discourse suggest that such historical sanction suddenly seemed inadequate, even inappropriate; that this heterotopic house of God, eternal and stalwart as it might be, might seem, in some secret corner of the heart (at least for a moment), to have its own psychologically shaken foundations to all the one hundred thousand homeless in Moorfields, in Lincoln's Inn Fields, in boats on the Thames, in the houses of friends. There is certainly a sense in which the allegorical comforts administered from afar change shape, and not always subtly, the closer the minister is to London. Familiar images spring suddenly into sharp, local, detailed relief. Robert Elborough, for example – the minister of the burned St. Laurence Pountney (a church dating from 1275 and not rebuilt after the Fire) unpacks Ezekiel's text in surprisingly specific ways:

> *The flaming flame shall not be quenched.* He doth not say, they shall not endeavour to quench it. In a common Calamity, who will not put to his helping hand? though in our sad disaster I wish every one had conscienciously [sic] discharged their duty: But notwithstanding their endeavours it shall not be quenched. Such, such shall be the rage and violence of it, as that aching hearts and helping hands, as that, to speak in our dialect and usual practice, Buckets, Engines, Ladders, Hooks, the opening of Pipes, and sweeping of Channels, shall not avail any thing at all: No, they would not withdraw the fewel of their corruption, and God would not withdraw the Fire of his indignation. *(London's Calamity, 4)*

The text pulls back out of details of individual duty and fire-fighting techniques and into larger spiritual matters, but the not-specially-biblical images of opened pipes and swept channels distinctly localize the full translation into the more abstract City of Heaven and House of God.

Nathaniel Hardy (he of the broken rhetoric) tries on several images to accom-modate the disaster in *Lamentation, Mourning, and Woe*, all of them either exhausted old clichés or silly new ones. At one point he compares London to a withered, scorched, burnt laurel leaf (21); at another to old Troy (a common trope before the Fire as well) (21); to a Camera Regis and a King's Coffer (25); and much to Pepys's disgust, he declaims: "this large *Volume* in *Folio* [is] abridged almost to an *Octavo*, there being, as is probably computed, scarce a *sixth* part remaining *within the Walls*" (21). Hardy had preached this sermon at St. Martin's in the Fields (safely west – though not by that much – of the Fire's limits) the Sunday after the Fire. Pepys writes: "to church again, and there preached Deane Harding [Hardy]; but methinks *a bad poor sermon, though proper for the time* – nor eloquent, in saying at this time that the City is reduced from a large Folio to a Decimo tertio" (*Diary*, VII:283, my emphasis). Hardy's own church was safely outside the sweep of the Fire, but as he notes in his epistle dedicatory, "London *was the* place *of my* Birth, Baptism, Education, *and* (*excepting those* years *which I lived in the* University *of* Oxford) in *and* about *the* City, *hath been the* place *of my* abode *and* habitation to this day" (A2v). As with Elborough's emphatic local detail, Hardy's personal connections with London may explain his eventual rhetorical shift from the inad⁄ equate metaphors of laurels and folios and Troys to a specific reference to James Howell's *Londinopolis* (a 1657 version of John Stow's *Survey of London*) and a very expressive, explicit litany of local sorrows:

> Let the *Merchants weep* for the *downfall* of that *Royal Exchange* (where they used to drive on their mutual Commerce) with the several *Wharfs* and *Keyes*, which were so commodious for landing their Goods.
> Let the several *Companies weep* for the *ruine* of their *Halls*, where they were wont to *meet* each other in love and unity . . .
> *Finally*, Let all the *Inhabitants* of this *City*, and her adjacent parts, *weep* to consider how many *Families* have not where to hide their *heads*, but are *scattered* up and down the *Fields* for *want* of their *Habitations*: Yea, how many *wealthy Citizens* are very much *impoverished*, and *some* of them brought to a *morsel of bread*. *(*Hardy, *Lamentation*, 23–24*)*

The loss of generic buildings and institutions is contextualized with specific mention of the Royal Exchange and the implicit but equally specific gesture towards the city livery companies whose halls burned down (including the Brewers, the Butchers, the Clothworkers, the Cordwainers, among others), and Christ's Hospital in Newgate Street. Thirteen years later, in a commemorative sermon, Henry Hesketh (1637?–1710), rector of Charlwood, Surrey, and after 1678 vicar of St. Helen, Bishopsgate, employs the same specificity of local detail to make his larger point:

> If the Stones were calcined in our Walls, and the Beams consumed to
> powder, it was because these had cryed each to other, as unable to support the

Load of our Frauds and Violences . . . If our great Conventions and Halls were not, it was but to impose a Fast for their former Plethories. And, in a word, if our City was made a fiery Oven, it was because we had contracted Dross, from which we needed refining.[39]

Each biblical allusion follows a locally specific clause; the biblically general larger point about the "fiery oven" acquires precisely historicized detail in calcined stones and powdered beams.

Biblical metaphors and allusions in general – which would rhetorically seem as if divinely lying in wait for this their aptest purpose – are suddenly troubled because in fact they are no longer metaphors. Their meaning no longer lies in absence but in presence. They are not the dead metaphors or nonmetaphors of classical rhetoric which have more or less imperceptibly slid into ordinary discourse; they are *abruptly* literalized, and tested in that literalization. The foundations *are* shaken, owls *do* inhabit temples, the flaming flame was *not* quenched, and God *hath* cast everybody out of their pleasant habitations. Allegory becomes documentary, and the emphasis of narrative shifts; detail of experience (calcined stones, opened pipes, swept channels, rubbished streets) combine powerfully with details of place to such an extent that *this place* is reexamined in hindsight; *this place* has been lost: *where is it and what was it*?

The fire poems are occupied with and shaped by the same concerns as the sermons, but they tend to deal with narrative and imagery in rather different ways. In their formal rigor (well, structure) and insistent optimism, they tend to create more compensatory heterotopias. The large body of poems, mostly by "divines or solid citizens or journalists, not members of the facile gentlemanly mob," as one editor of such poems puts it,[40] records a variety of voices speaking expressly and locally from the ruins and employing poetic structures as well as imagery to express the experience of the Fire but also to define and perhaps contain the boundaries of that experience. The imagery of collapse and chaos and transformation is equally present: John Allison (1645–1683), a Fellow of King's College, Cambridge, watches the fire's "fury still increas'd, and all / Houses and Churches Undistinguisht fall, / Resolv'd to know no limits, less than a City Wall";[41] John Tabor (b. 1607), registrar to the Bishop of Ely, claims that "Even the whole City in a manner lies / A ruinous heap to all spectators eyes";[42] Simon Ford (1619?–1699) – a Puritan under the Royalists, a Royalist under the Puritans, and finally Chaplain of Bridewell in 1670 – apostrophises: "Lo, here, a *City* to a *Chaos* turn'd."[43] And appropriately (if to some surprisingly) the City Poet Elkanah Settle, butt of Dryden and Pope, quite aptly articulates the conceptual and physical transformation within the linguistic: "Tis changd, without a Metaphor, I may say / From *Terr' del foego* to *Incognita*" (Settle, *Elegie*, 6). But verse form itself, often ostentatiously chosen, suggests the sharp conceptual contrast to the unbounded and unexpected destruction of the Fire not just by the effort of linear narrative, but also by varieties of strict formal containment and prescription. John Allison, for example, couches his version of the fire "In an humble Imitation of the most Incomparable Mr. Cowley his *Pindarick* Strain." The choice is conceptually apt, both for the pindaric accommodation of bombasity and the Cowleyan element of irregularity, fluctuation, surprise:

VII.

The Watches now in every street
Eccho the dreadful noyse of Fire,
Which calls with the same energy from bed,
As the last Trumpet shall the dead,
And bids them all draw nigher,
The shiv'ring multitudes in bodies meet
And some it raiseth by its light, and others by its heat.

Most of the poems, however, occupy more insistently symmetrical heroic coup-lets, as if the steady stately march of iambic pentameter is at least an effective psychological container for the fire, as in Joseph Guillim's (d. 1670, fellow of Brasenose College) *The Dreadful Burning of London*:

And here, although whole Streets but prove a Prey
To hungry Flames, through which they eat their Way:
How few among such multitudes engage,
To check their progress, or to quench their rage?

As the destructive Fire doth forward creep,
Its shining train whole Streets away doth sweep.
Which wandring Flames, lose and destroy their way,
And having ruin'd all, themselves decay.[44]

The destruction of whole streets – that conceptual enormity requiring repetition – is contained in neighboring stanzas; the voracious unpredictability of the flames is countered by the (tedious) padded predictability of the rhymes; indeed, the force of the wandring Flames seems dissipated by the very fact of being described so, decaying within the rhyme itself.

    The poems often actively assert their wish, if not their ability, to effect change through sheer poetic power, as if the invocation itself might push things along. Guillim, for example, in his epistle dedicatory to Sir William Turner, Knight and Alderman, confesses: "Having made a Poetical Attempt in describing the dismal Ruine of so Renown'd a City, I wish now I could so much farther play the

Poet, as to be like that *Thracian*, whose strains could make confus'd Stones rally into Order" (*Dreadful Burning*, A3); and Simon Ford apostrophises:

> This *Quill* should dig down *Mountains*, and my Muse
> The list'ning *Marbles* from their Beds seduce.
>
> Th' whole *Parian Quarrey* should obey her calls,
> And march a Volunteer to *London's Walls*.
>
> *(Londons Resurrection,* lines 19–22*)*

The vocabulary and stock of imagery seems initially as capacious as the biblical store, although generally classical in bent: Ford calls on Orpheus for his lyre and Amphion for his flute (as does Guillim), and Troy is the constant reference. A number of poems (by William Smith, Simon Ford, John Crouch, and Joseph Guillim, for example) are written in Latin or Greek, with or without English translations. There is also the large batch of poets for whom the classical imagery is either unavailable or inadequate – yet what Robert Aubin calls the "wretched conceits, puns, and dubious syntax and grammar" of the "Pie Corner muse" (Aubin, *London in Flames*, ix) may also be read as the conceptual efforts of a wide range of people to give voice and form to the unspeakable, the unthinkable.

John Tabor, like Nathaniel Hardy, confesses his own sense of linguistic incapacity, but channels it into firm, perhaps comforting and certainly reliable structures of heroic verse in *Seasonable Thoughts in Sad Times*. His preface to the reader announces that he was all set to write a poem about the war and the plague of the previous year:

> But then the startling and astonishing news of the Cities Conflagration
> turned my Muse to a new wrack of tormenting griefs, rending me as many
> others for a time capable of nothing but to stand in the way for News . . . till at
> length occurring the joyful report of the miraculous extinguishing of the
> Flames, and unexpected Preservation of the unconsumed part of the City
> and Suburbs, my mind became more sedate and quiet.   *(A4)*

Then all the horrors of the past few years get compressed into (admittedly rather versically challenged) couplets.

But Tabor's verses also begin to negotiate the enormity of change through the anticipation of perspectives over time:

> Upon *September*'s second day i'th'year
> Much talkt of *Sixty six, did there appear
> By two i' th' morning those consuming Flames,
> *Which did break out first in the Street* of Thames.
>
> *(Seasonable Thoughts,* 21*)*

The asterisk points the reader to the marginal note: "*Sept. 2. 1666. [by] two in the morning began this fire, which was not suppresst in all places till Friday morning following." Standing thus close to the Fire, the poet accommodates his sense of enormity by assuming language more appropriate to fifty years hence, and declaring its historicity by stepping outside the self-appointed boundaries of verse with a visually separate assertion of fact, typographically emphasizing separation, dissonance, distance.

Perspectives of distance often combine grammatically. In another of Ford's poems, for example, the living city is defined by and entombs its own past:

> The *City now* is the *once-City*'s Tomb,
> A *Sceleton* of *fleshless Bones* become.
> Its *Venerable Ruines* have the *Name*
> Of what it *was*, but *little* else the *same*.[45]

London *was*, now. London was, but is no more. In Thomas Brooks's sermon *Londons Lamentations* (1670), the London of the present gets buried in the grammatical past:

> *London* in those former times was but a little City, and had but a few men in it
> in comparison with **what it was now**. *London* was then but a great
> Banqueting-house, to **what it was now**: Nor the consumption of *London* by
> fire then, was nothing proportionable to the consumption of it by fire now . . .
> O what Age or Nation has ever seen or felt such a dreadful visitation as **this
> that been**. (26)

Over fifty years later, Defoe will employ much the same linguistic pattern in his novels to much the same effect as he superimposes an image of a past London onto a present, as in the scene in *Colonel Jack*, when Jack runs away with his first stolen bag:

> [S]o away he had me through *Long-alley*, and Cross *Hog lane*, and *Holloway
> lane*, into the middle of the great Field, which **since** that, has been call'd the
> *Farthing pye-house-field* . . . so we went on, cross'd the Road at *Anniseed Cleer*,
> and went into the Field where **now** the Great Hospital stands.[46]

A bit like Jack, Brooks offers the reader two Londons simultaneously, or rather, two pasts of London: its historical past, the London known; and the passing of that past, the London destroyed. These historical animals, in Pocock's words, are carrying out their perception of the new – the sudden collapse of familiar space – within the grammar of temporal collapse, testing old ways of perception and attempting new ways of articulation.

All genres of Fire narratives thus move in a sense forward and backward over place as well as over time; following the contours, the names, the places of the streets as the fire sweeps through them, plotting its course by the nature of the streets and buildings that determine it; and then backwards over the same ground as the Fire has reshaped it. The city as a whole has been changed; the narratives that attempt to deal with the change see the whole transformed into heap, the ordered city into jumbled ruin; the known into unknown.

Spaces of loss: public buildings, private dwellings, and streets

I will conclude this chapter with three brief historicized meditations on the destroyed public, private, and intermediary urban spaces, and their conceptual implications for later literary genres and works. These spaces of loss, recorded in Fire genres in terms of fragmentation and loss, get imaginatively rebuilt in later litereratures. The streets, literally emptied, closed, and impassable after the Fire, are imaginatively repeopled, becoming structures of meaning in poetry and avenues of possibility in prose. Public buildings and public spaces, figured as forlorn and treacherous in the immediate aftermath, become phoenixes of social meaning as they are reconstructed into fixtures of institutional identity. And private spaces – exposed and destroyed by the fire, made public in vulnerability, and demanding attention to personal detail in recovery – become the ultimate dwelling-place of narrative, the home for the most crucial retellings of private, individual, daily life.

In one of the more richly complicated printed consolations or quasi-sermons, O. S.'s *Counsel to the Afflicted*, the text introduces through the device of "Objections" a variety of anguished human voices in different situations, with different concerns and points of view, and either imagines or reports, in "Objection 17," a person consciously concerned with the disruption of public space: "It is not my own private loss that troubles me . . . but I am much afflicted to see *London* the glory of *England*, the chief and principal City of this Nation laid in ashes, and to see so many magnificent Buildings, so many goodly Churches, stately Halls, fair Houses, useful Hospitals, &c. demolished" (*Counsel to the Afflicted*, 118). The destruction of recognized public buildings meant that the larger, normally implicit, institutional framework for daily life was itself abruptly destabilized, rendering institutionality itself more visible. The Fire and rebuilding narratives ask: What were these framing public structures that grew up slowly to define us?

Consistently, the various Fire narratives list and name the range of public spaces and structures destroyed or changed. As with the litany of street names, although with different purposes and effects, a litany of buildings burned carries more semiotic weight than just a tabulation of damage; it implies a disintegration of fundamental structure, conceptual as well as architectural. Such a litany *also* supplies a form of textual reconnection. Lists *record* fragments; lists also *connect* them. The Fire and rebuilding coincided with and perhaps contributed to a cultural fascination for lists: newspapers tabulated victories and losses at sea, and gradually admitted advertisements that sorted properties and consumer goods (see chapter two); topographies and maps increasingly listed as well as depicted streets (see chapter three); the Royal Society was busy identifying and labelling the phenomena of both microcosm and macrocosm; Robinson Crusoe is as known for his inventory of goods and inventions as *Gulliver's Travels* is for its list of human vices and atrocities. In a sense, the *literary* details of everyday life live more in itemized lists than in visual description. Lists become part of the restructuring of the experience of urban space in London after the Fire, as well as of its rebuilding and reshaping. And a list of buildings destroyed marks a physically and perhaps conceptually larger emptiness.

Evelyn notes that the *way* that the Fire destroyed public space was by overextending it on the one hand: "it burned both in breadth & length, The Churches, Publique Halls, Exchange, Hospitals, Monuments, & ornaments, leaping after a prodigious manner from house to house & streete to streete, at great distance one from the other" (*Diary*, III:452). It took an effort; the Fire also seemed to implode the spaces between the structures:

> No Church, no Hall, no House, no Hospitall
> Can stand before it, but it ruines all:
> What will not burn, it breaks with piercing heat,
> And tumbling down with rubbish fills the street.
>
> *(Tabor, Seasonable Thoughts, 22)*

Evelyn, after his own litany of streets ("all *Fleetstreets*, old baily, Ludgate hill, Warwick Lane, Newgate, Paules Chaine, Wattling-streete now flaming"), adds another list – of the ornamental interstices of public spaces literally melted down: "The lead, yronworke, bells, plate &c mealted; the exquisitely wrought Mercers Chapell, the Sumptuous Exchange, the august fabricque of Christ church, all the rest of the Companies Halls, sumptuous buildings, Arches, Enteries, all in dust" (Evelyn, *Diary*, III:460). Thomas Brooks's sermon suggests that what formerly marked divisions and even held things apart now seemed to work *with* the Fire:

> [C]onsider the extensiveness of it. How did this dreadful fire spread it self, both with and against the wind, till it had gained so great a force, as that it despised all mens attempts? It quickly spread it self from the East to the West, to the destruction of Houses of State, of Trade, of Publick Magistracy, besides Mynes of Charity; it spread it self with that violence, that it soon crumbled into ashes our most stately Habitations, Halls, Chappels, Churches, and famous Monuments. Those Magnificent Structures of the

City that formerly had put stops, and given checks to the furious flames, fall
now like Stubble before the violence of a spreading fire.

(Brooks, *London's Lamentations, 20*)

In the margin beside this quotation, visually and textually reinforcing both
separation and enormity, sits this summary point: "Within the Walls of the City,
there were eighty one Parishes consumed. For every hour the fire lasted, there was
a whole Parish consumed." The public structures that had marked differences,
ordered space, checked fire, controlled threats, were now consumed whole,
"flaked and enervated," as the strange but apt Edward Waterhouse put it: "from
the East to the West it prostrated Houses, Halls, Chappels, Churches,
Monuments; all which it so flaked and enervated, that it has left few standing
walls, stout enough to bear a roof" (*A Short Narrative*, 68–69). Of Guildhall
("once the Glory of our Isle, / Become but now the Cities Funeral Pile"
[Guillim, *Dreadful Burning*, 9]) – the center of civic government, where lord
mayors and sheriffs were elected, where the Court of Common Council met, and
where important trials were held – only the exterior walls survived. Of the Royal
Exchange, built by financier Sir Thomas Gresham and opened in 1570 as a
covered meeting place for the country's merchants, the one thing that survived the
desolation of the interior was the figure of Gresham himself – a fact that seemed
full of latent significance to many chroniclers: "Sir *Tho: Gresshams* Statue,
though falln to the ground from its nich in the Ro: Exchange remain'd intire,
when all those of the Kings since the Conquest were broken to pieces" (Evelyn,
Diary, III:460). Pepys simply marks the fact: "The Exchange a sad sight, nothing
standing there of all the statues or pillars but Sir Tho. Gresham's picture in the
corner" (Pepys, *Diary*, VII:276). Whole poems would be devoted to the rebuilding of the Exchange alone, and royal reopenings of the city, arranged by Thomas
Jordan, made it a processional focal point; the rebuilt Exchange would occupy a
central imaginative place in the imaginative rebuilding of London's economy in
the works of Restoration and Augustan writers.

The city was shaken into pieces; fragments of public buildings pointed to but
no longer contained meaning. The Fire enacted a very disturbing transformation
of the public sphere, so to speak, and a list of its chief markers becomes an indi-
cator of the thing that is not. At the ruin of St. Paul's, Evelyn remarks the new
meaninglessness of architectural signs:

that beautifull Portico (for structure comparable to any in Europ, as not long
before repaird by the late King) now rent in pieces, flakes of vast Stone Split
in sunder, & nothing remaining intire but the Inscription in the *Architrave*
which shewing by whom it was built, had not one letter of it defac'd: which I
could not but take notice of . . .   (Evelyn, *Diary*, III:458–59)

The poems and narratives try to articulate the fragments of spatial meaning left in their city, to reconstruct a wholeness at least of meaning or implication:

> A half burnt Steeple was the Sign o' th' Street.
> A dumb deformity could nothing say,
> No, not so much as give ye time o' th' day.[47]

But the poems often confess themselves no more effective in articulating meaning than the scattered fragments they describe:

> But when the Churches and the Bellfries burn,
> The Bells are dumb, and their black towers mourn.
> What Fire is this, makes the bells cease to chime?
>
> (Guillim, *Dreadful Burning*, 8)

The frame of the question itself suggests the impossibility of an answer, the sense of poetic energy left open, drifting, itself ungrounded. Texts remain without their contexts; as with the street names, signs suddenly point nowhere. Empty space has supplanted designated place.

But perhaps most lasting in its literary effect on later writers – most particularly Defoe – was the sense of spatial *treachery* that marked the collapse of public buildings. The ruin of St. Paul's was particularly haunting. Pepys writes: "[Sept.] 7. Walked thence and saw all the town burned, and a miserable sight of Pauls church, with all the roofs fallen and the body of the Quire fallen into St Fayths – Paul's school also – Ludgate – Fleet street – my father's house, and the church, and a good part of the Temple the like" (*Diary*, VII:279). The sanctuaries have not simply disappeared, they have even more fundamentally betrayed their trust. Evelyn, with Pepys, remarks the collapse of St. Faith's, but more particularly in its ruined function as archival refuge: "the ruines of the Vaulted roofe, falling brake into St. Faithes, which being filled with the magazines of bookes, belonging to the Stationer<s>, & carried thither for safty, they were all consumed burning for a weeke following" (*Diary*, III:459). The destruction of the choir of St. Paul's into St. Faith's was an historical as well as structural collapse. In 1256 old St. Paul's had expanded over the territory of a small parish church, and in compensation had given the parishioners space in the crypt beneath. It was to a larger, lighter version of this crypt space that the publishers rushed to store their books during the Fire, relying on the thick stone walls for protection. The trust was misplaced, and in fact the space was permanently lost: the rebuilt St. Paul's did not reappoint internal space for the stationers ("The *Saint* was tortur'd when he broke his *Faith*!" shouts the royalist verse-writer John Crouch in *Londinenses Lacrymae* [6]).[48] "Even the Churches were no *Sanctuary*," says the anonymous author of *London Undone*, repeating the most obsessive cry. Guillim's poem houses structural betrayal and spiritual desolation within the formally ironic stability of heroic couplets:

> When to St. *Pauls* among the Books [the Fire] came,
> Learn'd Authors, for to shun the dreadful flame,
> To the magnifick Temple soon do flye
> For Refuge, as their only Sanctuary:
> Yet could not safety at the Altar find
> Though they had been like Saints themselves inshrin'd.
> Where shall we refuge seek, and pray? while thus,
> Heaven takes the very House of Prayer from us.
>
> *(Dreadful Burning, 9, 11)*

John Allison's pindaric odes express insecurity more structurally:

XV.

> When great Pauls was seen to fall,
>   People bid adieu to all,
>   And what hopes they had, resign'd,
> For they had little reason sure
> To think anything secure
>   When they cast their eyes behind.
>
> *(Upon the late Lamentable Fire)*

The physical temple of God, like its sermonic metaphors, was culturally collapsed, no longer (perhaps never?) what it seemed. Later Restoration and early eighteenth-century literature – and culture – would begin more widely and systematically to "read" the architectural spaces of buildings.

The issue of spatial treachery, like the later rebuilding issues of the pace of change, the extent of unfamiliarity, and the elasticity of boundaries, is often exaggerated in perception, or at least in post-Fire writers' accounts of cultural perception. London streets and buildings had long been notoriously dangerous in their physical instabilities. The prolific seventeenth-century artisan-writer Nehemiah Wallington (1598–1658), for example, writes over and over again about the sudden accidents and deaths of his neighbors, and the near-escapes of himself and his family, from collapsing chimneys, falling machinery, runaway carts, and fatal missteps, in the houses and streets of the city.[49] The old St. Paul's itself had long been functionally misoccupied by pedlars, con artists, stall-keepers, thieves, and gallants. But we don't speak ill of the dead: the study of literary rhetoric and cultural self-perceptions has of course as much to do with perceived change and self-representation as with actual change and accurate representation; the past by definition is fixed and thus seems stable; the Fire lit up all treacheries at once.

Not only were the public structures and signposts of London gone – the cultural and physical contexts or settings of daily urban life – but the smaller, closer, most profoundly meaningful of individual texts as well: the private spaces of ordinary life, the half-invisible details and habits of hundreds of thousands of private lives. Of course, "private" is not much of a social construct or concept in the mid-seventeenth century, even among the wealthy, and particularly not in the center of old London. The large shops of the more prosperous tradesmen often had the family living above the shop on one or two floors (with at least two people in each bedroom), and the upper floors and cellars rented or leased out to others of various classes and pursuits. (Todgers's in *Martin Chuzzlewit* has not evolved in use or size or convenience from its seventeenth-century foremodels.) And smaller houses could be even more packed, compressing whole families per room.[50] So "privacy" was not exactly dislodged by the Fire, and the homeless groupings in Moorfields would not be traumatized by the crowding *per se*, or by the lack of personal space. But "private life" in the sense of intimate, personal, domestic, *physical* details – the architectural spaces, however cramped and dark and dirty, that shaped the comings and goings of an individual's daily life, that *was* as well as *represented* the familiar, the secure, the given – all of that was fundamentally disrupted, all the more so from being repeated in thousands and thousands of cases, in 13,200 homes and shops destroyed, in 100,000 people evicted from their daily life. In that sense, private life as well as public life, personal as well as urban space, text as well as context, disappeared and would need to be redrawn as well as rebuilt.

Stockton in *Counsel to the Afflicted* records or at least imagines a number of those individual voices expressing several shifting concerns of domestic dislocation, social confusion, and personal vulnerability. One of his plaintiffs, for example, expresses repetitively the disconcertingness of disruption:

> I had a very sweet and commodious dwelling, where I lived very comfortably, and now I am greatly unsettled; I know not well where to dispose my self, I can't light on a house that pleaseth me, but am put to great straits, and am much troubled for the loss of my former habitation, and the inconvenience of my present abode.　　　　　(*Counsel to the Afflicted,* 93)

There is no such thing as ordinary life; people are destabilized, unfixed, marginalized within their own lives.

Standing around in Moorfields visually disturbs social barriers, and *all* the homeless find themselves for the moment in a conspicuous equality, as Evelyn observes:

> I left this smoking & sulltry heape, which mounted up in dismall clowds
> night & day, the poore Inhabitans dispersd all about St. Georges, Moore fields,

as far as higate, & severall miles in Circle, Some under tents, others under
miserab<l>e Hutts and Hovells, without a rag, or any necessary utinsils, bed
or board, who from delicatnesse, riches & easy accommodations in stately &
well furnishd houses, were now reduc'd to extreamest misery & poverty.

(Diary, III:457*)*

Anthony Wood, from his safe distance in Oxford, hammers out the providential
moral in repetitively concrete, intimate, insistent detail:

These that had a house to-day were the next glad of the shelter of an hedge or
pigstie or stable. Those that were this day riding wantonly in coaches, were,
the next, glad to ride in dung-carts to save their lives. Those that thought the
ground too unworthy to be touched by their feet, did run up to the knees in
dirt and water to save themselves from the fury of fire or the falling of houses.
Those that faired deliciously this day and nothing curious enough to satiate
their palatts, were within a few days following glad of a browne crust. Those
that delighted themselves in downe bedds and silken curteynes, are now glad
of the shelter of a hedge.   *(*Wood, *Life and Times,* 86*)*

Rich and poor alike are thrown in a heap and must scrabble for their physical and
social boundaries. The image of silken curtains as emblematic social boundaries
haunts Pepys as well: "To Sir W. Coventry at St. James's, who lay without
Curtains, having removed all his goods – as the King at White-hall and everybody had done and was doing" *(Diary,* VII:279). Presumably the king still didn't
sleep in a curtainless bed, much less in the shelter of a hedge, but Pepys as well as
Wood makes the cross-class generalization that all interior goods were removed
because all interior boundaries were threatened.

The most personal, intimate, and constant boundaries of private life – the curtains around one's bed, that promised warmth and darkness and privacy and protection from disease (so they believed) – were now rhetorically transferred to *outside.*
The spaces of intimate life were pulled open to public curiosity: Pepys and Evelyn,
and presumably many others, daily walked the streets or sat on bridges to observe
the progress of the Fire and the response of the people. Pepys, wandering among
the homeless in Moorfields, "drank there, and paid twopence for a plain penny
loaf" *(Diary,* VII:276). Distinctions between interior and exterior, privacy and
exposure, collapse at least momentarily with the distinctions of class and privilege.

Among the unsettled, bewildered crowds in Moorfields, each individual,
each family tries to pull together some sort of material life with tokens of the familiar, as Pepys observes:

Walked into Moore-fields (our feet ready to burn, walking through the town
among the hot coles) and find that full of people, and poor wretches carrying
their goods there, and everybody keeping his goods together by themselfs (and

a great blessing it is to them that it is fair weather for them to keep abroad night
and day). *(Diary, VII:276)*

Things assume great significance as the pegs of daily life, individually and collec-
tively the pieces of larger personal patterns of identity. Pepys himself is every bit as
materially conservative and detailed as Crusoe in his prioritization of and care for
his goods in the fear of the Fire: he and Sir W[illiam?] Penn dug a pit behind their
houses "and put our wine in it, and I my parmazan cheese as well as my wine and
some other things" (*Diary*, VII:274). A week later he confesses: "[Sept.] 14. . . . I
was troubled in being at home, to see all my goods lie up and down the house in a
bad condition, and strange workmen going to and fro might take what they would
almost" (*Diary*, VII:285). The Fire scattered or destroyed personal goods, or forced
people to scatter, bury, conceal, remove their goods, or in its aftermath left personal
effects lying up and down the house. Things, as well as people, had lost their place.

But what seems most to haunt many of the accounts of the loss of domestic
space is, as with the public buildings, the sense of spatial treachery in the ruin of
one's house – the physical and conceptual *context* for one's "things." Pepys,
looking as usual in vivid, personalized detail, describes the bewildered and dis-
believing attachment to domestic sites in the people and the pigeons in much the
same, sad, tolerant, associative terms:

> Poor people staying in their houses as long as till the very fire touched them,
> and then running into boats or clambering from one pair of stair by the water-
> side to another. And among other things, the poor pigeons I perceive were
> loath to leave their houses, but hovered about the window and balconies till
> they were some of them burned, their wings, and fell down. *(Diary, VII:268)*

As with the public spaces, sources of shelter become sources of threat. Fire narratives in general, of course, are accounts of suddenly treacherous interiors – the
investigations into papist plots, for example, opened up dozens of strange private
dramas. And providential literature characteristically emphasizes the hidden
local power of the unseen: William Gearing cheers his flock with the reminder
that the plague still lurks in the ruins of the city: "Death is neer, Death is in your
streets, Death is creeping in at your houses, and entring in at your windows"
(*God's Soveraignty*, 11). A city that had the year before been devastated in its most
private spaces and was thus already domestically destabilized, now had even the
illusory surface comfort of home and shelter unambiguously and in one sense
permanently destroyed. Pepys presumably speaks for many: "But much terrified
in the nights nowadays, with dreams of fire and falling down of houses" (*Diary*,
VII:287). Guillim's poem spends its first few stanzas in the silent vulnerable darkness of the bedroom:

> While urgent Sleep our heavy Eyes did close,
> And wrapt our mindes up in a soft Repose;
> Some glowing Coal, silent, and dark as night,
> Shakes its black Embers off, so shews its light.
> Which through some narrow room, did gently creep
> With a still foot, e're it abroad durst peep.
> Which will no longer now confined be,
> But steals forth with a kind of subtilty.   *(Dreadful Burning, 1–2)*

The origin of the fire is in the dark, in the night, in the intimacy of secret space, which can no longer *confine* the threat. Like the insistent public fear that the enemy was socially "within" – the Catholics, the fanatics, those extremists amongst us – and the spiritual certainty that the Fire was God's judgment for the interior sins of the city (sometimes actually located, as in the Sabbath-breaking in Moorfields), so many of the poems and Fire narratives reveal a lurking anxiety about the general interiority of fire, nurtured in our secret darkness, in a place where literal fact and psychological metaphor far too fully overlap.

What to some made things even worse was that the antidote seemed identical to the threat: one of the most effective, dramatic, and traumatic means of stopping the Fire was by pulling down houses. Pepys notes: "Now begins the practice of blowing up of houses in Tower-street, those next the Tower, which at first did frighten people more then anything; but it stop[ped] the fire where it was done – it bringing down the houses to the ground in the same places they stood, and then it was easy to quench what little fire was in it, though it kindled nothing almost" (*Diary*, VII:275). People naturally hesitated or resisted this measure – the Lord Mayor, Sir Thomas Bludworth, deplored the violence and what he foresaw as the city's future expense in recompensing property owners – and was much blamed afterwards for his lack of foresight and initiative (unjustly, as E. S. De Beer argues in his edition of Evelyn's *Diary* [see III:452n3, III:455n3]). It is a move both counter-intuitive – it demands destruction in the name of protection – and at the same time psychologically compelling – something akin to Crusoe's panicked instinctive response to throw down his enclosures, kill his goats, and plow under his crops, to save them from being destroyed by cannibals – the urge to destroy what is dear so it cannot be lost:

> And our distress in this the greater was,
> In that just Heaven had made our hands (alas)
> The active Instruments to tear down
> Our own beloved Mansions to the ground.
> *(Wiseman, Londons' Fatal Fire, 6)*

If, as postmodern cultural geographers argue, space is a socially produced dialectic, what are the short- and long-term consequences of being required to contribute to the destruction of your own domestic habitat, particularly for a greater civic good that essentially disappeared anyway? What effects would this have on the redrawing of London's lines, on individual rebuilding of personal space, of the cumulative reconstruction of public space? Part of the answer seems to lie in an apparent value shift within urban spaces, in a new prominence of streets and a new creation of distance between houses, a clearing of space between them, and so a conscious reification of private space, another articulated step into the wider context of changing European habits of living. And in literature, long after the things of houses and the pieces of daily life had been restored into homes, narratives would continue to expand within the conceptual contours of private dwellings and private lives.

London's streets disappeared during the Fire in several senses, and the narratives of Fire almost unanimously include representations of inaccessibility, unfamiliarity, dislocation, and the breakdown of network. Streets, like lists, normally link as well as separate space. But after the Fire street space was collapsed, neither linking nor separating but disfiguring and disrupting. First, it was literally not possible to get to places: "the streets [were] full of nothing but people and horses and carts loaden with goods, ready to run over one another, and removing goods from one burned house to another – they now removing out of Canning-street (which received goods in the morning) into Lumbard Streete and further" (Pepys, *Diary*, VII:270). Pepys marvels "to see how the streets and the highways are crowded with people, running and riding and getting of carts at any rate to fetch away thing[s] . . . [and] Tower-hill . . . was by this time full of people's goods, bringing their goods thither" (*Diary*, VII:272–73). The anonymous poem *London Undone* marks that "Places were lost where Coach and Cart might meet." After the Fire, Evelyn notes: "The bielanes & narrower streetes were quite fill'd up with rubbish" (*Diary*, III:461). On the fourth of September, Evelyn describes a ride through the city that in event as in narrative seems to trace transition into stoppage, moving through a list of streets that physically shift from hostility to resistance:

> The burning still rages; I went now on horse back & it was now gotten as far as the Inner Temple; all *Fleetestreete*, old baily, Ludgate hill, Warwick Lane, Newgate, Paules Chaine, Wattling-streete now flaming & most of it reduc'd to ashes, the stones of *Paules* flew like granados, the Lead mealting downe the streetes in a streame, & the very pavements of them glowing with fiery redness, so as nor horse nor man was able to tread on them, & the demolitions had stopped all the passages, so as no help could be applied. *(Diary,* III:454*)*

Avenues designed for access, for travel, for mobility, for passage, for transition, were filled and stopped with human panic and physical wreckage.

Second, part of the horror of the streets was not simply that their contours of buildings had disappeared, but that their very contours were changed, that the streets were "quite fill'd up with rubbish," as Evelyn says, or fallen into cellars and secret underground spaces, and one could not "have possibly knowne where he was, but by the ruines of some church, or hall, that had some remarkable towre or pinacle remaining" (*Diary*, III:461). On the first day after the Fire had been stopped, Evelyn describes "mountains" of strange emptiness that occupy space designed for passage, for connection:

> [Sept.] 7. I went this morning on foote from White hall as far as *London*
> bridge, thro the Late fleete streete, Ludgate hill, by St. Paules, Cheape side,
> Exchange, Bishopsgate, Aldersgate, & out to Morefields, thence thro
> Cornehill, &c: with extraordinary difficulty, clambring over mountaines of
> yet smoking rubbish, & frequently mistaking where I was.   (*Diary*, III:458)

Streets are always in some sense containers as well as markers of space; in London in the seventeenth century, they were even visually so, with barriers set up during the Commonwealth as a part of military defence.[51] But now, says Evelyn, "the vast yron Chaines of the Cittie streetes, vast hinges, barrs & gates of Prisons were many of them mealted, & reduc'd to cinders by the vehement heats" (*Diary*, III:461). By demolishing and distorting the traditional boundaries of the city, the Fire in a sense spilled open its barriers, drawing attention to structural containers by their absence.

John Tabor's poem *Seasonable Thoughts in Sad Times* returns again and again to the power of the fire to break street bounds:

> [The Fire] *did break out first in the Street of* Thames:
> And then blown on by a strong wind into
> The City, what e're Art, or strength could do
> Of men to stop, or slack its fury, by
> The Friday did in ruines lie
> The greatest part of that within the Wall,
> And much beside of that we Suburbs call:
> For it broke thorough *Newgate*, and went on
> To *Holborn-bridge*, and had through *Ludgate* gone,
> Up *Fleetstreet* into *Temple-bar* before
> Its fury stopt, and did burn down no more . . .
> What will not burn, it breaks with piercing heat,
> And tumbling down with rubbish fills the street:
> Through *London* streets, it comes and down all goes.   *(21–22)*

The Fire makes use of the streets and then sweeps beyond them; the streets, like the houses, seem to give up their last medieval identity and function in an act of self-destruction. In Guillim's poem it is as if the Fire knows exactly where to go and what to do when it gets there:

> The brightest of them [the flames] push tow'rd *Lumbard* Street,
> And lick up all opposing streams they meet.
> Where they the Jewels, and rich stones out-shine;
> And do the Gold but once again refine.   *(Dreadful Burning, 5)*

The materials are at hand, predefined in their function by their street, and so pre-destined in the alchemy of fire that would use and then permanently alter the significance of their names and the pattern of their lines.

Streets as markers of territory, as signs of place and direction, were emptied of their buildings and habitations and hence of their meanings. They had become nonlocators, or rather, markers of non-existence. Henry Griffith's postscript to his letter carrying the larger litany of streets quoted earlier visually portrays the frag-ment it describes: "Little of the city remaynes, save part of Broad and Bishop-gate streete, all Leadenhall street, and some of the adjacent lanes about Aldgate and Cretchett Fryers."[52] In Hollar's 1666 map of the burned city, based on Leake's survey of the ruins, the explanatory inset title includes the following key: "The blanke space signifeing [sic] the burnt part & where the houses are exprest, those places yet standing."[53] (See Figure 1.) Emptiness stands for emptiness; the burned city is represented not by black ashes and drawn ruins but by blank white space, with only the street names still standing. The empty space is in stark contrast to the familiarly detailed Hollaresque houses surrounding the ruined area, where human life and habitation is minutely inscribed and shadowed and three-dimen-sioned; the signifying emptiness foreshadows the future emphasis on two-dimen-sional groundplans in the decades of the rebuilding (see chapter two). The graphics of past and present co-exist here; the empty space, unlike the elevations of the surrounding surviving space, in fact signifies a metaphorical rather than strictly representational emptiness.

London's streets before the Fire had generally been subordinate, liminal space, designed of course for travel, transition, transmission, but typically narrow, cramped, dark, dirty, closed over with extended stories, and filled in with sheds and stalls and tenements – as *spaces*, experientially overshadowed by the combined domestic/commercial space of the City. Where the public edifices would be often magnificently rebuilt, and the private dwellings generally improved in structure, the streets would actually change less than any other physical aspect of the City – as chapter three will show, there was an intensely concerted effort to recover the ancient webbing in all its tiny detail.

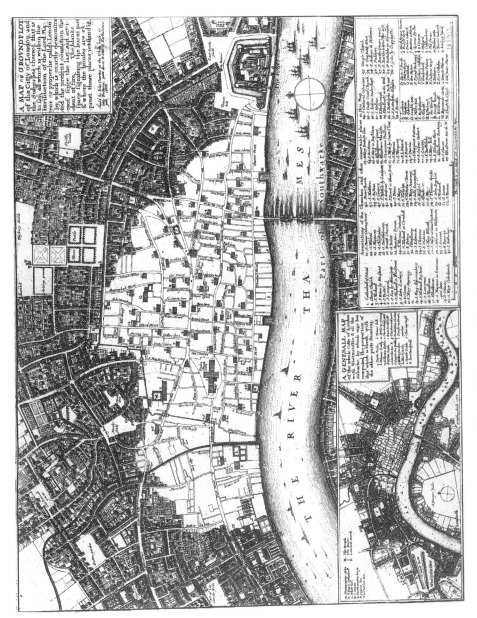

Figure 1 John Leake's survey of the ruins, engraved by Hollar (1666).

But that difference in emphasis between architectural and topographical space is fundamentally significant. Those street names – historically familiar to their inhabitants, relatively transparent and denotative to virtually any traveller – those place indicators of now lost, ruined, distorted, unrecognizable spaces, would over the next few decades command intense cultural interest and assume great cultural importance. In fact, the English interest in London's street names and meanings continued to escalate from this period through the eighteenth and nineteenth centuries in both literary and topographical works. To quote Kostof slightly out of context: "The street, it seems clear in this attitude, will no longer be thought of as the space left over between buildings, but as a spatial element with its own integrity" (Kostof, *City Shaped*, 215). The rhetorics of loss and rebuilding – the journalism, poems, sermons, plays, and novels – would most often if variously live in the streets, and thus most truly be topographies – etymologically, as Miller reminds us, the writings of *place*. London streets would become the semiotic structure redefining London, reinvested with social, political, and commercial meaning in a cross-cultural and profound attempt to reattach the street signs to their signified spatiality – to make *lived* space once again *known* space.

CHAPTER TWO

LONDINI RENASCENTI: THE SPACES OF REBUILDING

[O]n the 13 [September], I presented his Majestie with a Survey of the ruines, and a Plot for a new Citty, with a discourse on it.   John Evelyn, *Diary*[1]

If the rhetorics of Fire and loss momentarily fused together in their conceptualiza-tions of spatial anxieties, the possibility of redefining the city in the act of rebuild-ing it produced both a new and widespread cultural awareness of space itself, and (apparently) ideologically divided attitudes towards that spatial awareness. The Fire had destroyed 13,200 houses, the Royal Exchange, the Custom House, 44 of the City's Companies, the Guildhall and nearly all of the civic buildings, St. Paul's and 87 parish churches, as well as the furniture, records, wares, all the small uncountable wealth of *things* in individual lives, with a total damage estimated at £10,000,000 – a "staggering calamity" in the neighborhood of £5,000,000,000 today.[2] The blasted emptied ground seemed to some to beg for sweeping physical (and implicitly political, social, and economic) reform. The optimistically specific royal declarations of Charles, the elegant baroque plans of Sir Christopher Wren and John Evelyn, the practical grids of Robert Hooke and Richard Newcourt, the suggestions of Valentine Knight and Edward Jerman, all promised in different ways to open, order, regulate, and unify the city. Yet plot by plot, house by house, property line by property line, the "phoenix" of central London rose out of its ashes looking remarkably like its old, impenetrable, irreg-ular self. The architecturally and spatially "new" was systematically displaced into the suburbs or "out-parts" – physically (if not culturally) marginalized. Commonly, accounts of the rebuilding – from the eighteenth to the twentieth century – have seen it as poignantly wasted opportunity, an unparalleled example of civilian obstinacy and short-sightedness, a caving-in under the pressures and exigencies of immediate economic need. T. F. Reddaway has pointed out that the myth of a lost London originated in the mid-eighteenth century, and shows that it was not *simply* the case that Wren's plan was accepted by King and Parliament only to be defeated by stubborn citizens; rather, the new plans were never practi-cally viable in the first place.[3] Business and life could not wait eight or ten months for aesthetic or political refinement. Though I generally agree with Reddaway's argument, I want to argue that in some sense it *was* a cultural stubbornness that resisted wholesale urban change, and that resistance was not wholly mercenary. The fact of public and architectural rethinking of the city, combined with a closer look at both the actual processes of rebuilding and the various literary articulations of those processes, suggests a more deliberate, insistent, and widespread cultural preference for recovering the London known and lost, rather than creating a London new and unknown. Despite dramatic visual differences between the rebuilt London imagined by Evelyn and Newcourt and the rebuilt London actualized by Peter Mills and John Oliver, certain conceptual and strategic similarities emerge as well, tokens of a larger cultural attempt to bridge the shocking gap between past and present. The very conditions that made dramatic urban change possible made it unacceptable; the rebuilding of the city became part of a search for original meaning and original structure.

After a look at the practical demands and rhetorical structures of Charles's official rebuilding proclamation, this chapter will explore first the ideological premises and the actual processes of rebuilding in so far as they contribute to an awakening of a different – wider – kind and intensity of spatial consciousness among post-Fire Londoners, and second, the ways that the new genre of the newspaper published and publicized such changed awareness. Directly or indirectly reflecting the rules for rebuilding that Charles commanded in his first royal declaration on the subject, the respectively baroque and geometricized plans by Evelyn and Newcourt both imagine a newly reordered and socially regulated culture from the new lines of their redrawings. Yet, also like Charles's text, each also negotiates the common anxieties of making the new and foreign the known, of making the visible slippage between the familiar past and the incomprehensible present and future somehow navigable. Although none of the half-dozen or so ambitious ideological plans for rebuilding ever materialized, the excited discussion about them widened the circles of the rebuilding debates. The survey plans of Hooke, Mills, and Oliver, along with the calendars of the Fire Courts, articulate the piecemeal reproduction of the city and its point-by-point property wrangles. The newspapers increasingly negotiated the boundaries between public and private spaces in the rebuilding processes, repeating and clarifying the demands of the royal proclamations, localizing their instructions, familiarizing their expectations, and widening the territory of their applications.

The city that re-emerges – reclaimed or built over by the rebuilding processes – would literally provide the contours of the new literary landscape: *MacFlecknoe* could include a "Pissing Alley" because the surveyors chose to reinscribe it on the map (see Figure 4 and chapter four). But those new (or newly confirmed) boundaries in turn increasingly *required* new forms of imaginative definition and placement, as each attempt to recover or rebuild the old produced its own brood of unexpected strangenesses. As the boundaries were being redrawn and rein-

habited, the very acts of redrawing and reinhabiting contributed to the increasing
fluidity of social and commercial topographies – a fluidity which would accelerate over the decades of rebuilding. Various acts of non-compliance with the surveying demands show in part people not returning to their neighborhoods;
contours as well as contents of neighborhoods changed; signboards as well as
social signs disappeared from the streets often never to be re-established in quite the
same way. The early strategies and rhetorics of rebuilding become part of what
would be decades of increasingly varied generic attempts to reinscribe London
with familiar spatial meaning, or to negotiate the strange.

Ideal redrawings

A number of eminent figures – Sir Christopher Wren, John Evelyn, Richard
Newcourt, an army captain Valentine Knight, and City Surveyor Edward
Jerman – submitted plans for a new London shortly after the Fire was subdued,
and all the plans shared in varying degrees an ardent interest in opening and
reordering the commercial, social, architectural, and topographical spaces of the
City. Most were conceptually patterned on the European models of Andreas,
Campanella, and others, where the spatial arrangement of the city was designed
to regulate or at least monitor the social and civic relationships of the inhabitants.
All of the plans were designed to ease avenues for trade, to comply with the
baroque demands for "commodiousness" and uniformity, to fulfill an ideal of
architectural splendor, and, implicitly or explicitly, to create a city more
demographically governable. Valentine Knight's proposals, for example, advise
on the title page: "II. The City Built Stately, with large Streets, the Houses not in
danger of Fire, and the ground all put to best Profit. III. The People will walk easy
and dry, the Houses of Office and Streets kept sweet and cleane, and Goods delivered much cheaper."[4] I shall focus here on Evelyn's and Newcourt's plans because
each vividly images and articulates strikingly different social reforms within
spatial reconstructions, and yet each paradoxically can be read as similarly
engaged in making the city legible, the past transmissible. In a way, each carries
out the original, equally idealistic – and equally unsuccessful – rhetoric of
Charles's first royal declaration. And though none of the idealized reformative
plans was seriously considered – or rather, the exigencies and realities of rebuilding showed the surveyors and through them the Parliament the practical
impossibilities of such widescale reform – they remain as significant texts in the
awakening debate over the boundaries, possibilities, and implications of the
rebuilding of this urban space.

Although London – like most cities – has a literary history of self-congratu-
lation, the passionate desire of Evelyn, Newcourt, and others to alter radically the

contours of the city are contextualized by an equally prevalent pre-Fire view of London as architecturally and spatially deformed, and socially, politically, and physiologically dangerous in that deformity. In his 1666 reconstruction of Elizabethan England, Hollar notes that the buildings of Cheapside and near the Temple before the Fire "appear unshapely to a modern eye accustomed to see fabricks constructed after happier Models."[5] But not only to the "modern" (post-Fire) eye: narratively posing as a French traveller to London in *Character of England* (1659), John Evelyn elaborated on one of his favorite themes – the appalling architectural mess that was London: "a *City* consisting of a wooden, northern, and inartificiall congestion of Houses; some of the principall streets so narrow, as there is nothing more deformed, and unlike, than the prospect of it at a distance, and its *asymmetrie* within the Walls."[6] Though large, it is "a very ugly Town" (*Character of England*, 27): its best public buildings are "built about, and converted into rascally *Ware-houses*" (*Character of England*, 11). He analogizes that "the *Buildings* . . . are as deformed as the minds & confusions of the people" (*Character of England*, 29) such that "it is not an easy matter to distinguish the *Ladie* from the *Chamber maid*" (*Character of England*, 43). Two years later, in *Fumifugium*, an appeal to the restored king to clean up the city, Evelyn deplores the fact that "the Glorious and Antient City" (even Evelyn participates in the self-paeoning) should in fact be "so full of Stink and Darknesses . . . [and] compos'd of such a Congestion of misshapen and extravagant Houses; That the Streets should be so narrow and incommodious in the very Center, and busiest places of Intercourse."[7] London was poised for change, cried out for it, insisted Evelyn and others – Edward Chamberlayne, in the second edition of *Angliae Notitia* in 1671, also describes the pre-Fire housing as "low, dark, deform, *Wooden* Cottages" (11:201). In 1661 Evelyn foresees gardens (his darling desire), buildings, statues, progress, order, and elegance; in 1666 he will briefly believe it at hand.[8]

On September 13, 1666 – the same day that Evelyn submitted his plan to the King – Charles issued his first proclamation intended to govern the rebuilding: *His Majestie's Declaration To His City of* LONDON, *Upon Occasion of the late Calamity by the lamentable FIRE.* The declaration issues specific instructions for rebuilding and mandates compliance, threatening punishments for those "obstinate and refractory persons [who] wil presume to erect such Buildings as they shal think fit, upon pretence that the Ground is their own, and that they may do with it as they please" (*Declaration*, 3). The magistrates are directed to watch out for such obstructionists, and to "pul down whatsoever such men shal presume to set up" (3). The *Declaration* later assures the people that there is "nothing less in Our thoughts, then that any particular persons right and interest should be sacrificed to the publick benefit or convenience, without such recompence as in justice he ought to receive for the same" (*Declaration*, 8). But the royal direction for obedience and cooperation, and the threat of architectural destruction for disobedience and obstinacy, governs the shape of the whole – the assurance inserted belatedly after five more pages. Citizens were commanded to consent to the alteration of property boundaries, and to accept reimbursement for street fronts sacrificed to streets.

The declaration sets out specific topographical and social agendas. The streets – the fundamental contours of the new space – are publicly and regally accorded specific ranks in the spatial hierarchy: "We resolve that all Streets cannot be of equal breadth, yet none shall be so narrow as to make the passage uneasy or incon-venient; nor wil we suffer any Lanes or Alleyes to be erected, but where upon mature deliberation the same shal be found absolutely necessary" (*Declaration*, 5–6). No pesky little lanes or alleys will be permitted to clutter up and confuse the new and properly ordered streetlines, any more than troublesome citizens will be suffered to rebuild at their own discretion. In fact, the regulation of private space and the reorganization of public streets will include a redistribution of unsightly trades, in an effort to clean the air as well as the streets. The declaration plans to move the brewers, dyers, and sugar-bakers, all of whom produce the irritant smoke so obnoxious to Evelyn (who had recommended just such a displacement in *Fumifugium* in 1661), to new and clustered locations – to make "all those Trades which are carried on by smoak to inhabit together" (*Declaration*, 7). The royal text for rebuilding envisions a clean sweep of change, a chance to restructure social and commercial patterns within regulated and clearly hierarchized street patterns.

Yet this royal document, prescribing as well as describing change, also reveals a predisposition for recovering or recreating the old: "Lastly, that We may encour-age men by Our Own example, We wil use all the expedition We can to re-build Our Custome-House in the place where it formerly stood, and enlarge it with the most conveniences for the Merchants that can be devised" (*Declaration*, 9–10). As noted in chapter one, "formerly" becomes a prominent term in post-Fire vocabu-laries, negotiating change by signalling the compression of difference. Even in the king's plans for the new building, the newness is literally grounded upon the old; the places of the past help to fix the conceptualization as well as the construction of the new.

In this sense, the most crucial and elementary step towards beginning the rebuilding of the new London would be the survey of its past – of the individual boundaries of citizens' properties:

> in order to the reducing this great and glorious design into practices ...
> We do hereby direct, that the Lord Mayor and Court of Aldermen ... cause an exact Survey to be made and taken of the whole ruins ... [so] that it may appear to whom all the Houses and Ground did in truth belong, what Term the several occupiers were possessed of, & at what Rents, and to whom.
>
> (*Declaration*, 7–8)

The survey would sort things out, make order out of ruin, clarify the problems of redistribution, mark the transition between past and present. With a survey, London would literally know where it once stood and now stands.

The *Declaration* ends on an optimistic note, as if watching the unfolding of its commanded plans, almost as if it creates in its proclamatory power the "Plot or Model" of the city it envisions: "By the time that this Survey shal be taken, We shal cause a Plot or Model to be made for the whole building through those ruined places . . . We make no question but all men wil be wel pleased with it, and very willingly conform to those Orders and Rules which shal be agreed for the pursuing thereof" (*Declaration*, 8–9). It employs all its force of royal authority in its rhetoric to declare a new London into existence, to compress both the inconveniences of the past and the distresses of losing it into a powerful communal vision of the immediate future. Possibilities are expressed as commands; commands assume acts ("We make no question"); the future is rhetorically present.

The hope for willing conformity was in fact answered with great *conceptual* enthusiasm by the king's nearest and dearest. Evelyn actually submitted three plans for the rebuilding, along with a careful text that outlines methodology and ideology, which he published as *London Revived; Consideration for its Rebuilding in 1666.*[9] At first glance, the combination of text and projections presents an overt simplification and geometricization of the city, rearranging its architectural symbols as well as its patterns and essentially proposing a baroque plan of public buildings connected by straight, wide, navigable avenues, creating "constellations of monumentality."[10] But like the royal declaration itself, all of Evelyn's plans also reveal more of a symbolic (and for that matter literal) underground sense of recovery and preservation than is traditionally recognized, and which in its own way testifies to Evelyn's ambivalence about the powerful potential of the new space and the implications for shaping it.

All three of Evelyn's plans impose regular grids on the groundplan, cut across by axial radiants emphasizing architectural and cultural monuments. Each plan, informed by the working models of Paris and Rome, would reshape social life as it restructured urban patterns. Evelyn wants to clear the urban space of clutter, of the incremental houses and sheds and "raskally warehouses" – no houses whatsoever to be built near public stores and sanctuaries. Architectural structures are to be sorted by category – by social as well as commercial value. The removal of architectural clutter would correspond to the reorganization of social clutter, with a more rigorous sort of zoning quite along the lines of the *Declaration*:

> all of a mystery [trade] should be destined to their several quarters. Those of the better sort of shopkeepers, who sell by retail, might be allotted to the sweetest, and most eminent streets and piazzas. The Artificers to the more ordinary houses, intermedial and narrower passages (for such will hardly

be avoided) that the noise and tintamarre of their instruments may be the less importunate. The Taverns and Victualling houses sprinkled amongst them, and built accordingly. But even all these too, even the very meanest, should exactly respect uniformity. *(London Revived, 49–50)*

At the time of the Fire, the social topography of the City was, from the point of view of someone like Evelyn, the product of spatial chaos. As M. J. Power has shown through an analysis of the hearth taxes in central London in the middle and later seventeenth century, "haberdashers [were] living side-by-side with porters; lawyers beside pensioners, goldsmiths beside widows, all living in a random mix of large and small dwellings . . . where occupations and rich and poor are thoroughly jumbled."[11] Evelyn's reorganization of urban space would insure the reorganization of social space. Social declivities, so to speak, would not – like the physical declivities – be evened out so much as sorted and labelled. (Evelyn, of course, was a prominent member of the Royal Society, that institution dedicated among other things to parcelling and labelling.)

Open space, as well as occupied space, was also to be closely controlled: "Spaces for ample Courts, Yards, and Gardens, even in the heart of the city there may be some to the principal houses, for state and refreshment; but with great reservation, because of the fractions they will make, and therefore rarely towards any principal street" (*London Revived*, 50). "Fractions" are a danger both aesthetically and politically; as spatial interruptions, they not only break up the lines of design, they also interfere with political lines of site. European monarchs who had distrusted the conspiratorial confusion of the medieval town plans had redrawn their cities with wide, straight streets that would more easily accommodate a marching army than a lurking felon, self-proclaiming political centrality and surveillance.[12] As Fielding would declare a century later, central London seemed designed to conceal criminals in its dark twisted interior.[13] The great avenues of Paris were designed as lines of political surveillance and military access – in other words, *not* for the creation of a public sphere (where, in the words of the *Declaration*, "publick mischief may probably arise").

Yet Evelyn – and baroque urban planning in general – is not solely or perhaps even primarily concerned with social and political control of the city. The city architecture is designed to create a spatial awareness in the individual observer through the carefully negotiated relationships of buildings, the creation of vistas, and the planning of perspectives. As with many other continental trends, such urban planning, already introduced into London in the early seventeenth century by Inigo Jones, would eventually have made its way into London consciousness after the Restoration even without the dramatic possibility left by the Fire. But that possibility of complete architectural reform was irresistible to Evelyn. The buildings themselves should be ordered into "piazzas at competent distances, which ought to be built exactly uniform, strong, and with beautiful fronts. Nor should these be all of them square, but some of them oblong, circular, and oval figures, for their better grace and capacity" (*London Revived*, 37). As Kostof notes of Evelyn's basic plan, it emphasizes "the placement of public buildings and their visually meaningful interrelationships, and the possibility of exciting vistas" (*The City Shaped*, 218). Establishing architecturally meaningful relationships means recognizing and developing the symbolic legibility of buildings positioned in and influencing the perception of space. On Evelyn's plan, buildings are to be designed and placed in relation to each other in order to teach the viewer to read, to experience them interpretively from both a stable and a moving perspective. St. Paul's, for example, should be resituated in its old place, but the ascent from the Fleet to Ludgate should be no more than "graceful and just"; the descent towards Thames Street should be modified so that the new-built houses (to be facing the river) should present "a more becoming aspect, and an easier footing to the ranges above them, which would peep over one another successively, with a far better grace" (*London Revived*, 34, 35). An ascent which is "graceful and just" describes the experience of the viewer as much as the arrangement of the view – it describes *response*.[14] The perspectives are orchestrated: the "becoming aspect" and "easier footing," the peeping succession of views, makes gradually, digestibly open and available the contours of the city. As Lewis Mumford says of the baroque town: "one can take [it in] almost at a glance. Even what one does not see, one can . . . [imaginatively] extrapolate . . . once the guiding lines are established" (Mumford, *City in History*, 390). The reimagined baroque London would thus be a *known* city, available to the imaginative glance. The new would sidestep its self-produced strangeness.

In its difference, its figurative as well as literal foreignness, much of Evelyn's project also reads as part of the more urgent need to make the new knowable, available, open. But it also participates more explicitly in the cultural act of *recovery* as well as of reconstruction – the old city seeps in to fill even these brave new spaces. Very literally, Evelyn wants a chart of the submerged past: "[To] save a world of charge in making new [foundations], there would also be drawn, and accurately measured, a subterranean plan of all the vaults, cellars, and arched Meanders, yet remaining" (*London Revived*, 32–33). The plan of the ruined city must lie accurately and deeply beneath the construction of the new. The city must be plumbed; "all foundations upon this new ground [must] be searched to the old and more solid basis" (*London Revived*, 35). The old London is not to be obliterated – even conceptually – but incorporated, still implicit.

The varying interplay between text and image within the engravings themselves demonstrates the extent of conceptual recovery of the old in the ambivalent visualization of the new in Evelyn's idealized recreation. In the third sketch (see

Figure 2) the connections between old and new appear insistently, beginning with the title itself: "A Plan of London: Containing twenty five Churches only, reserved on their old Foundations, with all the principal Streets almost in the same part they formerly were, and Spaces for all the rest of the Houses, Lanes, and Alleys of note." Such an assertion bounds the top end of the plan; its visual foundation (besides the ever-flowing Thames) is a litany of place names and another spatio-temporal reference: "64. Market where stood the Stocks." The complexity of the newness is bounded by firm shading that simultaneously separates it from and suggests gradations into the familiar old – marked by place names that still mean what they mark. The central strangeness is further domesticated by the insertion of elevations – recognizable intimations of familiar structures that already exist or soon will be rebuilt: the Tower on the east end, the Temple on the west, St. Michael's on the northwest edge, and an unidentified little structure just to the northeast of Christ's Church. Furthermore, the very regularity of the new plan is inscribed by emphatic irregularity: the shading literally highlights the ancient, erratic boundaries of the city as they dribbled into being in slow, idiosyncratic parish history.[15] Finally, none of Evelyn's plans (nor Wren's, for that matter) even implicitly suggested what to later urban planners seemed obvious: destroying the medieval wall and gates and redefining city limits.[16] Even within the newest of the new, the spatial contours of ancient London remain conceptually fixed.

Richard Newcourt's plan, however, does break those conceptual bounds, although with an equal lack of practical success.[17] Newcourt was a topographical draftsman (d.1679) from Somerset and a friend of Sir William Dugdale, for whose *Monasterium Anglicanum* he drew views of religious houses engraved by Hollar.[18] His plan also attempts to reconcile the experiential tension between old and new, although in ways implicitly as well as explicitly different from Evelyn's. His first rebuilding scheme (see Figure 3), as John Bender puts it, "[in] extending the ancient walls and realigning parishes on a strict grid with a church at the center of each block, graphs the reorientation of London's growth during Defoe's lifetime more meaningfully than Wren's or Evelyn's."[19] The grid swallows the old boundaries and re-places everything, new and old, inside identical squares centered with identical elevations. The Thames is less a visual foundation than a natural boundary straightened and then forced from the bottom of the manuscript. The old City gates – Ludgate, Newgate, Aldersgate, Moorgate, Bishopsgate, Aldgate – surface ghostily, not in archeological recovery but as defunct markers of difference. They seem less designed to reorient the viewer than to remind him or her that the old London is irrevocably gone; the new must be negotiated differently. The whole plan is firmly bounded by a new sort of City Wall, with its own measured gates of entry, access strictly controlled.

Newcourt's plan, far more than Evelyn's, straightens out the city, bearing no

Figure 2   John Evelyn's third plan for redrawing London (1666).

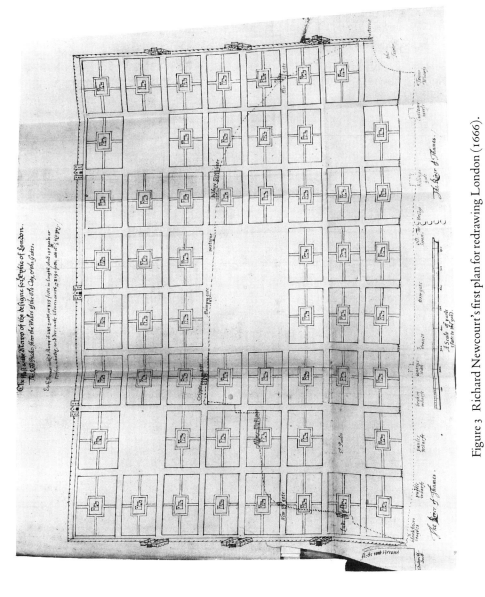

Figure 3   Richard Newcourt's first plan for redrawing London (1666).

visual resemblance to the actual London, old or new. Yet as Bender suggests, it becomes ideologically representative of the later London building (as dis-tinguished from the rebuilding of the City itself) in anticipating the commodification of real estate and its subsequent spatial as well as economic mobility – paradoxically, its instability. The parcelled, repetitive space of his plan comes graphically close to the mass-produced housing of Nicholas Barbon, who was, according to his contemporary Roger North: "the inventor of this new method of building by casting of ground into streets and small houses, and to augment their number with as little front as possible, and selling the ground to workmen by so much per foot front . . . [O]thers following his steps have refined and improved upon it, and made a super foetation of houses about London."[20] Although Barbon's motives as well as his methods are clearly very different from Newcourt's social and architectural planning, the latter's vision of division in some sense anticipates the efficient, profitable enterprise of Barbon and his imita-tive developers and prefigures the change in London from a baroque townscape to a capitalist city. The ideological extreme so apparent in Newcourt's implacable ordering and rigid systematization is made practical and profitable in the hands of later builders.

Yet repetitiveness itself is a form of epistemological reassurance; there is in Newcourt's dogged boxes the guarantee of "openness" and spatial knowability. As with the royal declaration and Evelyn's various plans, changes are ultimately predicated on some form of territorial recovery or the promise of *terra cognita*. The new city will be knowable through forms or patterns or titles of familiarity, and it will be knowable through its visual openness, its structural immediacy, its topographical *sense* or predictability. The old London, the given London, had vanished, and what was wrong with the misshapen, filthy, medieval city had a chance to be corrected. Yet it wasn't. As even the most revisionist reimaginings of London suggest, the pull towards recovery and legibility proves as strong as aes-thetic or social reform. The rhetorics of the royal proclamations and the submitted re-envisionings share a common denominator with the actualities of rebuilding in their effort to create known space – *ex nihilo*.

Actualities of rebuilding

In the event, none of the idealized plans for redrawing London ever got off the ground, so to speak. As the Earl of Clarendon put it, "very many, with more expedition than can be conceived, set up little sheds of brick and timber upon the ruins of their own houses, where *they chose rather to inhabit than in more convenient places*, though they knew they could not long reside in those new buildings."[21] In choosing rather to inhabit their old inconvenient spaces, Londoners enacted precisely that Carolinian anxiety that they would presume "the Ground is their own, and that they may do with it as they please." Since there were no accurate maps of the city, and no central plans of property ownership, the royal and elite optimism was misplaced, and the force of official imagination foundered. As T. F. Reddaway notes, an intelligible map of the ruins could not be made quickly enough to clarify and focus large-scale directions for change.[22] Ownership and tenancy issues were extraordinarily complicated, with buildings divided up into various dwellings, each often with separate leases and subleases of widely different term lengths. Just determining who owned what slowed official progress enormously. Londoners figuratively as well as literally, and architecturally as well as topographically, chose rather to recreate and reinhabit their old inconvenient spaces.

At the time, and indeed through this century, some regarded such resistance to change as mercenary, obstinate, and stupid. Evelyn had argued that the rebuilding ought to be "the joint and mature contrivance of the ablest men, Merchants, Architects, and Workmen, in consort" (*London Revived*, 31), but from the first no such consort was able to penetrate the fiercely piecemeal and locally idiosyncratic response to rebuilding. In 1668 Samuel Rolls was already complaining about the lack of conceptual cooperation in the rebuilding: "If the Owners of ground belonging to some of the highest and noblest Streets, had all agreed together to begin, and carry on their buildings all at once, or to part with their ground to others . . . then might we have seen ere now, a New Cornhill, a New Cheapside compleat, and entire."[23] Instead, he notes, "when all is said London at this day represents nothing more then our own divisions, together with the ill effects and consequences thereof" (Rolls, *Londons Resurrection*, 93). In 1734 James Ralph complained that though the Fire "furnished the most perfect occasion that can ever happen in any city, to rebuild it with pomp and regularity," in fact "the hurry of rebuilding, and the disputes about property prevented this glorious scheme [Wren's] from taking place."[24] Instead, the best buildings in London remain "generally hid in holes and corners, as if they had been built by stealth" (Ralph, *Critical Review*, 5). Disputes and stealth combined to signify short-sightedness and pig-headedness to a tradition of architectural and urban observers. Sir Christopher Wren's son, editor of the family history *Parentalia* (1750), blamed "the obstinate Averseness of a great Part of the Citizens to alter their old Properties, and to recede from building their houses again on their old Ground & Foundations" (*Parentalia*, 269). And in 1755 the author of *English Architecture* narrates an account of successive obstinacies that revolve consistently around a possessive territoriality – the "obstinacy of private persons, who insisted on their property and would build their houses on the old foundations."[25]

Certainly for economic and personal reasons, the city was largely rebuilt on its own old lines. As Reddaway notes: "property-owners and tenants were far too busy finding new quarters, keeping their businesses going or settling elsewhere. Few troubled to send in details and, without them, wholesale reallotment was impossible" ("London 1666," 7). The 1667 *Act of Rebuilding* prohibited over-hanging storeys, mandated the use of nonflammable building materials, enforced stricter building codes and regulations, and ordered some of the narrow streets straightened and cleared of the clutter of tents and stalls, but as Summerson notes, "[the] old land utilization was perpetuated in the new structures of red brick."[26]

Both popular and literary attitudes towards London suggest that even without the economic and social pressures to rebuild quickly on pre-existing lines, the majority of Londoners would have resented the imposition of a new order. Emil Kaufman and Sir John Summerson note that the Italianate introductions of Inigo Jones early in the seventeenth century (including most notably the piazza at Covent Garden built in 1639) were not appreciated outside the circles of the aris-tocracy until a century later – in the midst of the rebuilding debates. (And those *theoretically* central architectural debates were themselves displaced into the West End.) Jones's plans seemed, said a contemporary voice, "like Bug-Beares, or Gorgons heads, to the vulgar."[27] John Bender analyzes the ideology of control in those lines of order and admits that in the political fragility of Restoration in the 1660s "the imperious symbolism of ceremonial avenues cutting across the City surely would have gone against the grain of many Londoners" (*Imagining the Penitentiary*, 275n). To inhabitants who prided themselves on their independence from the court and on the impregnability of private ownership, who for the most part grew up within the walls of the city, and who were familiar with its faults and used to its peculiarities, the prospect of a wide, open, ordered city organized on continental models would have no conceptual place in this particular urban reconfiguration.

In the newly called attention to the configurations of urban space, those most directly concerned – and these crossed boundaries of class, gender, and trade – insisted on redefining personal boundaries at the direct expense of public improvement. The response to the loss and change of familiar *historicized* space was not to construct a new-and-improved city, but to recover and reconstruct the patterns and memory of the old. It was a process and product of increasing cul-tural self-consciousness; the recovery of London became the rediscovery of London; construction was reconstruction.

J. G. A. Pocock argues that, in a cultural response to the ruptures of temporal contiguity, reasserted continuity – the perpetuation of social usages and practices – becomes not simply transmission but a test of the capacity to act, to restructure, to rebuild, in the process of which institutionality is necessarily diminished. Pocock's argument is primarily temporal, but much of what he claims for the temporal processes of cultural readjustment has its spatial equivalent.[28] London, as a kind of institutional structure, or rather, as a complex combination of political, social, religious, cultural, institutional, and individual structures (not to mention the literally physical structures), ends up preserving itself along several of the routes outlined by Pocock. It preserves itself spatially in the midst of a space it does not otherwise modify – that is, the City recreates itself in its own image and thereby effectively displaces the architecturally reforming energies into the "out-parts"; it also adapts itself and its continuities within the exterior contingencies demanded by the practical and political requirements of rebuilding by conform-ing enough, by improving enough, by changing enough to make a discernible and therefore variously interpretable difference. And it is this combination of resistant self-recreation and compliant self-reformation that creates the dialectic between physical and experiential space that constitutes the cultural reperception of urban space in London. The governmentally directed attention to the emptied ruined spaces of the city meant that each citizen, each landlord, each tenant, each merchant, each shopkeeper, was required by policy and practicality to re-envis-age, reclaim, redefine, and rebuild the personal lines of city property; the cumula-tive response was to reaffirm the preexisting – to recreate consciously what had been pre-reflexively experienced. The present would set about to recreate the past in the context of the future.

The second royal proclamation, issued on October 24, 1666, marked the actual beginning of the official rebuilding. It outlined a soberer plan than the first, drawing on the experience-based recommendations of the appointed commis-sioners and city planners, abandoning plans for sweeping urban reformation and settling instead for general improvements on the old ground plan reinstated.

The committee appointed to oversee the rebuilding were six, three appointed by the Court and three by the City. The surveyors were to be "discreet and intelli-gent . . . Persons in the Art of Building . . . to see the said Rules and Scantlings well and truly observed" to prevent or "discover" "irregular Buildings."[29] The Court appointees were Christopher Wren (1632–1723), as yet an unpracticed and unknown architect, at the moment more prominent as professor of astronomy; Hugh May (1621–84), the controller of the Royal Works; and Roger Pratt (1620–85), a practical architect (who was knighted for his efforts in July 1668). The City appointed Robert Hooke (1635–1703), scientist and Royal Society Fellow; Peter Mills (1598–1670), a surveyor and builder; and Edward Jerman (d. 1668), Surveyor to the Fishmongers' Company and builder of the Royal Exchange. Pratt kept an account of his committee's proceedings:

> About the beginning of Octob: 1666 wee had our first meeting, wherein it
> beeing much controverted whether that part of the citty now burned, were

commensurable or not . . . [A]t our second meeting about Octob: the 8, wee ordered that Surveyours should bee appointed for the measurement of each particular Ward of the citty, and that the city should be sente too to issue out Orders commanding each Proprietor to cleere his foundations within 14 dayes at the farthest, in order to such measurement.[30]

Two of the three surveyors responsible for reclaiming the lines of the city were members of the City's rebuilding committee: Robert Hooke and Peter Mills, with the addition of John Oliver (c.1616–1701) – surveyor, architect, builder, glass painter, municipal councillor, and parish officer. They negotiated the tension between the government's requirements for each property owner or tenant to clear the property of debris, to hire one of the surveyors, and to begin rebuilding as quickly as possible, and the would-be rebuilders' doubts and difficulties about rebuilding in the middle of such confusion and change. One Thomas Hollier, a surgeon, claimed he "would be a builder again; but . . . knows not what restrictions there will be, so as it is unsafe for him to begin."[31] By the end of February draft proposals for the lines of the new streets were ready, and on March 5, 1667 the City's committee (Hooke, Mills, and Jerman) were ordered to stake out the streets. (The Court committee – Wren, May, and Pratt – remained primarily in advisory status.) The king requested a map so he could visualize the improvements more readily, and a version of John Leake's December sketch appeared (see Figure 1). By April 29 the whole package of committees and rules was officialized by an Act of Common Council, formally authorized by the king shortly afterwards; the replotting had begun.

The early surveyors played a crucial part in the cultural reperception of urban space. Along with the newspapers, they were primary agents in forcing public recognition of latent spatial boundaries and of changes in spatial meaning. They insured that each tenant would become aware in measured detail of his or her local boundaries and the relation of those spatial contours to their neighbors'. Their records made the private disputes and settlements public, available as a textual and visual redrawing of the City. Those same documents also record the lines of the past within the transformations of the present, creating another text to enable the cultural transition from old to new. Finally, the surveys literally produced the new spaces of the city, recommending the decisions that would reshape the landscape and delineate the territorial boundaries of future social and literary acts.

My insistence on a newly widespread awareness of spatial boundaries needs some qualification. City as well as estate surveying was commonplace in medieval and pre-Fire London for the assignment and acquisition of rent, among other things. Ralph Treswell's careful surveys show an equal attention to the spatial precision and minutiae that characterize the Mills and Oliver survey.[32] And presumably the tenants would be as equally aware of and watchful over the surveyor's

results and their immediate implications or effects. So, as with the linguistic arguments, I recognize that this sudden and widespread emphasis has its roots in a
simple difference in degree; as George Joye said of the ceremonies of the Last
Supper and the Passover Seder, there is "syche symilitude and propertie in them
bothe, the new so corresponding in all thingis the olde, that the olde declareth the
newe."[33] Yet if the degree of change is sudden enough and vast enough, it can
become a difference in kind as well. Though it may be impossible to prove a
difference in popular perceptions of space outside the textual and literary
differences I argue throughout this work, it seems likely that such a sudden, widespread, and systematic surveying scheme – and the frequent publications of such
a scheme – would have some trouble avoiding the social circles of gossip, comparison, and exchange.

The history and development of the private rebuilding was in a sense made
public, overseen and detailed in official records kept in the not-yet-rebuilt
Guildhall. Hooke, Mills, and Oliver (eventually just Mills and Oliver; Hooke
seems to have lapsed in his committee work) responded to each individual request
for surveying, and kept records – often with sketched illustrations – of each site
request, which were entered chronologically, with a cross listing under street
names, in day books by officers of the civic Chamber, so that the whole of the
rebuilding of the private sector of the City is meticulously inscribed piece by piece
in both spatial and temporal order. Between May 1667 and December 1673 a total
of 8097 sites were surveyed, with another 309 from January 1674 to July 1696. By
the end of 1671 the rebuilding of the private sector of the City was substantially
completed; the public sphere took noticeably longer (Jones and Reddaway,
"Introduction," *Survey of Building Sites*, 1:xxvi).

Mills and Oliver (and early on, Hooke) were virtually the first redrawers of
London and the most direct *producers* as well as arbiters of the specifics of the new
spaces of London. Their repeated choice of introductory verb reflects their
conceptualization as well as creation of appropriate new space in their
recommendations:

> 4
> Wee conceive that Turnagain Lane at Snowhill haveing no passage but
> Down to Fleet Ditch with divers steps for foot people and no horse nor Carts
> can go that way is not fitt to be opened all which wee leave to submitt to your
> Judgments.

> 5
> Wee conceive that Queenshead Alley by St. Nicholas Shambles being no
> thorowfair but for foot people upon sufferance and Gates shutt up when they
> please not fit to be opened all wee submitt.

6
to be staked out 9 foot and paved with freestone
Wee conceive that Panier Ally being a very short passage and when S.
Michaels at Queen Church is taken down it will be very near Cheapside that
Carting that way will be no advantage at all to any all which Wee Submit.
                    (Mills and Oliver, *Survey of Building Sites*, 11:22–22v)

The surveyors initially conceived and for the most part ultimately determined the
fitness of topographical space, to be recovered or relinquished, to come into or pass
out of urban existence. It is in fact their decision (see Figure 4) that Pissing Alley
should not only be preserved but also widened, thus permitting its later entrance
into poetic *terra firma* as definitive topographical signifier in Dryden's *MacFlecknoe*:
"Echoes from *Pissing Ally, Sh[adwell]* call, | And *Sh[adwell]* they resound from
A[ston] Hall" (see chapter four).

In defining the boundaries of private space for individuals and negotiating
disputes between them, the surveyors insured widespread and detailed individual
spatial awareness:

Jeanne Barnet Widdow
September the 14th. 1668
ONE foundation set out the day abovesaid Scituate in Ivy Lane belonging
to the said Mrs Barnett containing upon the front North and South 14 foot
from the middle of each party wall and in breadth at the back end East North
and South 14 foot 8 inches from the middle of each party wall and in depth
East and West from the front to the out of the back wall 30 foot Mr. Bell on the
Northside and the widdow Gressam on the South side.

   MEMORANDUM that upon the fifteenth Day of September 1668
upon the request of Mr George Willowbee Merchant Peter Mills Robert
Hook and John Olliver did view a certaine wall on the South side of Mr
Willobys garden joyning to the beare Inn in Bassingshall the which wall as
wee conceive belongs to the said Mr Willoby but the owner of the Bare Inn
had 3 Slitts in the said wall for Ayre into a Stable of about two foot in length
to 4 or 5 inches in breadth a piece and they were about 6 foot & a 1/2 from
the ground.
   Peter Mills

Mrs. Barnett, Mr. Bell, Mrs. Gresham, Mr. Willowby, and the apparently trucu-
lent owner of the Bear had all become acutely if not always accurately aware *within
inches* of their respective and tangent – private and shared – boundaries. And often
the shared boundary was not the relatively simple matter of a party wall (for which
the Rebuilding Acts gave specific directions) but larger conceptual and physical
spaces. In such cases, particularly when compensation was involved, mere text

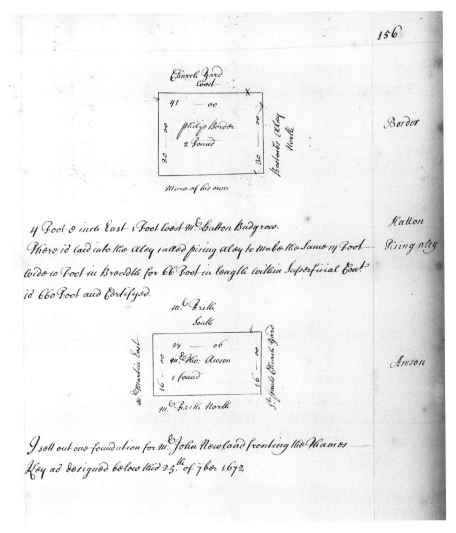

Figure 4 Pissing Alley: a surveyor's choice (1672).

was not enough; space needed *showing* in addition to *telling*. In Figure 5, for example, Oliver notes: "I sett out one Found[ation] for Mr. Henry Lascoe on Breadstreet hill" in which an intermediate structural space is "Covered with the house of Mr. Lascoe over Mr. Wharton," with the drawing asterisked to identify the problematic area (*Survey of the Building Sites*, IV:67v).

The final arbiter of boundary disputes was the Fire Court, consisting of three or more Justices of the King's Bench and Common Pleas and Barons of the Exchequer, who "amended boundaries by give and take, enlarged sites, provided for alternative sites and for joint development."[34] The Courts, which at the time

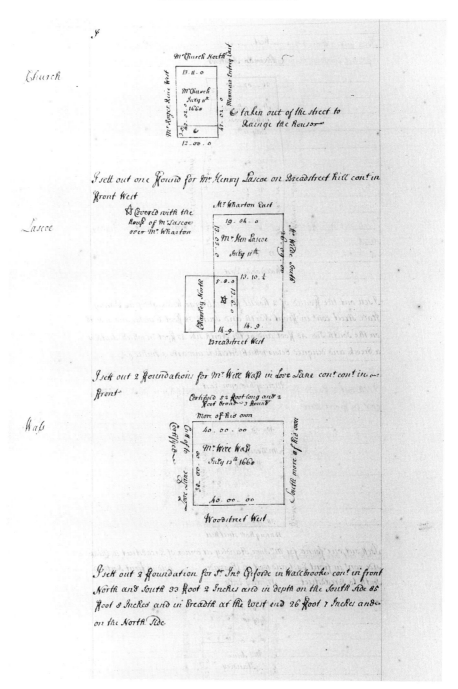

Figure 5 Mr. Lascoe's house covering Mr. Wharton's house (1672).

acquired and have since sustained a reputation for fairness and efficiency,[35] not only settled disputes but also promoted fire insurance and expedited rebuilding deadlines – often with their own persistent rhetoric of rebuilding that echoes the poetic and sermonic rhetorics of Fire and ruin discussed in chapter one, in phrases used most probably by the justices themselves in court: "that the messuage may no longer lie in its own ruins or may no longer remain buried in its own ashes."[36] The Fire Courts also helped to re-evaluate sites for land use, reinstating commerce and trade as well as private dwellings. They "endeavoured in the first place to find someone, freeholder, lessor, lessee, assignee, tenant for life, or tenant in occupation, who desired or was willing to rebuild. If none of the interested parties was capable of rebuilding then the Court cleared all interests by decreeing surrenders and even declaring leases void so that the site could be disposed of for rebuilding" (*The Fire Court*, 1:xv). On April 18, 1667, for example, the Court declared the site on which the White Horse Inn had stood to be "very conveniently situated for an inn and its continuation to be advantageous to trade," but as the parties could not be brought to agreement, the Court negotiated a recompensed redistribution of leases so that neighboring innlords could rebuild (1:14, A.43). Thus the Fire Courts not only contributed to the efficient rebuilding of the city and the widespread individual awareness of spatial boundaries, they *also* participated in a destabilization of real estate, in the rupture of ancient layered leases and cluttered settled tenancies, exposing and refiguring complicated spatial patterns.

Besides rebuilding their own private properties, citizens of London were expected to contribute to the various relevant institutional rebuildings, and in a sense the inhabitants themselves were surveyed and marked for rebuilding and reinhabiting. The Brewers of the Fifth Division kept watch over their members to see who contributed and how promptly to the rebuilding of Brewers' Hall; an official letter of March 2, 1671 warns:

> Gentlemen
>   Whereas I am informed that some persons in the 5th Division have not yet paid their subscripcon money And also that severall Brewers in that Division have not yet subscribed towards that worke These are therefore to desire you as well to collect the Arrears of Subscripcon money, as also, to take the Subscripcons of such as have not yet subscribed in that Division And to return the names of such as neglect to pay or refuse to subscribe to a Court of Assistants appointed to be holden at Brewers Hall on Tuesday – the 4th day of Aprill 1671 in the morning And also to bring with you an accompt of the money you shall have collected And hereof I desire you not to faile.[37]

Citizens were reminded on all sides of their rebuilding responsibilities. The parish churches offer another example of institutional and individual co-constructions. The list of householders for St. Bride Fleet Street, for example, outlines the various measures of its parishioners' property lines and names all its inhabitants in 1666, setting out to record dutifully those parishioners' compliance with the self-surveying law. But such records also begin to suggest the vagaries in compliance that themselves predict the unexpectedly changing demographies of the city as a result of the Fire. A representative sample of the List of Householders shows up both the structures and the slippages of self-surveying, as the list of names becomes another textual sign of different kinds of emptiness (see Figure 6).

As the rebuilding continued, signs of difference, of alienating change, of increasing *unknowability*, proliferated in spite of all of the varied attempts to reconstruct the known. The surveys themselves suggests such slippage. They supply a visual and textual link between pre- and post-Fire London, between the London which no longer existed and the redrawn and rebuilt London of Ogilby and Morgan's map of 1676. The streets and boundaries that *were* are charted in order to make sense of (and make possible) what *would be*. What they show and what they don't show is suggestive. On the one hand, they articulate both graphically and verbally which lines were redrawn, by whom, and with what sort of fuss. They record local businesses, taverns, and private houses, giving voice to the individual and private rebuilders (both owners and occupiers) of London. On the other hand, the surveys – like Hollar's map of the ruins (see chapter one) – also record new kinds of emptied spaces: "the surveyors were disinclined to record house names partly, perhaps, because the houses themselves had disappeared and the surveys were concerned with sites not buildings, and partly because such names were often the occupier's personal and profitable sign which he took with him when he moved" (Jones and Reddaway, "Introduction," *Survey of the Building Sites*, 1:xxiv). In participating in the redrawing of London's lines, they also record the loss of its signifiers.

One of the causes as well as consequences of this loss of signboards (and their signifieds) is the increasing fluidity of neighborhoods (see also chapters four and five). In spite of all the inhabitants who metaphorically as well as literally "chose rather to inhabit [their old sites] than in more convenient places," as Clarendon put it, there were a good number more who, once gone, were gone for good. (In terms of suddenness and sweep, such departures might well have contrasted noticeably with the more steady if irregular population turnover before the Fire.) As the 1670 post-Fire "Account of the inhabetants" of St. Benet Gracechurch reveals, the Fire changed the parish demographies in rather poignant ways: "gone out of the parish" gets quickly clipped to that repeated inexplicable "gone" (see Figure 7). By 1673, as Reddaway notes, the City government was beginning to panic at the rebuilt but *not* reinhabited houses. Various new incentives were offered to tempt businesses and householders back to their old territories (*The*

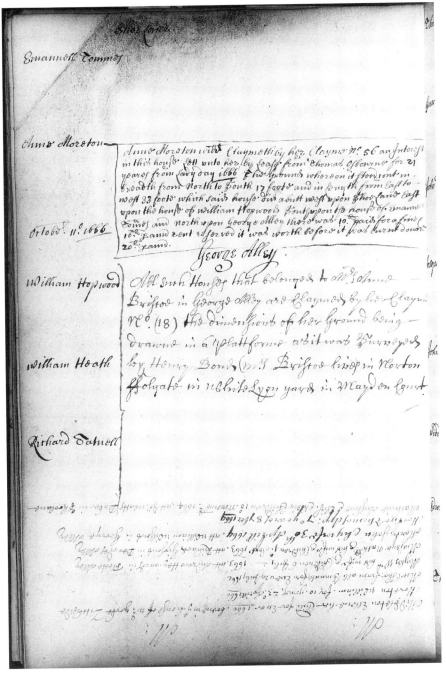

Figure 6 St. Bride Fleet Street List of Householders (1666).

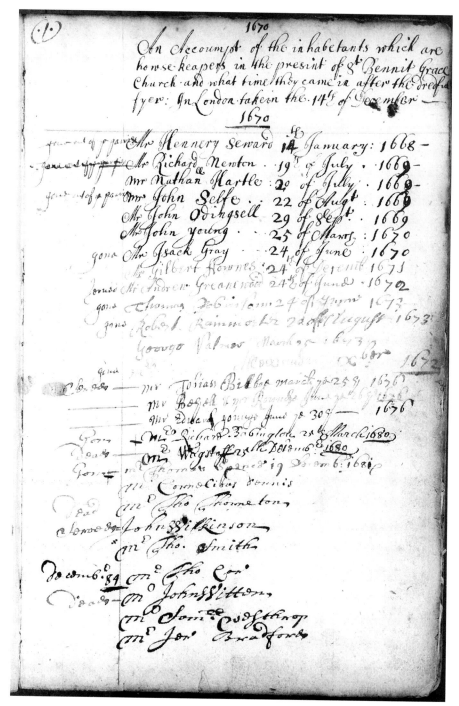

Figure 7 St. Benet Gracechurch Account of Inhabitants (1670).

Rebuilding of London, 300–308). In the meantime, private builders were capitalizing on the now humanly empty spaces and the abrupt fluctuations in demand. City space was bought and sold by Barbon and others in increasingly public and profitable ways:

> Wee are desired to give notice to all Gentlemen and others that have any ground to sell, or that desire to buy any in the City of *London*, to repair to the dwelling house of Mr. *James* Peters [sic] Scrivener at the Sign of the *Sugarloaf* near the Drawbridge on *London*Bridge, and there they may make their Entries where their Ground lies, and of the buttings and boundings and dimensions thereof, or where they would buy ground, either Fee simples or Leases, and speedily have Chapmen for the same; And, the entries of such Grounds to be sold, and the Chapmens Names that desire to buy, shall be made for six pence an Entry.
>
> *(London Gazette,* No. 209, November 14–18, 1667*)*

The new city that both the idealized and the actual reconstructions worked so carefully at assimilating was becoming in unforeseen *human* as well as economic ways increasingly strange rather than increasingly known. The shifting social and commercial territories so attentively analyzed by Defoe (see chapters three and five) were becoming a new sort of *terra incognita*. The full realization of this was in part cause and in part consequence of the increasing publicization of spatial awareness, which in turn would prompt new strategies of rhetorical response and recognition.

The public [iz]ation of spatial reperception

Where the surveys and Fire Court hearings made people individually aware of the various social and economic needs to make visible their private boundaries – thus massproducing social awareness of specifically local urban space – the newspapers published and thus publicized the larger preoccupations with urban spatial change, and record in form as well as content their own involvement with the change. In the decades after the Great Fire, the newspapers (primarily the *London Gazette*), underwent a typographical and generic shift in emphasis, from simply reporting court, war, and foreign news, to including news and advertisements of rebuilding and relocation, both commercial and private. They organized themselves by and concerned themselves more with *place*. Though the newspaper was always to some extent organized by place as well as time ("Harwich, January 30"; "Dublin, Jan. 27"; "Marseilles, Jan. 19"), its new systematic patterns of arrangement both emphasized the disruption caused by the Fire and enabled the rebuilding. In its changes in both form and content – by publicizing various shifts in urban space – the newspaper would play a significant part in shaping a more public awareness of the spatial implications of the rebuilding.[38]

In terms of published content, the newspaper simplified and repeated the Acts and proclamations of the rebuilding, ensuring the widest possible audience for the strategies of rebuilding and the awareness of spatial change:

> That the Lord Mayor and Court of Aldermen cause an exact Survey to be made of the Ruins, that it may appear, to whom the House and Ground did belong, what Term the Occupiers were possest of, what Rents were paid, and to whom the Reversions and Inheritances did appertain, for the satisfying of all Interests, that no mans right be sacrificed to the publick convenience. After which a Plot and Mode shall be framed of the whole Building, which no doubt may so well please all persons, as to induce them willingly to such Rules and Orders as shall be agreed to.   *(No. 87, September 13–17, 1666)*

In other words, the official administration of reconstruction publicly insists that everyone will recover what they have lost, and the more fully and quickly depend-ing upon the individual's cooperation with public decisions. All the citizens were simultaneously alerted to and advised to study the legal intricacies of their van-ished spatial structures. Such publicization would be of particular interest to widows, minors, charity-dependents, and others vulnerable to the prevailing power structures, in that a whole system of protective investment was wiped out: all the long leases, subleases, life interests, reversions, and assorted other land-holding investments of the property in the city meant that the destruction of 13,200 houses had implications far beyond the losses sustained by 13,200 freeholders, or even the combination of owners and tenants.[39] The whole com-munity was involved in the recovery or renegotiation of spatio-economic bound-aries.

The attention to legal and economic structures was physically grounded by what began in that royal and civic order for the citizens to survey themselves, which the newspaper repeated and localized for its readers: "the last Occupiers do within 14 daies after the date thereof bring into Beadles Booth, set up in the respec-tive Wards, for Publick Service, under his hand, a perfect Survey of the Ground whereon his House, Shop, or Warehouse stood, with their Appurtenances, and his Right and Term therein" (No. 89, September 20–24, 1666). The newspaper thus disseminated and reinforced the public recognition that all the citizens are both legally obliged and economically compelled to look *closely* at their propertied structures. They must find and define their own boundaries, understand the literal extent of their holdings and their relationship to the other inhabitants or owners or claimants on the house. That act of finding boundaries was in itself a massive labor: citizens were required to clear away the rubbish themselves. The fact that many people ignored such orders and that the governmental plan for massive private self-surveying died a fairly quick death perhaps indicates that actual reacquaintance with physical boundaries remained largely theoretical, but the point remains that *everyone* who owned or occupied a house in the City, of whatever size, on whatever sort of street, lane, court, or dismal little alley, knew that he or she was *supposed* to be formally aware of its boundaries. The inhabitants of the city were faced with deciphering both the literal foundations of where they had once lived, and to sort out the more abstract legal and economic structures that defined those spaces. Their acquaintance with the shape of local space was a matter of public decree.

Newspapers helped to negotiate these complicated legal as well as physical patterns of domestic habitation. Landlords and tenants had to sort themselves out before rebuilding could effectively begin. Rebuilding, of course, was going to cost a lot of money; who was primarily responsible? The *Gazette* announced the "Act for Erecting a Judicature for determining of Differences, touching Houses burned or demolished, by reason of the late Fire in *London*" (No. 129, February 7–11, 1666/7), and almost immediately landlords began organizing places and times in which to meet and negotiate with their assorted tenants:

> These are to give notice, That the Committee for Letting the Lands and Tenements, belonging to the *Chamber* of *London*, have appointed to sit at the *Guild-Hall*, on Wednesday Morning the *13th* of this instant *March*, and thenceforth weekly every Wednesday Morning during the said Moneth [sic]; to the end that the Tenants of any Houses burnt or demolished in the late dreadful Fire, may if they see cause, on those days apply themselves to the said Committee.   (No. 136, March 4–7, 1666/7)

For the next few years, the *Gazette* would publish the announcements of the court hearings, helping through its public voice to reorganize the chaos and to create a space for fair recovery, until their last chance:

> Whereas by the late Act of Parliament for reviving the Judicature for determination of differences, touching Houses Burned or Demolished, by reason of the late Fire which hapned in *London*, to continue until the 29th day of *September 1671* . . . These are to give notice to all persons concerned, to repair to the said Registers Chamber in *Hare-Court* in the *Inner Temple, London*, before the said 29th day of *September* now next coming, to Exhibit their Petitions accordingly; for upon or after the said day no Petitions can be received.   (No. 486, July 11–14, 1670)

The *Gazette* basically re-issues what the King or the City have decreed, but its public and communal reinforcement and simple repetition of the issues, keeps cultural attention fastened on both the large and the small, the disrupted public and the private spaces of the City.

The *Gazette* participated in as well as published both the facts and consequences of loss and the piecemeal of rebuilding. Just months before the Fire, the *Gazette* had publicly resisted the pressure to admit advertisements:

> Being daily prest to the Publication of Books, Medicines, and other things, not properly the business of a Paper of Intelligence. This is to notifie once and for all, that we will not charge the *Gazette* with Advertisements, unless they be matter of State; but that a Paper of Advertisements will be forthwith Printed apart, and recommended to the Publick by another hand.[40]

But shortly after the Fire it civilly changed its mind. By October, the *London Gazette* had come out in full-force cooperation with the relocation enterprise:

> *Such as have settled in new Habitations since the late Fire, and desire for the convenience of their correspondence, to publish the place of their present abode; or to give notice of Goods lost or found, may repair to the corner House in* Bloomsbury, *on the East-side of the Great Square before the House of the Right Honorable the Lord Treasurer, where there is care taken for the Receipt and Publication of such Advertisements.*
>
> (No. 94, October 8–11, 1666)

Loosening its strictures about advertising meant essentially that the newspaper gave voice to more and more citizens concerned in the efforts of rebuilding and relocating – publishing more and more of the *public*.

The format of the paper itself contributed to its effectiveness, creating a sense of things findable and space knowable. From the start the advertisements occupied the same predictable space on the page. The *London Gazette* was in those days a single folio sheet, with two columns of print on recto and verso. The relocation advertisements, after the first week or so, consistently appeared in the lower quarter of the first column on the verso of the issue. Later, as relocation information as well as advertisements would increase and intensify, more space would regularly be occupied.[41]

Increasingly, what the public wanted published included the relocation notices of a wide variety of trades. These notices suggest the extent of commercial disruption and offer rhetorical possibilities for reestablishing continuity:

> These are to give notice that Mr. *Richard Royston* Bookseller, who formerly lived at the *Angell* in *Ivy-lane*, and the Shop-keepers who formerly dwelt in the *Round-Court* in St. *Martins*, are now placed in St. *Bartholomew's*-Hospital near *Smith-Field*. (No. 118, December 31–January 3, 1666/7)

Many persons were displaced and used the newspaper to advertise both their relocation and their continued dependability:

> *Thomas Rookes* who before the great Fire lived at the *East End* of S. *Pauls*,
> and there made the *best Ink* for *Deeds* and *Records*, now lives in *Ludgate* street,
> between *Ludgate* and the West end of S. *Pauls* at the Sign of the *Lamb* and *Ink-*
> *bottle*, and there makes the best ink.   *(No.* 661, March 18–21, 1672*)*

> *Alderman* Backwell *is at present placed in Doctor* Goddards *Lodging, in* Gresham
> *Colledg, where his Affairs are managed as formerly in* Lombard-street.
>   *(*No. 86, September 10–13, 1666*)*

Here, as in the Fire narratives and the idealized rebuildings, "as formerly"
becomes the vocabulary of reassurance, part of the rhetoric of reconstruction. As
Pocock argues, "continuity," or the way that a society describes itself as perpetu-
ating and transmitting its forms, becomes, in response to "contiguity" (the unpredictable assailants of social or natural order that threaten our ability to think and
act), a *means* of acting, not necessarily dependent on the existence or survival of the
institutions themselves (*Virtue, Commerce, History*, 92). In other words, the newspapers' attention to and insistence on local temporal or commercial continuity in
the face of overwhelming "contiguity" is part of the movement of psychological
and cultural rebuilding in the first new acts of physical rebuilding:

> The Shop-keepers that were formerly in the *Royal Exchange* in *Cornhil*, are
> now removed to *Gresham-Colledge*, Where they have built themselves Shops,
> both above and below Stairs, and carry on their ancient and respective trades.
>   *(*No. 113, December 13–17, 1666*)*

In some cases, however, the effort to bridge the temporal and spatial chasms
actually calls attention to the disruption of functional meaning in space, and highlights the overturning of spatial reference. Public spaces, for example, in some
cases are *transferred* into private ones:

> *We are desired to Certifie, That the Affairs of the* Custom-House *are now*
> *Transacted in Mr.* Jo. Blands *House, formerly known by the name of the Lord*
> Baynings *in* Mark-Lane, *where the Farmers and Officers of His Majesties Customs*
> *with their Clerks and Attendants, will be ready on all occasions at the usuall times for the*
> *Dispatch of all Affairs belonging to them.*   *(*No. 87, September 13–17, 1666*)*

Although public and commercial space had traditionally occupied private space
(or the other way around – shops and services on the ground floor, domestic spaces
above), and would continue to do so though to a lessening degree throughout the
rebuilding, still space had largely been *designated*, even in small local operations; to
squeeze the practical functions as well as the emblematic significance of the
Custom House into Mr. Jo. Bland's house meant a conceptual as well as historical
and spatial reconfiguration; the public inconveniently collapsed into the private.
    One way of keeping the relocations between public and private more pri-

vately sorted, coherent, and accessible was to publish detailed topographical directions. As with the narrative accounts of the Fire itself, incessant repetition of street names and relations seemed to offer the reassurance of temporal as well as spatial navigability – using the known past to negotiate the strange present:

> *These are to certifie, That the* Kentish *and* Sussex Post-Office, *formerly kept at the* Rand-House *in* Love-lane, *is now removed to the House of* Mr. John Dyne, *in the Passage to and from* Tower-Hil, *near the Pump in* Crutchet-Fryers.
>
> The First-Fruits Office *is kept in* Coney-Court *in* Grays-Inn, *and will be open on* Munday the Eighth day of October *instant*, 1666.
>
> The Porter will further inform you.   *(No. 93, October 4–8, 1666)*

This particular advertisement bolsters topographical confidence with the promise of a live human being just waiting to direct "you" personally where you need to go. Public space still functions as reliable public space, if momentarily disconcerted.

Over time, the newspaper advertisements worked precisely towards publishing the properly reestablished patterns of commerce inhabiting commercial buildings, suggesting the restabilization of commercial space by showing trades resettling not just in their new but back in their old places within the rhetoric of continuity:

> It is thought not unfit in respect to persons concerned and remote, hereby to give notice, That Sir *Robert Viner* and several Goldsmiths who since the late dreadful fire have continued their affairs in *Broadstreet* and *Wincester street*, are now removed for their greater conveniency to their several Houses in *Lumbard street* as formerly.   *(No. 479, June 16–20, 1670)*

> These are to give notice, That *Edward Bartlet Oxford* Carrier, hath removed his Inn in *London*, from the *Swan* at *Holborn-Bridge*, to the *Oxford-Armes* in *Warwick-lane*, where he did Inn before the Fire. His Coaches and Waggons going forth on their usual days, *Mondays*, *Wednesdays*, and *Frydays*. He hath also a Hearse, with all things convenient to carry a Corps, to any part of *England*.   *(No. 762, March 6–10, 1672/3)*

The newspapers helped put the pieces back together, publishing the reconfigured meanings of social and commercial space, redrawing the cultural lines of London.

The small individual pieces of the city needed putting back together as well, and eventually private space was also admitted into the advertisements. In addition to publishing new addresses, the *Gazette*, the *Mercury*, and others devoted an increasing amount of space to the recovery of lost or destroyed property, first occasioned by the Fire, and later, lost property in general:

If any person have found any Books or Writings belonging to *Arthur Trevor*,
Esq., deceased, or to *John Trevor*, Esq.; lost in the removal in the late dreadful
Fire, Let them give notice thereof to Mr. *Leakes* at the *Crown* in *Fleet-street*
where they shall receive full value of the Books, and be well rewarded for the
Writings.   *(*No. 125, January 24–28, 1666/7*)*

These are to give notice, That all Persons concerned in the Lead melted at
Porters Key London, by the great Fire in *September 1666*, that they make their
claim for it of *Robert Buckle* at the house of *John Moor* in *Mark-lane London*,
within one Month after publication hereof.
                               (The City Mercury, No. 26, September 2–5, 1667*)*

"Property" also of course includes records, and by implication, all the personal,
social, and cultural contexts of a life, as well as its material structures. Persons
could advertise their recovered property in prosperity: "A goldsmith relocated, has
recovered his fortunes and advertises to pay his debts in full" (No. 135, February
28–March 4, 1666/7). The newspaper became a crucial genre of relocation, an
instrument of reconstruction, publishing the descriptions of whatever new territories in the city were generated by the Fire, and clearly helping to mark and aid the
reconstruction of public and private space.

Newspapers in a sense also literally contributed to the physical rebuilding of
the city, supplying materials and workers through its advertisements:

All persons who are willing to serve and furnish this City with Timber,
Brick, Lime, Stone, Glass, Tiles, Slates, and all other Materials for Building,
may in Person repair to the Committee of Common Council at *Gresham*
House, *London*, on Mundays, Wednesdays, and Fridays, in the Mornings
weekly; who will be ready to receive and treat with them upon any Proposals
they shall make, which are desire may be in Writing.
                                    *(*No. 115, December 20–24, 1666*)*

Owners could find builders, builders workers, and workers work through the
paper. The newspaper helped to regulate the daily details of the financial boundaries of rebuilding, the small scale as well as the large, the private as well as public
restructuring. The connections between physical materials, their prices, and their
availability – a whole equation for rebuilding in its smaller local details – finds
stability and authority in print, in the public page that would circulate consistency
in practice along with news *of* practice.

Finally, the newpapers reported on the rebuilding itself. The *London Gazette*,
for example, carefully monitored the progress of the rebuilding of the Royal
Exchange: "*London, Oct. 23.* This day being appointed for the laying a Foundation
of the *Royal Exchange* in the place where it formerly stood . . . His Majesty with the
usual Ceremonies placed the first stone" (No. 202, October 21–24, 1667). Just a

few weeks later "his Royal Highness . . . went to the *Royal Exchange* . . . to lay the first Stone for a second Pillar" (No. 205, October 31–November 4, 1667). Building went on apace, and the *Gazette* was happy to announce the rehabitation of the Royal Exchange and its architectural promise of commercial restabilization:

> *London, Sept. 29.* Yesterday the Merchants met for the first time, in the *Royal Exchange*, with much satisfaction beholding that excellent Structure raised with greater luster from the Ashes of the Old, and is a work which in every way holds proportion with the rest of the goodly buildings of the reviving City. *(No. 404, September 27–30, 1669)*

A year and a half later, the *Gazette* announced that "the late Shop-keepers in *Gresham Colledge* (together with several other Tradesmen with them) are now returned into the *Royal-Exchange*, that most Stately and most Magnificent piece of Building" (No. 566, April 17–20, 1671). The physical power of the new build-ing argues by architectural definition for its economic power, and the *Gazette*, by seeing the merchants and shopkeepers back inside, and confirming the luster and stateliness of this new and improved version of England's commercial structures, does its part to reinforce the strength and persuasiveness of what has been rebuilt. The verbal reinforces the architectural: "Our City Buildings go on beyond expectation: the Survey last week was 2508 Foundations laid; and many of them in good forwardness, and some finish't: which is the more considerable, for that less than three moneths since, there were not above 400 Foundations lay'd" (*The City Mercury*, No. 32, October 3–10, 1667).

Thus the newspaper did more than report progress and publish hope; it marked the contours and locations and extent of change, laying its own form of foundation for the cultural perception of changing city spaces. In publicizing the processes (especially the successes) of rebuilding, it also published a rhetorical groundplan for the imaginative reperception of city space, a rhetoric concerned overtly with phoenixes and visible magnificences, but as with the envisioned and actualized groundplans, equally concerned with recovery, with familiarity, with strategies for making the new known, the strange meaningful.

Rhetorics of rebuilding: "while they fix the Bounds"

This section is a postscript to the chapter, and a prescript to the later literary chap-ters. I want to foreground some of the general patterns of anxiety that demanded various imaginative constructions in the decades of and after the rebuilding. Those patterns tend to follow or combine the usual panegyric with some sort of doubt about the extent and implications of change, and more specifically with a persistent need to confine as well as define the change, perceived as both spatial and economic. In the poems of rebuilding, rhetorical energy is consistently spent on limiting the bounds of rebuilding energy, unconsciously but not coincidentally echoing Robert Hooke's characterization of the lay person's nervous view of spatial dimension and power – those who have

> no true notion of the vastness of the Universe, and the exceeding minuteness of the Globe of the Earth in comparison therewith, who have *confined their imagination & fancies only within the compass and pale of their own walk and prospect* . . . [Yet] the same God that did make *this World that we would thus limit and bound,* could as easily make it millions of millions times bigger, as of that quantity we imagine; and all the other appearances except this of Parallax would be the very same that now they are.[42]

It is precisely the unexpected immensity of the rebuilt city – both physical and epistemological – that unsettles the confidence of the rebuilding poems, and that increasingly makes urgent room for visual and textual efforts to fix and limit and comprehend the changing spaces of London in the rush of published maps and topographies in the 1680s through the 1730s, and in the increasingly topographic poems, plays, and early novels.

I will focus briefly here on a few very early rebuilding poems for the ways that they articulate concerns in later literary projections of the rebuilding. Simon Ford's long celebratory poem of the rebuilding, *Londons Resurrection, Poetically Represented* (1669), in many ways a signature poem of the period, figures just such a tension between the stabilizing forces of rebuilding and an early intimation of their future consequences:

> Hark, how the clatt'ring *Tools* confused sound
> Divides the Ear! The *Pick-axe* rends the ground
> To load the *Spade.* Its Loads bestow'd between
> The sifting *Ridder,* and the searching *Skreen.*
> The *Saw* the *File,* the *Ax* the *Grindstone* whets;
> The knotty Tree this *hews,* the other *eats.*
> The *Arm* the *Plane,* the *Maul* the *Chissel* drives.
> Through heart of Oak the groaning *Auger* dives.
> The glowing *Steel* the weighty *Sledges* stroke
> Beats into Form; which quench't doth *hiss* and *smoak.*
>
> *(lines 113–22)*

The poem drives home the sensual immediacy of the rebuilding, the litany of individual acts that reproduce the lost city, the reassurance of operative causality. The poem actually has another whole stanza devoted to the heroic efforts of screws, rundles, ropes, balance engines, cylinders, and beams, all working in model machinic harmony to reconnect and stabilize all parts of the urban structure. The surveyor stands in comforting monarchical relation to all this concerted effort, carefully fixing the bounds of topography and by implication activity:

> Thus goes the *Building* on. Confused grounds
> Just *Verdicts* part; and (while they fix the Bounds
> To publique Streets by the *Imperious Line*)
> *Surveyors* like unbounded *Sov'raigns* reign,
> *Each House* clasps with its neighbour; and the *Square*
> *Each Front* unto its fellow⁄wall doth *pair*.
> And *Sister⁄Piles*, whiles thus they intermarry,
> Like *Sister⁄Faces*, uniformly vary.   *(lines 141–48)*

There is direction and purpose to all this energy, a direction that will contribute to the ideal of unity in variety, of soft, safely gendered "sisterly" compliance. But – also like most seventeenth⁄ and eighteenth⁄century rhetorics of rebuilt space – Ford's poem shivers a little in process. The confused sounds that divide the ear are never fully sorted out by all that long stanza of detailed production; the term trans⁄ fers to "confused grounds," left hanging at the end of the line only to be "parted" rather than resolved or reconciled by the (surveyors' or Fire Court's) Verdicts in the next, and wandering into epistemological and topographical confusion at the very height of triumphant resurrection: sight confutes thought, and the returning Londoners lose themselves in their new/old streets:

> Till they, who by the *Old, New London* Size,
> Confess their *Thoughts* confuted by their *Eyes*:
> As old Acquaintance, when mens Fortunes mend,
> Find him a *Courtier* whom they left a *Friend*.
> Till *Citizens* themselves, returned, *stray*
> In the new⁄modul'd Streets, and *lose* their *way*.   *(lines 345–50)*

Ford's poem ends with an uneasy speculation about the negotiations between space acquired and space given up:

> Yea, (though *Front⁄buildings* shall be *backward* thrust
> T'enlage [sic] each Passage to dimensions just)
> *London*, thou shalt not *less* by *lessening* grow;
> Whiles each House gains *above* what's lost *below*,
> Its breadth *squeez'd* into *Height*; and from the *skies*
> *Stealing* the room the cramped *Ground* denies,
> Thus thy own *Thames* both robs and makes amends:
> While it *pays* this shore what from that it *rends*.   *(lines 525–32)*

The parenthetical "though" and half the choice of terms (thrust, lost, squeez'd, stealing, cramped, denies, robs, rends) suggest the discrepancies in the utopian imaginings; even as early as 1667 there's a sense of space inverted or mis-manipulated, of the city pushed and pulled into various configurations, neither large enough to hold change, nor firm enough to contain it.

No one had a true notion of the upcoming vastness of the rebuilt London; *most* would carefully confine their imagination within the compass of their own walk (and in fact order their walk to confine their imagination); most would "limit and bound" the staggering consequences of the new in the habits or vocabularies of the old; and yet within all this is also the excitement of the new itself, the possibil-ities of its newness being commanded by the new technologies – of telescope, of microscope, of surveying, of mapping, of novelizing.

Perhaps the most striking architectural instance of rebuilding rhetoric was the Monument itself (see Figure 8). Ordered by a 1667 Act of Parliament, designed by Christopher Wren,[43] with sculptures by Caius Gabriel Cibber, and situated on the source of the Fire itself, this piece of city sculpture makes visible a number of political and cultural assumptions and desires about the rebuilding. The trans-lation of the Latin inscription on the north, for example, claims: "A little space of time saw the same city most prosperous, and no longer in being" (Welch, *History of the Monument*, 20). A little *space* of time could compress enormous cultural changes, figured in equally permanent senses of stone and Latin verse, yet opening wide in meaning and implication. The south side of the Monument translates: "Haste is seen everywhere, London rises again, whether with greater speed or greater magnificence is doubtful, three short years complete that which was considered the work of an age" (Welch, *History of the Monument*, 22). Haste and magnificence become the reigning preoccupations; the rebuilding must move on apace, and must submit entries that will support the inflated rhetoric of rebuilding. The Monument is thus both a recording of and a charge to the rhetoric of rebuilding: to fulfill promises as well as descriptions. It is suggestive that when later maps reintroduced building elevations into their groundplans, the Monument was often drawn casting a literal or verbal shadow: "The monument or Pillar where the fire began" (see Figure 9).

The Monument

Figure 8 Engraving of the Monument (1720).

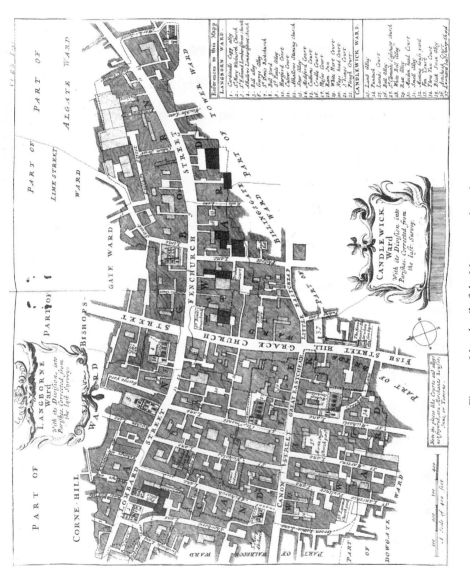

Figure 9 Map detail of the Monument (1720).

CHAPTER THREE

REDRAWING LONDON
MAPS AND TEXTS

A Large New and Exact MAP, with a true Description of the City of London, *and its Ruines,* **as it now stands** *faithfully surveyed . . . A distinction of the* Wards **formerly well known, now marked** *in this MAP with prickt Lines. Their divisions and bounds as they were set forth. The names of the Streets, Lanes, and Alleys, wharfs, and Passages. As also the Places where the Churches were. And the several Halls of the Worshipfull* Companies, *where they* **formerly stood** *. . . As also the manner of the re-building of the said* City; *and the number of* Churches **to be re-built** *with other Things,* **well worthy to be known both of Natives and Foreigners.**
(*An Exact Surveigh* by Leake & Hollar; *The Mercury*, No. 21, August 15–19, 1667; my emphasis)

To make lived space once again known space required the recharting of it, in a mapping that recontiguates *were* with *are*, *formerly* with *now*. Much of Restoration and early eighteenth-century literature topographically reconceptualizes as well as redefines London, relating parts to wholes, mapping content to form, spatializing relationships, localizing patterns, visualizing boundaries, recovering the old and figuring the new. The sheer topographical specificity of the period's literature *remaps* and *describes* its setting, finding and fixing the here-and-now. But its mapping and describing have generally been considered metaphorical; the pre-occupation with present time and local space a function primarily of the new political and social milieu of the restored Court. This chapter will prepare the historical and cultural ground for the argument in part II that in fact the *literary* remapping of London is part of the *literal* remapping, grounded both imaginatively and technologically in the innovations of cartographic reappropriation, borrowing explicitly and implicitly from its vocabulary and conceptual apparatus. The remapping itself coincided with a textualizing of the city, a verbal as well as visual attempt to find, define, and secure the topographical contours of the city. In cartography, the ornamental bird's-eye-views and elevations of the fifteenth through the early seventeenth centuries were replaced with two-dimensional groundplans that recorded the most obscure courts and alleys; in textual topography, the narrativized antiquities of Stow disappeared under a welter of alphabetized and cross-referenced *lists* of street names.

But the longer term consequences of rebuilding – grounded as well in the fast-changing economic climate – also generated a different and growing sense of spatial disorientation: as fast as the new spaces were mapped, they changed. Discernibly ambitious new building in the western suburbs, with discernibly different architectural assumptions, added more of the new to the sense of shape, structure, and topography of the city, and effected even greater abstract change in the city's social and commercial patterns. Shops, trades, neighbors, and social customs, dislodged from their medieval patterns, re-settled in new places, and as London's surging trade economy increasingly governed shifting social as well as commercial trends, transience generally replaced stability. Urban space became in part a function of shifting spatial practices, grounded, as Defoe argues, in the abstractions of a credit economy: "By this very Article of publick Credit, of which the Parliament is the Foundation (and the City, are the Architectures, or Builders) all those great Things are now done with Ease, which, in the former Reigns, went on heavily, and were brought about with the utmost difficulty."[1]

The changing emphasis of England's economy from trade to credit has gener-ally been described by economic historians as creating a metaphorically fluid ground in commercial and social worlds for roughly the five decades after the revolution of 1688. The creation of public credit and national debt meant that land, or even bullion, was no longer the central guarantor for or means of exchange, replaced by the "airy substance of paper credit," the value of which was measured by the waxing and waning of public confidence.[2] As Colin Nicholson argues: "New forms of property [became] the currency of social activ-ity and mobility . . . Uncertainty and flux were threatening to displace fixity and favoured forms and . . . new kinds of activities were generating inherently unsta-ble procedures" (*Writing and the Rise of Finance*, 5). And as P. G. M. Dickson notes, only a minority believed that the political, social, and economic conse-quences of this financial revolution would offer any real advantages to England; most registered alarm, disapproval, and "a nostalgia for an ahistorical past."[3]

Spatial changes in London share – perhaps even sponsor – the economic metaphors; both literally and figuratively unsettled the familiar landscape. In space as in economics, the writings of those who opposed the changes reveal "a nostalgia for Aristotelian notions of freehold and real property as the foundations of personality and value" (Nicholson, *Writing and the Rise of Finance*, 4) – for the fixity and stability of the (ahistorical) past. But for that minority who accepted or even promoted such change, rhetorical and practical strategies from the 1680s on adjusted from *recovering* the old to *navigating* the new.

The London section of Defoe's *Tour*, an analysis of which closes this chapter and this first part of the book, supplies a useful conceptual and rhetorical connec-tion between the cartographic, topographic, architectural, and literary strategies and rhetorics of rebuilding that occupy the first part of this study, and the imaginative rehabitation of London in the plays, poetry, and early novels of the period discussed in part II. The *Tour* borrows from the technical vocabulary of surveyors in creating a Line of Measurement that grammatically as well as metaphorically not only marks but elastically follows the bounding growth of the city. The Line employs narrative as well as motion to encircle and descriptively contain the city by *moving with it* rather than trying to stop it, accommodating its language and imagery to the changing perceptions of urban space.

Maps: refiguring space

Before the Fire there were relatively few maps of London.[4] Most maps of London between 1550 and 1660 were printed on the continent or engraved by foreigners, and were sponsored by royal or military events.[5] Over the next hundred years or so a few other maps of London were published, but they were almost entirely derivative of the Tudor maps. In some sense this sparseness was due as much to lack of *need* as to any lack of interest: "Travellers were few and such major buildings as existed were built over many decades, so that the layout of even the larger cities scarcely changed from generation to generation. In consequence there was little need for planned guidance in the form expected today" (Moreland and Bannister, *Antique Maps*, 40). Just before the Fire the topographical interest in London showed signs of picking up – inevitable in light of the ever-increasing urbanism: in 1658 appeared the bird's-eye survey of Richard Newcourt's and William Faithorne's bird's-eye-survey and the bird's-eye view of Wenceslaus Hollar. Hollar was later commissioned by Charles to survey London completely when the Fire literally and theatrically interrupted him. The Fire also, in a manner of speaking, literally and theatrically interrupted the whole tradition of three-dimensional cartography in London, and generated a very different perception of cartographic discipline.

Maps have always functioned as historical agents in the public perception of space as well as of national identity. Most maps before 1550 were produced for the Crown to conceptualize and consolidate the sense of a nation, allowing viewers to take "effective visual and conceptual possession of the physical kingdom in which they lived" (Helgerson, *Forms of Nationhood*, 107). As J. B. Harley argues: "maps were one of a number of instruments of control by landlords and governments; they were spatial emblems of power in society; they were artefacts in the creation of myth; and they influenced perception of place and space at a variety of geographical scales."[6] The Braun and Hogenberg and the "Agas" maps, for example, present orderly banks of houses in fairly untangled streets, presumably as part of the royal propaganda (see Figure 10).[7] The detailed elevations allow one, as the

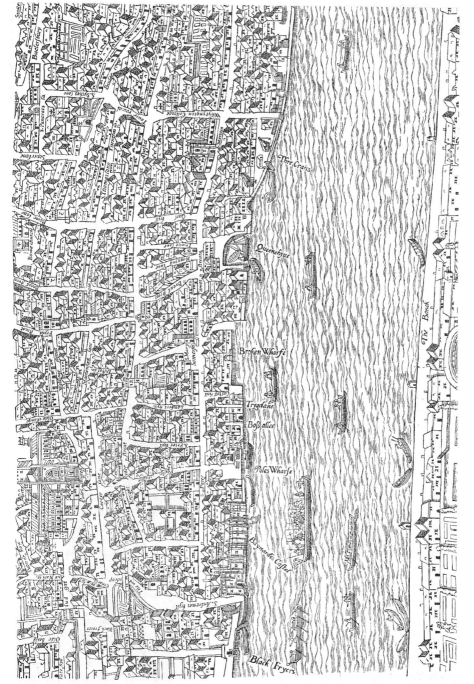

Figure 10 The "Agas" Map (*c.* 1552).

early surveyor John Fitzherbert puts it, to "see ye goodly stretes, the fayre build-
ynges . . . [and] ye great substance of ryches contayned in them."[8] Maps produced
visions of country and city that reflected representational choices, that created
images as much about how the mapped site *ought* to look (according to either
patron or mapmaker) as about how it actually did.

Such maps also contributed to an increasingly different *conceptualization* of
space, as J. R. Hale argues, which helped travellers to connect impressions of their
journey with their route as a whole, landowners to "see" their estates, and citizens
to visualize their country.[9] At the time of Elizabeth's accession land holdings were
still verbally described from manorial records, sometimes with diagrams;[10] by the
mid-sixteenth century picture maps were used increasingly by statesmen, land-
owners, and military engineers.[11] Harley argues that Saxton's atlas of 1579,
which features iconic fragments of landscape, transformed the viewer's sense of
place "from a state of separation to one of proximity, and this viewer was placed
'inside' a countryside which would have otherwise been invisible to him"
("Meaning and Ambiguity," 24).

Changes in map production and map techniques depend upon the amount of
information that the map is required to express and is perceived as *able* to express:
"limited appreciation and use of mapping [before the sixteenth century] is hardly
surprising as the detailed topographic information which can be imparted by a
text can never be expressed in its entirety on a map; not until maps could be made
approximating to a required level of information could they provide more than a
very generalised *aide-mémoire*" (Tyacke, Introduction, *English Map-Making*, 16).
Virtually all pre-Fire maps were pictorial bird's-eye-views and map-views
(combinations of groundplans and views), in which buildings and landmarks
are privileged over topographical accuracy. They reproduce visually known
space. Harley argues that the "apparently careless delineation [of landmarks]
connotes a set of values rather than a purely technical backwardness" ("Meaning
and Ambiguity," 32). The early bird's-eye-view celebrates the elevations of
buildings, the visual details of structure, offering a totalizing possibility, a sense of
visual control that offers the viewer the illusion of a "celestial eye," as in Faithorne
and Newcourt's 1658 view of the West End (see Figure 11).[12] The sense of space
is entirely present, fixed, available; the structural detail offers a representational
realism that seems to confer visual power over space – and had become a new way
of perceiving space in the Renaissance.

The disadvantages of the bird's-eye-view, from a modern cartographic perspective, may be the same as their contemporary advantages: alleys and yards are
often obscured; "[l]ess room is available for labelling, administrative boundary
lines cannot be drawn in with exactness and it is frequently impossible to gauge the
true width of streets and the real extent of buildings. In short, precision of

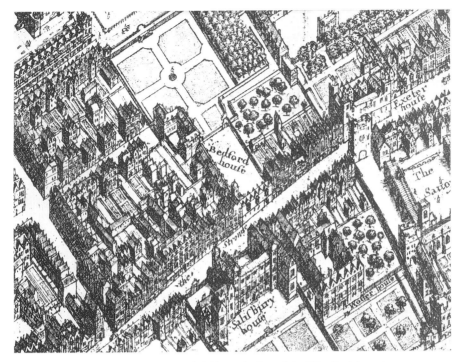

Figure 11 Newcourt and Faithorne's plan of the West End (1658).

measurement is sacrificed to visual impact" (Fisher, Introduction, *Collection of Early Maps*, [n.p.]). Harley argues that society did not "press the map-maker to solve the problem [of inaccuracy in] relief depiction . . . [because] there was no demand for such precision" (Harley, "Meaning and Ambiguity," 32). That isn't *quite* true, of course. The Civil War demanded accurately representative maps, and got them: *A Plan of the City and Suburbs of LONDON as fortified by Order of PARLIAMENT in the Years 1642 & 1643*, for example, is orderly, geometricized, with clean lines of access, almost like the Dutch maps (see Figure 12). And land-owners could have strong personal interests in knowing precise boundaries. Fitzherbert, in *The Boke of Surueying*, encourages topographical specificity pre-cisely for social and economic reasons, showing "how a lordshyppe or a maner shuld be surueied and vewed, butted & bounded on euery parte, that it may be knowen for euer, whose euery parcell thereof was" (33v).[13] But the *requirements* for precision are different and have different implications from those that will emerge because of the Fire: here, the land is viewed, butted, and bounded on every part to secure it to its owner; temporal as well as social continuity and stability is preserved – one keeps what one has, on Fitzherbert's recommendation. Similarly, Fitzherbert recommends a certain kind of thoroughness in surveying a city

81

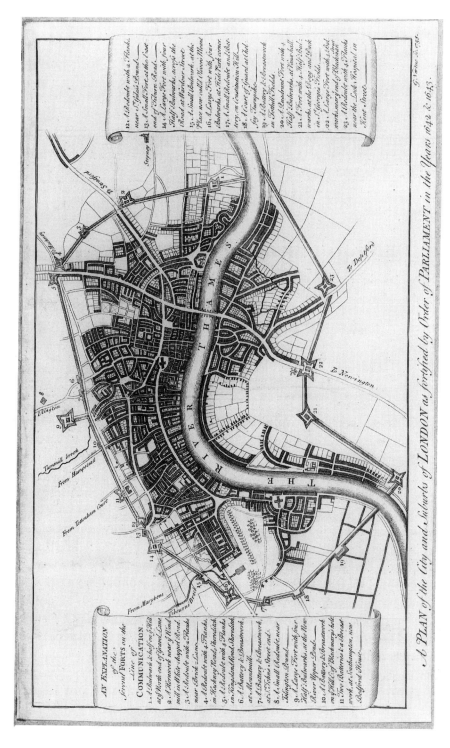

AN EXPLANATION
of the
several FORTS on the
Line of
COMMUNICATION.

1. A Redoubt & half on Wind
mill West end of Gray's Inn Lane.
2. A Hornwork near y Wind
mill in White chapel Road.
3. A Redoubt with 2. Flanks
near Brick Lane.
4. A Redoubt with 2. Flanks
in Hackney Road, Shoreditch.
5. A Redoubt with 3. Flanks
in Kingsland Road, Shoreditch.
6. A Battery & Breastwork
at Mountmill.
7. A Battery & Breastwork
at S. John's Street end.
8. A small Redoubt near
Islington Pound.
9. A Large Fort with four
Half Bulwarks, at the New
River Upper Pond.
10. A Battery & Breastwork
on y Hill of Blackmary hole
Tine Batteries & a Breast
work at Southampton, now
Bedford House.

12. A Redoubt with 2. Flanks
near S. Giles's Pound.
13. A small Fort at the East
end of Tiburn Road.
14. A Large Fort with four
Half Bulwarks, across the
Road at Wardour Street.
15. A small Bulwark at the
Place near old S. Vincent Mount.
16. A Large Fort with four
Bulworks at Hide Park corner.
17. A small Redoubt and battery on Constitution Hill.
18. A Court of Guard at Chel-
sey Turnpike.
19. A Battery & Breastwork
in Tuthill Fields.
20. A Quadrant Fort with 4.
Half Bulworks at Vaux hall.
21. A Fort with a Half Bulwarks, at the Dogg and Duck
in S. George's Fields.
22. A Large Fort with 4. Bul
works, near y end of Blackman
near the Lock, Newinot in
Kent Street.

Engraver's mark: G. Vertue fecit 1738.

A PLAN of the City and Suburbs of LONDON as fortified by Order of PARLIAMENT in the Years 1642 & 1643.

Figure 12 A Plan of the City and Suburbs of LONDON as fortified by Order of PARLIAMENT in the Years 1642 & 1643.

(although he acknowledges that such thoroughness hasn't yet been attempted), but that thoroughness depends primarily on establishing the *social* network of spatial relations, and privileges buildings over space, or rather, building *owners* over topographic spaces: "to shewe who is lord of the house nexte unto the sayde brydge, and who is tenaunte" (*Boke of Surueying*, 34v).

In general, although some sixteenth- and early seventeenth-century topographers perceived a certain value in topographical accuracy and specificity, it was either linked to further securing social privilege or seemed unattainable. The title page of Samuel Waler's map of the manor of Garnetts, Essex (1622) advertises "A true and perfect Plott of all the Demesne Landes belonging to the Mannor of Garnetts" that will show, among numerous other items, "euerie Gatehouse, Barnes, Stables, Douehouse, Orchards, Yardes, Gardens, High waies, Drift waies, Ponds, Pathes, Pound, Stiles, Gates, Bridges" (quoted in Harley, "Meaning and Ambiguity," Plate 4). Such a spirited listing would become a model for post-Fire topographies attempting to comprehend the strange vastnesses of the rebuilt City, but as an antecedent to such maps and texts Waler's map marks the early side of the shift from country to city, and from place detail as property definition to place detail as spatial orientation. London itself did not yet have such a close catalogue – either cartographically or textually – except of course for John Stow's *A Survey of London* (1598), which is actually closer to Fitzherbert's economic genealogy in privileging owner and history over space and structure. John Speed apologizes for the small and therefore distorting scale of Norden's inset map-view of London in their 1611 atlas, and promises to furnish a "trew plott" at a time of "further leasure," but as John Fisher points out, neither Speed, nor Aaron Rathbone, nor Wenceslaus Hollar ever carried out their sometimes approved or commissioned plans to survey the city (Fisher, Introduction, *Collection of Early Maps*, 2). Until the Great Fire London's cartographic depictions remained pictorial: topographically inaccurate but visually complete and imaginatively comprehended.

The real demand for cartographic precision came when the very floor of cartographic tradition disappeared, when the culture of London needed to explore and make known the lost, the destroyed, the rearranged. "Careful delineation" suggests a different set of values: signs had *lost* their signifieds, the map symbols attached to nothing; building elevations were become empty fictions; London had to rebuild from the ground up – literally, visually, and conceptually.

The Fire destroyed virtually all of the existing map-stock of London plans, and London in order to be rebuilt needed to be *found*. Property lines are of course the skeleton of any city, and logically co-exist with property ownership. But in the case of such sweeping destruction, the lines must be recovered in order to reclaim the property; the lines *precede* their ownership at least conceptually, rather than coextend with it. An elevation – the traditional bird's-eye-view – was both practically and symbolically inadequate. As the City surveyor John Holwell declared with implicit contempt: "Those that are minded to draw the Map of any Town City or Corporation, only with the Uprights of the Houses, will have no need to measure either the House, Courts, or Allies thereof."[14] Leake's survey of the ruined spaces, etched by Hollar, combines in a transitional generic moment the bird's-eye-view that still captures and contains "the ryches of the fayre streets," the three-dimensional structuring of lived space, with the bare spaces and topographical precision of the modern groundplan, in which the "blanke space signif[ies] the burnt part & where the houses are exprest, those places yet standing"[15] (see Figure 1 in chapter one). The two-dimensional plot literally as well as figuratively represents blank space, emptiness, the inexpressible.[16]

The two-dimensional plan would dominate cartographic representations of London until the early decades of the eighteenth century. In 1677 finally appeared *This Most Accurate Survey Made by JOHN OGILBY Esqr And William Morgan* – "very nearly the first linear ground plan (or 'plot' to use the contemporary term) of a British town."[17] John Ogilby (1600–1676), former dancing-master, translator of Homer and Æsop, and a target in *MacFlecknoe*, moved in the same circles as Hooke, Wren, Flamsteed, and the Royal Society generally. The plan of London, part of a larger project to remap the nation in *Britannia*, used "the most mathematically precise and scientific surveying methods" (Hyde, ix), sweeping away the traditional elevations, the oblique angle, and most of the visual detail in the interests of accurate and *comprehensive* topographical detail (see Figure 13).[18] All the dark tangled corners of London that earlier mapmakers had tactfully concealed now assumed equal topographic importance: the use of keyed numbers in the small corners where a name would not fit insured that not even the tiniest spaces could escape.[19] As William Leybourn, surveyor for the Ogilby and Morgan map, declares, the best way to plot London is to notice "besides the *High streets*, and *Lanes*, all *Courts* and *Allies*, all *Churches* and *Church-yards*, and the 2 Temples, all *Inns* of *Court*, all *Colledges*, the *Guild-Hall*, and all eminent *Halls* or *Corporations*, all *Market places* and *Market houses*, &c."[20] The new survey, the new map techniques, exhibit as a central concern the actual interrelation of all the real spaces of the city, the grounding of place itself. The property lines do not declare themselves as lines of *property* but as lines of *place*; owners are not named, as they were in the *Survey of the Rebuilding* (see chapter two). Though the larger property owners are indexed – on Figure 13, for example, A14 marks the house of Lord Gray – the view of the house is scraped from the map, and the owner expunged into the index. Only common property, which by function as well as by geographic position reorients the viewer to the shape of the city, is identified: Leaden Hall, Market for Leather; St. Peters Cornhill Church & Yard; Lime Street; Holborn Bridge;

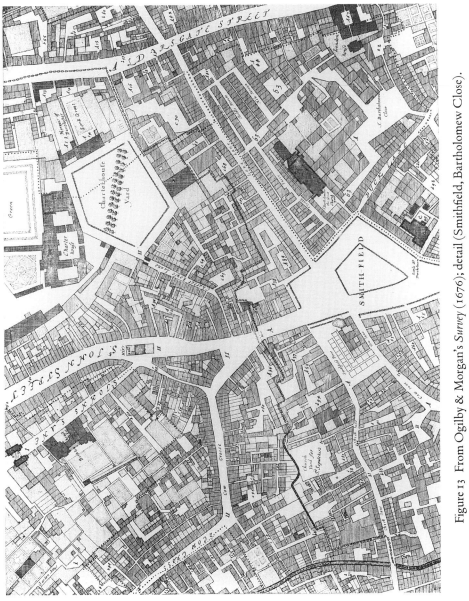

Figure 13 From Ogilby & Morgan's *Survey* (1676); detail (Smithfield, Bartholomew Close).

St. Andrew Holborn Church Yard; the New Canal. A variety of new or newish symbols sorts out the fluctuation of changes: the "prickt Lines" for the boundaries of wards, smaller dots for parishes and liberties, chain links for the boundary of the City, double lines for the City wall, and the thin snaking transgressive line for the extent of the Fire. The map in the way it images and defines the lines of the city marks a shift in the meaning of place. For at least two decades, the groundplan, shorn of isometric projections, would dominate the English maps of London. Even Hollar, who obviously took loving delight in his delicately engraved elevations, swept out his own view of the city in a map he published based on Ogilby and Morgan's survey. Only on the edges of the Thames, and in the northern spaces of the city, do the remnants of familiar representation remain – a further displacement of the projections of Leake's survey.

The first groundplans after the Fire are essentially non-narrative, non-mimetic; the topographical spaces are cleared of visualized, imagined life. They signalled change; but they also reacted against themselves, and quickly reintroduced familiar representational features of the past. Morgan's map had not been particularly popular. Both bulkier (it measured 8' x 4') and less decorative than other maps, it expired after one edition. The changes in later maps suggest that this austere groundplan was *too* new, too different, too alien; it recovered the old city conceptually but not imaginatively. The later maps and surveys increasingly reincorporate bits of three-dimensional detail, reconstructing and repopulating the cartographic genre as the city itself three-dimensionalized. In 1681–82, Morgan, reaching for the popular market (Barker and Jackson, *History of London in Maps*, 43) consolidated the compromise, providing a model that would be used until the middle of the eighteenth century. His new map reinstates the elevations of certain important buildings, including the Monument and its shadow (see Figure 14).[21] Later popular mapmakers, such as John Strype in 1720 (see Figure 15), George Foster in 1738, and John Rocque in 1746, continued to retain that vivid visual detail. In a sort of reverse colonization, such detail would have recovered the old city more effectively for its citizens by firmly planting visually familiar figures (even if they were re-buildings) onto those unknown topographies to reinhabit the *terra incognita*.

Cartographic interest had begun to revive just before the Fire, partly through Charles's interest in map-collecting, partly because the Navigation Act of 1651 had restricted the supply of Dutch atlases, and partly because London's expansion in the west began to be noticeable and – to some – vaguely worrisome. But the Fire catalyzed both interest and need, and map-making as well as map-buying became part of the wider cultural interest in recovering the city. The Fire destroyed the City's map-stock, and many of those who had previously sold maps now undertook to publish them as well. English cartographic publication was at

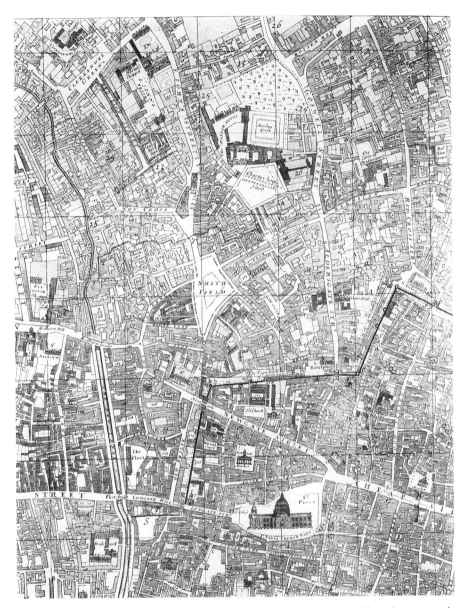

Figure 14 From Jefferys's edition (*c.* 1749) of Morden & Lea's map (1720) based on Morgan's map (1682); elevations reinstated.

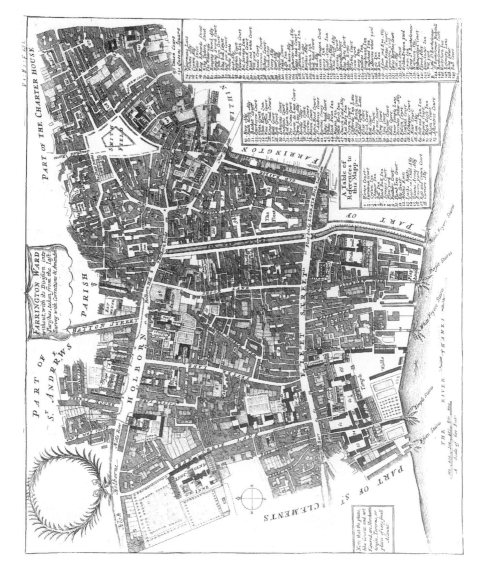

Figure 15 From Strype's *Survey of London* (1720); Smithfield, Bartholomew Close.

one of its most prolific periods from 1665 to the early decades of the eighteenth century, and the market for maps, which since the Renaissance had widened from Court to statesmen, landowners, and the educated, now widened further to the expanding reading public, which included tradespeople as well as merchants. Maps were becoming more versatile, serving as book illustrations as well as wall decorations, and could be sold as topical mementoes. Tyacke notes that "intermittent warfare on the continent and such events as the 'Glorious Revolution' of 1688 provided a continual incentive for the map-sellers to complete for customers."[22]

As with the news of the destruction and rebuilding of London, its remapping was also charted in the public newspapers through increasingly plentiful advertisements, adding the vocabulary of cartography to the discourse of cultural self-spatialization. The advertisement from *The Mercury*, quoted at the head of this chapter, offers itself as new and exact and "faithfully surveyed," bringing together the old and lost (the "*Wards* formerly well known") into new symbolic awareness ("now marked . . . with prickt Lines"), and the nature of the new, both actual and potential, "well worthy to be known both of Natives and Foreigners" (*The Mercury*, No. 21, August 15–19, 1667). The 1670s saw an increase in production and sales of maps of both England and London:

> A new Map of *London, Westminster*, and Borough of *Southwark*, with their Suburbs, shewing their Streets, Lanes, Allies, Courts, with other Remarks, as they now are, in one imperial sheet of paper, price 12 *d*. with descriptions, 1 *s*. 6 *d*. pasted upon Cloth with Rowle and Ledge 4 *s*. Sold by *Robert Green* at the *Rose* and *Crown* in *Budge-rowe*, and by *Robert Morden* at the *Atlas* in *Cornehil*.　　　　　(*London Gazette*, No. 1036, October 21–25, 1675)

Maps entered the arena of popular *events* as well as of public spaces, as in John Ogilby's attempt to further fund his production of *Britannia* through a form of public auction, to be held on the premises of a popular coffee house:

> Mr. *Ogilby*, for the better enabling him to carry on his *Britannia*, by an actual Survey, &*c*. has lately erected his standing-Lottery of Books, at Mr *Garways* Coffee house in *Exchange-Alley*, near the *Royal Exchange London*, which opening the 7 of *April* next, will thence continue without Intermission, till wholly drawn off: Where all future Adventurers, may by them selves or Correspondents, daily put in their Money upon the Author, according to his Proposalls so generally approved of.
> 　　　　　(*London Gazette*, No. 768, March 27–31, 1673, and No. 769)

Ogilby's death didn't stop the publicization process; his stepson, William Morgan, continued the lotteries to help boost sagging finances, as the completion of the survey seemed to drag on beyond the original subscribers' patience.[23] And through games, cards, and texts which advertized their accessibility, map-sellers could fit a conception of the world into a recognizably English context, "whereby Geography may be easily and familiarly learnt by all sorts of People."[24] The popularity of maps may also be gauged to some extent by the plague of counterfeits, as in Ogilby's *Itinerarium Angliae*, or Book of Roads, in which "Mr *Ogilby's* name is to each sheet . . . to prevent Counterfeits" (*London Gazette*, No. 1065, January 31–February 3, 1675/6). And finally, by their *size*: Ogilby offered his "Tables of all the Roads, with the computed and measured distance betwixt every Town, and the distinction of Marks and Post-Towns, fitted for a Pocket-Book," and sold them "at his House in *White-Fryers*," as well as through his regular booksellers.

In the house, in the street, in the pocket, and in popular culture, maps had become part of everyday life, and visually marked the new and widespread cultural awareness of spatial relations and representations. Spatial relations could be "easily and familiarly learnt by all sorts of People"; and the newspapers, in advertising the production and sales of maps, and underscoring the local directions for where to go to get them (near this church, over against that tavern, in the shops and houses of booksellers, stationers, milliners, and mapmakers) thus not only publish the sale of maps, they publish the contours of space itself.

Anxieties of rebuilding

But those contours changed virtually as soon as they were marked, and shifted in often unpredictable social and commercial – as well as geographic – directions. Not all of the building energy in London in the later seventeenth century centered on the City; in fact, many of the shopkeepers and tradesmen who had been forced by the Fire to relocate found themselves setting up new areas of commercial enterprise in the increasingly fashionable and rapidly expanding West End – several miles beyond the gates to the old City. Six years after the Fire only three-quarters of the eighty thousand people who had evacuated the City had returned. "The houses were there, but the people were not returning to fill them."[25] People had built a new life beyond the City walls, and many found it inconvenient, undesirable, or in some cases impossible to return. Much of the social and economic energy of London drained out of the City center and into its "out-parts," creating a surge in new building that outflanked and undermined the rebuilding. From the 1680s to the 1730s London's physical dimensions swelled at rates that overpowered all previous spurts of growth.[26] Defoe, in trying to define the limits of London in 1724, flings up his hands, defeated by the constant changes:

> [T]he City of *London*, for so it is still to be called, is extended to *Hide Park Corner* in the *Brentford* Road, and almost to *Maribone* in the *Acton* Road, and how much farther it may spread, who knows? New Squares, and new Streets rising up every Day to such a Prodigy of Buildings, that nothing in the World does, or ever did, equal it.   *(Tour,* 1.5.316*)*

The building in the "out-parts" differed significantly in *kind* from the rebuilding in the city, which architecturally and topographically ended up preserving the close medieval patterns, the familiarity of the English past. The new building revived the interest in baroque geometricization and order introduced by Inigo Jones in the early seventeenth century and interrupted by war and the Commonwealth. Two aristocratic patrons of architecture, the earls of Southampton and St. Albans, had started building schemes around Bloomsbury and St. James's Squares before the Fire; these schemes afterwards inspired similar projects (see Figures 16 and 17). George Rudé shows that "they firmly established two important new principles of urban development: the presence of the land-lord's own house in the square . . . and the principle of a complete unit of develop-ment, comprising square, secondary streets, markets, and even a church."[27] The squares created their own economic and social needs, and markets, shops, and inns, as well as smaller houses and tenements for the tradespeople and their ser-vants, mushroomed among the new squares.

With the massive building and rebuilding going on all over London came a proliferation of treatises, pamphlets, and guides, both theoretical and practical, and their popular reception indicates, as Manley argues, the dissemination of a "new urbanism" shifting from the pre-Fire urbanism.[28] Although, as with the maps, we can't reliably extrapolate audience from print history, the number of editions as well as their changing format at least suggests the *perception* of a popular market. William Leybourn's *The Compleat Surveyor* went through four editions in his lifetime and one after. John Holwell's *A Sure Guide to the Practical Surveyor* was advertised in the *London Gazette* issue of August 29–September 2, 1678, as was *The City and Country Purchaser and Builder* by S. P. [i.e., Stephen Primatt], Gent. – "The Second Edition, much enlarded [sic], by *William Leybourne*" (No. 1515, May 24–27, 1680). The first edition of this work (1667) describes itself as responding directly to citizens' – not professionals' – needs. Primatt offers his treatise as a way of helping "the Noble suffering Citizens . . . very willing and desirous to build" but who were "impeded by certain Differences arising amongst them, as to their respective Interests in the [Ground], and late Houses, others through their unskilfulness in building were not less indisposed to it for that many of them are compelled to trust to the Conscience and Fidelity of Workmen and Surveyors" (*City and Country Purchaser,* A3v-A4). The work then offers tables of rates, supplies, rules for purchasing and measuring

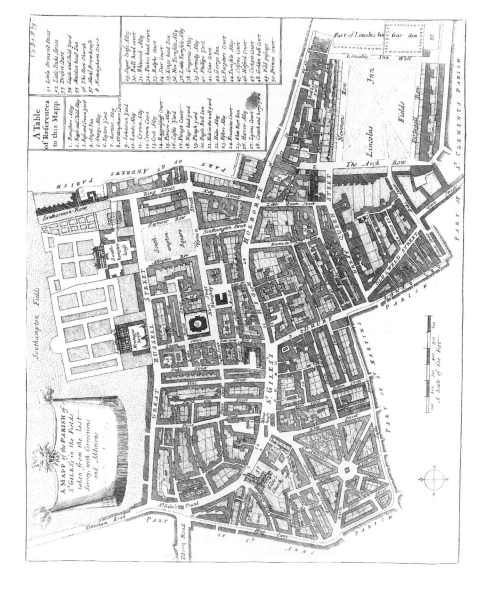

Figure 16 From Strype's *Survey* (1720); Southampton Square.

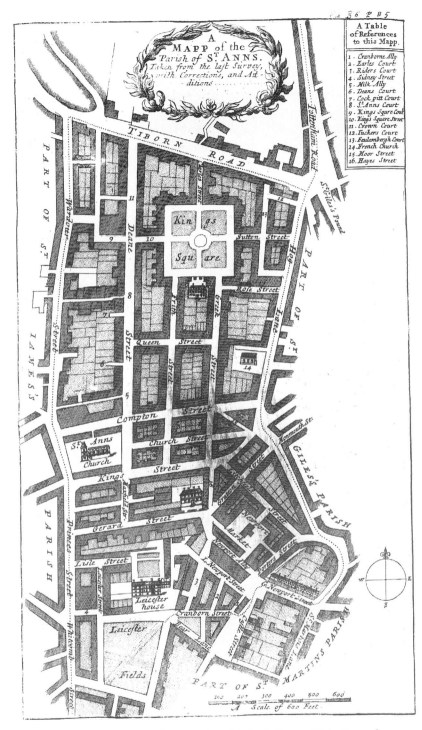

Figure 17 From Strype's *Survey* (1720); King's Square (Soho Square).

land, various examples of groundplans, valuations for street frontage, shop windows, and so on.

The appearance in 1715 of Colen Campbell's *Vitruvius Britannicus* and Giacomo Leoni's edition of Palladio's *The Four Books of Architecture* prompted a series of theoretical as well as practical architectural publications for noticeably wider audiences. *Vitruvius*, a list of important classical English buildings, included among its more august subscribers the names of masons, carpenters, and joiners. It was instantly popular, and was followed on the one hand by theoretical treatises by Shaftesbury, Jonathan Richardson, Daniel Webb, and half a dozen others; and on the other, by a sturdy succession of books and pamphlets compiled by and expressly for craftsmen.[29] Works by Batty Langley, William Halfpenny, Thomas Chippendale, Robert Morris, and others brought the principles of taste in building simply and colorfully to the lay as well as professional eye, essentially *describing* the professional not only to himself but to the public.[30] Langley's *The Builder's Chest-book* (1727), for example, develops a series of "lectures" on the five orders of architecture in a dialogue between an apprentice architect and Palladio himself. The first question is: "What is an Architect?" Palladio firmly responds: "A Person Skilful in the Art of Building" (1). By the first half of the eighteenth century "the humblest carpenter and bricklayer" began to assert their prerogative to discuss, criticize, and create questions of architectural significance (Summerson, *Georgian London*, 36). From the exigencies and experience of participation in rebuilding came a wider number of voices confident of pronouncing upon it. Issues of space, in structure as in boundary, had become matters of public discourse, of daily life, of cultural commonalty.

But the issues of rebuilding were not simply a matter of public discourse; they were also matters of public anxiety. Just as the burned-out city was rebuilding itself back into recognition, the rest of London went and got strange. *So much* was new, to accommodate all these new inhabitants, all these new fashions. The out-parts as well as the center of the city encountered strangeness, though in different ways.

The various texts of the rebuilding mark several overlapping shifts in public attitude. In 1668, Samuel Rolls had complained about the scattered, haphazard, and disorganized attempts to rebuild the city, comparing a generally unimpressive London to an uneven forest, an old orchard, and finally wondering, "must it commence a village before it commence a city?"[31] By the early 1670s, the tone of the Londoncentric publications had changed: London did not remain long within the imagery of stasis and decay, and city-describers were singing paeons to the resurrected city; works such as Edward Chamberlayne's various editions of *Angliae Notitia* (1667–1707), John Brydall's *Camera Regis, Or, A Short View of London* (1676), Thomas DeLaune's *The Present State of London* (1681), all celebrate the recovered glories and increased girth of the city.[32] But by the 1680s, more and more broadsides and pamphlets seem to pick up on the doubts between the lines in the rebuilding poems, and work to calm a rising anxiety: "As there has been great mistakes about the Damage and Nusance by the Increase of New-buildings in the suburbs; so by this we may see the mistake to be as great about their number and value."[33] Another apologist broadside claims that "the increase of New-Buildings hath of late occasion'd such Clamour."[34] Most recuperative pamphlets made their position clear in large-print titles. Nicholas Barbon, the famous mass-marketer of urban space, published *An Apology for the Builder: Or, A Discourse Shewing the Cause and Effects of the Increase of Building* (1685), in which he argues that London, for its

> number of good Houses, for its many and large Piazzas, for its richness of Inhabitants . . . must be allowed the largest, best built, and richest City in the world . . . [But] the whole Nation is astonished at the flourishing condition of this Metropolis, to see every year a new Town added to the old one; and like men affrighted are troubled with misapprehensions, and easily imposed on by the false suggestions of those that envy her grandeur, and are angry with the Builders for making her so great.   (*Apology*, 2)

The sheer quantity of printed reassurance assumed necessary suggests a measure of the growing cultural anxiety that London was fast growing socially, economically, and experientially out of control.[35] The loss of the old urban background and the burgeoning intrusiveness of the new combined to increase the sense of topographical unsteadiness, the strangeness of this lived world.[36]

So much had changed: not just the face of the old world, but its very social and commercial *patterns*; not just the contours of urban space, but its *nature*. The early attempts to recover the familiar past in fact helped to generate more of the strange and new. The lines of the streets, the structures of the buildings, the patterns of commerce, the habits of daily life, all were transformed. The city of London had to be renegotiated on every level; the maps, the architectural treatises, and the textual topographies were all, along with the literary productions of the period, part of the cultural attempt to rechart that *uncanny* territory.

Texts: new grammars of space

Both the narrative techniques and conceptual concerns of London topographies changed after the Fire in ways that correspond to changing concerns in carto-graphic, architectural, and literary practices and assumptions. Maps adapted to new visual needs, but even maps – those fixed graphic spaces – were not enough to contain and practically re-present London. As William Stow claimed in 1722:

"But suppose a very large Map could be drawn, still the Inconveniency would be such, that the Inspector must have a magnifying Glass to read what he looke for, without such a Book as this, to direct in what part of the Town it lies" (*Remarks on London*, A4). *Textual* topographies (as distinct from visual or graphic ones) appeared in new forms and remarkable quantities to attempt their own generic mastery of the city. Topographies before the Fire, modelled almost exclusively on John Stow's 1598 *Survey of London*, conceptually presume and narratively reflect a *relative* sense of urban fixity even within the vocabulary of change, a correspondence between place name and place behavior or commercial function. The spaces and patterns of London's streets are presented as more or less knowable, reliable, and relatively static. But as London is destroyed and rebuilt, re-covered and re-membered, reperceived and redefined, the experience of inhabiting its new spaces demands new habits and new forms of expression. Defoe's *Tour thro' the Whole Island of Great Britain*, published in 1724–26, differs strikingly from earlier descriptions of London in its grammar, imagery, and implications, and the differences both depend on and reflect a new consciousness of space – topographical, commercial, and even structural – as fluid, shifting, unreliable, unpredictable. Borrowing the vocabulary of surveying and the grammar of motion, Defoe's *Tour* offers new generic strategies for a cultural and textual remapping (if not a containing) of estranging modern space.

Here, as throughout this study, I want to be careful to distinguish between documented historical change and various cultural perceptions and expressions of change. The historical question of London's social, political, and topographic instability has been much debated.[37] In the argument that follows I want to emphasize two different points. First, part of this great sense of changed urban space is indeed perceptual and comparative: Londoners after the Fire and during the Restoration more generally perceived and described themselves in terms of drastic change – economic, social, political, religious, and urban – looking back nostalgically towards an "ahistorical past" of topographical reliability and fixity. These various literary and technological self-representations have respectable genealogies. At the same time, however, I do not want to minimize the existence of actual change. The financial revolution was, if not predicated on, certainly enabled by the disruptions and possibilities of rebuilding, of marked shifts in previously more-or-less settled social and commercial urban spaces. What Colin Nicholson argues about the economic revolution applies equally to the spatial transformation: "The texts [that contemporary writers] produced express a struggle for meaning and value in what was for them an era of devastating change" (*Writing and the Rise of Finance*, 18).

Before the Fire, descriptions of London were rather few and relatively single-minded. William Camden's *Britannia* (1586) was widely read and admired (translated from Latin into English in 1610 and frequently reprinted through the seventeenth century), but its scope was both larger in territory and narrower in focus than would be expected or found in any specific topographies of London. Yet that scope – the antiquarian interest in the traces of the past defining the contours of the present – would characterize all specific topographies until after the Fire. Stow's *Survey*[38] achieved immediate popular success, being reprinted in 1599, 1603, and 1633, but then disappeared from print until John Strype's beautiful (but unwieldy) edition in 1720 – the text of which was based on the never-published description Ogilby intended to append to his 1676 map of the city.[39] Though there had long been a tradition of London-centered literature in the drama, poetry, pamphlets, ballads, and broadsides of the sixteenth and early seventeenth centuries, non-literary works centering on London in the 1640s and 50s tended to occupy themselves (not surprisingly) with papal plots, military strategies, and tax structures. For much of the early and mid-seventeenth century, Londoners had other things to worry about than their topographic profile. So for its apparent ability to satisfy a minimalist contemporary need for self-description, Stow's *Survey* became a fixture of the genre. It furnished a literary and conceptual model to more than a hundred years of descendants who relied heavily (and often silently) on his information and followed his formal and grammatical patterns for a topography that in many ways defined and fixed the genre as something that defined a fixed space.

The phrase "defined a fixed space" in many ways oversimplifies the realities of sixteenth- and early seventeenth-century London. Lawrence Manley, among others, has demonstrated the disturbing power, the "bewildering profusion of social roles," the "terror of deterritorialization," of the "increasingly mobile environment of London" (*Literature and Culture*, 77).[40] City literatures, in the forms of description, complaint, or celebration, generally accompany noticeable change, and Manley quotes an epigram by Thomas Freeman in which "the whole city becomes a monument to helter-skelter motion" (*Literature and Culture*, 427). Both Elizabeth and James were actively concerned to limit the growth of the city, and both failed to contain its surging changes. But the argument that follows emphasizes textual *trends* that, while drawing on familiar tropes and traditions, also indicate change. The rapid development of the genre of textual topography, its sharp increase in numbers of publications and popularity of editions, and its rhetorical strategies, all testify to a post-Fire sense of change, and a change of interest, that in its own way includes, not surprisingly, a nostalgic oversimplification of its own past. The spaces of the past, from the point of view of the rebuilding-present, do in fact seem fixed, stable, known; and the grammar of the new texts reflects a different sense of motion, a different "grammar of space."

Henri Lefebvre argues that for medieval communities, ancient, monumental buildings housed social meanings and fixed spatial relations; manors, monasteries, and cathedrals were the focal points anchoring a stable network of lanes and roads.[41] Spatial relations were in some sense visible, concrete, self-declarative. Richard Helgerson notes that Elizabethan England, in its efforts to identify and visualize itself as a nation, produced a series of works commonly called surveys, descriptions, and chorographies. These terms suggest a fixed object of vision, a territory *waiting* to be covered visually and verbally – contrasting noticeably with the proliferation of "tours" and "journeys" in the late seventeenth and early eighteenth centuries (Helgerson, *Forms of Nationhood*, 133). By the early seventeenth century, chorographies had generically settled into architectural and genealogical reference works, "where county gentry can find their manors, monuments, and pedigrees copiously set forth" (Helgerson, 133). The manors and monuments confirm the significance and stability of a newly mapped nation. The spaces of early England are pinned in place by the physical structures and genealogies of the gentry.[42]

Stow's *Survey* and its faithful followers describe the traditional emblems of the city in as much or more detail as they describe the streets and buildings, recording the manors and monuments, the pedigrees and anecdotes, of the city's past and present luminaries. The groundplan is defined in terms of its history as much as its geography; every house has its story, and such stories fix the structure within its historical and social context of past and present. For example, one small corner of Tower Street Ward housed both a villain and a voyeur:

> Then at the west ende of Towerstreet haue ye a little turning towards the North, to a fayre house sometime belonging to one named *Grista*, for he dwelled there in the yeare 1449. And *Iack Cade* captaine of the rebels in *Kent*, being by him, in this his house feasted, when he had dined (like an unkind guest) robbed him of al that was there to be found worth the carriage. Next to this is one other fayre house, sometime builded by *Angel Dune* Grocer, since possessed by Sir *Iohn Champneis* Alderman & Maior of *London*, he builded in this house an high Tower of Bricke, the first that ever I hearde of in any priuate mans house to ouerlooke his neighboures in this citie. But this delight of his ey was punished with blindnes, some yeres before his death. *(Survey, 97)*

Different fair houses hold different stories, but the houses and the stories are located in relation to each other, within this chronological and topographical continuum called London.

Of course the city changes, and of course Stow recognizes and records such change. But change is almost always slow, incremental, crustacean – one literal example in Stow also serves metaphorically:

> In this old Fishstreete is one rowe of small houses . . . now possessed of fishmongers, [which] were at the first but moueable boardes (or stalles) sette

out on marketdayes, to shewe their fish there to be sold: but procuring license to set up sheads, they grewe to shops, and by litle and litle, to tall houses, of three or 4. stories in heigth [sic], and now are called Fishstreete.

(Survey, 280–81*)*

Houses and streets grow slowly into each other; the peculiar grammatical constructions almost suggest that the moveable boards themselves displayed fish, procured licenses, and in their conglomerate growth, *became* Fish Street. The growth itself is predominantly interior, organic, settled rather than unsettling. The fields of Whitechapel and Smithfield, the larger streets in Cheapside, the streets circling St. Paul's, have all gradually been "enclosed" and "encroached upon" by sheds and shops and tenements. Stow marks outward growth, but fastens on inner congestion. The very slowness of the change emphasizes what remains the same.

This emphasis on slow change is copied in Stow's pre-Fire successors. In his 1657 work *Londinopolis*, for example, James Howell discusses the "insensible augmentation" of the suburbs since Henry III, the "insensible Coalition" of Westminster and London, and the "insensible Coalitions" of people that have brought London to its world-class glory (*Londinopolis*, 341, 346). Thus recordable change is of antiquarian more than contemporary interest, as Stow had declared: "What *London* hath beene of auncient time, **men may here see,** as what it is now euery man doth behold" (*Survey,* A3; my emphasis). The past may be covered over, like many of the old streams, but it is still present, immanent, accessible; the *temporal* present is physically *present.* London is available to behold and survey.

The structure of Stow's text reinforces its sense of fixity and stability. Each description of a ward begins with its bounds: "This Warde of *Faringdon* within the walles, is bounded thus: Beginning in the East, at the great Crosse in West Cheape, from whence it runneth West . . . Then againe into Cheape, and to Foster Lane . . . Then backe again into Cheape" (*Survey,* 249). Each street, lane, and alley is named and noted, the ichnography outlined. Once bounded, the ward can be entered and mined for its monuments, antiquities, stories, and histories. Interior streets narratively dead-end into buildings:

[At] the North ende of Aue Mary Lane, there is a short Lane which runneth West some small distance, and is there closed up with a gate into a great house . . . *Iuie Lane* . . . runneth North to the west ende of Saint *Nicholas* Shambles. And then west *Pater Noster Rowe*, till ouer against the golden Lyon, where the Warde endeth for that streete. *(Survey,* 250–51*)*

Stow records the changes within these boundaries, and ends each description with a brief, firm, factual account of the aldermen and the tax structure of the ward. Historical change remains narratively contained.

Social and commercial change seems equally as slow and, at least on Stow's construction, as self-contained. In a rather extended discussion of the London markets, Stow carefully tracks who moves, but balances that account with who remains:

> Men of trades and sellers of wares in this City haue often times since chaunged their places, as they have found their best advantage. For whereas Mercers and Haberdashers used to keepe their shoppes in West Cheape, of later time they held them on *London* Bridg, where **partly they yet remayne**. The Goldsmithes of Gutherons lane, and Old Exchaunge, are now for the most part remoued into the South side of west Cheape: the Peperers and Grocers of Sopers lane, are now in Bucklesberrie, & other places . . . But the Brewers for the more part **remaine neere** to the friendly water of Thames. *(Survey,* 62; my emphasis*)*

Nearly every instance of removal is stabilized by a counter-example; and the paragraph ends with the point that, though the "*Patten* makers of S. *Margaret* Pattens lane [are] cleane worne out," "horse coursers and Sellars of Oxen, Sheepe, Swine, and such like, **remaine** in their *olde* market of Smithfilde, **&c.**" (*Survey,* 63; my emphasis).

Just as the generic scarcity of pre-Fire descriptions of London suggests a sense of topographical stability, if not stasis (why would anyone need new descriptions of very old ground?), so their narrative and grammatical structures share in suggesting a *relative* sense of containment.[43] The traditional vocabulary for topographies relies on a grammar of stasis. In John Fitzherbert's important *The Boke of Survueying* (1587), for example, "The cytie of the maner Dale **standeth and lyethe** betwene the Kynges hygheway leadynge from the towne of A, unto the towne of B" (xxxvii; my emphasis). For Stow and his successors the topography of London is primarily fixed by verbs of stasis and by passive constructions of "to be" – streets and structures are grammatically inert: "after that is Grubstreete, more then halfe thereof to the straightning of the streete, next is Whitecrosse streete, up to the end of Bech lane, and then Redcrosse street wholy, with a Parte of Goldinglane, even to the Posts there placed, as a bounder . . . and so haue you all the boundes of Criplegate warde without the walles" (*Survey,* 231–32). Each paragraph ends with a textual boundary that confirms the topographical: these be the lanes, there stand the posts, and here we have the bounds of the whole.

There has always been a generic convention of verbs of motion – boundaries running and stretching and extending themselves. A 1637 translation of Camden's *Britannia* notes that "at the West end of the City, other Suburbs runne a great way in length, with goodly rowes of houses orderly ranged . . . Neither lesse Suburbs runne out on the North-East and East" (*Britannia,* 432–33). Stow's text also offers a few counter-examples of relatively energetic passages. In Cripplegate Ward, for example, we have "Lad lane, which runneth east to Milkestreete corner"; Love Lane, which "runneth downe to the Conduite in Aldermanbury streete"; and Addlestreet, "out of the which runneth Phillippe lane downe to *London* wall" (*Survey*, 230–31). But these early uses of "run" rather straightforwardly apply for their meaning to "extend, be continuous" rather than to literal rapid motion – the sense it will assume with Defoe. (And anyway, *these* goodly houses are behaving themselves; something later writers *want* desperately to believe.) And in Stow's passage, these lanes are only allowed to run around *after* they have been secured on either end by a "be" and an "is", with lots of sedentary streets "lying" around for stability: "These be the lanes on the east side" (*Survey*, 231).

In general in these early topographies, both grammar and imagery confidently imply possession and control, in spite of the patternless anarchy of the ancient streets. The language assumes possession. For John Fitzherbert, people *hold* places; even cottages, though situated in relation to lord's manor, are grammatically (if not legally) within the tenant's grasp: "P. Q. holdeth a cotage of the lord at his wyll and . . . it conteyneth in brede by the hye way foure perches, and in length syxe perches, and a halfe and payeth &c." (*Boke of Surueying*, xxxviii). In Stow, *we have* the bounds of Cripplegate Ward; "Then haue yee *Brodestreete*, whereof the warde taketh name"; "Then haue you Baynards Castle, **whereof this whole Ward** taketh the name" (*Survey*, 137, 297; my emphasis) – the shape of the whole *belongs to us*. Howell repeats (or rather, copies) the patterns:[44] "Then have ye *Burchover* Lane . . . [where,] in the Reign of *Henry* the Sixth, had ye (for the most part) dwelling there, *Frippers* or Upholders" (*Londinopolis*, 81; see *Survey*, 154). The observer is confidently in control, "[directing] our pace" (*Londinopolis*, 87 – *not* plagiarizing Stow here), and "[steering] our course" (*Londinopolis*, 119) in his visual, verbal, and vehicular possession.

These passages express a *phenomenological* more than a political sense of possession. In some ways, of course, Stow *et al.* did their level best to reinscribe class boundaries, to delineate the wrong side of the tracks. One common field outside the wall, for example,

> is so incroched upon by building of filthy Cotages, and with other prepesterous like inclosures: and Laystalles, (that notwithstanding all Proclamations and Acts of Parliament made to the contrary) that in some places it scarce remaineth a sufficient highway for the meeting of Carriages and droves of Cattel, much lesse is there any faire, pleasant, or wholesome way for people to walk on foote.   (*Survey,* 348*)*

My interest here is with the way that *all* topographers try to make the space they are dealing with open, accessible, familiar, negotiable, and stable for the reader – the way they assume or create (given their historical contexts) the solid ground upon which people may "walk on foot."

Such sense of possession comes in part from the sense that whatever motion occurs is generated by the observer – the ground stays put. Such activity tends to increase as the genre develops. Stow himself stays fairly sedentary; he claims to "haue attempted the discouery of *London*" (*Survey*, A2v), but his discovery is archival rather than experiential: in addition to having "seene sundrie antiquities," he has also found that "through search of Recordes to other purposes, dyuers written helpes are come to my handes, which few others haue fortuned to meete withall" (*Survey*, A2v). When he appears in the first person, it is through his memories rather than as a physical presence in the streets. But later topographers quickly developed the trope of a guide, briskly leading the reader through the London maze. For example, Howell's *Londinopolis*, in a moment of daring originality, departs from Stow and insistently frames itself in terms of guide and guided, describing itself as "An Historicall Discourse or Perlustration of the City of London, the Imperial Chamber, and chief Emporium of Great Britain." The conflation of linguistic and physical acts (talking and walking), both attributes of description, centers entirely on the observer, the one who walks through and comments on (a *fixed*) London. Places stay firmly in place, although observer and reader are quite frisky:

> [A]nd so [we will] lead you in at her Gates, whence you shall walk along her *streets*, and visit her *Churches* . . . Then, we shall bring you to refresh yourself at her *Conduits*, and *Aqueducts*, her *brooks, bourns,* and *Wells*; Afterwards, we shall gently lead you along over her *Bridges*, and . . . accompany her *Stream* all along, till she comes to pay tribute to the *Ocean*; Then we shall make a perambulation in her severall *Precincts, Divisions*, and *Wards*.
>
> *(Howell, Londinopolis, 1)*

The language remains consistent throughout the text: it is always we who move, covering the pre-existing territory briskly or leisurely, as our unquenchable guide directs. The topographical narrative spatializes actions; the observer and perambulator determine the spaces to be covered and assessed; the city waits to be entered, walked, discussed.

Such a grammar of space changes as dramatically as the cartographic presentation of London's spaces after the Fire. Helgerson's claim for a rhetorical shift from surveys, descriptions, and pre-Fire maps to the motion-based tours and journeys of the late seventeenth and eighteenth centuries historicizes Michel de Certeau's distinction between verbal descriptions of place as "maps" which "see" – presenting a tableau ("there are") that implies the knowledge of an order of places – and "tours" which "go," spatializing actions and organizing movements ("you enter, you go across, you turn") (*The Practice of Everyday Life*, 119). Much as the post-Fire maps create a new visual schema of London, the post-Fire topographies change in formal, grammatical, and conceptual response to the instabilities and spatial disorientation of the rebuilding by inventing a new grammar of space. Things *move*.

Modern space, according to Defoe (as well as to Lefebvre and Soja), is *produced*; it is not a background for movement, a site for building, or an absolute Cartesian category, but a function of spatial practice. The cultural change in perceptions of space is in part the product of changed movements within a particular spatial world. Lefebvre locates a general European transition in the sixteenth century, in the military and economic wars of acquisition, during which space and time were urbanized as capitalism produced the abstract spaces of the world of commodities. It was then, he argues, "that the town recognized itself and found its image. It . . . began to represent itself graphically; . . . plans proliferated, plans which as yet had no reductive function, which visualized urban reality . . . These were true tableaux, bird's-eye views; the town was putting itself in perspective" (*Production of Space*, 278). But London only caught up with the rest of Europe in these moments of rebuilding after the Fire, when the new groundplans and the new buildings proliferated, and the city – like the nation earlier – was forced to put itself into visual perspective, as Defoe chronicles:

> It is . . . a particular and remarkable Crisis, singular to those who write in this Age . . . that the great and more eminent Increase in Buildings, in, and about the City of *London*, and the vast Extent of Ground taken in, and now become Streets and Noble Squares of Houses, by which the Mass, or Body of the whole, is become so infinitely great, has been generally made in our Time, not only within our Memory, but even within a few Years.   *(Tour*, 1.5.326*)*

Defoe appends *A Brief Description of the New Buildings erected in and about the Cities of* London *and* Westminster *and Borough of* Southwark, *since the Year 1666*, and carefully emphasizes the stark differences between his own account and that "described by Mr. *Stow*, or any other Author, who wrote before the Fire of *London*" (*Tour*, 1.5.326) in terms of transformed and transforming space: "so many great Houses were converted into Streets and Courts, Alleys and Buildings, that there are, by Estimation, almost 4000 Houses now standing on the Ground which the Fire left desolate, more than stood on the same Ground before" (*Tour*, 1.5.328). The houses of the past are *converted* into the four thousand houses of the present through a syntactically odd mediation – as if by their prior conversion into streets, courtyards, and alleys. But where Stow's grammatical conflation of buildings and streets (in Fish Street) intensifies the inward, upward incrementation, Defoe's suggests an implosion.

According to the *Tour*, the motions of *trade* produce the motions of space: "We see several Villages, formerly standing, as it were, in the Country, and at a great Distance, now joyn'd to the Streets by continued Buildings, and more making haste to meet in the like Manner" (*Tour*, 1.5.317). The villages that "stood" at a diffident distance in the past now move spatially as well as temporally into the present, and move at a run, pushed and drawn by trade. In the disrupted and redistributed commercial patterns, trade no longer simply resides among the butchers in Eastcheap or the goldsmiths in their counting houses, but in the abstract spaces produced by public credit, the postal system, the new network of roads, and in the shifting spaces of a far more transient and commercially fluid series of neighborhoods. In *The Complete English Tradesman*, published the year after the first two volumes of the *Tour*, Defoe warns: "It is true, we have seen a kind of fate attend the very streets and rows where such trades have been gather'd together; and a street famous some years ago, shall, in a few years after, be quite for-saken" (*Tradesman*, 1:99–100). The commercial space of London is fluid and can be treacherous: "When a shop is ill-chosen, the tradesman starves, he is out of the way, and *business will not follow him who runs away from it*" (*Tradesman*, 1:99; my emphasis). The *meanings* of place have changed and keep changing, and can no longer be found among the place *names*. Space no longer seems static, fixed, grounded, but runaway, and Londoners must pay attention to the shifts in spatial implication in order to survive. From the 1680s to the 1720s, descriptive topogra-phies increasingly wrestle with the dimensions of the rebuilt city in ways that attempt to define and incorporate its new elements, first to re-fix it, to find and contain its invisible new boundaries, and eventually, through Defoe, to *accommo-date* it rather than resist or overpower it.

The topographies of these decades express a growing sense of uneasiness at the increasing unknowability of metropolitan London. Robert Burton (aka Nathaniel Crouch) claims in his *Historical Remarques and Observations of the Ancient and Present State of London* (1681) that "it would too much inlarge this small Volume to give an Exact Account of the City of *Westminster*, and other parts which now seem swallowed up in *London*" (*Historical Remarques*, 114). William Stow, in his *Remarks on London* (1722), accuses contemporary maps as "more for Ornament than Use" and "not [describing] a fourth part of the Places contain'd in 'em: Moreover, was a Map 30 Foot long, and 20 deep to be projected, yet would it not comprehend the whole Town to an exact Scale of Feet" (A4). He notes: "So large is the Extent of *London*, *Westminster*, and *Southwark*, with their Suburbs and Liberties, that no Coachman nor Porter knows every place in them; therefore this Book may also be a Guide for them, and prevent, as hath been too often done, their losing any more Portmanteaus, Trunks, Boxes, or Parcels" (*Remarks on London*, A 5v). The spaces of London are in some sense even a threat to property. If the professional citymonger cannot be depended upon to negotiate the spatial confusion of London, what must be the fate of "all Gentlemen, Merchants, Tradesmen, Chapmen, [and] Country People?" (*Remarks on London*, A 5v).

The new topographies attempt a cartographic comprehensiveness.[45] Edward Hatton's *A New View of London* (1708) claims to contain "the Names of the Streets, Squares, Lanes, Markets, Courts, Alleys, Rows, Rents, Yards and Inns in London, Westminster, and *Southwark*"; William Stow's *Remarks* claims in its title page and again in its preface to "[shew] where every Street, Lane, Court, Alley, Yard, Green, Close, Square, or any other Place, by what Name soever call'd, is situated" (*Remarks on London*, A 4). In a telling little grammatical moment that wrests the implications of topographic control from the topographer to his spaces, Stow adds: "There is no Place which (to the best of my Knowledge) *I have escap'd*" (*Remarks on London*, A 5; my emphasis). The grammatical subtext suggests that the burden of place is inescapable. More straightforwardly, Burton's *Historical Remarques* allows little to escape him: though following the general format of John Stow, with the description of each ward beginning with a list of streets and ending with a list of aldermen, the text then intensifies the language from stasis ("is," "are") to containment: "*Farringdon Ward* within, wherein are contained *Foster* lane, *Mugwell* street, *Pentecost* lane" (*Historical Remarques*, 106); "*Queen Hythe Ward*, which comprehends" (107); "*Castle Baynard Ward*, containing part" (108); and so on. Many of the guides, including Hatton's *New View*, William Stow's *Remarks*, and the *New Remarks of London* are simply alphabetized, cross-referenced *lists* of streets and their relations to each other:

> Love lane, between Wood str. W and Aldermanbury, near the Church E. Stow has it called so from the amorous and wanton Persons formerly here remarkable.   (Hatton, *New View*, 49)

> *Ropemaker's Alley*, in little Moorfield by Moorfields, L. At the end of this Alley is an House, which has the Privilege to keep a Latch, or Door, which lets one into *Grub Street*, for which the Passenger is to pay the tenant thereof one Farthing; from which Custom it is called *Farthing Latch*.
>   (Stow, *Remarks*, 66)[46]

The common denominator in these descriptions is to find, catch, and tie together *all* the corners and pockets and replicated spaces; to have, in a pocket companion (as with the maps), the sense of having London in one's hand, as a bird's-eye view hands it to the eye.[47]

In some ways all of this is still old news, a bewilderment as old as London's oldest streets, in place for centuries and indeed *losing* as much as maintaining coherence over time. William Stow graphically reproduces an ancient confusion:

some People are so ignorant, especially in the Country, as to think *London*, *Westminster*, and *Southwark*, is all *London*, because contiguous to one another; which is a grand Mistake; for if you should send a Letter to a Friend in *King-Street*, which is in *Westminster*, but write at the bottom of the Superscription, *London*; how should the Postman know, whether you mean *King-street* by *Guildhall*, *King-street* on *Great Tower-hill*, *King-street* in *Spittle Fields*, *King-street* in *Prince's street* near *St. Anne's* Church, *King-street* near *Golden Square*, *King-street* in *Dean-street* by *Soho-square*, *King-street* in *Covent-garden*, *King-street* by *Hay's Court* near *Newport Market*, *King-street* in Upper *Moor-fields*, *King-street* by *Old-street Square*, *King-street* by *Bloomsbury Square*, *King-street* by *St. James's Square*, *King-street* near the *Six Dials* [sic], or *King-street* in the *Mint*?
(Stow, *Remarks*, A5)[48]

But in fact postal urgency is itself a recent phenomenon, part of the modern sense of space, of distances acquiring new meanings, new dimensions, new relations to time; Stow capitalizes on the already baffling groundplan of London to market the necessity for his own meticulous reference work.[49] In the past – before the rebuilding of London, the explosion of trade, and the improvements in travel – the vast reduplication of streets would have mattered to few, since most people stayed neatly put in their neighborhoods.[50] Presumably any city that *expected* much popular intercity movement would at least have hesitated before adding King Streets thirteen and fourteen. The overwhelming quality of the modern spaces of London lay in its new layers of Lefebvrean and Defoean abstractness that intensify the confusion of old space while dislodging its familiarity.

The cultural perception of London's spaces from the 1680s to the 1730s was that they refused to be fixed, and the topographies, for all their self-glorified comprehensiveness, simultaneously admit defeat, as the author of *New Remarks of London* (1732) confesses:

I spent above six Months in making my Collection . . . And yet, after all, I will not deny, but here are many Alleys and Courts within the Bills of Mortality, which are not inserted in this Work; but then I must beg Leave to observe, that they never had any Names given them, or, at least, that they are so far lost, that the ancientest Inhabitants in or near those Places, never heard of any particular Names by which they are known and distinguish'd, nor are they to be met with in any Parish-books, though the ancientest of them have been searched to find them out.
(vii)

The oldest spaces keep their secrets; the newest spaces escape their bounds; neither maps nor alphabetized lists can comprehend them. Lists – as well as maps in Certeau's sense – are "constituted as proper places in which to *exhibit the products* of knowledge, [and] form tables of *legible* results" (*Practice of Everyday Life*, 121). But the fast-growing London is precisely *not* legible, and resists exhibition as a product of knowledge. Neither maps nor groundplans nor lists nor tables can represent with any adequacy or accuracy the protean urban space.

On the other hand, as Certeau suggests, "*stories* about space exhibit . . . the operations that allow it" (*Practice of Everyday Life*, 121; my emphasis). The generic rumblings in London topographies mark a rough, erratic, inconsistent but discernible change from map to tour, from fixity to motion, from historical anecdote to comprehensive list to narrative story. Surveys and descriptions, while never entirely disappearing, increasingly find themselves in the company of "guides," "tours," and "journeys," and the insistent number of "new views" and "new reviews" are themselves marked by the new grammars of space.

The new journeys and tours narratively expand to explore and explain the new spaces they enter. A different sense of the place and power of "story" is part of it. Although Stow told endless stories about his London spaces — as in the unkind guest and unfortunate voyeur cited above — those stories are short and tied forever to their sites; they are anecdotes rather than narratives. Furthermore, Stow's stories are always past, completed, a form of document. Someone like John Macky, on the other hand, in *A Journey through England* (1722) describes in terms of scene, character, and present action the social as well as structural interiors of his territory, tracking the shifting variables of place: who inhabits what and where, and what goes on inside? For example, he sorts the coffee houses according to their various social and political appropriations and then *enters them*:

> The *Scots* go generally to the *British*, and Mixture of all sorts go to the *Smyrna*. There are other little Coffee-Houses much frequented in this Neighborhood, *Young-Man*'s for officers, *Old-Man*'s for Stock-Jobbers, Pay-Masters, and Courtiers, and *Little-Man*'s for Sharpers: I never was so confounded in my Life, as when I enter'd into this last: I saw two or three Tables full at *Faro*, heard the Box and Dice rattling in the Rooms above the Stairs, and was surrounded by a Set of sharp Faces, that I was afraid would have devoured me with their Eyes. I was glad to drop two or three Half-Crowns at *Faro*; to get off with a clear Skin, and was overjoy'd I was so got rid of them.
>
> *(Journey, 168–69)*

Macky's story moves in the sense that he allows his sentences, although structured in the past tense, to retain the uncertainty of immediate experience: "When I enter'd into this last . . . I was afraid." The narrator himself runs from place to place, pinning trades to place and faces to trades, describing the structures of buildings, the atmospheres of neighborhoods, the prevailing urban trade winds. The format of the work, which, like Defoe's, presents a series of familiar letters to

"Dear Sir," anticipates a Richardsonian writing to the moment. The end is not necessarily contained in the beginning; things are changing as we speak.

Such is essentially the strategy adopted and perfected by Defoe in the *Tour*: his topography, particularly in the section on London (Letter 5), employs an open-ended generic form (the familiar letter) and a unique kind of narrative applied to the latest formal innovations of the post-Fire London surveyors.[51] As Pat Rogers has noted, the language and imagery of the *Tour*, unlike those of earlier descriptors of London, *presume* motion and change.[52] Geoffrey Sill objects that such an emphasis on Defoe's literary art has "the adverse effect of taking the *Tour* out of the social context in which it was written, and stripping from it the social and historical function it was written to serve."[53] But those rhetorical strategies that Rogers analyzes so thoroughly and persuasively are in fact precisely calculated to address and influence a specific cultural anxiety – a form of rhetoric that springs from the very material of its culture. The literary art of the *Tour* is *steeped* in its social and historical contexts.

The *Tour* begins (disingenuously) by admitting its own futility as description. Like Macky's *Journey*, the formal structure of the *Tour* is letters, each describing a "circuit" or "journey" that, in the first two volumes, begins and ends in London. But places simply change too quickly to permit full incorporations. The introduction, which emphasizes the effort to record "the present State of Things," also confesses that the concept of a present *state* – of an identifiable and static situation that opens itself to description – is something of a polite fiction, since the material to be recorded escapes beyond the edges of text and tour moment by moment and step by step: "Even while the Sheets are in the Press, new Beauties appear in several Places" (*Tour*, 1.1.4). Each volume of the *Tour* concludes with an appendix listing and occasionally describing the new building projects begun or completed in the interstices of the writing and printing of the book. And many of those addenda are left suspended, textually and imaginatively incomplete for every reader of the first edition: "Since the Closing this Volume there are several Great and Magnificent Buildings begun to be Erected, within the Circuit of these Letters, which however, not being finish'd, cannot now be fully describ'd" (*Tour*, 1.3.250). What remains undescribed remains in some sense invisible, unknown, uncontained. The circuit of letters cannot expand enough to hold its chosen content.

Yet the admission of failure in some ways suggests a prescription for success. The central letter of the original two volumes, Letter 5, focuses entirely on London. Though Defoe claims that London is "infinitely difficult" to describe "in the narrow Compass of a Letter" which in Strype's edition of Stow's *Survey* "so fully takes up Two large Volumes in Folio" (*Tour*, 1.5.316), still, the title of this narrow compass declares that it "contains" a description of London "*as taking in the city of* Westminster, *Borough of* Southwark, *and the Buildings circumjacent.*" The narrator explains more precisely that "*London*, as a City only, and as its Walls and Liberties line it out, might, indeed, be viewed in a small Compass; but, when I speak of *London*, now in the Modern Acceptation, you expect that I shall take in all that vast Mass of Buildings" (*Tour*, 1.5.316) – named, numbered, and wondered at in the rest of this long paragraph. That is, there are two Londons: the old city fixed within its medieval bounds, and the new city, with its "new Squares, and new Streets rising up every Day", restructuring its skyline and redefining its boundaries at each new moment. The structure of the letter and the journey – writing to the moment and travelling on apace – rhetorically move with the changing landscape, the circuits encircling their objects and rhetorically accommodating their true nature, their real difference.

Defoe's narrative also *shapes* as it describes, and suggests a different strategy of spatial management that borrows from the new language and techniques of post-Fire surveying. Defoe's language of motion translates into a language of control:

> I have, as near as I could, caused a Measure to be taken of this mighty, I cannot say uniform, Body; and . . . have here given as accurate a Description of it, as I can do in so narrow a Compass, as that of a Letter, or as I could do without drawing a Plan, or Map of the Places.   (*Tour*, 1.5.318)

Defoe could, of course, have appended a plan or map; each letter is already prefaced by one of Herman Moll's maps. But a map or a plan has lines that, once drawn, do not move; change eludes and makes obsolete the contours of a graphic text. Defoe instead chooses narrative to create lines that move with the movement of their objects. He *causes a measure* to be taken, which he then redefines in the title of the preliminary section: "*A* LINE *of Measurement, drawn about all the continued Buildings of the City of* London" (*Tour*, 1.5.318). This Line begins a description of the topographical boundaries of the city.

A topographical line, as defined by the London surveyor William Leybourn in *The Compleat Surveyor* (5th edn. 1722), "is created or made by the moving or drawing out of a *Point* from one place to another . . . and according as this motion is, so is the Line created, whether *streight* or *crooked*" (3). Who controls the motion controls the shape of the line – and also its power: "in a Circular Line . . . the Point in its motion returneth again to the place where it first began, and so maketh the Line infinite, and the ends or bounds thereof undeterminate" (Leybourn, *Compleat Surveyor*, 3–4). A moving, circling Line not only defines boundaries but also creates space, reserving infinity and indeterminacy for itself rather than for the space it contains.

Defoe's Line as description verbally and textually encloses the city, defining and following a topographic and narrative line that threads together structures and places with verbs of motion:

The Line begins . . . at Peterborough House, the farther House *West* upon the River *Thames*, and runs *N.W.* by *W.*, by the Marshes to *Tutthill Fields*, and passing by the *Neat Houses*, and *Arnold's Brewhouse* . . . goes *North* behind the Stable-Yard Buildings . . . then crossing the Road . . . holds on *East* till the New streets formed out of *Hide House Garden*, cause it to turn away. . . [S]loping *North East*, it passes by *Pimlico* . . . inclosing the Garden Walls . . . it takes in a Burying Ground and some Buildings . . . but then turning short *South*, it goes towards *White Chapel Mount*, but being intercepted by New Streets, it goes quite up to the *South* End of the *Dog-Row* at *Mile End*.

(Tour, 1.5.320*)*

(There are about nine pages of this.) The Line itself takes on the energy of travel: far more athletic than those old Stowean streets that run and stretch, this Line runs and goes and crosses and takes in and leaves; it turns and turns short and turns away; it meets buildings, encloses gardens, and dodges interceptions. Occasionally the Line reacts, but more often it *acts*, becoming a marker and even an agent of change as its identity merges into the narrator's. It becomes almost a living thing, its patterns of movement recalling the swift, precise, and complicated escapes of Defoe's fictional characters. In *Colonel Jack* (1722), for example, the young and newly minted criminal Jack sprints after his comrade within a desper-ately accurate topographical memory:

I [ran] after him, never resting or scarce looking about me, till we got quite up into *Fenchurch-street*, thro' *Lime-street*, into *Leadenhall street*, down St. *Mary Axe*, to *London-Wall*, then thro' *Bishop gate*, and down old *Bedlam*, into *Moorfields* . . . . so away he had me through *Long-alley*, and Cross *Hog lane*, and *Holloway lane*, into the middle of the great Field, which since that, has been call'd the *Farthing pye-house-field* . . . so we went on, cross'd the Road at *Anniseed Cleer*, and went into the Field where now the Great Hospital stands.[54]

Like Jack, Defoe's London Line marks spaces and changes; it establishes, records, and crosses boundaries. As in the novels, the *Tour*'s line of topography merges with the line of narrative; the Line of boundary merges with the author or agent who defines the boundaries:

N.B. *The Town of* Greenwich, *which may, indeed, be said to be contiguous to* Deptford, *might be also called a Part of this Measurement;* **but I omit it**, *as I have the Towns of* Chelsea *and* Knights Bridge *on the other Side, tho' both may be said to joyn the Town, and in a very few Years will certainly do so.*

(Tour, 1.5.323; *my emphasis)*

The Line and its author combine to define and contain the slippery city — *format-ting* it, in David Trotter's sense: "by *London*, as I shall discourse of it, I mean, all the

Buildings, Places, Hamlets, and Villages **contain'd in the Line of Circumvallation** . . . by which **I have computed** the Length of its Circumference above" (*Tour*, 1.5.325–26; my emphasis). The narrator omits and predicts, defining the Line of Circumvallation; the Line (which the narrator creates and authorizes) crosses and intercepts streets, it bypasses some houses and connects others, it slips behind and marches before the recognizable structures of London.

Defoe's Line, an improvement in energy and ingenuity on its few post-Fire predecessors' such as Brydall's (1676), Hatton's (1708), and Strype's (1720), would become the generic model for later topographic Lines of distinction, such as Burton's *New View . . . Continued by an Able Hand* (1730) and the anonymous *New Remarks of London* (1732). The formal structures of these topographies loosened themselves to accommodate narratively as well as incorporate descriptively the rapidly expanding and radically changing urban contours of London, elastically but firmly tying them all together in a narrative that combines a tour with a view, and moves from map into story. The grammar of space suggests a grammar of motion.

PART II
INHABITING LONDON

CHAPTER FOUR

THE ART OF WRITING THE
STREETS OF LONDON

> I securely stray
> Where winding alleys lead the doubtful way,
> The silent court, and op'ning square explore,
> And long perplexing lanes untrod before.
> (John Gay, *Trivia; Or, the Art of Walking the Streets of London*, 1716)

> I cross'd the Street indeed, and went down the first turning I came to, and I
> think it was a Street that went thro' into *Fenchurch-street*, from thence I cross'd
> and turn'd through so many ways and turnings that I could never tell which
> way it was, nor where I went, for I felt not the Ground I stept on, and the farther
> I was out of Danger, the faster I went, till tyr'd and out of Breath, I was forc'd
> to sit down on a little Bench at a Door, and then I began to recover, and found
> I was got into *Thames-street* near *Billingsgate.*
> (Daniel Defoe, *The Fortunes and Misfortunes of the Famous Moll Flanders,* 1722)

From Charles II's 1666 proclamation reopening and rehierarchizing the streets to
John Gay's mock-heroic "security" and Moll Flanders's insecurity in the doubtful
winding alleys, London's streets underwent a profound physical change that
found its cultural expression in the various topographically obsessed forms of
Restoration and early Augustan literature. The streets which the Fire had emptied
of signs and filled with rubbish were, over the decades of rebuilding, gradually
emptied of rubbish and reinvested with meaning. T. S. Reddaway claims that
"the change, though almost unbelievable, passed without comment."[1] That
claim is what these chapters in part II challenge; the comment was *everywhere*,
directly and indirectly, explicitly and implicitly, in the kinds and contents of the
imaginative literatures of the period. Hollar's survey had marked "blanke space
signifeing the burnt part" (see Figure 1). As the people of London gradually
rebuilt and reoccupied their houses, the literature repeopled the streets, filling in
those blank spaces with a new cultural awareness behind the literary version of the
old bird's-eye-view.

    Some of the power of the new narratives of urban landscapes derives from a
much older literary tradition of inscribing London's streets with social, commercial, and traditional topographic meaning – the Renaissance epigrams, cony-

catching pamphlets, and Jacobean city comedy – that as Lawrence Manley argues emerged from and negotiated a different but also specifically *urban* crisis. I want to keep in focus the ways that the new literature and new spatial representations swallowed whole or in part the rhetorical patterns of the past. The rupturing of spatial stability brought on by the Fire and the rebuilding (or at least, the radically *experienced* instability which defensively or nostalgically *reconstructed* a past stability) ignited a widespread cultural effort within the City to remap itself imaginatively, to resignify its spaces, to rename itself. Literary genres engrafted other forms and strategies of cultural texts that had *explicitly* dealt with the aftermath of destruction and reconstruction – the sermons, journalistic accounts, guidebooks, and maps discussed in part 1. In particular, the constant litany of street names in the sermons and journalized accounts, the indexing and itemization of streets in the topographies, the grammatical and imaginative change from a relative sense of spatial fixity to a relative sense of spatial motion, and the cleanswept two-dimensionality of the surveys and groundplans replacing the three-dimensional bird's-eye-views, all found themselves in the employ of poetry, drama, prose fiction, and some rather urgent urban genre-crossers in between.

"Streetness" itself becomes a generic convention, different mainly in degree but at some points in kind from pre-Fire representations:

(1) The *presence* of streets occupies more kinds of literatures – not just the subliterary groups – and genres by more canonical writers;
(2) Street meanings are more often spelled out in post-Fire literature, although along many different agendas, because individual meanings were far less stable;
(3) Characters – particularly in the spaces of fictional narrative and early novels – become less types, less emblems of Jonsonian humors, with identities determined *by* place, and more determined to construct their own or others' identities *from* place (or series of places);
(4) Street names in poems and prose fictions often appear as lists or indices, categorized, sorted, and labelled, with the same strategies as the proliferating textual topographies;
(5) Shifting perceptions of spatial identity, boundaries, and meaning find different expression in transitional, innovative, and overlapping genres.

After a meditation on the nature of the rebuilt streets, this chapter will look closely at these rhetorics and strategies of "streetness" in the poetic structures of John Dryden's *MacFlecknoe* (1682), Alexander Pope's *Dunciad Variorum* (1729), and John Gay's *Trivia* (1716), and in the narrative innovations of Richard Head's *The English Rogue* (1665), Ned Ward's *The London Spy* (1698–1700), and Daniel Defoe's *Moll Flanders* (1722), with some glances at lesser-known figures and works along the way. I will consider not only the ways in which their conceptual concerns overlap, but also how their generic differences try to represent or enable or alter the imaginative perception and actual negotiation of urban change.

Conceptualizing streets

In any city at any period there is always a spatial hierarchy of streets that depends on historical, commercial, and/or social function; more than physical difference lies in the spaces between avenues and alleys, and the differences vary within historical and cultural contexts. The basic physical hierarchy of London's streets is fairly typical for the period:

> A street was a major thoroughfare, wide and perhaps paved; a lane a narrow thoroughfare; a yard or court an enclosed space entered from a turning off the street or lane; and an alley a very narrow way between buildings. The four names suggest a progressive decline in space and physical graciousness.[2]

Such a marked "decline" explains why the lanes and courts and alleys were loftily overlooked by the Renaissance bird's-eye-views — they didn't "fit" topographically or conceptually with the concern to present a rich, spacious, *coherent* sense of a national capital. Even after the widening of the streets, each small turn in a walk through London could mean a vast turn in social, political, commercial, and experiential meaning. The City of London remained unusually heterogeneous; as Power's detailed analysis of the hearth taxes in London before and after the Fire suggests, London certainly in 1666 and apparently for many years after maintained a traditional rather than modern urban occupation of the city, with "haberdashers living side-by-side with porters; lawyers beside pensioners, goldsmiths beside widows, all living in a random mix of large and small dwellings" ("Social Topography," 221).[3] In the City of London turning down a street in a particular district never necessarily entailed a turn into the known,[4] and in fact all of the literature examined in this chapter shows a *rhetorical* jumbling and jostling of elements that captures and exploits or seeks to sort and contain the topographical and social intercrowding — "the miscellaneity, clutter, indiscriminateness, and accumulation that urban pace and urban energy produce."[5] As Spiro Kostof notes more generally about street plans: "Streets that read as straight and uniform on the city plan may be compromised by the capricious behavior of the bordering masses."[6] London's City streets, rarely even remotely straight to begin with, seemed to some to be compromised by the capricious behavior of their inhabiting masses. The literature of the late seventeenth and early eighteenth centuries shows that Londoners well understood that it was not enough to recover the streets and reinstate street names; reinhabiting the new city demanded that the occupant also map that *behavior*.

Although the groundwork of rebuilding London after the Fire required the surveyors to relay the street plan, and that included reaffirming street hierarchy, in a sense *all* streets, wide or narrow, assumed equal importance because no space was perceived as stable any longer. The systematically individuated attention bestowed on even the murkiest corners of the City by the surveyors and cartographers settled into a more general and unflagging cultural awareness of the changed significance of street spaces. That change was both physical and phenomenological. On the one hand, as Henry Harben says, the streets "*were* built as *streets* with some definite line of frontage and not as *footways* to and from individual houses."[7] Although "utopian hundred-foot roads were abandoned at an early stage" (Reddaway, *Rebuilding of London*, 289), the chief traffic routes were widened and their gradients somewhat levelled, and even the lanes and sidestreets were required to be fourteen feet wide – enough for drays to pass each other safely. An Act of Parliament (April 29, 1667) laid down rules for enlarging and more or less levelling the streets, and those rules paid close and equal – if strictly hierarchized – attention to each class of streets:

> That the street called Fleet Street, from **the place where the Greyhound Tavern stood** to Ludgate, and from thence into St. Paul's Churchyard, shall be further enlarged to be of the breadth of forty-five foot . . .
>
> That the ground **where the Middle Row in the Shambles stood,** and the ground of the four **late houses** in Newgate Market, between Warwick Lane end and the **late Bell Inn,** there, and also the ground **where the Middle Row in Old Fish Street stood,** shall be laid into the streets . . .
>
> That Love Lane in Thames Street shall be enlarged to be of the breadth of ten foot. (my emphasis)

Pedestrians had their own post-protected spaces in the high streets. And the *spaces* of the streets themselves changed, opened. Buildings were set further back from street boundaries, and new fire regulations insisted that they be built straight up from first to final storey. There was more light, more air, more room *above* street level – more dimension to the physical spaces of the streets.

These physical improvements altered the phenomenological experience and significance of the streets. Where street space in London before the Fire tended to be subordinate or "weak" public space in Spiro Kostof's sense – liminal footspace or transitional connector; dark, dirty, cramped, enclosed; stuffed with stalls and sheds and scythed by swinging streetsigns – street space after the Fire at least officially shared the spatial status of the structures – the public and private buildings – it had previously simply connected. To quote Kostof slightly out of context: "The street, it seems clear in this attitude, will no longer be thought of as the space left over between buildings, but as a spatial element with its own integrity" (*The City Shaped*, 215).

As it turned out, however, the physical improvements in the streets proved vastly incommensurate with eventual need. After the streets were physically and conceptually opened up, they were squeezed back down by the increasingly fast and furious pace of traffic. On the one hand, the growing availability and affordability of inner-city travel "made life more attractive for the upper [and eventually middle] classes" (Stone, "Residential Development," 179) but on the other, the confused and crowded roar of the streets which began in the early seventeenth century with the influx of coaches and sedans and general domestic traffic, as well as the constantly increasing commercial traffic,[8] assumed critical proportions in the late seventeenth and early eighteenth centuries, and contributed to the powerful dark side of street imagery in the period. Increasingly the eighteenth-century city planners, like the literature, "sought to make the city a place in which people could move and breathe freely";[9] but opening up the streets and street habits to permit more moving and breathing *also* meant that more *kinds* of people – as well as more kinds of literatures – were enabled to move and breathe freely. In a sense, the changing hierarchy of streets operated both metaphorically and analogically with literary genres, cotemporaneously destabilized, with old traditions newly recovered and new genres meeting new needs. The literature of the underworld matches step for step the new encomia of the streets. Physical mobility affects social mobility; spatial negotiation entails social navigation; charting streets turns to narrativizing them.

The ambivalence which had always in some sense infested the streets of London in its cultural and literary textual expressions intensified with their changed, charged power. As the streets offered new spaces for literal (and literary) as well as social mobility – as their significance as boundaries was redrawn and redefined – they also reinforced the perception of the shakiness of topographical and social boundaries *qua* boundaries. For example, as with the official narratives, the sermons, the early post-Fire maps and topographies discussed in part I, the rules laid down for the enlargement and improvement of the streets navigate by what had been lost – "the place where the Greyhound Tavern stood"; "the ground where the Middle Row in the Shambles stood"; "the ground of the four late houses in Newgate Market." Rebuilding is reorienting: *new* place is designated by *former* place. And rebuilding is disorienting: in the ensuing decades of rebuilding, people increasingly moved, or seemed to move, through the structures of society as they moved more easily – whether more visibly or more hiddenly – through the streets. The streets bounded the areas and implications of London and simultaneously promised transmission through them. The rush and crush of traffic carried enormous symbolic weight that the imaginative literatures tried to shoulder and redistribute, containing it within traditionally ordered structure, sound, meter, and meaning (Dryden, Pope, Swift, Gay) or flowing with it into narrative open-endedness and apparent formlessness (Head, Ward, Brown, Defoe).

The semiotic weight was heavy as well. London's street signs entered a period of literal and figurative instability; in a fascinating way, the physical and the symbolic implications of street signs often collided in the experience of the London walker.[10] Although street signs were not systematically replaced by numbers until 1762, the shift from the visual charting of London to its numerical sorting – the erasing of some forms of visual detail – began with the Acts for Rebuilding the City. The shift was marked by two very different axes of change. As the physical structures and positions of the signs were simplified, their meanings were on the one hand deliberately complicated and on the other socially obscured.

In the mid-seventeenth century, colorful wooden signboards hung out over the streets, and though they virtually completed the job of cutting off light and air, and in their competitive size or neglected age often crashed down on pedestrians or caused the collapse of the building itself, they at least made the city visually negotiable. The earlier signs had been fairly straightforward, visually denotative, with a single simple device closely related to the trade signified, as the Dagger and Pie in Cheapside (1660) really offered the dagger-pies that appear so plentifully in the Jacobean city plays; the Frying Pan marked the ironmonger; the Harp and Crown sold musical instruments; the neighborhood goldsmiths conducted business under the Gilt Fox, the Golden Anchor, the Golden Bull, and the Golden Artichoke (Hilton Price, "Signs of Old London," *LTR* IV:28). The signs meant what they said, and you could see what they meant.

After the Fire, the signs lost some visual prominence: rebuilding regulations required (but could not always enforce) that they be displayed flat against the building.[11] Pictorial signs were also gradually replaced by verbal signs. And the images that remained swung loose from any obvious referents. By the early eighteenth century the devices had multiplied and shifted away from the trade represented. As Addison complains in the *Spectator*:

> Our Streets are filled with blue Boars, black Swans, and red Lions; not to mention flying Pigs, and Hogs in Armour . . . I would enjoin every Shop to make use of a Sign which bears some Affinity to the Wares in which it deals. What can be more inconsistent, than to see a Bawd at the Sign of the Angel, or a Taylor at the Lion? A Cook should not live at the Boot, nor a Shooemaker at the roasted Pig; and yet, for want of this Regulation, I have seen a Goat set up before the Door of a Perfumer, and the *French* King's Head at a Sword-Cutler's.[12]

As with the street names, meaning peels away from street signs; these are almost literally floating signifiers creating or perhaps created by their own topographic disorder.[13] In marked *contrast* to the early conditions of rebuilding and reordering and temporal change, Edward Copeland notes in an article on *Clarissa's* much later London: "London and its systems operate in utter truthfulness. The rules are as dependable as those of fairy tales: if Clarissa names the street, 'Dover Street', to a chairman, she will discover Lovelace's plot. If she sends her letters to a proper posting inn, she will get her mail."[14] If it is true that London institutionally settled down somewhat by the mid-eighteenth century – and the maturing of postal systems, law enforcement, urban planning, and economic practices suggest it did – it was in contrast and response to the increasingly unbearable, ungovernable topographic, social, and semiotic confusion produced in part by the rebuilding and rethinking of London. In the earlier, transitional period, the city that had been to some extent navigable by illiterate sight now required knowledge of different kinds of codes. As the streets were physically cleared and opened, making it easier to *see*, they increasingly required to be *read*.

Many of the cartographic and literary efforts of the rebuilding period were designed to reattach signs to signifieds, to read the signs of the streets in the names of the streets, to repossess their meanings. Naming a street identifies – to someone who speaks the same topographical language – a complete cultural space. *Renaming* the street either creates or recaptures a cultural identity. The literary renaming (and in a sense, the resigning) of London's streets drew upon and acquired some of its cultural authority from a much older tradition of naming (and containing) the significance of London's streets in the proliferation of epigrams in the 1590s to the 1630s. Lawrence Manley describes that subliterary burst as a response to the "terrifying and unknowable world of material and social profusion" produced by the great shifts in social change and the possibilities of social mobility in the neofeudal urbanization of Elizabethan London.[15] The poetics of the London epigram, Manley argues, attempt "to define the indefinite or fix the elusive in formulas; and second . . . to *be* definitive by inscribing that formal literally or metaphorically 'on' the matter defined" (*Literature and Culture*, 418). The early sixteenth-century jester John Heywood, for example, defines existing places and cultural spaces in a comforting, containing verse list that sometimes asserts topographical identity and that at other times implies an ironic social obverse:

> Still thou seekest for a quiet dwelling-place:
> What place for quietness has thou now in chase?
> London bridge? That's ill for thee, for the water.
> Queenhithe? That's more ill for another matter. . .
> Bread street? That's too dry, by drought thou shalt be dead.
> Philpot Lane? That breedeth moist humours in thy head. . .

Creed lane? They fall out there, brother against brother.
Ave Mary Lane? That's as ill as t'other.
Paternoster Row? Paternoster Row?
Agreed: That's the quietest place I know.[16]

Although much of the post-Fire literature also attempts to "define the indefinite or fix the elusive" through various streetly explorations, those explorations resist formula; their "fixtures" are different. The *Dunciad* transforms genre; *Moll Flanders* creates genre. Part of the difference in generic approach derives from the difference in cultural assumptions. Heywood's poem, in looking for a quiet space to dwell in this new urban urgency, plays systematically on the *existing* denotative aspects of London streets, even as it watches those denotations subverted by rising commercial and social changes. The names still *mean* something – enough to enable even puns of change. The names actually begin each line, and though each name is followed by a question mark, and in the course of the poem the sense of denotative street meanings shifts into treachery, where the streets end up meaning the opposite of their original designation ("Creed lane? They fall out there, brother against brother"), that comprehensive sense of meaning remains contained within the evolving structure of the poem itself. As Manley argues, the London epigram, "by sorting names and places . . . laid a lucid order over an obscure substrate of possibilities" (*Literature and Culture*, 424). Like Stow's 1598 *Survey of London*, Heywood draws on an ancient sediment of place meaning to mark what changes by what remains the same. The post-Fire literature would also draw heavily on Stow and the older Jacobean forms – on the pre-existing street names and the pre-existing literary tradition – for the same purposes of ordering the new social confusion of urbanization. But the literatures of rebuilding enabled a contemporary rebuilding of genres to incorporate and accommodate multiple layers of new experience: the increasing speed of urbanization after the Fire and during the rebuilding; the increased rush and crush of traffic because of the widened streets; the increasing unreliability of street names as denoters of social or commercial space, due to more frequent trade relocations (see chapter five).

In a number of senses, then, the streets of London come to *characterize* the period, defining the boundaries of the literatures as much as the literatures define the boundaries of the streets. As Peter Earle puts it, "the London of this period [1650–1750] has come down to us in a series of literary and artistic images, so detailed and apparently realistic that one feels one could almost walk in its streets."[17] That's exactly the point: the literary and artistic images combined with the journalistic, sermonic, and cartographic efforts to make the streets walkable, knowable; to explore the "op'ning squares" and unwind the "long perplexing lanes" – the new streets of new generic possibilities.

Sorting streets: formal verse satire

Most critical and cultural discussions of Augustan topographical poetry emphasize the physicality, the materiality, the clutter and claustrophobia of the streets.
Richard Sennett points to Hogarth's engravings of Beer Street and Gin Lane to
show the tactile, sensory difference between eighteenth- and twentieth-century
ways of occupying streets (*Flesh and Stone*, 18). Even the orderly Beer Street reveals
not simply a fairly contented, stable crowd, but also one very physically connected,
closely touching. In the pre- and post-Fire London, the street-traveller, unlike a
modern counterpart, requires in fact a great deal of physical effort to navigate the
streets, and is necessarily aware of the people and the buildings and the detritus of
the streets in order to move; to paraphrase Sennett, the body moves actively, awake
in space, to destinations in the process of fragmenting, with street travel itself as the
process of connecting (*Flesh and Stone*, 18).

Much of the formal verse satire of post-Fire London lives in the street, but pre-
tends it doesn't want to. Many critics have noted the obvious topographic density
of Augustan satire, but, as Pat Rogers puts it, most consider the abundance of
contemporary physical detail "a mere trick in the fingers," or "a sort of local
colour."[18] Rogers's study sees that the particular choices of emphasis ("squalor,
pestilence, ordure, poverty"), as well as their mode of physicality and their tone of
disgust, are more than classical satiric inheritances, but "also a particular response
to the conditions of the time" (*Hacks and Dunces*, 4) – "the way London is laid out
testifies to the life which is led there" (*Hacks and Dunces*, 9). Much more of life itself,
in fact, was lived in the street: historic events, public occasions, celebrations and
punishments, were not simply "public" but "*open-air*" (*Hacks and Dunces*, 64–5).
Manley, for example, analyzes the waxing and waning of the coronation and
mayoral pageants in London from the 1540s to 1702, noting the sharp decline of
the shows immediately after the Fire, but seeing at the same time a quick surge of
"a return of the older patterns, which were forever altered by more deeply rooted
changes" (*Literature and Culture*, 292). The public pageants, which supply the
structures of *MacFlecknoe* and the *Dunciad*, were as much celebrations of London
and its achievements as they were markers of monarchs and mayors, and their
published descriptions provided the reading experience of walking through and
witnessing the traditions of connections between place and place name, between
location and event. John Ogilby's *The Relation of His Majestie's Entertainment
Passing through the City of London, to His Coronation* (1661), for example, marks a
route as clear and detailed and visualized as the maps he would be making fifteen
years later, describing the arches, the sculptures, their significance, and their *place*;
in tracking Charles through the streets he combines the known power of the city
with the promised power of the returning monarchy – the precise inversion, of

course, of the figures of Shadwell and Theobald or Cibber. But in both the pageantry and the poems, the power of the description itself depends upon the condition of *known space*, the given significance of Leadenhall Street, Cornhill, the Exchange, Cheapside.

Pat Rogers also argues that the images of plague and fire "became the climactic symbols of Augustan satire," drawing their "potent imaginative charge" from "the recent memory of the twin catalclysms of 1665–6" (*Hacks and Dunces*, 96). But where he sees such poems as *MacFlecknoe*, "Description of a City Shower," *Trivia*, and the *Dunciad* as largely "defensive idiom[s]" which do not so much create coherence as "assert and defend an existing order" (*Hacks and Dunces*, 96),[19] *safeguarding* old identities, I want to thicken that description in the context of rebuilding to suggest in fact a combination of the temporal and generic descriptions. This poetry, I agree, asserts and defends an order, but it rather asserts and defends the *existence* of that order – an order which in fact *no longer exists*, or rather, stands more in need of recreation than preservation. In other words, Augustan topographical poetry recreates or reestablishes the order it affects to presume, drawing upon the old Jacobean city energies and similes to resettle its foundational ground. But at the same time it does create a form of coherence and invents new identities; it employs and in the process lends energy to new forms of technology, new shapes of space. On the one hand, much of this poetry seems intent on containing change, fixing motion to place, pinning dunces into eternally stable identities. Spaces in these poems *guarantee* meaning; the form of the poem emphasizes closure, end of sentence. On the other hand, I want to emphasize how much these poems spring from and contribute to new vocabularies and strategies of managing urban space. Much of their social and aesthetic sorting both draws from and creates *new* topographical meaning as it defends the old. The poems place themselves within and depend upon the contemporary significance of London streets; but as that significance was in the process of visible change, the ambiguities and ambivalences of the streets themselves seep into the poems, and the poems in fact insist on their own definitions and certainly intend to impose them without.

At one point in Dryden's *MacFlecknoe*, "Ecchos from *Pissing-Ally, Sh[adwell]* call, | And *Sh[adwell]* they resound from *A[ston] Hall*." "Pissing Alley" obviously counts on denotation; place name is informed by function, presumably, and confers the power of its name to the new chief of the literary state. But Pissing Alley itself was a product of the new city in so far as it was (or rather, four of them were) consciously revived by the surveyors. "Pissing Alley" does not appear in Stow, in Pepys, in the *London Encyclopaedia*, in Bell, or in Reddaway; but on November 22, 1669, George Cony (life has its own puns) paid 6*s* 8*d* for the staking out of his foundation in Pissing Alley in Friday Street, and Edward Cooper paid for two surveys on July 6, 1670.[20] There were actually several Pissing Alleys: in St. John's Street; between Bread Street and Friday Street, just west of Paternoster Row; in King Street, Oat Lane; and in Paternoster Row. According to Mills's and Oliver's *Survey*, they all survived their respective surveying decisions and thus became candidates for the landscape of Dryden's poem; the most likely, however, are the Pissing Alleys in King Street or Paternoster Row for size and location near the Thames, where the trebles are squeaking and the basses are roaring. This version of the alley was recovered between September 14 and 25, 1672: "There is laid into the alley called pissing alley to make the same 14 Foot wide – 10 Foot in Breadth for 66 Foot in length within superficial [Count] is 660 Foot and Certifyed" (*Survey of Building Sites*, v:156). Given that a number of lanes and alleys were considered unfit to be opened up, the preservation of Pissing Alley can't be taken for granted: Turnagain Lane at Snowhill, for example, "haveing no passage but Down to Fleet Ditch with divers steps for foot people and no horse nor Carts can go that way is not fitt to be opned" (*Survey of Building Sites*, 11:22; March 27, 1667). About thirty alleys and passages around Thames Street were closed, including Too Little Lane, Dunghill Lane, and Pisspot Alley on Tennis Court Lane, with the Pissing Alley "to the North door of Pales Church to be opened to 9 foot" (11:23v).[21] Thus the landscape of *MacFlecknoe* – the spaces that shape and move the sounds within the world of the poem – owed its being in some measure to the surveyors' reshaping of the ruined city. There is a double temporal move here: calling upon the linguistic eternity of the name and significance of Pissing Alley also emphasizes the contingency of present place.

That contingency of present place is both reemphasized and resisted in *MacFlecknoe* through some of the same rhetorical strategies as those of the guidebooks, the sermons, and the maps – of underpinning the new *with* the old and negotiating the new *by* the old:

> Close to the Walls which fair *Augusta* bind,
> (The fair *Augusta* much to fears inclin'd)
> An ancient fabrick, rais'd t' inform the sight,
> There stood of yore, and *Barbican* it hight:
> A watch Tower once; but now, so Fate ordains,
> Of all the Pile an empty name remains.

Stow had described in his *Survey of London* (1598) the Barbican in richly suggestive terms:

> On the northwest side of this Citie, neare unto Redcrosse streete there was a Tower commonlie called *Barbican*, or *Burhkenning*; for that the same being placed on a high ground, and also builded of some good height, was in olde

time used as a *Watch Tower* for the Citie, from whence a man might behold and view the whole Citie towards the South, as also see into *Kent, Sussex*, and *Surrey*, and likewise euery other way east, north or west.[22]

But the tower promising visual command of the city had long since vanished for Stow, not to mention Dryden – Stow claims it was "plucked down" by Henry III in 1267; the name had been empty for centuries. The Fire reinforced the emptiness, the sense of "pile" as ruin as well as mass: Mills's and Oliver's *Survey* records a number of surveyed sites around the Barbican and Aldersgate Street. "From its old Ruins Brothel-houses rise" invites the question – *Which* old ruins? From the thirteenth century or the seventeenth? – particularly since the rising "prostitution" of writing and performing was so directly connected to the restoration of the monarchy and the implications of rebuilding. That the poem calls on such a distant past in such an archaic voice allows a temporal trick of making the literary and dramatic present and recent past appear even infinitely further away from the remote (and perhaps constructed?) past of cultural watchtowers, of aesthetic command.

There are perhaps double allusions to the rebuilt City in the "Monument of vanisht minds" (Wren's Monument was completed in 1677; the anti-Catholic message was added in 1681) and in the inclusion of John Ogilby – translator of Virgil, yes, but also surveyor of streets – among those who "almost choakt the way." As Hunter has argued: "It is urban clutter that we spy in satire as much as satiric clutter that we find in urban art . . . In any case, the great distinctive literary forms of the English eighteenth century – satire and the novel – both have something crucial to do with urbanness, and both are characterized by an addiction to representing human space filled beyond comfortable capacity" (*Before Novels*, 125). As many critics have noted, the area from "near *Bun-Hill*" to "distant *Watling-street*" encloses not much; the new world of the city is choked by newness itself; it *overinhabits* itself. *MacFlecknoe*, written (probably) ten years after the Fire, in 1676, the year of the *Survey* and a decade into the rebuilding, has moved into another, much worse urban space than Dryden had envisioned in *Annus Mirabilis* (1666):

> Already, Labouring with a mighty fate,
> > She shakes the rubbish from her mounting brow,
> And seems to have renew'd her Charter's date,
> > Which Heav'n will to the death of time allow.
> More great than humane, now, and more *August*,[23]
> > New deifi'd she from her fires does rise:
> Her widening streets on new foundations trust,
> > And, opening, into larger parts she flies.   *(lines 1173–80)*

Of course, *Annus Mirabilis* is in a completely different genre and serves a completely different purpose from *MacFlecknoe*; yet both poems are suggestively representative of the dominant rhetoric describing London in their respective times. Ten years later, the rubbish is still there, although in perhaps a different form; Augusta is bespattered; the streets, widened, permit more and worse traffic; in the world of *MacFlecknoe*, as with the *Dunciad* and Swift's city poems, the streets do not open into larger parts but in a sense close down, stultify, choke all ways.

Pope's *Dunciad* also charts the city, sorting the goats in text and notes into predefined (or redefined) spaces.[24] Smithfield, home of the new Muses, Pope's note glosses:

> is the place where Bartholomew Fair was kept, whose Shews, Machines,
> and Dramatical Entertainments, formerly agreeable only to the Taste of the
> Rabble, were, by the Hero of this Poem and others of equal Genius, brought
> to the Theatres of Covent-Garden, Lincolns-inn-Fields, and the Hay-
> Market, to the be reigning Pleasures of the Court and Town.
>
> *(Dunciad Variorum, 1:2n)*[25]

The historical connections of Bartholomew Fair were still entirely contemporary for Pope's readers – a "semantic coral reef," in Rogers's words, "in which there were encrusted myriads of fossilised allusions, practically all of them pejorative in character" (*Hacks and Dunces*, 157–58). The fair itself continued until 1855; thus the social meanings Pope articulates here are even more pronounced in their strategy of containment and identification of seepage. The voices of the modern world in the decades of the rebuilding employ a vocabulary eerily like that of the Fire sermons and poems, where place collapses into place, meaning slides into meaning. For the *Variorum*, in the move in the fifth stanza of the opening, where "Here" and "Hence" begin a number of the lines that point to and culminate in "all the Grubstreet race," we see at once an emblematic futility of place name – all roads lead to Grub Street – and its emblematic power – you, pitiful object of satire, have been *named* by Grub Street, pinned into place.

But the way that this conservative move of sorting is played out in the poem offers another indirect representation of and comment on the contours of this particular universe. Much of the sorting out occurs *underground* in Pope's poem – in the footnotes rather than in the poem itself. In the text of the poem, place is a given, its familiarity assumed. But even there, even where place name calls up instant image, immediate identification, the subterranean world of the notes can either destabilize or concretize the assumption of the line:

> But far o'er all, sonorous Blackmore's strain,
> Walls, steeples, skies, bray back to him again:

> In Tot'nam fields, the brethren with amaze
> Prick all their ears up, and forget to graze;
> Long Chanc'ry-lane retentive rolls the sound,
> And courts to courts return it round and round:
> Thames wafts it thence to Rufus' roaring hall,
> And Hungerford re-ecchoes, bawl for bawl. *(DV* 11:247–54*)*

Pope's note glosses the imitation of *Æneid* in the progress of sound, but the topographical allusions are progressively modern: Tottenham, distant and Saxon, known by 1600 as prosperous, full of almshouses and charities; Chancery Lane, renamed in the late fourteenth century, glossed by Pope as temporally and socially retentive, recycling transgressions and transgressors; Hungerford Market, a relatively new (1682) and, by Pope's time, markedly unsuccessful rival market to Covent Garden, a commercial and topographical failure that even in sound is twice-removed from originality, re-echoing rather than echoing, closing the sentence with the finality of disintegration.

Fleet Ditch disembogues dead dogs as the procession moves by Bridewell;[26] Pope's note disembogues further interpretive possibilities by connecting *subtextually* the progress of the Dunces to the Lord Mayor's Day procession:

> It is between eleven and twelve in the morning, after church service, that the criminals are whipped in *Bridewell.* – This is to mark punctually the Time of the day: *Homer* does it by the circumstance of the Judges rising from court, or of the Labourer's dinner; our author by one very proper both to the *Persons* and the *Scene* of his Poem; which we may remember commenc'd in the evening of the Lord-mayor's day: The first book passed in that night; the next morning the games begin in the *Strand*, thence along *Fleetstreet* (places inhabited by Booksellers) then they proceed by *Bridewell* toward *Fleetditch*, and lastly thro' *Ludgate* to the City and the Temple of the Goddess.
>
> *(DV* 11:258n*)*

Pope's note emphasizes the mayoral procession, the "discursive trajectory" of which, as Manley notes, is "essentially open-ended and incomplete; it did not lead to the end of time but traced a profane and continuing route through it" (*Literature and Culture*, 282).[27] No eternity here (in the *Variorum*, of course, Universal Darkness does not actually end the poem); none of the atemporality of a royal procession; rather, fragmentariness, contingency, "profanity" at once affirm and are contaminated by their moral and aesthetic equivalents in the upper world of the poem. The topographical notes themselves operate almost like satiric streets-as-*limen* that Manley sees negotiating between divergent or even incompatible interests: expanding, explaining, connecting – but subverting, contaminating, distancing. Or from the perspective of form as metaphor, the notes (mis)behave *like* the overflowing ditches, overwhelming and polluting the disingenuously "clean" text and "straight" narrative above.

Pope abridges Stow to gloss the gates of Lud (*DV* 11.332n); the story is one of decay, destruction, and rebuilding, of "new heads on their old bodies." Ludgate itself had been damaged in the Fire but was since restored. Pope's note suggestively *doesn't* mention what Stow spends more time on: its function as a prison for "debt, trespasses, accomptes, and contempts" – as opposed to Newgate, the prison for "treasons, fellonies, and other criminall offences" (Stow, *Survey*, 33). The "gates of Lud," then, submerge the image of a prison for petty criminals (such as Henley and Blackmore, poetically speaking), but simultaneously point to it in the sub-textual quoting of Stow, the original definer of London as place; the submerged image rises articulately and is confirmed by the note at the end of Book 11: "*Fleet* A Prison for insolvent Debtors on the bank of the Ditch" (*DV* 11:395n) – where anonymous "others" among the sleeping bards "made their safe retreat" (*DV* 11:396).

The street spaces of the *Dunciad*, as with *MacFlecknoe* and Swift's city poems, are generically different from the streets through which the novelistic characters move: as Aubrey Williams and others have pointed out, the procession of the dunces is a remarkably static event.[28] Little moves except on the organic level of decay. These streets do not permit transformation; the lines of the poem attach spatial identity to their victims and the subterranean notes fix the identification. (As "A Description of a City Shower" points out, filth itself declares its spatial identity: "Filth of all Hues and Odours seem to tell / What Street they sail'd from, by their Sight and Smell.") The spaces of the new city for Pope do *not* appear fluid, elastic, living; or rather, the poem's structure, meter, rhymes, and imagery, combine to *immobilize* the swift shifting modernity, to stop it in its tracks, to pre-serve the vermin in textual formaldehyde or to dissolve the differences in a "tum-bling down the Flood." By drawing on Stow and presuming the contemporary reader's topographical knowledge, the poem defends by repositing an older order of street identification and so contains the streets as well as the hacks.

At the same time, however, such poems spring from and most vividly preserve the world they pretend to annihilate. The transgression of order, both aesthetic and spatial, is contained precisely by presupposing and imposing an order that in fact is rapidly disintegrating (hence the need for a *Dunciad* in the first place). The final triplet of "City Shower" still lives as richly and rudely and ringingly, spilling its wonderfully fetid imagery into readers' awareness over and over again, the triplet itself of course pushing repetition. The notes of the *Dunciad* overwhelm the terranean text, busily creating world upon world of vivid jabbering dunces. These poems, then, offer a paradox of space, another aspect of their well-argued paradox of modernity,[29] and in expending so much energy to refix the boundaries, to contain the motion, to sort the clutter, they simultaneously enter the fray as the loudest, sharpest, strongest voices articulating modernity and overfilling space.

In Gay's *Trivia; or, The Art of Walking the Streets of London* (1716)[30] – as in the city poetry of Pope and Swift as well as in the fictional narratives of Ward and Defoe – we see the same physicality of space as well as its motion, the creation of social and moral identity through topographical placement, the blurring of social boundaries, the reading of signs, and the formal, poetic (re)organization of space. But we also see a kind of celebratory energy – as Rogers puts it, "a kind of urban hormone which sets the activity of the whole town in motion" (*Hacks and Dunces*, 164) – that is closer to Defoe's narratives, to Defoe's response to the demands of the new.

The opening stanza of Book 1 (*Of the Implements for walking the Streets, and Signs of the Weather*) presents fairly straightforwardly the obvious real paradoxes of London's streets: the goddess Trivia, as the meeting of three ways (i.e., as the Streets Themselves), will literally as well as figuratively transport the poet securely through the spacious streets; but it is the inherent nature of London's streets that, spacious as some may be, there is nothing like a grid (or "Naples' smoother streets" [*T* 1:93]) and everything contributes to straying: winding alleys (like Trivia herself, the nature of London's streets) lead, but lead a doubtful way, and "long perplexing lanes untrod before" recalls the reiterated cry of the textual topographers who boast of commensuration and complain of incommensurability. No matter how exhaustive the survey, the perambulation, the documentation, some corners of London insist on remaining untrod, undefined, uncontained.

The poem insists on the joys and virtues of inhabiting the streets with some immediacy, of walking rather than riding, in terms that do not seem ironic, since they make sense:

> Let beaus their canes with amber tipt produce,
> Be theirs for empty show, but thine for use.
> In gilded chariots while they loll at ease,
> And lazily insure a life's disease . . .
> Rosy-complexion'd health thy steps attends,
> And exercise thy lasting youth defends.   (*T* 1:67–74)

The pleasures of exercise are expanded in the context of and in contrast to what everyone had been complaining about for a century: the streets "pestred" by coaches rumbling, shaking, perplexing the way (*T* 1:99, 100, 104).

But at the same time – and precisely because of the modern condition of the coach-pestered streets ("Here laden carts with thund'ring waggons meet, / Wheels clash with wheels, and bar the narrow street" [*T* 11:229–30]) – the poem offers a variety of instruments for achieving distance: canes, shoes, pattens, umbrellas, surtouts, wigs, etiquette, perhaps the georgic digressions themselves. The Walker retreats in Book 11 to the open spaces of Pall Mall (*T* 11:257ff) and the "close abodes" and bye-streets "Where wheels ne'er shake the ground; there pensive stray / In studious thought, the long uncrouded way" (*T* 11:273–74) – in other words, the oldest streets of all, least changed by Fire, least changed by change. After all, the art of walking the streets of London was precisely a miniature version of the art of negotiating the new spaces of London itself, requiring literal and conceptual instruments: canes, maps, topographies, the bird's-eye-view of literature.

As in "A Description of a City Shower" ("Here various Kinds by various Fortunes led, / Commence Acquaintance underneath a Shed"), physical proximity threatens social distance: the barber's apron, the perfumer's touch, the baker's flour contaminate walkers wearing black; the chimney-sweep, the small-coal man, the dust man stain those "that youthful colours wear"; and the chandler and the butcher threaten all (*T* 11:25–44). Visual distinctions literally blur; physical distance maintains them, as does street etiquette – the polite creation of space:

> Let due civilities be strictly paid,
> The wall surrender to the hooded maid;
> Nor let thy sturdy elbow's hasty rage
> Jostle the feeble steps of trembling age:
> And when the porter bends beneath his load,
> And pants for breath, clear thou the crouded road.
> But, above all, the groping blind direct,
> And from the pressing throng the lame protect.   (*T* 11:45–52)

Politeness preserves as well as protects the differences of gender, age, class, ability; at the same time, the Walker notes, some social distinctions should be muddied: shove the fop and bully into the ditch.

Trivia marks out the literal as well as the social signs of the street, but for Gay, unlike for Addison and others, the signs are reliable: the creaking of the swinging signs signifies rain (*T* 1:158–59); "Be sure observe the signs, for signs remain, / Like faithful landmarks to the walking train" (*T* 11:67–68). But this is a new age, and the signs must be *read*. At the Seven Dials (laid out by Thomas Neale in 1693 with a column of seven facets with dial faces in the center of the seven converging streets), the illiterate visitor struggles with the unreadability of the topographic space:

> Here oft the peasant, with enquiring face,
> Bewilder'd, trudges on from place to place;
> He dwells on ev'ry sign with stupid gaze,

> Enters the narrow alley's doubtful maze,
> Tries ev'ry winding court and street in vain,
> And doubles o'er his weary steps again.   *(T* 11:77–82*)*

The streets can only be untangled through the act of reading, which encompasses
signs, topographies, maps – and requires as well the art of writing the streets of
London.

But reading too long or too much carries its own danger – the digressive
episode of Cloacina, "Like the sweet ballad ... Too long detains the walker on his
way; / While he attends, new dangers round him throng; / The busy city asks
instructive song" (*T* 11:217–220). Book 11 of *Trivia* supplies, as do the textual
topographies and all the multiple forms of London literature, an index of street
identities:

> Shall the large mutton smoak upon your boards?
> Such, *Newgate*'s copious market best affords.
> Would'st thou with mighty beef augment thy meal?
> Seek *Leaden hall*; St. *James*'s sends thee veal;
> *Thames-street* gives cheeses; *Covent-garden* fruits;
> *Moor-fields* old books; and *Monmouth-street* old suits.
> Hence may'st thou well supply the wants of life,
> Support thy family, and cloath thy wife.   *(T* 11:544–51*)*

Gay's catalogue is rather cheerier than Pope's or Swift's or Ward's; Moorfields
comes out quite well in this sunnily accurate little moment. For the Walker, as for
Edward Copeland's version of Clarissa's London, signs are reliable, street identities stable enough, the urban possibilities promising.

Trivia of course has its own nightworld in Book 111, yet that too is explicitly
negotiable as long as you "fix [your] eyes intent upon the throng" (*T* 111:15) and
"Stand firm, look back, be resolute, beware" (*T* 111:24). The moon appears in the
very first stanza to contribute light enough to discourage the villain; the rest of the
poem opens up the dark spaces and renders them, if not harmless, at least manage-
able: "Then shalt thou walk unharm'd the dang'rous night" (*T* 111:113). The
close, dark, unprotected spaces, the prostitutes, the pickpockets, the alleys changing shape and meaning in the darkness (*T* 111:127–29), the mohocks, the aggressive chairmen, the lurking cellar, all get their measured attention, and all shadow
the spaces of the daylit city, yet the poem is a happy one and comes the closest to the
self-confident topographies in promising and appearing to believe in the mastery
of the corners.

Not least in this comparison between *Trivia* and the guidebooks is the index,
supplying another layer of textual accommodation of space, another ordering of
streets, another form of access to the city:

Asses, their arrogance,	2, 13
Alleys, the pleasure of walking in one,	2, 271
Arundel-street,	2, 484
Bully, his insolence to be corrected,	2, 59
Butchers to be avoided,	2, 43
Burlington-house,	2, 494

Cheapside, fallen coaches, Drury Lane and virtue, the author's dislike of cheese, "Legs, their use," shins, signs, umbrellas, walls, "*Wednesday*, how to know it" – all parcelled, sorted, accessible, informative, contained. London is *signed*: "High-rais'd on *Fleet-street* posts, consign'd to fame, / This work shall shine, and walkers bless my name" (*T* III:415–16). The poem inscribes itself as sign; like Swift's and Pope's, it contains the darkness within formal verse – like the Fire poems, the heroic couplet itself suggests structural and conceptual containment; but unlike Swift's and Pope's, Gay's poem reads confidently, optimistically, the need for negotiation or containment not urgently ideological but practical, sensible. For Trivia "the scavenger bids kennels glide / Within their bounds, and heaps of dirt subside" (*T* I:15–16) – the couplet, like the kennel, keeps things tidy, but even when in the "rainy floods" the "kennels break their bounds" the poet doesn't seem vastly upset; his imagery remains "cleaner" than Swift's, softer than Pope's. In some sense, Gay's poem is closer to the agendas and tones of the textual topographies, and perhaps to Defoe's narratives, than to his fellow Scriblerians' outwardly similar verse satire. Genres, as well as attitudes, as well as streets, were distinctly unstable and open for redefinition.

Reinhabiting the streets: prose fiction

Much of the prose fiction of the late seventeenth and early eighteenth centuries works in the contextual crisis of rebuilding to rename and rewalk the streets, to refashion a "complete cultural space" from this lore of the past and the experience of the present. Walking the streets increasingly invades the prose literature in tempo with the proliferating street guides. Richard Sennett argues that in the urban city *now* "space has . . . become a means to the end of pure motion – we now measure urban spaces in terms of how easy it is to drive through them, to get out of them . . . As urban space becomes a mere function of motion, it thus becomes less stimulating in itself; the driver wants to go through the space, not to be aroused by it" (*Flesh and Stone*, 17–18). Sennett is referring primarily to the smooth highways, fast cars, and sleek technology that make speed and motion inherently desirable in our society, but he traces how such an emphasis derives from an eighteenth-century shift in cultural perceptions of space from static and hierarchized to motion-based, with Harvey's discovery of the circulation of the blood becoming the metaphor for economic and social health in terms of free and even rapid movement. As the various economic tracts of the late seventeenth and early eighteenth centuries show, particularly in Defoe's *Tour*, the perception of space as fluid, elastic, circulatory, living, already informs the literary representations of inhabited space. In London after the Fire, all the traditional walkings of streets – the royal and mayoral processions, the Stowean peripatetics, the lurkings of the cony-catchers – found a new form of expression in increasingly longer prose narratives and into the novel itself. Where the form of epic and structure of heroic couplet found a way visually and aurally to contain the frenzied motion of the streets, prose narratives found a way to release it.[31]

The prose fiction of London during the rebuilding revives some of these older patterns of literature and culture and combines them with new attitudes and strategies that bring the streets themselves to life, as places to inhabit as well as move through, as spatial elements with their own integrity, as Kostof says, rather than simply space left over between buildings. The streets of the new literatures open up ways of negotiating real space through imaginative space, of conceptually grappling with changes in tempo, contour, possibility. This section will look primarily and in some detail at three important literary and cultural works that mark the heightening interest in street representation across the six or seven decades of the major reconstruction and expansion of London: a historically and generically transitional work, Richard Head's *The English Rogue* (1665), which feeds richly on the Elizabethan and early Stuart urban genres but which in its immediate post-Fire popularity seems to satisfy a new need and provide a new model for later work; Ned Ward's *The London Spy* (1698–1700) – with some lengthy sideways glances at the works of Tom Brown – which combines the cony-catching resonances of Head's work with the increasing spatial meticulousness and grammatical energy of the proliferating guides to London streets; and Defoe's *Moll Flanders* (1722), which structurally and imaginatively realizes the full symbolic potential of the new power of London streets.

The English Rogue (1665),[32] by Richard Head (1637?–1686?), while coming straight out of the literature of the streets going back through Heywood and Nashe and Greene, is also a transitional work that not only employs the old fixture of character types ("the most eminent cheats of both sexes") but also plays very firmly in the streets. As an example of pre-Fire street literature, *The English Rogue* offers first, a character usually working in rather than moving through the streets, and second, streets as known quantities for both character and reader, in a narrative that reflects the possessive grammar of pre-Fire topographies. But the work's printing history suggests it found an immediate popularity in the decades after the

Fire: after the first licensed (and cleaned-up) edition was published in 1665 by
Henry Marsh, its success prompted the bookseller Francis Kirkman to write a
second part to the work after failing to persuade Head to write it himself; it was
licensed in 1668, and appeared in 1671, along with a third and fourth part, and
advertisements for a fifth. In 1680 a uniform edition of the four parts appeared.[33]
A combination of the printing history and a look at its formal qualities suggests
why *The English Rogue* works as an example of new literature, as a transitional or
genre-crossing piece capable of supplying ideas and energies into the literary
changes of the rebuilding. Though the work springs from a tradition of rogue literature, that tradition had, at least according to Michael Shinagel, "exhausted the
inherited lore of jest-books, beggar-books, conny-catching pamphlets, and the
like" (Introduction, *The English Rogue*, viii). Semi-autobiographical and proto-
novelistic, *The English Rogue* was available for generic revamping, a perfect candi-
date for the literary and cultural contexts "before novels." The interest in street
literature which had clearly flagged in the decades before the Fire suddenly
reignited (so to speak). The work at once assumes the reader's intimate knowledge
of London streets and their overworld and underworld significance, and also
moves toward the kind of restless London street narratives of Ned Ward, Tom
Brown, and Daniel Defoe.

Meriton Latroon, coming into London as a young man already trained in the
arts of feigning crippledness and begging for a living, finds his good and bad
fortune to be most often determined by his own ready knowledge of place. He suc-
ceeds quite well begging in the pleasure grounds of Moorfields[34] (*ER* 61), but gets
ahead of himself with "a company of Rogues, cheats, Pickpockets, &c." in
Lincoln's Inn Fields (*ER* 66) – home of the lawyers – and, caught in the act of
stealing a loin of veal, "was kickt the Gantlet from the Standard in *Cheapside* to the
conduit at the lower end thereof" – that is, from one end of the emblematically
prosperous, commercial, property-valued street to the other (*ER* 70). He continues: "This unhappy adventure made me betake my self to my old course of
begging, resolving as yet not to deal in that trade I had little experience in" (*ER*
70). His life in the city quickly accustoms him to the shifting modes of dress,
behavior, possibility, mobility; like Moll Flanders over fifty years later, Latroon the
shape-shifter learns to pull his identity and even his gender from the street itself:
"Coming into *Burchin-Lane*, I went to a Salesman, and bought (pretendedly for
my Maid) an ordinary yet handsome Peticoat and Wastcoat, furnishing my self
with all the Appurtenances requisite for a Servant maid" (*ER* 133).[35] Like Head
himself, who in John Aubrey's words "could transform himself into any shape,"[36]
Latroon wears the disguises offered by the social mobility and anonymity of the
urban streets. But in *The English Rogue*, the place meanings are fixed; Latroon just
has to read them correctly. He dreams of "all the meat in *East-cheap*" when he's

starving (*ER* 155); he cozens a turnkey of Ludgate, a jeweller of Foster Lane and a scrivener in Bow Lane, and is arrested – like Moll Flanders, exactly when he is "walking the streets securely" (*ER* 273[37]) – by a man with a mouth "as largely vaulted as that within *Aldersgate*; . . . take both head and face together and it appeared like the Saracens on *Snow-hill*" (*ER* 273) – and away he's carried to the King's Head in Wood Street. He *finds* his identity in the street, ready-made; Moll, on the other hand, will as often create identity within or confer it upon a street.

A trope that later prose narratives will consistently adopt is the street as simultaneously refuge and escape, reflecting the deep ambivalence towards urban-ness that characterizes literature on both sides of the Fire. Latroon gloats: "the largeness of that Vast City [of London] would afford conveniency for my concealment," but at the same time the intersection of place and occupation is also a threat: "But then my cloaths much troubled me, knowing nothing would betray me sooner than they" (*ER* 142 [ch. 14]). *The English Rogue* as a whole seems to operate in much the way that Manley argues for the whole Elizabethan city *œuvre*, as a "representation of disorder and mobility" that was at the same time "typically a function of the quest for stasis" (*ER* 77) – clearly an agenda equally interesting to the world of rebuilding.

The ambivalence towards street space as refuge/trap is countered, in the *Rogue* as in later narratives, by the rhetorical gambit of containing by describing. *The English Rogue* makes visible the dark, crawling underworld that in fact inhabits the shadows of the same streets the in-law London citizen travels daily. But opening it up, of course, also seems to contain it, both conceptually and in this case practi-cally, like a textual topography. Rather like Moll, Latroon declares himself a pen-itent who is writing this juicy narrative to warn fine upstanding citizens of their danger. His advice, if not his penitence, is concrete and presumably reliable:

> If you are robbed, there is no help but to indeavour to surprize the Thieves by
> a strict pursuit . . . In the first place, scowre the next Road, not streight before,
> but either on the right or left-hand; for they know *Hue* and *Cries* never cross
> the passages, but go straight along . . . [I]f you are robbed in the eastern
> quarter, pursue them not in the direct Road to *London* with *Hue* and *Cry*, for
> by some other way they are fled; but haste to the City, and in *Westminster*,
> *Holborn*, the *Strand* and *Covent-Garden* search speedily, for there they are.
>   (*ER* 52; ch. 63)

"For there they are." As with Stow's possessive grammar – "here have you," "there have we" – Latroon promises that if we combine knowledge of the streets with a knowledge of street habits, the city is ours, open, available, navigable, reli-able. The threat of the city street is contained by itself; avenues of escape are avenues of pursuit. At the same time, however, the fundamental hierarchy of the streets is challenged: here, the "direct roads" are treacherous, the straight path futile; the answers for in-laws as well as outlaws lie in the corners, the labyrinth, the nature of the old City itself, which was soon in the very process of being *recovered* rather than reorganized. The popularity of street literature maps onto the larger cultural investment of cartographic and topographic preservation rather than "improvement."

Head's work, written before the Fire but consumed enthusiastically after-wards,[38] thus revives some of the older, familiar patterns and images of an urban literature already designed to express, explain, and absorb the urban experience, and offers itself as a model for adapting those older traditions to newer formats and changing implications. A form of literature that had clearly been flagging to some extent even before the Civil War, the underworld narrative sprang into new life with the rebuilding and the new layers and tempos of strangeness it produced.

Ned Ward, though born after the Fire (1667–1731), was very much a product of the rebuilding city, and his notorious *London Spy*[39] is a narrative record of a teeming, boiling, noisy, crowded, churning London, a jumble of loose signifiers awaiting redefinition. His street signs, too, are social signs, but their meaning is far less fixed, as often perverted as adjusted; the signs swing crazily in the streets. His topographical analysis is as particular as any of the contemporary guides; London is anatomized by place function, place reputation, and place influence, but it is also filled in with the faces and habits and sights and sounds and smells that the maps and topographies leave carefully alone. The Spy gives voices and bodies to the crowds that Stow and his textual descendants left simply "pestring" the ordered or re-ordered spaces of the city. Like the Elizabethan cony-catching pam-phlets, epigrams, and ballads, but with more narrative detail and narrative motion, *The London Spy* offers its own handle on the pestering, festering, burgeon-ing urban space.

For many modern readers, and perhaps for contemporary readers as well (given Ward's status in the *Dunciad*, for example), the text seems linguistically overstuffed; there is almost *too much there*. Ward draws upon the tradition of city simile and proverb in assigning meanings to places, but his similes seem to crowd the sentences, yoking like and like, like and unlike, like and wildly unlike. Many times the narrator employs straightforward indentification, assuming readerly street knowledge. One place is often defined *by* another, different, place: at a tavern near Aldgate he finds the oaths flying about "like *Squibs* and *Crackers* in *Cheap-side*" in a mayoral show (*LS* 1:5). A man passing as "*a Gentleman of good account in the* North *of* England" insures his reputation through his bills that "*pass as Current in the* Lombard-street *as the best Merchants in the City*" – and the financial reputation mutually secures the social (*LS* 1:6). A former wine-cooper's apprentice now passes "*as Compleat a City Beau . . . as you shall see in* Lombard-Street Church *of a Sunday, or in* Drapers-Garden *an hour before Dinner-time*" (LS 1: 6–7). We hardly *need* a knowledge of the city; the act of simile itself supplies the topographical significance – meanings reinforce each other, as we now *know* City beaus stroll Drapers' Gardens (see Figure 18).

But deeper knowledge of the shifts in street etymology destabilize even these apparently straightforward similes. Before the Fire, for example, the garden belonged to Drapers' Hall, taking over Thomas Cromwell's house in Throgmorton Street and stretching to London Wall, and "was only open to those prepared to pay £3 for the privilege";[40] after the Fire it was opened to the public – a place, then, doubly destabilized. What once was function-specific – the drapers dried their linen there in the sixteenth century – has now moved into open, fluid, general use; but in the transition it creates the appearance of functional reliability – this recent apprentice merely *looks* like a city beau strolling the city gardens. Meaning is simultaneously fixed and troubled; the layers of past and present conflict beneath and yet are tied together by the wrench of simile.

The catalog is relentless – hundreds of pages fleshing out the kind of new/old list combining the topographical indexing of the new guidebooks with the ancient litany in Heywood's "On Seeking a Dwelling Place" – old patterns creating or challenging new need for security. We have the ostlers in Bishopsgate Street and Smithfield, the Water Lane Protestant, the whore of Bartholomew Fair, the antiquary of Gresham's College, the Fleet Street bumsitter, the mercer's daughter in Cornhill, the Moorfields artist, the Amminadab (courtier) in Finch Lane, the smell of a Southwark ditch, the tallyman from Houndsditch, the Yorkshire bullock in Smithfield market, the Lincoln's Inn mumpers (genteel beggars) and the Long Lane clickers (shopkeepers' touts who solicit custom for the secondhand clothes shops there), all provide social markers to topographic place at the same time as the topographic place insures the social marking. The identification seems scattershot, but also assured, universal, almost atemporal. *The London Spy* charts spatial meaning with a vengeance, drawing upon custom, traditional knowledge, oral literatures, and ancient identities, affirming spatial meaning onto the vast fluctuating disruptive urban experience. The text supplies the darkside of the security of the topographies.

The same patterns dominate similar texts by similar writers. Tom Brown (1663–1704), like Ned Ward born outside the city and apart from the Fire, also was fascinated to the point of obsession with the physical and social contours of London. (The *Dictionary of National Biography* describes his knowledge of London as "extensive and peculiar.") One of his narrators says: "*London* is a World by it self; we daily discover in it more new Countries and surprizing Singularities, than in all the Universe besides . . . [T]he *Inhabitants* themselves

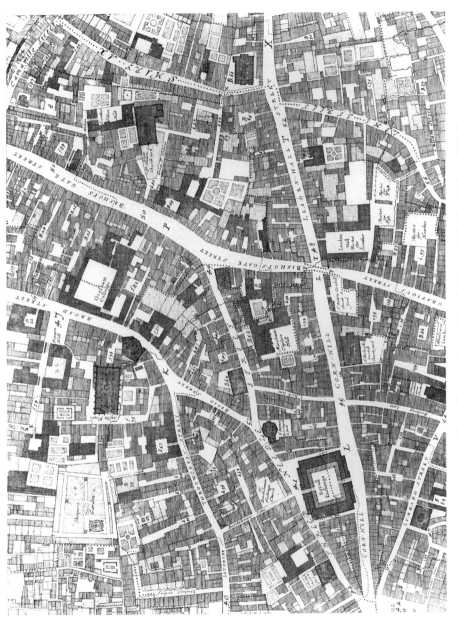

Figure 18 Ogilby and Morgan's map (1676): Drapers' Gardens; Pinners' Hall.

don't know a quarter of 'em."[41] In *A Comical View of the Transactions, That will happen in the Cities of London & Westminster* (1707) he creates an entire satiric itemization of place:

> *Thursday* 17 . . . Justice to be had at *Doctors Commons* when people can get it . . . At Night much Fornication all over *Covent-garden*, and five miles round it . . .
>
> *Sunday* 3. Beggars take up their respective Posts in *Lincoln's-Inn-fields*, and other places by Seven, that they may be able to Praise God in capon and *March*-beer at Night . . . Great Thumping and Dashing of the Cushion at *Salters-hall* about Eleven; One wou'd almost think the Man was in Earnest, he lays so furiously about him. A most refreshing smell of Garlick in *Spittle-fields* and *Sohoe*, at Twelve. *(Works* I:44–43, 53)

As in *The London Spy*, Brown's narrative orchestrates places and people seeming to inhabit *each other*; what is pointed out as characteristic is simultaneously reaffirming, self-affirming. The proverbial quality and context of the narrative points to the known by way of the unknown, or rather, submerges the unknown by disclosing the known.

But as with the London Spy's opening self-severing from the ancients (he tosses off Augustine, Virgil, and Descartes with, respectively, a fig, a fart, and a turd [*LS* 1–2]), these texts separate and dislodge meanings as often as they assert or reaffirm them – replicating, in a textual sense, the mobility of meaning in the cultural world. Ward's relentless similes behave like the overelaborated street signs, layering contradictory or simply peculiar "devices" over a simple point until the sense of meaning itself shards away. A head-dresser's shop "is as seldom to be found without a *Whore* as a *Booksellers Shop* in *Paul*'s Church Yard without a *Parson*" (*LS* 11:26). Parsons are yoked with punks, booksellers with hairdressers; the high is undermined by the low, the low not elevated by the high; the text produces a systematic reduction of all aspects of the city not simply into the streets, but into the gutters. The overdetermined similes entwine all classes, genders, ages, and occupations of London. A particular distillation of brandy, says a "reverend *Doctress* of *Debauchery*," will at once "make a *Parson* dance *Sallingers-round*, a *Puritan* lust after the Flesh, and a Married Man Oblige his Wife oftener in one Night, than without it he shall be able to do in Seven" (*LS* 11:27).

As the earlier similes had implied, the apparent differences between high and low, respectable and reprehensible, vanish in the corners of the night, in the shadows of the streets, as in Swift's city poems and Defoe's urban novels. The City itself, "Augusta" as the Spy explicitly refers to it, in the wee hours changes shape and identity, slinking into moral as well as physical darkness as the Spy and his companion move towards "the *Dark-houses* at *Billingsgate*" (*LS* 11:31): the appar ently "amorous squallings . . . [of] cats" turns out to be the cries of an abandoned baby "at the door of an Eminent Shop-keeper in *Grace-church-street*" (*LS* 11:31). The suggestion is that the "differences" between night and day in London are constructed, and constructed to be visible, but they cannot carry the weight of their lived experience; day collapses into night.

All the physical activity of the streets, which simultaneously promises and threatens a corresponding social mobility, is equally captured in the grammatical motion of the text. As with the textual topographies of this period, Ward's text moves, and moves fast, through the streets of London, its verbs rambling, stum-bling, strolling, blundering, groping, thundering around London. The Spy cannot stay in one place; he promises to give himself "the pleasure of two or three hours Ramble in the Streets" (*LS* 1:23). As in Gay's *Trivia*, the pleasure is as much in the art of walking the streets themselves, motion for its own sake, knowl-edge from exploration, darting into large buildings and small corners with equal gusto, "prying into the dark Intrigues of the Town, to experience what Pastime the Night-Accidents, the Whims and Frolicks of *Staggering Bravados* and *Strolling Strumpets*, might afford" (*LS* 1:23). There is a power in making motion, the power of making space itself. Tom Brown's narrator watches the physical and lin-guistic ordering/disordering of space by the vehicles:

> Some Carry, others are Carried: *Make way there*, says a gouty-leg'd
> Chairman, that is carrying a Punk of Quality to a *Morning's Exercise . . . Make
> room there*, says another Fellow driving a Wheel-barrow of Nuts . . . One
> draws, another drives . . . Here a sooty Chimney-sweeper takes the Wall of a
> grave *Alderman*, and a *Broom-man* jostles the *Parson* of the Parish.
> *(Brown, Works* 111:16–17)

The motion creates social as well as physical disorder; those in charge of motion – the drivers, the chairmen, the carriers rather than the carried sort the space and tempo of the streets, but at the same time *everyone* who is in the streets participates in and contributes to that motion, that experience: "[the citizens] are always in Motion and Activity. Their Actions succeed one another with so much Rapidity, that they begin a Thousand Things before they have finish'd one, and finish a thousand others, before they may properly be said to have begun them" (*Works* 111:27). Tom Brown and his Indian, Ned Ward and his Spy, and all their con-temporary cultural companions are moving within a moving city and are movers among movers.

Defoe's urban novels offer perhaps the most vivid rendering of the *strength* of London street space in Kostof's sense. In a way, the whole new drama of motion is peculiarly suited to novelistic narrative: telling a temporal story *means* offering a narrative line out and away; the enclosure of a poem or the static setting of a drama are opened up in these novels where genre itself provides a different form of habita-tion and the topographical line of escape. Defoe both employs traditional patterns and expands into new possibilities in the narrative spaces of his urban novels. For example, as with the royal proclamation for remarking the streets (and the official narratives, sermons, and maps discussed in part 1), one way the various cultural projects orient the new is by linguistically marking the old. In *Colonel Jack*, for instance, Jack runs "through *Long-alley*, and Cross *Hog lane*, and *Holloway lane*, into the middle of the great Field, which **since** that, has been call'd the *Farthing-pye-house-field*... so we went on, cross'd the Road at *Anniseed Cleer*, and went into the Field where **now** the Great Hospital stands."[42] The reader runs with them, and to allow the eighteenth-century reader to follow more quickly, Jack posts the more recent names and landmarks with the words "since" and "now." Jack pulls the reader into his city – or rather, his cities: in the act of reading and recognizing London, the reader occupies simultaneously the London of Jack's past and present. If there is a psychological or historical obstacle, he kicks it away. We know every twist in that long breathless escape to the fields. We may not know Jack's real name, we may not know the company he keeps, but we know where he sleeps, where he eats, and where he counts his money.

Defoe's urban characters are notorious for evading the truth, for concealing their identities, for keeping close cover. But they display an equally remarkable ten-dency to broadcast their whereabouts. Neither Jack, Moll, Roxana, nor even the respectable H. F. will trust us, the readers, with their real or full names, any more than they trust their acquaintances within fictional space. But they *do* privilege us with an address of sorts, through their carefully charted movements. They offer us a topographical identity in lieu of a legal or (in Homer Brown's sense) a personal identity.[43] George Starr has said that we "seize on place-names" in *Moll Flanders* "as fixed points in an otherwise fluid landscape, and the very fact that its features lack definition gives a special potency to proper names, such as they possess on old maps of newly discovered regions."[44] But in a sense Defoe's novels are *new* maps of newly discovered *old* regions. Defoe's urban novels present narrative versions of the post-Fire two-dimensional ground plan, which sweeps the visualized build-ings off the streets in order to access all corners, to see the City even more com-pletely and comprehensively than a three-dimensional, minutely detailed bird's-eye-view can afford. For Defoe's urban characters, the dense, ancient netting of inner London is open, available, given. They do not wander tentatively down unfamiliar alleys, nor consult the map when writing their adventures: although "scarce looking about," in their chronology of action as well as in recol-lected narration they always know *exactly* where they are. By choosing a Restoration (rebuilding) setting for his novels, and by explicitly mapping its terrain, Defoe opens an avenue between past and present, allowing readers to find not only entertainment in strangeness and adventure, but also comfort in what remains familiar and still seems close. The unchanging lines and names of the city streets reinforce continuity in time and place with the past, offering an imaginative refuge from a bewildering present.[45]

In *Moll Flanders*, the streets of London provide refuge and identity, although there is also a sense in which for Moll all roads lead (very nearly literally) to Newgate. Her strategies of narratively mapping her space – of bringing into sharp, detailed focus the names and patterns of the London streets in order to strengthen her routes of escape – end by mapping her path to prison. Moll's streets are in very many ways the streets of all Londoners of the rebuilding, simultane- ously avenues of pursuit and concealment, spaces both liminal and destinal, offering escape and threatening betrayal. Moll finds, at least for a time, some secur- ity in the topographical interstices of the old city; her vivid and precise narrative mapping of those streets suggests the pleasure and perhaps the relief Defoe (and his contemporary readers) felt in escaping temporarily with her into the spatial and temporal margins of an older, darker, yet historically given city.

Moll's pre-criminal life is essentially as placeless as it is nameless. Colchester, Northampton, Virginia, Bath, all appear as places hardly more specified or individuated than the Elder Brother, the Gentleman-Tradesman, the Bath gentle- man, or the banker. When Moll returns to London pregnant by the vanishing Jemy and keeping the lovelorn banker on a string, she assumes a new identity within a new (and significantly double) address: "I came to *London* the next Day after we parted, but did not go directly to my old Lodgings; but for another name- less reason took a private Lodging in St. *John's-street*, or as it is vulgarly call'd St. *Jones's* near *Clarkenwell*" (*MF* 159–60). Moll the banker's-betrothed disappears into St. John's Street; Moll the future thief and whore tenants St. Jones's. The double name suggests the diverging paths; St. John's Street "was originally a road for pack-horses only . . . [but] in the days of the stage-coach . . . it was the starting point of the main road north from Smithfield via the Angel" (*London Encyclopaedia*, 745). Moll's life in the streets essentially begins here, at this doubly named originating point, for the banker turns out to be her last chance for respect- able security; he loses his fortune and promptly dies.

The visual and topographical vagueness in this first part of Moll's life van- ishes abruptly after her first crime – the theft of a bundle from an apothecary's shop in Leadenhall Street:

> I cross'd the Street indeed, and went down the first turning I came to, and I
> think it was a Street that went thro' into *Fenchurch-street*, from thence I cross'd
> and turn'd through so many ways and turnings that I could never tell which

> way it was, nor where I went, for I felt not the Ground I stept on, and the farther I was out of Danger, the faster I went, till tyr'd and out of Breath, I was forc'd to sit down on a little Bench at a Door, and then I began to recover, and found I was got into *Thames-street* near *Billingsgate*. (MF 192)

This scene of topographical confusion marks a radical shift in the novel to the precise occupation of London streets. In this first crime, the beginning and ending points of her reaction are signposted; she is lost in between. But not for long. The places where Moll steals are indicated only vaguely, but her routes of retreat are almost invariably charted with topographical precision. The shops, the inns, and the houses which offer the laces, tankards, and bundles for Moll to steal are the sources of her danger as well as her wealth; she sees Newgate in their outlines.[46] The streets, on the other hand, offer a network of escape – she "found" herself in Thames Street near Billingsgate – street intersected by place, positioned on a map. Like Jack, Moll constructs her narrative maps with the same fervent need for spatial orientation and escape.

Streets – the space between houses – are in some ways by definition and in contrast to houses unstructured, fluid, something to be moved through, transitional, transformational; Moll acquires in these named streets her professional identity, her titular – if fluid and only loosely signifying – name (*MF* 214). Occupying a single address means inhabiting a fixed identity. The streets offer Moll escape not only in the way they physically invite her to disappear into dark alleys and obscure courtyards, but also in the spaces they provide her – as for the English Rogue and the London Spy – with personal disguise and psychological concealment. And in that concealment lies power. When Moll impersonates a maidservant waiting for her mistress at the Barnet stage-coach stop and makes off with a very comfortable bundle, her route of escape is also her place of transformation:

> I walk'd away, and turning into *Charter-house-Lane*, made off thro' *Charter-house-Yard*, into *Long-Lane*, then cross'd into *Bartholomew-Close*, so into *Little Britain*, and thro' the *Blue-Coat-Hospital* into *Newgate-Street*.
>
> To prevent my being known, I pull'd off my blue Apron . . . I also wrapt up my Straw-Hat . . . and so put the bundle on my head. (MF 239)

The anonymity of the London streets allows Moll – like Head's Meriton Latroon – to become whatever she wants: a wealthy gentlewoman with her own gold watches tempting thieves; a maidservant; a man; a beggar. The combined command over personal and topographical exteriors – the ability to assume a different identity in the carefully charted streets – seems to grant her power over more conventional and respectable street-walkers. Once she has a sense of command of the streets Moll can slip easily into the pockets of the town, respectably visible and securely invisible.

Keeping secret space preserves safety; topographical anonymity proves even more important than nominal invisibility: "[M]y Name was publick among [the other thieves] indeed; but how to find me out they knew not, nor so much as how to guess at my Quarters, whether they were in the East‑End of the Town, or the West; and this wariness was my safety upon all these Occasions" (*MF* 221–22). But "topographical anonymity" is precisely what Moll does not conceal from the reader. We are given every detail, corner by corner, of her routes; we are invited not into a place but into a series of places closely connected, a simultaneously tempo‑ral and physical line of movement that anticipates Defoe's characterization of the boundaries of London itself in the *Tour* (see chapter three): moving but con‑nected, elastic but directioned, less contained than accommodated. The narrative line becomes a topographic line.

Such a connection between street and story invites – even insists – on pushing the interpretive possibilities further. As the example from Morden and Lea's map shows (see Figure 14), Moll's route after she almost kills the child in Bartholomew Close describes a path that at its beginning and end is equidistant from Newgate:

> I took [the child] by the Hand and led it a long till I came to a pav'd Alley that goes into *Bartholomew Close*, and I led it in there . . . the Devil put me upon killing the Child in the dark Alley, that it might not Cry; but the very thought frighted me so that I was ready to drop down . . . and I went thro' into *Bartholomew Close*, and then turn'd round to another Passage that goes into *Long‑lane*, so away into *Charterhouse‑Yard* and out into *St. John's‑street*, then crossing into *Smithfield*, went down *Chick‑lane* and into *Field‑lane* to *Holbourn‑bridge*, when mixing with the Crowd of People usually passing there, it was not possible to have been found out. *(MF 194)*

The first half of this route is repeated and reversed later (in the maidservant passage quoted earlier [*MF* 239]), and explicitly concludes in Newgate Street.

But in Defoe's world, as in many layers of London's literary representations, the streets are as threatening as promising. The reader of *Moll* is the potential victim of Moll; on the other hand (from Moll's point of view), the in‑law citizen may learn the streets as thoroughly as the outlaw. In the end, Moll's carefully charted streets seem to spiral after all into the center they had tried so hard to circle. The building that haunts her thoughts also overshadows her streets, and she finds herself trapped in a tangled circle of both thoughts and streets: "I was ingulfed in Labyrinths of Trouble too great to get out at all" (*MF* 203). The streets could close round her as well as open before her; the socially central power of street space seems stronger than she thought: first providing refuge, it now collaborates in her capture.

Yet not *exactly*; Moll is caught, "not [in] a Mercers Shop, nor a Warehouse of a Mercer, [but in] what look'd like a private Dwelling-House" (*MF* 272). As Crusoe, H.F., and Roxana all discover, the greatest threat to personal security may lie concealed in other people's private space (see chapter six). The streets, then, have their own experiential power and promise, marking a new kind of habitable space that separates itself from the structures traditionally bounding the streets: the houses, the shops, the halls, the structures of social and physical stability, the places to be in rather than to move from or between. In the larger space of the novel, Moll's life in the streets *is* transforming even while it seems to capture her: Moll's imprisonment in London becomes the site of her repentance, leading her indirectly to her final prosperity back in Virginia and finally back in England itself – when once again places are generalized. Specific topography has served its purpose.

Part of the contemporary appeal of Defoe's urban novels may thus derive from their particular combination of stability and motion to produce avenues of spatial escape for the reader. The novels resurrect for the contemporary reader the medieval tangle of streets and offer a different way of ordering them, of finding one's way around a city at once familiar in its ancient place names and strange in its recent rebuilding. The streets that Moll negotiates remain constant under the changes in their structural appearances. Moll's best-laid plans, like H.F.'s, pre-suppose an intimate knowledge of the interrelation of the London streets. Stuart Miller argues otherwise: "Though Defoe's place names may be plotted on a map, in the reading they give the impression not of an ordered map, but of a jumble, a labyrinth in both subject and object, in Moll and in the city, in the individual and in the world."[47] Such a characterization of Defoe's fictional spaces misreads the presence of these streets and the great care with which they are charted, because the reader Miller imagines is a twentieth-century reader less intimately acquainted with and invested in the patterns and powers of those street names. Mapmaking is an attempt to open, order, and know space. The fact that Defoe's characters remember with such precision the complicated avenues of retreat reveals the extent to which the map of London existed in sharp, still relief in their minds, as something to be drawn and depended upon *instantly* in moments of desperate fear. The routes are convoluted, but they conform to the twisted patterns of the medieval city, and the ease with which Moll and Jack and H.F. dart through these streets precisely measures their psychological mastery of topographical space. For Defoe's characters, for his contemporary readers, and for himself, the urban novels – like the new maps and topographies – discover (if not impose) an order within the dark corners of the city, and a psychological centrality in its margins. Defoe produces a London at once familiar and strange, an older city obscured as much by passing time as by sudden growth. In spite of – or perhaps because of – their structural and spatial ambiguities, Defoe's urban novels offer his readers much of what he hoped to find for himself: the occasional *possibility* of structural and spatial refuge within the past familiarity of the buildings and streets that had come to seem so elusively new. In the act of reading *Moll Flanders* the reader recovers the past city in moving through streets retained in the present. For Defoe as much as for Pope, Swift, and Gay, the art of inhabiting the streets of London was in part the art of *writing* the streets of London.

CHAPTER FIVE

NEW NARRATIVES OF PUBLIC SPACES: PARKS AND SHOPS

I have seventeen Modells of the City of *London* of my own making, and the worst of 'em makes *London* an other-guess *London* than 'tis like to be.
(Thomas Shadwell, *The Sullen Lovers,* 1668)

In most towns, but particularly in the city of *London* . . . [m]any trades have their peculiar streets, and proper places.
(Daniel Defoe, *The Complete English Tradesman,* 1725)

In the first narrative wake of the Fire, the newspaper and diary accounts, the sermons, and the poems incessantly listed the names of the streets and the public buildings that had vanished, as a way not only to record but to reconnect the sites and shapes of space. And in the first reconstructive wake of the Fire, the surveys and new maps redrew the streets, the fundamental webbing of the essential *place-ness* of London. Lists and streets came first – the connectors, the foundations, the skeletons of shape. Only with the spatial boundaries redrawn could the city be rebuilt and reinhabited; only with the streets recovered could the rebuilding and rehabitation begin; only with the lists marking loss could the narratives expand. The loss of the public world, the markers of civic institutionality, occupied the first observers and mourners. O. S. sighs in *Counsel to the Afflicted* (1667): "I am much afflicted . . . to see so many magnificent Buildings, so many goodly Churches, stately Halls, fair Houses, useful Hospitals, &c. demolished" (118) – the churches and halls precede the "fair Houses" and his own sense of personal, private loss; for John Evelyn, the *sumptuousness* of London's public monuments demands reitera-tion: "The exquisitely wrought Mercers Chapell, the Sumptuous Exchange, the august fabricque of Christ church, all the rest of the Companies Halls, sumptu-ous buildings, Arches, Enteries, all in dust" (*Diary,* III:460). The destruction of the known markers of public life – the buildings of trade and commerce, of relig-ion, of civic pride – signified a visual destabilization of the larger, normally implicit, institutional framework for daily life, rendering institutionality itself more explicit. The public structures that had marked differences and ordered social, political, economic, and religious space had been consumed: the "public sphere" itself need redefining as well as rebuilding. Some of the emblematic struc-

148

tures and symbols of public life, such as St. Paul's and the Royal Exchange, have been discussed in chapter one. This chapter will focus on two spaces and two strategies: the public parks, as they are repeatedly inscribed by the virtually hegemonic conventions of Restoration comedy; and the shops, as Defoe's generically innovative *Complete English Tradesman* gives them life and place.

Restoration London was, in its social spheres, a place of parks, and in its economic expansion, a place of trade. Both parks and shops are species of public territory that caught new cultural and literary attention after the Fire. Drama, one of the most visibly dominant genres of the Restoration and new in all sorts of ways, has been thoroughly discussed by historical and recent criticism for its public reappearance, its new audience, the emergence of the actress, the ethos of the rake, the revival of city comedy, the technological innovations, and the production of spectacle. But what has had less attention is the way that Restoration comedy – in these cultural and historical contexts of Fire and rebuilding – so emphatically locates itself *outside* the boundaries of the ruined City. The plays of Etherege, Shadwell, Wycherley, Pix, Congreve, Centlivre and others play themselves out primarily in the untouched (if not *old*) spaces of St. James's Park and Hyde Park, offering an audience however elite, however removed from the immediate distresses and inconveniences of rebuilding London, a retreat into the *known*, the secure, the green spaces of uninterrupted social life. It was not until the early 1700s that the City began to emerge in city comedy as something respectable, as a place imaginatively *inhabitable* by the (admittedly expanded) audience of drama. Although this phenomenon of course springs from the increasing respectability of trade itself (and the profits it was so clearly wielding to many aspects of society), it also suggests a larger comfort in the rehabitation of a rebuilt City. Things had begun to work again.

The "dramatic" move back into the City corresponds to a larger sense of things up-and-running, of trade firmly reestablished and the spaces of trade reformatted and tracked. Defoe's *Complete English Tradesman* (1725), like the *Tour*, articulates in occasionally novelistic ways the topographical, structural, and conceptual shifts in the new phenomena of architecturally self-advertising shops, arguing both the importance of place for trade and the importance of spatial appearance for the function of trade. The rebuilding of the Royal Exchange had signified the larger public emblem of financial recovery; Defoe's work looks more closely at the pragmatics of rehabitation, of properly locating and properly announcing the details of local trade, of presenting and maintaining appearances and actualities of prosperity, of successfully renegotiating the economic spaces of London. As his urban novels re-peopled the streets of London, the vivid characters of the *Tradesman* people the shops and narrativize the abstract spaces of modern trade.

As Lawrence Manley argues for an earlier time which had already incorporated a sense of change and movement, the idea of the City can fluctuate, seem
fluid, produce new identities, new genres, precipitating "a spatial orientation
because the mobilities it creates open for some the possibility of choice at any critical moment in time."[1] In the dramatic presentation of the parks and the narrative
occupation of the shops, literary genres participated in or adapted themselves to
the larger cultural reconstitution of London's public spaces and their implications for private lives. The emphasis on the urban in Restoration and early eighteenth-century literature charts the intersecting boundaries of public and private
interests, commercial and recreational space, domestic trade and domestic life.
This chapter follows the cultural and literary tensions between a need to reconstruct a recognizable public space and the narrative strategies and generic innovations involved.

The (dramatic) refuge of parks

"More than any other form of art, drama depends upon the city," argues
Renaissance critic Anne Barton, for in the city "drama can afford to build a house
of its own."[2] The city supplies the audience that fills and therefore finances the
theater houses, and at the same time furnishes material for the playwrights.
Restoration drama, particularly the comedies,[3] has its own well-known penchant
for London settings, but while its characteristic urban settings and strategies are
deeply embedded in the structures and assumptions of Elizabethan and Jacobean
city comedies, it also develops quite significant differences in approaches to and
emphases on place that spring in part from differences in audience, economy, cultural and political values, and the presence of women on the stage, but *also* in part
from a different sense of the restructuring and rehabiting of public spaces after the
Fire.

What seems curious, however, in a period where nearly every other literary
and technical genre seems preoccupied with the names and shapes of the lost
topography of the City, Restoration comedy notoriously spends much of its time
in historical and topographical settings that in some sense *need* no reinvestment of
meaning. Rather, the plays draw upon and reconfirm the structures and strategies
of Jacobean city comedies in mapping predictable behaviors back into the *unde-
stroyed* parts of London: St. James's Park, the Mall, Rosamond's Pond, Mulberry
Gardens – with relatively few direct references to the City streets themselves.
Moreover, these park spaces are not simply *whole*; they are also more or less *new*.
The Mall in St. James's Park was laid out in 1660 as part of Charles II's landscape
improvements; Spring Gardens, closed during the Commonwealth, was
reopened in the Restoration; Hyde Park, originally a hunting ground and opened

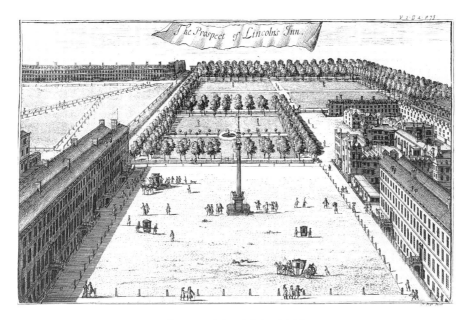

Figure 19 Lincoln's Inn Fields.

to the public at the beginning of the seventeenth century, was enclosed by Charles
II in 1660 to become the parading ground of the nobility and gentry. All the parks
– public or semi-public – formed part of the new court life of the Restoration that
from its relative freshness would not even carry the weight of traditional nomen-
clature or cultural function – the space was experientially clean, available for a
different kind of topographical recovery.

The theaters themselves, like their productions, lay in untouched territories;
both the reopened theaters of the King's and the Duke's Companies first performed in Lincoln's Inn Fields (see Figure 19). The history of the reopening of the
theaters is well-documented, but rather confusing and worth recapping.[4] In 1660
Charles gave Sir William Davenant and Thomas Killigrew exclusive rights to
form their own companies, the Duke's Company and the King's Company
respectively. Killigrew's company began playing at Gibbon's Tennis Court in
Vere Street, Clare Market, until 1663, when they moved to the larger Theatre
Royal in Bridges Street, Covent Garden – roughly midway between the City and
the Court. (It was closed from 1665 to late October 1666 because of the plague
and Fire, and burned down in 1672, rebuilt by Wren in 1674.) The Duke's
Company began playing in Salisbury Court in November 1660, moving to the
new Lincoln's Inn Fields Theatre in June 1661, and then to the Dorset Garden
Theatre, built by Wren, in 1671. (Killigrew's company also used the Dorset
Garden Theatre while the Theatre Royal was being rebuilt.) The two companies

merged in 1682 (the King's Company absorbed by the more financially success-ful Duke's Company), and united they exercised virtual control over public drama until 1695, when the leading actor, Thomas Betterton, formed his own company at Lincoln's Inn Fields.[5]

The reopening of the theaters *in London* in 1660 was of course a public mark of royal approval; the theater was sanctioned as part of urban London life – but a specific part and place of urban life. The most obvious reason that Restoration drama deals so little with City life is the usual one: the Restoration playwright and the Restoration audience were emphatically *not* of the City, but (with some excep-tions) members of the Court, of prominent literary and social circles. The theater area, between the City walls and the court at Westminster, known as the Town, had begun to be developed in the early seventeenth century and by the Restoration had become "the permanent, fashionable center for England's elite" (Manley, *Literature and Culture*, 483).[6] The City housed the Puritans, the moneymakers, the recalcitrant Commonwealths. What had that City to do with cultivated urban court life?

Yet the newspaper and diary accounts show that the loss of the old City in the Fire traumatically affected many more people than those immediately displaced. Pepys's and Evelyn's diaries, the King's concern, the Anglican sermons preached in the West End, the variety of verse, all record a sharp and general sense of loss. So why is there virtually no mention of the Fire and the rebuilding in any of the mainstream Restoration comedies? Shadwell, perhaps because he was a City poet, refers to the Fire and the rebuilding in *The Sullen Lovers* (1668) and *Epsom-Wells* (1673); Sir Positive At-All, who claims expertise in all aspects of life, has out-modelled even John Evelyn in his plans for a new City (see the quotation heading this chapter), and Clodpate, the country squire in *Epsom-Wells*, is "an immoderate hater of *London*" who keeps the second of September a Festival and "swears the Frenchman that was hang'd for burning on't was a Martyr" (1.i.5). But in general the plays are profoundly silent on the subject; the dramatic streets are empty, because everyone's gone to the parks.

Thus both the real and the imagined settings of the "city" comedies are set apart from the strangeness of rebuilding going on in the oldest part of London. Yet in their very distance they may be functioning as part of the literary redrawing of London: these real and imagined settings consistently and insistently reconfirm the topographical security of the places that they do inhabit, and so participated if much less visibly (or by negation) in the restabilizing of urban space. There is almost no shift in the *kinds* of topographical emphases in Restoration drama before and immediately after the Fire, perhaps because what was most deeply objection-able about the earlier city comedy tradition – the forceful presence of the City and its Citizens – was already elided in the first years of reopening, and perhaps because – thus purged of the less welcome elements – the topographical emphasis on the more or less specifically detailed spaces of St. James's, Hyde Park, Spring Garden, and Covent Garden served the larger project of reiterating reliable place names, reaffirming the existence of safe, sure ground.

Yet as Henri Lefebvre argues, "walls, enclosures and facades serve to define both a *scene* (where something takes place) and an *obscene* area to which everything that cannot or may not happen on the scene is relegated: whatever is inadmissible, be it malefic or forbidden, thus has its own hidden space on the near or the far side of a frontier."[7] The emphatic insistence on the parks as the "scene" where virtually *everything* takes place in Restoration city comedies suggests its "obscene" area, in the silenced, excluded, or metaphorized City, that would only gradually reenter the dramatic spaces, more or less when the Citizens entered the gentrified cultural spaces of London life.

In much pre-Fire drama, the city is assumed. Often during the Restoration not only the Elizabethan and Jacobean comedies themselves but also their paradigmatic strategies would be reenacted on the post-Fire stage. The legacy was large: between 1580 and 1642 over one hundred plays with London as their setting were performed and published (Barton, "London Comedy," 160). But these plays had at least one crucial difference from the typical Restoration settings of London: they tended to occupy the City itself, and to allow their audience – a far more socially stratified audience, featuring among others London apprentices – "a vision of themselves that was at once glamourized and anchored firmly in their own urban reality" (Barton, "London Comedy," 176). A gentrified version of this claim obviously applies to the new and primarily elite Restoration audiences as well,[8] but the social topography differs. The early city comedy *featured* the City. Early Restoration comedy, both before and after the Fire, would *run* from the City, partly from the same, and perhaps from different reasons: it was the problematic site of trade, and the problematic site of loss and rebuilding.

But the pre-Fire Restoration plays undoubtedly employed the structures and assumptions of earlier city comedy. The Elizabethan and Jacobean legacy threw into sharp relief the givenness of the London cityscape in several ways. First, London itself could literally be taken for granted – the implied setting needing only the barest topographical referents, and even those carrying more social than cartographic weight. As Douglas Bruster argues, for Jacobean "city comedy" (he disputes the label), "the concept of *place*, once crucial to a social analysis of the plays, is ultimately less important in Renaissance drama than a concern with material life which underlies the themes and structures of the drama."[9] The city comedies of the Jacobean period *assume* topographical identification for their reproduction and critique of social space. In this sense, London can appear either

as the implied home, preknown, or as the implied mystery, distant and uncom-
prehended – in either case, not particularized. Second, in the more topographically detailed plays, the street names have significance for character and plot,
enabling the kind of satisfactory urban sorting that Manley argues worked to keep
pace with the proliferating subdivisions, stratifications, and positions of a burgeoning urban and increasingly capitalist society. Topographical signifiers and
social signifieds work with each other in elastic similes that, like lists and in a way
like streets themselves, could simultaneously separate and link a complicated
collection of urban characters and habits.

Some forms of pre-Fire city plays depend fairly silently on the known. John
Wilson's *The Cheats* (1664) opens with a prologue that promises "[No] frisks
abroad – NO – Our Scene's all at home."[10] The entire play, though set explicitly
in London, has *no* topographical references. Being at home, what need? Richard
Brome's *A Joviall Crew: Or the Merry Beggars* (1641, 1661), reprinted in 1684 and
1686, has a nondescript, generically English country setting with one projected
journey (or "fling") to London to see the Spring Garden and the races in Hyde
Park, but the journey itself is dropped – one of the heroines, Rachel, points out:
"We have seen all already there" (c4v). In John Tatham's *Knavery in All Trades:
Or, The Coffee-House* (1664), the setting is implicitly London, though no specific
place markers are given with the acts; the opening of the third act, for example,
simply recalls the relatively new but vastly popular interior of the coffeehouse:
"The Coffee-House discovered, three or four Tables set forth, on which are placed
small Wax-Lights, Pipes . . . Enter *Mahoone*, trimming up the Tables, his Man
ordering the Fire-pots and *China-Cups*, his Wife in the Barr, his Maid imployed
about the Chocolat" (D3).[11] The street space is not specified but the urban space is
particularized; the street is implicit, the scene is new enough to be rendered, familiar enough to be recognized, and appropriate action anticipated. For one from the
inside, the City is already a given; it doesn't need to be spelled out.

In contrast, some plays work from more specific topographies, more explic-
itly asserting the preknown or knowable quality of London. Jasper Mayne's *The
City Match* (1639, 1659) occupies quite specific territories throughout London
and Westminster, with the assumption that London is or can be a *known* territory.
The play positions characters and actions within a vivid topographical context –
from Moorfields, Pimlico, the Exchange, Gresham, Guildhall, Fish Street, the
Thames, Cheapside, Broad Street, the Strand, to Westminster Hall, Spring
Garden, Park Corner, and out to Ipswich and Shooters Hill. The play's epilogue
defines itself as "what was first a comoedy i'th' street: / Cheapside brought into
verse, no passage strange / To any here that hath been at th' *Exchange*" (Mayne,
City Match, 73). In William Davenant's *The Wits, A Comedie* (1665), the hero
Young Palatine describes himself and the Elder Palatine as "Two that have . . . /

Convers'd so long in the town here, that you know / Each Sign, and Pibble in the Streets" (i.i.13). As Thomas Sprat, Bishop of Rochester and historian of the Royal Society, had declared earlier that year: "the *Streets* and the *Alleys* of *London* stand still and represent themselves always in the same fashion to our eyes, and it is enough to know them perfectly only to travel them often through."[12] London, as stage-setting and as backdrop for living, is ultimately a known, stable quantity – it *stands still*. The plays present the "known" on stage; the spectacle of everyday life.

The most elaborately detailed topographies in pre-Fire city comedies tend to string together packages of similes (though not as elaborate as Ward's in *The London Spy*) that unite place and behavior, expectation and location. In Mayne's *The City Match* place defines character, or character recalls place, through simile: the templar Bright, the merchant Warehouse and the Exchange seamstress Mistress Holland characterize the sleeping Timothy Seathrift "Just like a Salmon / Upon a stall in Fishstreet"; "The like to this fish that we shew, / Was neer in Fishstreet Old or New" (*City Match*, iii.ii.28–30). In Abraham Cowley's *Cutter of Coleman Street* (1663) both place ("London") and time ("1658") are supplied, as well as a series of straightforward place similes, each of which anchors a character or the expectation of a character within a specific topographic identity: Sir Jolly contemplates a marriage-and-money scheme that "were as hard a composition as one's own, as ever was made at *Haberdashers Hall*" (*Cutter of Coleman Street*, i.iv.6). Haberdashers' Hall, burned down in the Fire, was earlier associated with the importation and later production of pins, and thus connected with women's allowance of "pin-money" for pocket expenses.[13] Much of the play depends on the audience knowing that space defines the Puritan – Coleman Street, refuge in 1642 for the five members of Parliament whom Charles I had tried to arrest in the House of Commons (and a prominent street in *Journal of the Plague Year*), was a Puritan stronghold well into the eighteenth century, and in this play gets quite populated with the Congregation of the Lovely (*Cutter of Coleman Street*, iii.xii.39) and the Congregation of the Spotless (iv.v.46). Place – and place-jokes – would be self-evident to the audience of these early city-placed comedies.

The pre-Fire city comedies draw upon the same rich cultural lore of London that informs the other genres of encomia and complaints, a lore accumulated over centuries and apparently as fixed and familiar as London itself. Although the various forms of writing the city testify to its historically steady need to be written, to be visualized, to be conceptually managed, such need would take a different turn after the Fire, and carry a different urgency. Restoration comedy would in some ways rely heavily on the earlier forms, essentially importing a stability of structure, a tradition of expectation, as part of the recreation and presentation *of* stability, structure, traditional expectation. With their varying ways of attending to the streets of London, the post-Fire comedies offer conceptual structures of recovery, tolerance, or escape.

The post-Fire comedies remain strikingly the same as both Jacobean and pre-Fire plays, given the spatial and textual upheaval surrounding them caused by the Fire and rebuilding, but they also register some differences, and in both similarities and differences they suggest a cultural function at least not in conflict with the more overt redefining and reinhabiting of the city in other fields and other genres. Lawrence Manley makes a claim about verse satire in the Restoration that perhaps as aptly applies to Restoration drama: "Urbanity has here entered a narrower range, and fallen prey to a kind of *genrism*. It has become more exclusively the province of a particular class of urbanite and a privileged mode of expression" (*Literature and Culture*, 371). It is often difficult for some of us to keep the plots straight precisely because they seem so much the same – all those Dorimants and Dorilants and Millimants milling through doors in pursuit of witty sex in the same unmarked rooms and the same known parks. The most well-known come from a nest of hundreds, suggesting an insatiable appetite in the audience for the same – as their prologues and epilogues continually point out. From the point of view of my argument, studying the spatial representations and orientations of post-Fire literatures, "the same" includes a remarkably stable and utterly known sense of place: the parks. The places and their meanings, whether vaguely assumed or intimately detailed, *never* lose their spatial and social meanings; they are as constant as the love of wit and the hope of sex, and thus as crucial a part of the cultural and literary discourse.

As with the Elizabethan and Jacobean city comedies and the pre-Fire comedies, the sites and streets of London are assumed in the setting; the plays supply little specific geographic detail, and that detail is generally presumed to be *known*, identifiable, "common" public space. The first generation of post-Fire plays, like the earliest Restoration comedies, differ from those earlier city comedies in that they rarely occupy the City itself, spending most of their time in the Town, presenting different kinds of protagonists and presuming a different kind of audience. The few City references in the plays tend to be linguistic – metaphoric or similic identifications of character with place, while real movement (plot development) almost always takes place in the parks. Both City and park meanings, as public space meanings, are confirmed over and over again; the meaning rarely changes, is rarely challenged. Much as the post-Fire topographies created a new grammar of space, Restoration plays as a genre set up a *vocabulary of place* that reaffirmed the stability and recognitive value of key semiotic and historic public spaces.

In virtually all of the post-Fire comedies of the seventeenth century, London's sites and streets are assumed in the setting; often London itself is not mentioned, though some recognizable public site will enter to confirm the suspicion. The plays supply varying degrees of topographic detail, though generally sparse (the detail tends to increase later in the century with the more visibly emerging financial and social power of the City and with the increasing stabilization of the rebuilding). Shadwell's *The Sullen Lovers* (1668), beyond having the specific reference to the rebuilding in Sir Positive At-All's model of London, has a more specific time than usual for its setting ("SCENE LONDON"): "In the Moneth of *March*, 1667/8." In Edward Revet's *The Town-Shifts* (1671), the scene again is implicitly London, full of garden walls and unnamed streets, with a reference here to Hackney and there to Longacre. Edward Ravenscroft's *The Citizen turn'd Gentleman* (1672) has even less topographical identity: beyond "SCENE: *London*," there are no topographical referents; just country lists and indoor scenes. Nevil Payne's *The Morning Ramble* (1673), identifies Act III in "A Tavern" and Act V with "Scene the Park," but the rest of the acts are not explicitly located.

As the rebuilding progresses, the spatial orientation sometimes gets more detailed. For example, in Shadwell's *The Miser* (1672), though all of the action centers in Covent Garden, the Park, and Mulberry Garden, a few more names are thrown in, such as Bow Street off Covent Garden Market and Gray's Inn Walks. *The Mall: Or the Modish Lovers*, by J.D. (1674),[14] locates itself immediately in St. James's Park "with the adjacent Places" – more specifically, as the play unfolds, in Pel Mal [sic], under some trees on the bank of the Duck Pond, and with a nod towards Wild Street Alley (in Covent Garden, off Great Wild Street, off Drury Lane (see Figure 20). Act I scene ii opens with Perigreen (alias Camila, a Spanish Lady in Disguise) reading the superscription of a letter and matching address to house: "For Mrs. *Woodbee* [privately married to Lovechange] at her house in St. *James's* street, − − London. − − Sure 'tis hereabout." And in Thomas Durfey's *Madam Fickle* (1677), located SCENE COVENT GARDEN, the widow Fickle lodges in Bridges Street (off Russell Street in Covent Garden) and the Epilogue invites the censorious critic to meet him tomorrow in Lamb's Conduit Fields.

Thus from 1667 through the early eighteenth century, most Restoration comedy, and especially the better-known or recently recovered plays for which the above serve as simplified context – such as William Wycherley's *The Country Wife* (1675), Sir George Etherege's *The Man of Mode* (1676), "Ariadne's" *She Ventures and He Wins* (1695), William Congreve's *The Way of the World* (1700), Mary Pix's *The Beau Defeated* (1700), Susanna Centlivre's *The Basset Table* (1705) – situate themselves in the same basic spot of ground, with the same communal signboards delineating the same social space.[15] Any references to the City tend to be *linguistic* identifications of character with place, or predictions about character from place, in metaphor or simile. Almost none of the plays ventures beyond epithet or simile into the City or the eastern suburbs. Sir Positive At-All in Shadwell's *Sullen Lovers* – he who claimed he had built the best model for London – also claims an astonishing sexual prowess – but his sexual conquests seem to lie in linguistic geography (as his architectural ones remain in the hypothetical), covering London northeast to southwest (if rhetoric's a test): "Why there is not a Lady of Pleasure from *Blackwall* to *Tuttle-Fields* that I am not intimately acquainted with" (II.ii.30). In Revet's *The Town-Shifts* (1671), Thomas Faithfull (of the Parish of St. Giles in the Fields) suggests that his friend Lovewell has "been drunk ever since in a Chimney corner, with some Weavers Wife, without *More Gate*; and at last been beaten out by her Husband, and that makes him melancholy" (I.v.11), but again, the spatial reference is metaphoric rather than actual, and there is no real movement in real places *except* Hyde Park and Mulberry Gardens. Harriet in *The Man of Mode* (1676) admits that some women "have an Eye like *Bart'lomew*, big enough for the whole Fair, but I am not of the Number, and you may keep your Ginger-bread" (III.i.34), and Horner in *The Country Wife* (1676), sounding rather like the London Spy, if not quite so crude, says to Pinchwife: "that grave circumspection in marrying a Country Wife, is like refusing a deceitful, pamper'd *Smithfield* Jade, to go and be cheated by a Friend in the Country" (I.i.11); and later: "Thou art as shye of my kindness, as a Lumbard-street Alderman of a Courtiers civility at Lockets" (IV.iii.72). (Of course, Pinchwife *should* be as wary of Horner as an alderman of a courtier in Locket's; located in Charing Cross, it became a meeting place of the gentry after the theater, where like as not it was the Cit as much as the Fop who received the brunt of the satire that evening.) And in *The Way of the World* (1700), when Foible claims that Mirabell called Lady Wishfort "superannuated" and "old frippery," Lady Wishfort sputters furiously, "I hope to see him hung with tatters, like a Long Lane penthouse, or a gibbet-thief," and Foible "loyally" responds: "He! I hope to see him lodge in Ludgate first, and angle into Blackfriars for brass farthings with an old mitten" (Act III). Long Lane was known for secondhand clothes (and a "penthouse," says Johnson, is " shed hanging out aslope from the main wall"), so Lady Wishfort's simile places Mirabell visually at the site of tatters and frippery, while Foible's "wishfort" sends him imaginatively if not actually into the City sites of prisons.

As these examples suggest, the linguistic rather than spatial or actual movement into the City keeps a conceptual distance for the audience; the park space or interior domestic space is visibly present in the scenery or stage hints; any disruptions are sexual and social rather than spatial, or if spatial, springing from a *human* confusion about or misperception of spatial significance – not from any inherently unreliable spatial locators. The *characters* may be roped into unpleasant connections through the linguistic trap (as Pinchwife grimaces: "A Pox on [Horner] and his Simile" [1.i.11]), but the audience appreciates the wit by remaining *outside* its spatial field.

Rather, Restoration plays as a genre set up a vocabulary of place that reaffirmed the stability and recognitive value of key semiotic and historic public spaces: Covent Garden, St. James's, Mulberry Gardens, Spring Garden, Pall Mall, the New Exchange – all places visited by the nobility, the gentry, and those who served them or preyed on them in the dark. All of them repeat and reconfirm that vocabulary, hanging social space on topographic pegs and not only using place to push plot but also using plot to reaffirm known space. Without hoping or even wishing to cover all the territory, I've sketched out the cultural and literary significances of the central park spaces below.

Covent Garden: (See Figure 20.) Covent Garden, once the produce garden for Westminster Abbey ("Convent Garden") was granted to John Russell, first Earl of Bedford, after the dissolution of the monasteries and developed by Francis Russell, the fourth Earl (1627), who built a number of houses designed by Inigo Jones. Strype described it as in "one of the best Parishes in the Cities of *London* or *Westminster*" for "its fine, streight, broad streets, replenished with such good Buildings, and so well inhabited by a Mixture of Nobility, Gentry, and wealthy Tradesmen."[16] The new square consisted of St. Paul's Church (Covent Garden Church) on one side and of tall terraced houses on the other three, all facing an elegant courtyard known as the piazza. The piazza was spacious and open, but surrounded by narrow streets and small dark courts ("*Drury*'s mazy courts and dark abodes," *Trivia*, 111.260). The houses, completed in 1639, at first found wealthy tenants, but shortly afterwards the new squares to the west, such as St. James's, began to draw them away and the district became more mixed, especially when a flower, fruit, and vegetable market in the square began to develop popularity by 1670. By 1730 most of the original houses had given way to more and more shops and coffeehouses, gambling dens, brothels and bath houses.[17] By the time of the Restoration, the fashionable elite were already moving west and the worlds of entertainment and market were moving in. "Covent Garden Church" thus became doubly coded, referring directly to St. Paul's and obliquely to the rendezvous site – actual or metaphoric – for prostitutes or illegitimate lovers: "Gallants, leave your leud whoring, and take wives, / Repent for shame your *Covent-Garden* lives" (Shadwell, *Epsom-Wells*, epilogue).

Covent Garden's priority in the Restoration vocabulary of place is wonderfully asserted in *The Country Wife* in the first conversation between Sparkish, Horner, and Harcourt on the semiotics of signboards, their places signified, and their ultimate meanings:

Figure 20 Covent Garden.

SPARK. Nay then, since you are so brisk, and provoke me, take what
follows; You must know, I was discoursing and raillying with some Ladies
yesterday, and they hapned to talk of the fine new signes in Town.

HORN. Very fine Ladies I believe.

SPARK. Said I, I know where the best new sign is. Where, says one of
the ladies? In *Covent-Garden*, I reply'd. Said another, In what street? In
Russel-street, answer'd I. Lord says another, I'm sure there was ne're a fine

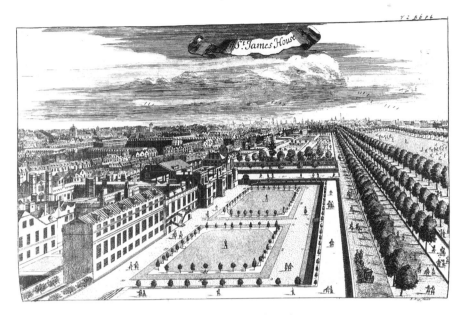

Figure 21 St. James's Park.

new sign there yesterday. Yes, but there was, said I again, and it came out of
France, and has been there a fortnight ... Did you never see Mr. *Horner*; he
lodges in *Russel-street*, and he's a sign of a Man, you know, since he came out
of *France*, heh, hah, he.   *(1.i.9–10)*

Rather more richly than many of the plays, this scene actually seems to entangle
spatial meanings; much like the anxiety expressed in the *Spectator* about the semiotic unreliability of the new signboards (see chapter four), the joke (or the trouble)
here is that Horner signifies different spatial meanings to different "readers" –
emptiness and impotence to Sparkish (with as he thinks the ironic relish that
Covent Garden is itself a sign for sexual promiscuity), but full semiotic realization
to the audience. In that sense, then, Horner *restabilizes* the sign of the place, the sign
of the times. The signs all mean what they claim to mean; neither the place nor the
markers have changed. (At least not yet.)

St. James's Park: (See Figure 21.) The oldest of the royal parks, first made into a
playing and hunting ground by Henry VIII and his heirs and then neglected
during the Commonwealth, St. James's was enlarged and redesigned on French
models by Charles II. In 1660 he basically created the site of Restoration drama:
he built a tree-lined avenue paved with ground cockleshells where he could play
pall mall; he combined small ponds to make a canal "for Ducks and Waterfowl"
(Strype, *Survey*, II.6.77). He left Rosamond's Pond alone (where "the blest Lover

shall for *Venus* take, / And send up Vows from *Rosamonda*'s Lake" [*Rape of the Lock*, V.135–36]); he planted "curious Rows of Lime Trees round about" (Strype, *Survey*, II.6.77), and stocked deer. The Park was a favorite haunt of the King, and thus of the Court, and retained its glamour certainly through the King's death in 1685 (although in the 1670s it was beginning to become "public" in ways not fully appreciated by the fashionable). But through the 1670s it was still known as a haven of the elite. Zechiel in Durfey's *Madam Fickle* (1677) hopes and then regrets that the manly Manley "dares not draw in the *Mail*" (II.i) – unlike Hyde Park, St. James's and its "adjacent parts" are not as typically the sites for violence. For Margery Pinchwife, St. James's Park and Mulberry Gardens are the "best Fields and Woods to walk in" (II.i.15), as Alithea smilingly answers her; and although the places resonate with intrigue for the audience, and at least with sophistication for Alithea, they also almost bear the weight of Margery's naïveté in so far as they *are* and have been for, oh, the length of social memory, the "best" places to walk in – they retain their meaning even in, and partly through, the situational irony.

Hyde Park: St. James's is the oldest, but Hyde Park is the largest of the royal parks, covering 340 acres. Also converted by Henry VIII into a hunting ground, it was opened to the public in the early seventeenth century, used for military defense in the 1640s, and used as a popular pleasure ground again in the 1650s. At the Restoration Charles reclaimed and enclosed it. He made popular the Ring, where the nobility and gentry rode in circles admiring themselves and each other in their sedan-chairs and coaches. The park was known as a duelling ground, and by the 1680s had become the prey of highwaymen. William III strung lights along Rotten Row ("*route du roi*") to discourage them, but with no success. Payne's *The Morning Ramble* (1673) features an invitation to "a duel in Hide-Park" (III.i). But Hyde Park from the 1670s on also seems to be the most socially defining public space. As young Bellair comments to Harriet in *The Man of Mode* as they walk in the Mall: "Most people prefer *High Park* to this place." Harriet responds: "It has the better Reputation I confess; but I abominate the dull diversions there, the formal bows, the Affected smiles, the silly by-Words and Amorous Tweers in passing" (III.iii.46). Though Harriet might not appreciate the formal shape of Hyde Park, she recognizes that for Dorimant "all beyond *High Park*'s a desart to you, and that no gallantry can draw you farther" (V.ii.88). Although in the interests of love (or money) Dorimant admits that it has in fact comprised "the utmost limit of [his] Love" (V.ii.88), and he's willing to try out the sounds of "Kaw, Kaw, Kaw" (as Harriet characterizes the pastoral) for her sake (V.ii.95), still, the powerful social boundaries of this public park space seem to enclose not just the characters but the genre itself. In *The Way of the World* (1700) Millamant insists on breaking *out* of the socially binding public space by hypothetically refusing to go with Mirabell after their marriage "to Hyde Park together the first Sunday in a new chariot to provoke eyes and whispers, and then never to be seen there together again" (IV). The place of the park is a *fixed*, perhaps fixing site, resonant with social meaning and behavioral implication.

As the City itself recovered social and spatial equilibrium, the city comedies gradually get more specific, exploring and setting up newly detailed ways of investigating and investing with social meaning more and more of the City streets themselves. In the continuation of what Manley argues as the distinctive character of the West End in bringing "a gentrifying city together with an urbanizing gentry" (Manley, *Literature and Culture*, 483), the Restoration comedies chart an increasing tolerance for and even sanction of the role of the City characters not simply as conies for the elevated version of elite cony-catchers of town and court, but as admittedly respectable members of plot and audience. Manley notes that "the restored order that was promised [by the Restoration], and to some extent the one that was eventually and fitfully delivered, had more in common with the revolutionary movement toward expansion, diversity, progress, and increase than with the ancient regime that had preceded it" (Manley, *Literature and Culture*, 566). As the audience changed, so the public sites of drama and their dramatic representations began to shift in their social and topographic meaning, at least to some extent. In a sense, the parks got darker and the City got lighter. On the one hand, the public spaces of the parks became more and more "public" – that is, open to and inhabited by a wider swath of classes, not just the highest and lowest. The spaces of the parks thus became potential spaces of cultural anxiety first for the upper classes and later for the middle classes, no longer supplying the fixed social ground counterpointed against the shifting of the City.[18] On the other hand, the City and its occupants were becoming richer, more powerful, more upwardly mobile, and more frequent theater-goers. Drama shifted from mocking the Cits to essentially inviting them in.

In Wycherley's *The Gentleman Dancing-Master* (1673), the prologue is addressed to the City, "newly after the Removal of the Duke's Company from *Lincoln's-Inn-Fields* to their new Theatre, near *Salisbury-Court*." Salisbury Court, off Fleet Street, was indeed closer to the City than the theaters in Lincoln's Inn Fields or Covent Garden – near Bridewell and the Fleet, near St. Paul's, midway between the City and the Inns of Court. (See Figure 14.) Wycherley's prologue explains:

> Our Author (like us) finding 'twould scarce do,
> At t'other end o'th'Town, is come to you . . .

Where needy Wit, or Critick dare not come,
Lest Neighbour i' the Cloak, with looks so grum,
Shou'd prove a *Dunne* . . .
And still we know [you] are ready to ingage
Against the flouting, ticking Gentry who
Citizen, Player, Poet, wou'd undo,
The Poet, no; unless by commendation;
For on the Change, Wits have no reputation;
And rather than be branded for a Wit,
He with you, able men, wou'd credit get.

The prologue, however acidly, charts a shift in social, literary, and spatial territory,
seeing a market change with a change in audience, a change in expectations, a
change in critical behavior, and a change in dramatic supply to this new set of
demands.

The plays begin to stock a different set of characters and in more specific City
locations. In *The Gentleman Dancing-Master*, the heroines (or rather, the heroine
Hippolita and her aging maid Prue) incorporate the Town and the Suburbs in
their duet of rambling desires: Hippolita mourns being confined from plays, the
Park, Mulberry Gardens, Spring Garden, church itself, while Prue echoes with
"*Ponchinello* or Paradise," Tottenham Court or Islington, a pint of wine at the
Prince in the Sun, the Organs and Tongs at the Gun in Moorfields, and, yes, like
Hippolita, a Man (1.i.1–2). All the usual Restoration watering holes show up
(Covent Garden, the Inns of Court, St. James's), but so with equal vivacity do
mercers' shops, Mustard Alley, Ludgate, Lombard Street, and the very clothes of
the City men sitting in the Pit: because the sober citizens in their "Velvet Jumps,
Gold Chains, and grave Fur Gowns" will not "break our Windows," "We there-
fore, and our Poet, do submit / To all the Chamlet Cloaks now i' the Pit"
(Epilogue). Payne's *The Morning Ramble* (1673) opens with Merry embedded in
some corner of the city where "the Smiths, Shoo-makers, Pewterers, and Sadlers
in our street have no measure to call up their Prentices by, but the noise of my
Fiddles playing me to my Lodgings" (1.i.6) – a literary example of what M. J.
Power has described as "a random mix of large and small dwellings . . . where
occupations and rich and poor are thoroughly jumbled."[19] In Edward
Ravenscroft's *The London Cuckolds* (1683) – published in the City – the "SCENE
LONDON" is exactly the City of London, centering around the Change (in this
case the Royal Exchange), Garraway's Coffee House, marriage in the Minories,
Bartholomew babies, business in Lombard Street, a "Blockheaded City
Attorney," and a "dull City husband, as insipid and ill relisht as a *Guildhall* dish on
a Lord Mayor's day." Although the focus on the citizens of London is not exactly
flattering (the epilogue comments: "A vision like to that methinks i'th'Pit / I see,

and every *Cuckold* is a Cit" while "There's not one *Cuckold* amongst all the Tory's"), the sheer inclusion of so many different characters in their detailed habitations marks a change in cultural territory and literary attention. The City was beginning to resist being imaginatively ignored and elided.

Not only does the City increasingly appear, it appears in increasingly better lights. Sir Richard Plainman ("Formerly a Citizen, but now lives in *Covent-Garden*"), in Centlivre's *The Basset-Table* (1706), comes out not too badly or ridiculously in his position as father to Valeria and uncle to Lady Reveller. Mrs. Rich, a "Fantastick City Widow" in Mary Pix's *The Beau Defeated* (1700), is an unsavoury character precisely *because* she abandons her past, rejecting the City sources of her (husband's) wealth as she finds her gaudy finery slighted by a duchess: "I shall dye. To disrespect me in the open street! . . . I'll absolutely break all commerce with those little *Cits*" (I.i.1–2). Her maid contemptuously explains to Lady Landsworth: "though my Mistress is fled to *Covent Garden*, she is as much despis'd by the real Quality, as she is cajol'd by the Pretenders to it" (I.i.4). Her well-drawn, sensible brother-in-law chastises: "Still abusing the City, 'tis a shame, Mrs. Rich, a burning shame. I tell thee, thou proud vain thing, thou gilt Ginger-Bread; the City is famous for Men substantial in their Persons, their Purses, their Credits, when your Limberham'd, this end of the Town *Beaux*, are the half product of Nature, wretchedly piec'd up by Art, weak in their Bodies, their Brains, their everything" (II.i.14). And in the context of this play, he turns out to be right.

The spaces of the dramatic city shift in meaning and possibility. As more and more servants and apprentices attended the theater, more plays were directed to them, and more attention was paid to the perceived shifts in social boundaries. The prologue to *The Basset-Table* is addressed to the "Brethren of the Upper Tire" and spoken by the character of Buckle, who, along with the maidservant Alpiew, orchestrates much of the plot subtleties in the play:

> Therefore, dear Brethren, (since I am one of you)
> Whether adorn'd in Grey, Green, Brown, or Blue,
> This Day stand all by me, as I will fall by you . . .
> But may your Plenteous Vails come flowing in,
> Give you a lucky Hit, and make you Gentlemen;
> And thus preferr'd, ne'er fear the World's Reproaches,
> But shake your Elbows with my Lord, and keep your Coaches.

Freeman the vintner and his wife Urania in *She Ventures and He Wins* are as fully rounded characters as seventeenth-century comedy ever cares to produce, displaying wit, judgment, and integrity in their mediations between the gentry and their well-concerted and well-justified "revenge" against the conceited, amorous, stupid Squire Wouldbe. Gradually, the City re-enters the genre of drama after a historical life as absent insult, present insult, and, if with some ambivalence, occasionally with respect.

And as the representations of the City changed, so did those of the parks. After Charles II's death in 1685, the public parks in general slipped into what some perceived as a steady social decline. St. James's was no longer the sole province of sovereign and court, and by Queen Anne's time it would become a notorious site for prostitutes and Mohocks. And Covent Garden had long since begun its slide into social alleyways. The change in the parks – or the widening change in the perception of the parks – signalled a change in the dramatic representation of who inhabited the parks, and *how*. As the parks shifted in their topographical meanings, they became sites for changing identities. In Ariadne's *She Ventures and He Wins* (1695), for example, Dowdy, now Squire Wouldbe's wife (though he, as the *Dramatis Personae* announces, is of "poor extraction"), and her mother Beldam, a pawnbroker, enter St. James's Park in their finest frippery; Beldam puzzles how "the Misses" manage not to sweat under their masks, and Dowdy boasts, "Oh, I have learnt to wear one since I was a Gentlewoman" (IV.v.32). Both women bristle at being mistaken for "this end of the town folks" (IV.v.33). On the other hand, St. James's allows Charlot and Juliana to cross gender more successfully than Dowdy and Beldam cross class: the play opens with the wealthy, independent heroines dressed in men's clothes as Charlot plans to find a husband; Act I scene iii opens in St. James's Park with Lovewell crossing the stage, "*Charlot* and *Juliana* following him in Mens Cloaths." They test his mettle as men, and Charlot proposes; he accepts in a later scene in the park when she reveals her face. They have a wedding breakfast at "the Blew Posts in the Haymarket" (III.v.24), and then the rest of the main plot revolves around Charlot disidentifying herself, pretending to jilt Lovewell and playing on his preconceptions of the park: "Death, Hell, and Furies! What can this mean! Am I thus Jilted at last by some lewd Woman! O Sot! that I could think one of *Charlot*'s Birth and Fortune wou'd marry at that wild Rate. She only took up that Name to gull the easy Coxcomb, unthinking Fool" (III.v.26). Charlot even has him arrested and tempts him with a false Charlot, but he remains true to the person – whoever, whatever she was – whom he met and married in the park. St. James's allows both Charlots to exist, and both to be successful. In Centlivre's *The Busybody* (1709), the generic "Park" is the site for female possibility, the open space in the city where the women can enter veiled and escape precisely through its customs. Miranda, to escape unmasking herself to Sir George, tells him: "I have it – Sir George, 'tis fit you should allow something; if you'll excuse my face, and turn your back (if you look upon me, I shall sink, even masked as I am) I will confess why I have engaged you so often, who I am, and where I live." Sir George agrees, and she slips away behind his back (I.i). Isabinda, the daughter of Sir Jealous Traffic who prefers the confining customs of the Spanish, lives in a house that fortunately for her, in terms of plot and concept, opens on the Park. In general, the parks function both as fixed spaces for social and sexual intrigue – solid ground to play around on – and later as changing sites for changing opportunities.

It seems suggestive, if wildly speculative, that the "narrow genrism" marked by Manley of formal verse satire has pretty much the same lifespan of a "narrow genrism" – or rather, fixed form – of Restoration comedy, that is, roughly from the decades of rebuilding to a period of spatial stability, as if the boundaries of genre itself have something to do with the stability of a culture in a period of decentering and recentering. Park space becomes a different kind of public space, with a different meaning in its traditional dramatic representations; genre confirms public space at a time when all spatial signifiers were shifting rapidly – those in the peripheral vision of the Town the most elusive and threatening, those in immediate focus the most available for definitive confirmation. Thus during the first decades of the Restoration and rebuilding, the settings of the plays *sort* rather than confuse or blur boundaries, restoring a sense of place through a vocabulary of spatial reiteration and a reiteration of visual continuity.

"Peculiar streets, and proper places": the city in shops

The sites of trade, both large and small, are in some ways the Lefebvrean "obscene" of the dramatic habitation of the parks – the spaces that early Restoration drama kept firmly *inside* the City walls. But by the time that the City was climbing over the walls and into the theaters and parks, by the time that the citizens and apprentices not only appeared but sometimes appeared well *inside* as well as *at* the plays, other early eighteenth-century writers such as Addison and Defoe began to pay more detailed literary attention to those people and their places. The nation with "the spirit of shopkeepers," as Swift contemptuously described it,[20] in a sense developed *out of* the restoration of its shops. The increase in domestic and foreign trade both supported and was nourished by the expansion and prosperity of London in the decades of rebuilding. The spaces of London increasingly became spaces of commerce, part of Lefebvre's "production of abstract space," and as Colin Nicholson and David Trotter argue, the sites of new forms of property and new possibilities for identity.[21] As these spaces "materialized," they paradoxically became abstractions; their success depended simultaneously on movement and regulation, elasticity and containment, expansion and control. The redrawn streets housed *new* "peculiarities," as Defoe called them; identifying place meant at once recognizing and defining what was proper to it.

The shops and markets of London assumed new interest and attracted conscious attention after the Fire and in the exigencies of rebuilding. They are in some ways peculiar places, sites of overlap between public and private worlds, where private needs are publicly met, or public business is privately transacted. The markets sold first to "housekeepers," and only later in the market day to retailers; shops traditionally combined domestic and commercial spaces within one struc‐ ture. The decades of rebuilding witnessed the redefinition of those spaces; the early eighteenth century witnessed their refragmentation. The complex, sophisti‐ cated, abstract shifts in the contours and significance of local commercial spaces required their own form of cartographic recovery and topographic discovery. In the 1670s, the surveyor and City Measurer William Leybourn drew plans for the permanent sites of the new City markets, plans which, like the new maps of the City, graft the new onto the known and make visible the concepts and boundaries of changed public places. By the 1720s, Defoe, always a most attentive observer of the patterns of commerce, was both anxious and experienced enough to produce a new kind of manual that would enable the tradesman (necessarily a customer and consumer as well) to chart and occupy the oddly private public spaces of shop and warehouse.

Before the Fire, the main public or common markets, where country people would bring meat, poultry, dairy goods, fruits, and vegetables to sell in the City, had all been held in the main streets – Leadenhall Street, Gracechurch Street, in Cheapside, and off Newgate Street.[22] The goldsmiths in Cheapside were partic‐ ularly vocal about the encroaching stalls, the smells, the noise, and the obstruction of foot and wheeled traffic. The markets had always been regulated (with more or less effectiveness) by the City authorities, who were particularly charged with pre‐ serving territorial boundaries: the country people were not authorized to sell outside the market and market hours, while the freemen, who had the right to trade from shops, were not supposed to encroach into the market space. After the Fire, which swept away markets and shops alike, the City pushed to clarify and strengthen the spatial and commercial boundaries. The markets were taken off the streets and given permanent public spaces of their own; by August 1677 Leybourn was paid £20 "towards his paines in plotting the severall publique marketts of this City" (*Orders of the Markets Committee 1676–77*; quoted in Masters, Introduction, *Public Markets*, 11). His plans were to record the precise dimensions of every fixed stall in order to gauge respective rents from the farmers (see Figure 22).[23] The table of reference on the verso of the plan shows that the markets recreated the old concepts in new places and oriented the new to the known, marking, for example, the "Gate way out Leadenhall Street," "Prices Paved Alley," "Collerman behind," "New Passage to Prices Buildings," "Passage to Spread Eagle Inn," "Against Vandeputts Buildings," "Place for Higlers." As with homeowners and tenants – the occupants of private places –

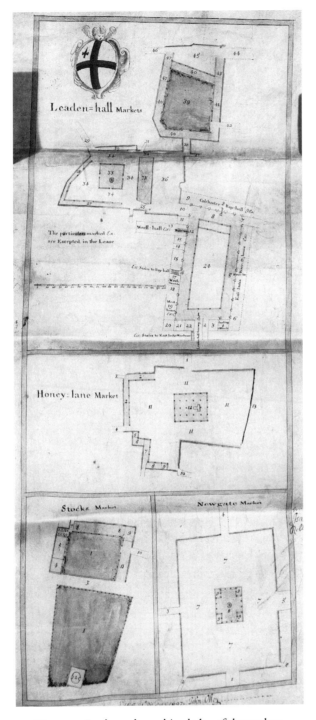

Figure 22 Leybourn's combined plan of the markets.

the owners of stalls and shops, and purchasers from stalls and shops – necessarily became communally aware of reconfigured spaces and the dimensions of their boundaries (see Figure 23).

The structures of wider world trade also acquired new literal and literary prominence after the Fire. The royal reopenings of the City at the Restoration, arranged by Thomas Jordan, made the Royal Exchange a processional focal point; the rebuilt Exchange would occupy a vivid imaginative place in the works of Restoration and Augustan writers (see Figure 24). In Addison's well-known encomium, for example, he emphasizes its prominent position as a structure that institutionalizes nationality, that houses England's commercially public space, and moreover, offers the private citizen a choice of public identities:

> There is no Place in the Town which I so much love to frequent as the *Royal-Exchange*. It gives me a secret Satisfaction, and, in some measure, gratifies my Vanity, as I am an *Englishman*, to see so rich an Assembly of Country-men and Foreigners consulting together upon the private Business of Mankind, and making this Metropolis a kind of *Emporium* for the whole earth . . . Sometimes I am justled among a Body of *Armenians*: Sometimes I am lost in a Crowd of *Jews*; and sometimes make one in a Groupe of *Dutch-men*. I am a *Dane, Swede*, or *French-Man* at different times, or rather fancy my self like the old philosopher, who upon being asked what Country-man he was, replied, that he was a Citizen of the World.   *(Spectator 69, May 19, 1711)*

The real power of the Exchange is not just its commercial trade but what that trade produces: the "uncertainty and flux" generated by new forms of property that "radically [revised the] sense of identity and possibility" (Nicholson, *Writing and the Rise of Finance*, 5). The New Exchange, built on the Strand in 1608–9, competed with the Royal Exchange after the Fire on both commercial grounds and literary sites, are known for its sumptuous shops – particularly of mercers and drapers – that catered for the nobility and gentry, is part of Restoration drama's vocabulary of place. Margery Pinchwife in *The Country Wife* (1675) learns from Alithea that the New Exchange is the best place for "close walks" (II.i.15), and the play devotes an entire seduction scene there, as Margery stands enchanted with its "power of brave Signs" (the Bull's-Head, the Ram's-Head, and the Stag's-Head); Pinchwife snarls: "Nay, if every Husbands proper sign here were visible, they wou'd be all alike . . . all Bulls, Stags, and Ram's heads" (III.ii.41). The Royal Exchange and the New Exchange become literary sites for social and identity exchange.

But the fixed markets, the rebuilt shops, the larger structures of commercial exchange, were emphatically *not* markers of fixed territory. England's commercial spaces were defining themselves as much by the abstraction of public credit,

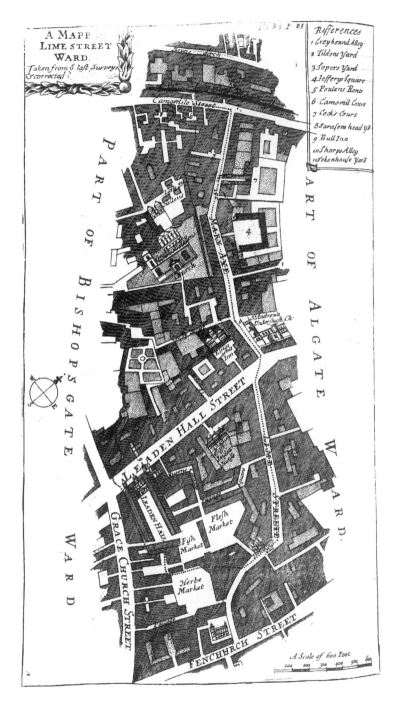

Figure 23   The market spaces.

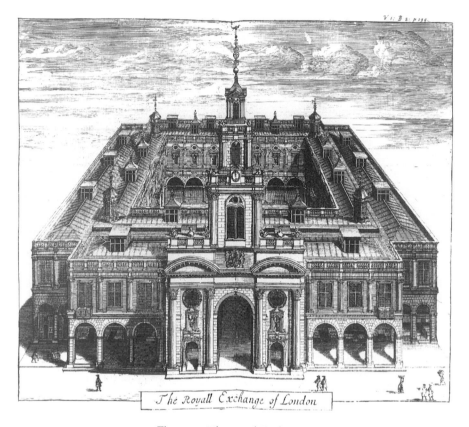

Figure 24 The Royal Exchange.

which as Defoe explains has "no *Whereness*, or *Whenness*, *Scite*, or *Habit*,"[24] as by the rebuilt structures themselves, marked out equally by the intersections of *pace* and *place*. Thus it was an oddly invisible territory, a system of boundaries that overlay the now rebuilt and re-known topographical streets and architectural structures to produce a new generation of *terra incognita* that would require new strategies of navigation and habitation. Defoe supplied them.

After five years of a fictional occupation of urban spaces, Defoe turned back to didactic narrative structures to explore the relationship between physical structures and cultural spaces. Defoe is known for employing the strategies and formulas of history for his fictions;[25] but he also uses novelistic strategies to equal effect in his instructional, descriptive, analytic, and didactic explorations of the buildings and spaces and structures of the nation. *The Complete English Tradesman* (1725) is a text that blends economic theory with local example, general instruction with vivid illustration. Its dominant surface concern is the financial success of the individual tradesman.[26] But that success, Defoe tries to show, is predicated on a delicate and complex integration of physical structures, topographical implications, and psychological patterns. That is, the *Tradesman* is just as keenly interested in the relationship between the particular parts of a trade economy and daily life as it is in individual success: between the houses, the streets, and the shops, and the larger, more abstract whole of trade networks and national credit. The *Tradesman*, like the *Tour* (discussed in chapter three), explores ways both to fix and traverse the shifting patterns of modern spaces. The structure of the text, like the structures *in* the text, offers the reader instructions on how to combine, control, and inhabit the apparently competing worlds of mercantile success and social aspirations.

The *Tradesman* outlines one strategy for managing commercial urban space while it employs another. It identifies boundaries, or rather, categories of boundaries, and marks their interrelations: the *place* of the shop in the City, its *appearance*, and its *contents*, all have their correlatives in the tradesman himself, who learns how to occupy his shop by regulating his time, his duties (religious, commercial, and social) and their places (the closet, the counter, and not-the-theater), the boundaries of his domestic and business spheres, and most importantly, *himself* and his behavior within each category. The *Tradesman* enforces its lessons with narrativized examples; Defoe stocks his scenarios with vivid characters who make the world of the shop and its mysteries imaginable, recognizable, knowable. And what these strategies achieve, or claim to achieve, is "completeness" – a comprehensive coordination of parts with wholes (goods and shop, shop and street, street and district, district and City, City and nation), of reciprocal relations between spaces and structures (gendered and social, domestic and commercial, private and public) – a grasp of the social and psychological production of commercial space and the effect of spatiality on physical and psychological space.

The tradesman must understand *place*. He must learn to sort his business within the patterns of the city, to negotiate the significance of the particular configurations of London streets and public markers. Defoe had explored the often rapidly shifting boundaries of London (as well as of towns and cities all over Britain) in the *Tour*; he is here more locally concerned to impress upon the new tradesman (the inhabiter of a new kind of visible and self-conscious commercial space) the simultaneous existence of fixed boundaries and moving lines. Each area of the City had resettled or resorted itself in the rebuilding into various new or revived commercial categories, the boundaries of which were not necessarily self-evident; as the street names had become less denotative, their signs requiring definition, so *location* more generally was become *interpretive* because of its fluctuation:

> It is true, we have seen a kind of fate attend the very streets and rows where
> such trades have been gather'd together; and a street famous some years ago,

shall, in a few years after, be quite forsaken; as *Pater-noster-row* for mercers, *St. Paul's* church yard for woollen-drapers, both the *Eastcheaps* for butchers; and now you see hardly any of those trades left in those places. *(CET* 1:99–100)

Defoe reconstructs and adapts for a changed London a Stowean vocabulary as well as topography of commercial place:

> In most towns, but particularly in the city of *London*, there are places as it were appropriated to particular trades, and where the trades which are plac'd there succeed very well, but would do very ill any where else . . . as the orange-merchants and wet-salters about *Billingsgate*, and in *Thames-street*; the costermongers at the *Three Cranes*; the wholesale cheesemongers in *Thames-street*; the mercers and drapers in the high streets, such as *Cheapside, Ludgate-street, Cornhill, Round-court*, and *Gracechurch-street*, &c . . . Many trades have their peculiar streets, and proper places. *(CET* 1:98–99)

Defoe points out, in language that suggests a self-evident character of commercial districts, but which is actually obvious only after it has been learned: "Pray what would a bookseller make of his business at *Billingsgate*, or a mercer in *Tower-street* . . . ?" *(CET* 1:99). The streets and spaces of London imply the boundaries of success or failure:

> [A] particular trade is not only proper for such or such a part of the town, but a particular sortment of goods, even in the same way, suits one part of the town, or one town and not another; as he that sets up in the *Strand*, or near the *Exchange*, is likely to sell more rich silks, more fine hollands, more fine broadcloths . . . than one of the same trade, setting up in the skirts of the town, or at *Ratcliff*, or *Wapping*, or *Redriff*. *(CET* 1:101)

The shopkeeper orchestrates the relation between place, structure, and custom: "he must learn, as well as he can, how to furnish his shop suitable to the place he is to trade in, and to sort his goods to the demand which he is like to have there" *(CET* 1:102). Making a mistake in location is a terrible misstep: "When a shop is ill chosen, the tradesman starves, he is out of the way, and business will not follow him that runs away from it" *(CET* 1:99). Commerce moves, but it does not follow. The tradesman must catch up with the pace of his City. The concrete spaces of the streets and structures of shops are fixed in the sense that they provide the *conduits* for trade; the canny tradesman must comprehend and fix for himself the patterns of the abstract, shifting spaces of trade itself.[27]

The narrative strategy in the *Tradesman* emphasizes the importance of respectable bounds for the individually characterized tradesman and functions as a sort of counterpoint to the fictionalized point of view in Defoe's urban novels. The successful tradesman must be at least as aware of the implications of place as the successful thief. In *Moll Flanders*, the significance of commercial place is central to Moll's success. When Moll glides into the silversmith's shop in Foster Lane (which Strype identifies as "a place of good resort for Silver Smiths, who forge and work Plate for the Goldsmiths, who sell it"),[28] she is charged (justly) by a neighboring goldsmith with attempting to steal the "loose Plate [that] lay in the Window." She resists her accuser, claiming: "I came in to buy half a Dozen of silver Spoons, and to my good Fortune, it was a Silver-smith's that sold Plate, as well as work'd Plate for other Shops" (*MF* 269–70). Knowing the lay of the mer-cantile land allows for all sorts of sophisticated forms of exchange. In the *Tradesman* as well as in his urban novels, Defoe supplies his contemporary readers as well as his fictional characters with the narrative maps to help them negotiate the territories of urban life.

The "complete" tradesman must also have a thorough knowledge of "place" in terms of the provenance and patterns of his stock: "where produc'd, or where made, and how to come at them, or deal in them, at the first hand, to his best advantage" (*CET* 1:5–6). The tradesman's commercial vision must be both wide-angled and well-focused, with a panoramic sense of source and product, or distant cause and local effect, of places of origin and routes of distribution – "superimposing [an] articulated space on the randomness of geography" (Trotter, *Circulation*, 5). That is, the abstract networks of trade will format and make intelligible (hence profitably marketable) the specific goods that will occupy (however briefly) the shelves of the shop.

With almost novelistic attention to interior detail, the *Tradesman* insists that the appearance of the shop must conform to its location, and its goods must conform to both. Letter XIX, "Of Fine Shops, and Fine Shews," is wholly devoted to ana-lyzing the exteriors and interiors of shops. Defoe distinguishes between "furnish-ing" a shop (supplying it with goods) and "fitting up" a shop, or furbishing its appearance "in painting and gilding, fine shelves, shutters, boxes, glass-doors, sashes, and the like" (*CET* 1:312). In some ways, the concrete space of any par-ticular over-furnished shop – the details of its appearance and the claims implicit in that appearance – seems for Defoe to detach itself from the abstract space of its *true* interior, the solid credit behind its stock. He draws attention to the compli-cated tension between exterior and interior, appearance and content, and to the finely drawn line between architectural transparency and commercial hypocrisy in the slippery relations of commerce.

The appearance of the shop changed dramatically in the early eighteenth century in ways that one would expect Defoe to applaud. While the shop did not, according to Summerson, exactly achieve "full architectural consciousness" until the middle of the century, improvements in the technology of glass manufacture replaced its small-paned mullioned casement windows with the larger-paned and more literally transparent sash-windows.[29] (Defoe had already approved of the new sash-windowed modernity of Burghley House in the *Tour*.) The concept of the show-window, with a variety of goods artistically displayed, should have pleased the Defoe whose character H.F. fretted so insistently over the essentially meaningless signifiers of the marked doors during the plague. And indeed, Defoe concedes, "there is much to be said for setting goods out to the best advantage too; for in some goods, if they are not well-dress'd, well press'd and pack'd, the goods are not really shew'd in a true light" (*CET* 1:301). And the tradesman who "does not make a good shew . . . comes abroad like a mean ordinary fellow, and no body of fashion comes to his shop; the customers are drawn away by the pictures and painted shelves" (*CET* 1:313). But a good exterior is only a necessary and not a sufficient condition for success. Defoe's ultimate advice on the appearance of the shop is that it achieve architectural self-declaration, a public transparency: "Let the shop be decent and handsome, spacious as the place will allow, and let something like the face of a master be always to be seen in it; . . . this takes as much with the wiser observers of such things, as any other appearance can do" (*CET* 1:316). The shop that keeps the promise of its design will "preserve" the customer, and through the customer, the trade itself, within its properly located, identified, and organized spaces.

The boundaries of habitation are a key concept in the *Tradesman*. The success or failure of personal as well as commercial life depends on finding, understanding, and personally regulating the dangerously shifting boundaries of modern space. The greatest threat the modern tradesman faces is the constant temptation to extend his boundaries, to conflate in the wrong way the social and commercial world, the private and public habitations of new space. After emphasizing the tradesman's need for the widest possible conceptual (commercial) knowledge, the text begins very firmly to define and constrict areas of behavior within well-bounded structures and territories. The tradesman must learn first to fit his social and intellectual life into the conceptual sphere of his shop, and then to confine himself physically and psychologically within those self-constructed bounds:

> He that will be a tradesman should confine himself within his own sphere: never was the gazette so full of the advertisements of commissions of bankrupts as since our shopkeepers are so much engaged in parties, form'd into clubs to hear news, and read journals and politicks; in short, when tradesmen turn statesmen, they should either shut up their shops, or hire somebody else to look after them.   (*CET* 1:47)

Defoe worries about the rapid dissolution of social as well as commercial boundaries. He nervously watches tradesmen flocking recklessly out of their shops and into coffeehouses, taverns, and theaters, dissipating their attentions and ultimately their profits within a social as well as spatial confusion: "This is an age of gallantry and gaiety, and never was the city transpos'd to the court as it is now: the play-houses and balls are now filled with citizens and young tradesmen, instead of gentlemen and families of distinction" (*CET* 1:67). Defoe is watching from the other side of the Town as the Cits begin to inhabit the benches in the theater and the roles in the plays. The young ("modern") tradesmen, wearing swords and swordknots, infest social spheres above their own, inhabiting new public spaces and confusing their boundaries, displacing the "proper" occupants of theaters and depleting the spaces (and in the long run the *sources*) of their own prosperity. In order to succeed at his trade and to sustain his success, the tradesman should rather confine himself within the boundaries of his trade – commercially, socially, and structurally: "[T]he tradesman's proper business is in his shop or warehouse, and among his own class or rank of people; there he sees how other men go on, and there he learns how to go on himself . . . there he hears all trading news, as for state news and politicks, 'tis none of his business" (*CET* 1:49). Without him, the shop has no "body," no "face," no "authority"; it lies open and empty and meaningless without the signifying presence of the owner. The empty shop lies open to quite the wrong sort of customer – Moll Flanders, for example, sees in that silversmith's shop in Foster Lane "a tempting Bait indeed, and not to be resisted by one of my Occupation; for the Shop had no Body in it, as I could see, and a great deal of loose Plate lay in the Window" (*MF* 269). The shop depends on its keeper for definition as well as for existence.

Fully as risky as collapsing or abandoning the proper physical and social spheres of shop and warehouse is confusing the different spheres and spaces of daily life. "The duties of life," says the author, "must not interfere with one another, must not jostle one another out of place, or so break in as to be prejudiced to one another" (*CET* 1:61; E 8r).[30] He offers two very detailed, novelistic illustra-tions of the consequences of jostled duties and misplaced attentions:

> When the tradesman well-inclin'd rises early in the morning and is mov'd . . .
> to pay his morning vows to [his Maker] either in his closet, or at the church
> where he hears the six o'clock bell ring to call his neighbours to the same duty;
> then the secret hint comes cross his happy intention, that he must go to such or
> such a place, that he may be back time enough for such other business as has
> been appointed over night, and both perhaps may be lawful and necessary; so
> his diligence oppresses his religion, and away he runs to do his business, and
> neglects his morning sacrifice to his Maker.   (*CET* 1:64; E 8v)

On the other hand, he is at financial risk if, in his shop or his compting house, "the same deceiver presses him earnestly to go to his closet . . . to prayers" and he may find that he "[says] his prayers so long and so unseasonably 'till he is undone" (*CET* 1:65; F11). The duties of the private must never be confused or conflated with the duties of the public; public space must never be misconverted into private space, and public spaces themselves must never be confused. The shop must define itself as a *place of business*. To misoccupy the spaces of shop and church is as self-destructive as avoiding them. The complete tradesman must learn to sort and emplace his responsibilities.

One mistaken notion of separate boundaries, however, and one of the more unfortunate consequences of the new economic and urban patterns for Defoe, is that the tradesman has begun to shut out his wife from the shop, and have her "sit above in the parlour, and receive visits, and drink tea, and entertain her neighbours, or take a coach and go abroad" (*CET* 1:355). Custom, he concedes, has made it seem "ridiculous for the women to appear in [certain kinds of] shops" (although he challenges the verdict of mere custom), yet the situation has got out of hand, and most merchants seem uneasy permitting their wives in their shops (*CET* 1:355). A wife so separated from the shop means not only a division of profits but a division of labor and, in time of need, no sympathetic reinforcement. Such a fracturing of space into gendered territory limits the actions and the possibilities for both husband and wife. Defoe offers several arguments for the wife's or widow's place in business as part of the organic unity of English trade.[31]

Though the boundaries that the tradesman must recognize and negotiate seem fairly firmly prescriptive, they are in fact (as with all Defoean boundaries in the end) rather fluid and tricky. For one thing, it is not always so easy to sort out public and private life when at this time the public and private space of the tradesman were closely conflated. The tradesman's house was typically the floor above his shop; the whole family tended to be involved in the business. This could work to the tradesman's advantage on those rainy days when "To Shops in Crouds the daggled Females fly, / Pretend to cheapen Goods, but nothing buy" (Swift, "Description of a City Shower," lines 33–34). Since to be a "complete tradesman" is to be "a perfect *complete hypocrite*" (*CET* 1:114), it helps to be able to leap upstairs and vent like "a man chain'd down in *Bedlam*" or a "*Lybean* lion" (*CET* 1:115), although this image, as critics have noted, is uncomfortably extreme.[32] The point seems to be to emphasize the separation of public and private, commercial and domestic spheres, within the close confines of a particular shop-structure, articulating the possibilities of self-control by shoving the irate tradesman imaginatively upstairs. The same structure can house different identities, and while Defoe never anywhere advocates child- or wife-abuse, he here effectively makes the point that the tradesman can inhabit different identities in different spaces if the rules of successful commerce require it—like his fictional urban characters, the tradesman can *act a part*. Knowing the boundaries of domestic and commercial space, particularly within small specific locations, enables the tradesman to become as fluid, as well as regulated, as the commercial territories he is trying to navigate.

The other difficulty with charting these boundaries is Defoe's own consistent ambivalence about the upwardly mobile social possibilities for the tradesman:

> How are the antient families worn out by time and family misfortunes, and the estates possess'd by a new race of tradesmen, grown up not in families of gentry, and establish'd by the immense wealth, gain'd, as I may say, behind the counter; that is, in the shop, the warehouse, and the compting house? . . . A *Shoemaker* in *London* shall keep a better house, spend more money, cloath his family better, and yet grow rich too: It is evident where the difference lies, an *Estate's a pond*, but a *Trade's a spring*. (*CET* 1:373–75)

Defoe seems here eager to blend the traditionally separated spheres of tradesmen and gentry, spheres that in the beginning of the text he had been so anxious to keep cleanly apart, uneasy over the sight of so many shopkeepers abandoning their shop for the theater, and flinging off the respectable apron for the fashionable sword. Anticipating the interests of the *gentleman*, he dwells rather triumphantly (and autobiographically, as Paula Backscheider notes and Michael Shinagel elaborates)[33] on the number of tradesmen invading the Herald's Office to locate or purchase coats of arms for their coaches, their plate, their furniture, and "the pediments of their new houses" (*CET* 1:377). He implicitly justifies the difference by the relative economic position the tradesman occupies. The *new* tradesman has no business leapfrogging from the domain of business to that of leisure; success (secured wealth) alone can permit upward mobility. Once a tradesman has *filled* his space, so to speak, he can begin to think about expanding it. What is all that money for, if not to widen its own circle of productivity?[34]

The *Tradesman* argues for an essential reciprocity between parts and wholes, for a management of public and private spaces that requires a knowledge of specific territories and of larger abstract connections – of the balance between separation and integration. The personal, social, and economic unity that *The Complete English Tradesman* advocates on the local level – within the house, within the neighborhood, within the City – expands at the end of the text to incorporate the national society and economy, and merges conceptually with the *Tour*. Defoe's economic theory here, that "an *Estate's a pond*, but a *Trade's a spring*," in fact, repeats the sense of ever-widening circles of economic energy in the *Tour*. As Peter Earle notes, Defoe implies that "high wages [lead] to high demand which [leads] to high employment which [leads] to high wages."[35] Defoe extrapolates on his earlier breakdown of the London streets and their commercial specialization and interdependence to encompass the entire national network of goods and services:

As the demand for all sorts of *English* goods is thus great, and they are thus extended in every part of the island, so the tradesmen are disperst and spread over every part also; *that is to say*, in every town, great or little, we find shop-keepers wholesale or retale [sic], who are concern'd in this circulation, and hand forward the goods to the last Consumer: From *London* the goods go chiefly to the great Towns, and from those again to the smaller markets, and from those to the meanest villages; so that all the manufacturers of *England*, and most of them also of foreign countries, are to be found in the meanest village, and in the remotest corner of the whole island of *Britain*, and are to be bought, as it were, at every body's door.   *(CET* 1:398)

Defoe, the ever-unifying traveller, then walks through that door – again conflating at the moment of separating the spaces of private and public commercial territory – and exultantly inventories the furniture of the poor man's dwelling, tracing each item – the hangings, the cane chairs, the tables and chests of drawers, the bedding (down to the blankets, sheets, and feather ticking), the rugs, the kitchen utensils, the earthenware, the glassware – to its county of original manufacture, and he builds an image of the abstract space of trade on specific images of individual doorways, shopcounters, and economically comfortable houses (*CET* 1:403–4). The power of the British nation, he insists, lies not in conquest but in trade (*CET* 1:382–83). That is, the "completeness" of the nation depends less on its absorp-tion of foreign elements or its colonization of foreign spaces than on its apparently unique ability to unify its own disparities and to organize its own internal eco-nomic and social spaces.[36] In a sense, the *Tradesman*, like the *Tour* and the urban novels, offers specific agendas for *inhabiting* – even *colonizing* – the new spaces of England itself. The shops of London have become part of the organizational public structures of *national* completeness.

Spiro Kostof describes the Grand Manner of the European baroque building – which had been sifting into London urban planning from the early seventeenth century, and would accelerate in the "Out-Parts" during the rebuilding – as aspir-ing "to turn the composition of urban spaces, the spatial experience of moving through streets and squares, itself into a spectacle" (Kostof, *The City Shaped*, 222). He notes, of course, that "the city as theater is not the exclusive preserve of the Grand Manner. In every age urban spaces – streets and squares – have served to stage spectacle in which the citizenry participated as players and audience" (ibid.). But some periods are more intensely self-staged than others. In post-Fire London, the spatial experience of moving throughout the city was redrawn in vir-tually every genre, each with its own imaginative advantages and its own peculiar urgencies. Familiar genres altered; new genres emerged. Older forms of drama were refitted within the demands of a new cultural attitude towards the city. The theater made the recognizable public spaces of the parks visible, reaffirming known territory through a shared cultural spectacle. Public space was imagined and occupied on the stage. Londoners could and did see themselves and their city represented over and over again in hundreds of similarly structured and identically placed comedies. The boundaries of public space were indubitably established and unmistakably inhabited. At the other end of town, and at the other end of the period of rebuilding, Defoe created different genres of urban spectacle, making the public as well as secret spaces of London equally visible to his audience. In a sense, Defoe's world is the "obscene" of the elegant Restoration comedy, the "hidden" or "inadmissible" cultural corners or historical moments of London, and virtually all of his narratives vividly repeople those places. The world of the shop, which increasingly supported the world of the stage, became as visible and knowable to itself in the *Complete English Tradesman* as the world of the Town defined or received itself through its drama. The sheer variety of literary genres devoting themselves to the conceptual recovery of the city's public spaces and the meanings of those spaces was as much a part of the cultural rebuilding as the reconstruction of the Royal Exchange.

Public and private, of course, define themselves in relation to the other, and each movement of literary or architectural definition of some public space assumes or asserts its other: we witness on the public stage in the scenes of public parks the seductions of most private life, or we see, as members of an audience, the secrets of the dark in closet and bedroom; we see in the tradesman's shop the perilously close and conflicting boundaries of domestic and commercial life. Virtually every genre of literature in London after the Fire tried its hand at some sort of urban reconstruction and reconception, wandering its streets, exploring its public spaces, creeping into its corners. I want to suggest that part of Defoe's contemporary popularity – and the increasing power of novelistic narrative in general – was that his novels, and his novelistic texts, most thoroughly, completely, and successfully mapped all the territories of the city – the lost city, the rebuilt city, its public spaces and its private lives.

CHAPTER SIX

NARRATIVES OF PRIVATE SPACES: CHURCHES, HOUSES, AND NOVELS

The Fire emptied and the rebuilding resignified not only the public structures and spaces of London, but also the boundaries of ordinary life, the details of half a million private lives. As discussed in chapter one, "private" is not a self-evident category; even among the wealthy, domestic space could be densely populated well into the eighteenth century. Roger Chartier delineates a fluid set of definitions for "private" (*privé*) in the late seventeenth century that includes not only the "'familiar' but also something like the English 'at home'" and which does not "require isolation, retreat, or protective walls."[1] Such fluidity seemed at this time to call for a "clear boundary . . . to be drawn between the function of public representation and the private sphere of intimate retreat" (Chartier, "Community, State, and Family," 399). This study has attempted to show through historical intersections of cultural and literary texts that the Fire and rebuilding *focused* public attention on various structural implications of isolation, retreat, and protective walls, the ambiguous boundaries between public and private, and the various attempts to draw or to resist drawing boundaries. Both public and private spaces, in their paradigms as well as their idiosyncratic overlappings, had been violated by the Fire, and the distinction between them in the late seventeenth and early eighteenth centuries was in flux, their spaces often topographically, socially, politically, and functionally overlapping. Nevertheless, as the public markers of London were being redefined and reinhabited, so were its private spaces of religious and domestic habitation. Urban as well as country houses were increasingly designed with privacy in mind, creating the spaces not only for private life but for the private experience of reading – and increasingly, of reading *novels*, as various cultural critics have argued.[2] As with the sorting of public spaces, however, marking the boundaries of privacy was troubled and ambiguous. The immediate sources of shelter had become sources of threat, and the spaces of intimate life were opened beyond the daily community of gossip to shocked published documentary. The construction of private space was haunted by ghosts of the traditional suspicion that it was less devoted to God than to self, by the political suspicion of what goes on in uncontrolled, unsupervised space, and by projections of what might socially ensue from individuals reading alone in the dark, so to speak. Moreover, the increasing emphasis on the intactness of the domestic sphere was continually threatened by historical and natural events that included such prosaic elements as the fragility of housing and the interpenetration of neighborhoods, as well as by the intrusion of political and religious monitors, so that the idea of home or church as *refuge* was simultaneously challenged by the facts of spatial treachery.

This chapter will look at two basic aspects of private space, the church and the house, primarily through the works of Defoe. The church – most intuitively a public marker – was at least temporarily transformed by the Fire from public to private space, changing the nature of its cultural and literary occupation for the decades of the rebuilding. I will take a quick glance at Anglican churches which, when they appear at all in Restoration drama, masquerade as sexual spaces, as the sites for private intrigue. I will go into greater detail about Dissenting churches, partly because, as a number of literary and cultural critics have argued, the Dissenters in some sense helped to produce the wider readership for the future novel in their emphasis on self-examination, literacy, and the semiotics of ordinary life,[3] and partly because of their relationship to Defoe. Though Dissenting meeting-houses, which may appear as social and spatial jokes in drama, have no serious imaginative literatures of their own – for reasons of course having as much to do with their religious ideology as anything else – they do have a profoundly troubled symbolic and structural history that would contribute (along with the various natural disasters of plague and fire) to Defoe's perception and persistent literary explorations of the implications of contemporary spaces and structures – beginning with his first religious poem, "Fleeing For Refuge To The hope Sett before us" (1681).

The chapter will then turn to the more obvious candidates for narratives of private space: houses. I look at some of the historical and architectural changes in the design and building of houses and then, through readings of Defoe's *The Storm* (1704), *Robinson Crusoe* (1719), and *Roxana* (1724), at the cultural implica-tions of these literary explorations of ways to define, inhabit, and *misinhabit* private space. As Defoe so attentively followed the new lines of public space in the *Tour* and the *Tradesman*, so he would also work his way into the private spaces of the rebuilt city, marking the lines of refuge and vulnerability in domestic habitation, and opening up what would be "the importance of the novel in publicizing 18th-century private life."[4]

Finally, this chapter investigates the relationship between the increasing cul-tural attention to private space and the narrative possibilities of the new genre of the novel as a literary space that supplied new ways of *visualizing* space. I hope to contribute to discussions of "the origins of the novel" the context of *space* – of familiar space destroyed, and spatial habitation disrupted; of patterns of occupa-tion and semiotics of interpretation reinscribed; of new urban spaces demanding new narrative spaces. I will argue that all of these earlier cultural literatures that redraw, redefine, and reinhabit London form part of the complex context of a need for and a love of leisured description of ordinary life in familiar settings.

A skyline of churches

In the most literally visible way, churches may have been the most immediate markers of social and public life that needed narrative as well as architectural reconstruction. Wren may not have succeeded in realizing his baroque street plan, but he did carve a new and dominant skyline through the rebuilding of the churches. In *Parentalia* Wren is said to have intended to rebuild "all the Parish Churches in such a Manner as to be seen at the End of a Vista of Houses, and dispersed in such distance from each other, as to appear neither too thick, nor thin in Prospect."[5] The steeples of the rebuilt churches would gather and focus the gaze of the pedestrian, combining but moving past the perception of the private houses towards a series of public images that would supply consistent visual and cultural significance through the traditional associations of the state religion. The churches would in effect *imply* the city, their vista the skyline. By 1685, when most of the 51 projected out of 87 lost churches were rebuilt, Wren had achieved, according to Spiro Kostof, "the most remarkable revocation of a Gothic profile on a citywide scale."[6] The city as a whole was reshaped in its visual line, its contoured whole; the public projection of the city was gothic in outline and therefore connected visually and culturally to the past, but it was also undeniably and unforgettably new, thus suggesting another form of accommodation of the new urban spaces with traditional structures of social order.

Such a skyline – such a dramatically "public" reconstruction of the way the City could be seen and known as *spectacle*, as potentially available to anyone with access above and beyond the street – could reconfigure the entire shape and meaning of the City itself as something visible, open, strong, unified, defined. And yet the mayoral processions now ended in the mayor's own house; after the burning of St. Paul's, the concluding evening prayers were replaced with indoor entertainment at the Guildhall, suggesting a shift, as Lawrence Manley argues, "from civic community towards bourgeois privacy."[7] Furthermore, churches are conspicuously absent – or only negatively present – from the literary "street level" point of view as sites for narrative plot and imaginative rehabitation. The Anglican churches become sites pretty much for sexual intrigue – for *private* negotiation – in Restoration drama; Dissenting churches do not seem to appear imaginatively at all.

Wren's churches were rebuilt, of course, on their old, cramped, idiosyncratic sites, where the original church might have been "anything but rectangular and be built up against other buildings on two or even three sides."[8] But Wren invariably perpetuated a unicellular plan on these unaccommodating sites, with sightlines directed towards the pulpit and no "dark or hidden spaces" and no separate, "papist" chancel, with large, clear-glass windows, for "a rational moderate Protestantism" (Gomme, "Architecture," 93).

These were the churches to reinhabit; but these Anglican churches rebuilt in the City, as well as those untouched by the Fire in the West End, seem largely uninhabited – or rather, *misinhabited* – by the literature of the Restoration. It is as if they are literarily silenced – "the Bells are dumb" as Joseph Guillim's poem *The Dreadful Burning of London* (1667) laments. Perhaps that is unsurprising. For one thing, church space had a literary history of doubling as sex space – see, for example, the diatribe against the secular and sexual misinhabiting of St. Paul's in John Earle's *Micro-cosmographie, or, A Peece of the World Discovered* (1628). As Restoration drama was more interested in conventional sinning than in conventional reform, drama's settlement of Covent Garden continued the tradition; as discussed in chapter five, "Covent Garden Church" was equally a code for St. Paul's Covent Garden and a brothel; alternatively, St. Paul's Cathedral was simultaneously a place of Anglican worship and a place of social, sexual assignation. St. James's Church features in Vanbrugh's *The Relapse* (1696): Lord Foppington replies to the question which church does he most "oblige with his presence," "Oh! St James's, there's much the best company." "Is there good preaching too?" Amanda goes on to ask. "Why faith, madam," he replies, "I can't tell. A man must have very little to do there, that can give an account of the sermon." In Wycherley's *The Gentleman's Dancing Master* (1673) Hippolita is not allowed to go to church because men might be there. And in Aphra Behn's *The City Heiress* (1682), set *"Within the Walls of* London" church space has a fairly extended treatment as private (sexual) space. The prologue, written by Otway, accuses the audience: "You care as little what the Poets teach / As you regard at Church what Parsons preach. / ... At Church, in Pews, ye most devoutly snore." Lady Galliard, a rich City widow, asserts the lovestruck Sir Charles Merriwill, is "now at Church, I'm sure, not for Devotion, but to shew her Charms, and throw her Darts amongst the gazing Croud" (1.i); Tom Wilding, the discarded Tory nephew of Sir Timothy Treat-all ("an old seditious Knight, that keeps open House for Commonwealthsmen and true blue Protestants" [*Dramatis Personae*]), declares he has "an Assignation here at Church," which Sir Charles finds "an odd place for Love-Intrigues." Wilding explains that women are "forc'd to dissemble Religion, the best mask to hide a kind Mistress in" (1.i). Although the rest of the drama occupies streets and chambers, the private drama of the play requires the church space as the site of original assignation and interpretation. In general, Anglican churches were occupied by comedic drama more as private spaces for private assignations and contemplations than as places of public worship. Like the public/private spaces of the shop, churches will be inhabited more frequently in the later wider spaces of the novel.

Church space in hiding

Dissenting churches are even more absent as religious sites in imaginative litera-ture. For one thing, they were not exactly available as imaginative sites for fiction, given the Dissenters' difficulties with fiction itself.[9] But even culturally they were scarcely inhabitable – perhaps a space must be culturally inhabitable before it can be fictionally inhabitable? Along with the plague of 1665 and the Fire of 1666, some of the citizens of London also had to contend with infectious and inflamed religious hostilities. While St. Paul's was rising magnificently above ground through Wren's reconstruction, flanked by the reinforcements of new Anglican steeples, Dissenting chapels were forced underground, so to speak, into spatial invisibility and flux.

On St. Bartholomew's Day, August 24, 1662, the Act of Uniformity ejected from their churches all ministers who refused to take the oath of allegiance to the Church of England and conform to its basic practices.[10] An earlier proclama-tion, suspecting all those "under pretence of serving God, [who] do daily meet in great numbers in secret places," had ordered that "no Meeting whatsoever of the Persons aforesaid . . . shall at any time hereafter be permitted or allowed [to meet], unless it be in some Parochial Church or Chappel in this Realm, or in private Houses by the persons there inhabiting."[11] In the genre of response, Thomas Lye (1621–84) preached a farewell sermon on August 17, in which he advises:

> There are secret Ordinances. It may be thou canst not be so much in the *Pulpit* as thou would'st, oh! be more in thy *Closet*: it may be thou shalt not have so many opportunities to hear so many *Lectures*, be more conscientious in thy *meditations* in secret: it may be thou shalt not have that freedome with God in *publick*, be more earnest with God in *private*.[12]

The public worship of God must legally and socially become private, even secret. The Act of Uniformity sent ministers, congregations, and the churches them-selves into odd forms of hiding.

First, the very spaces and structures of Dissenting meeting-houses were pub-licly and systematically appropriated by the dominant political and religious structures. The Dissenting community primarily occupied the close network of lanes and alleys in and around the financial district of London – the part to burn.[13] The Fire itself seemed to offer a more powerful justification for space-steal-ing, as the *London Gazette* announces:

> [T]he places under-named, of late made use of for Conventicles and Unlawful Assemblies, are now by His Majesties particular Command in Council, appointed to be used every Lords Day for Celebrating Divine Worship and Preaching the Word of God, by approved Orthodox Ministers … for the benefit of the Inhabitants of the Parishes near adjoyning respectively, where the Parish Churches have been consumed by the Fire.

The notice goes on to detail the topographical and architectural specifications of the spaces to be remarketed, and does so in the ancient genre of real estate sales-ship:

> In *Hand Alley* in *Bishopsgate-street*) a large room, purposely built for a Meeting-house, with three Galleries, thirty large Pews, and many Benches and Forms, known by the name of *Vincents* Congregation …
> In *Mugwell-street, Mr. Doolittle's Meeting house*) built of Bricks, with three Galleries, full of large Pews, and thirty eight large Pews below, with Locks and Keys to them, besides Benches and Forms …
> *(London Gazette,* No. 478, June 13–16, 1670)

The specific places of Dissenters' worship were publicly stolen, divided up after the Fire for orthodox rehabitation. Thus for a large number of City-dwellers who were to become financially and, eventually, socially prominent in London in the decades after the Fire, the sense of physical and cultural space was destabilized and rendered treacherous, unfamiliar, elusive, from political and religious as well as natural threats.

Second, the Dissenters had to occupy space differently. The legal and social pressures to be quiet, private, and concealed meant that Dissenting ministers moved their congregations into *other* public and private spaces, but occupied those spaces secretly. Schoolrooms, warehouses, public buildings, and barns supplied continually shifting premises as each new location was betrayed and exposed. Pinners' Hall, for example, in Pinners'-Hall-Court, Old Broad Street (see Figure 18), where Samuel Annesley (the Foes' minister) later preached, and where Defoe in 1681 transcribed six sermons of John Collins, was variously rented out to several congregations on Saturdays and Sundays, and, when not in use by the Pinners' Company, also during the week (Whiting, *Studies in English Puritanism*, 448). Dissenting spaces belonged to someone else; they were bor-rowed, contingent, temporary, unreliable.

Not only did the topographical space of the Dissenting church shift into abstraction, so the makeshift meeting-spaces themselves evolved into architectural paradoxes. The general theory of Dissenting architecture highlights the self-con-scious simplicity, the deliberate disornament, of the meeting-house. Donald Davie has characterized the Puritan aesthetic legacy, in form as well as function, as one of integrated simplicity: "From the architecture, from church furnishings, from the congregational music, from the Geneva gown of the pastor himself, everything breathes *simplicity, sobriety*, and *measure*" (*A Gathered Church*, 25).[14] When toleration began to replace persecution in the 1670s and Dissenters were no longer prevented from erecting their own meeting houses, they tended to rebuild on their former patterns of squares or simple oblongs (rather than the Anglican cruciform), with double rows of windows, and a plain (by contemporary standards) interior (Drummond, *Church Architecture*, 42). The meeting-house in Little St. Helen's that Annesley eventually established in 1672 under Charles's Act of Indulgence was representative: "a moderate-size building, with three good galleries, and . . . conveniently situated" within the densely Dissenting area around Bishopsgate (Wilson, *History and Antiquities*, 1:363). But during the 1660s, when persecution was most intense, a dim and inconspicuous corner in the City was not enough: the meeting-houses had to be able to protect their ministers and to disguise themselves. The Conventicle Act forbade Nonconformists from gathering together in groups of more than five for purposes of worship. City officials and unofficial informers combined to enforce the Act, harassing, dispersing, and arresting Dissenters in their meeting-houses and homes. Dissenters responded with more ingenious ways of gathering together and concealing their minister:

> In some cases a trapdoor opened into a lower chamber; in others a hatchway on the stairs could be shut at a moment's notice, and the preacher who had been using the lower part as a pulpit could escape to the upper floor and thus find refuge in a neighbouring house. Sometimes a curtain was hung across the room in such a way that on entering a stranger could not see who was preaching, and when the meeting was disturbed a cloak would be thrown over the minister's dark habit and he could make his escape amid the confusion that ensued. Narrow escapes were common, and often the magistrates missed almost by accident the victim they chiefly sought.
>
> *(*Cragg, *Studies in Puritanism*, 41–42*)*

Thus for many years, even some of the most famous Dissenting meeting-houses were emphatically *not* simple, and unlike the Anglican churches, courted "dark and hidden spaces." In fact, for most of Defoe's first twenty years,[15] the term "meeting-house" – the space designed for communal worship – was essentially an abstraction, a shared conceptualization, rarely applicable for long to any one physical structure, and carrying in its name not only the semiotic reversal of public-turned-private-turned-secret, but also a stigma of social and spatial unacceptability, an image of "dingy squat buildings in back streets" (Drummond, *Church Architecture*, 46).

I have tried to keep clear throughout this study that the massive spatial destabilization of London after the Fire was on various grounds – religious, political, social, economic, and architectural – pre-shaken, poised like other aspects of the nation and the Continent for change. But in the different ways the Fire and rebuilding affected those grounds, it seemed both to catalyze and calcify the various manifestations of spatial destabilization, to bring them into sharper and even more urgent ideological and practical relief. Thus the places and structures of the Dissenters, even before the Fire pushed them out of their preference for architectural and ceremonial "simplicity" into strategies of disguise and escape, would after the Fire escalate those patterns as the rebuilding itself cooperated in spatial persecution and Dissenters retreated into the margins of the City and the corners of City structures.

Defoe's works in virtually every genre distill the patterns of spatial and architectural dislocation and insecurity that characterize the intersections of his life and his times. Natural disasters and religious persecution historically combined to disturb, dislocate, and destroy the patterns and structures of public and private life: home, church, the city itself. During Defoe's childhood, the plague and Fire proved that the world was not simply unstable or uncertain, but that it could be *annihilated*.[16] Enormity waited none too subtly upon the edges of daily life.

The church, symbol of refuge, was itself in need of sanctuary. In Defoe's earliest known work, the fair-copy manuscript of seven verse meditations written in 1681,[17] the first and longest poem centers on doubt and fear, safely contained within images of religious sanctuary. Entitled "Fleeing For Refuge To The hope Sett before us," its form and imagery capture many of the physical, religious, social, and spatial instabilities Defoe had experienced growing up in London during the plague, the Fire, and the persecution of the Dissenters. The poem is also disturbingly prophetic of the financial and legal terrors lying in wait for him during the next thirty years. Written during a time of his life about which we know little more than that he was deciding to become a merchant rather than a minister, this poem gathers together the kinds of anxious concerns about the reliability of refuge that would permanently shape Defoe's interest in spatial and narrative structures.

The 214-line poem opens upon a hunted, terrified figure fleeing for sanctuary to one of the "Cittyes of Refuge" (line 2). The first four verse paragraphs (of fourteen) are liberally fortified with various images of refuge: that term itself appears in each (2, 31, 35, 39), along with the related images of "The Sacred Port" (13), "The securer Towne" (16), "The Willing Gates" (21), "The Long'd Ports" (23), and "That Paciffick Gate" (24). "Refuge" appears twice more (97, 162), and "home" three times (73, 99, 124). After the allegorical introductory stanzas, which dramatize the biblical theme of cities ordained by God to protect Jews guilty of manslaughter,[18] the refuge is quickly identified with God and Christ

(28–31, 96–97), and the poet assumes the role of fleeing sinner. The greatest part of the poem then focuses on the supplicant's needs, his wants, his insufficiencies, with the central stanza fastening on fear: "Thy Generall Call has No Excepcon Made, / To Any But to Such as are Affraid: / And all Thy Promises So Full Appear, / There can be No Unworthyness but Feare" (104–7). The poem concludes with a vision of the glorious security and relief of heaven:

> Then Take me To Thy Self, and Heaven Display,
> Where Sin Shall Cease, and Sorro' flee Away:
> There all Thy Glory shines, There I shall See,
> Thee as Thou art, and be a God like Thee:
> There Thy Full Presence Ever shall Appeare,
> Heaven Were No Heaven, if Thou Wer't Not There. *(209–14)*

The form of the poem reinforces this pattern of the fear of pursuit framed by the hope of refuge. The inner verse paragraphs (except for the most central lines of fear, 104–13) follow no consistent pattern of indentation, meter, or line length, suggesting the broken gestures of panic, the unstructuredness of fear:

> Chiefly I come,
> (Ah That I were at home!)
>
> And From My Self,
> That Fatall Shelf,
> On which my Soul Would Splitt & Drown,
> Lord I Have Nothing of My Owne!
>
> In vain I Flee,
> If thou Direct me Not The Way To Thee.
> In Vain I Make Assay,
> For he'l Oretake That does Persue to Slay.
> Awake my Grace,
> And Let my Sence of Danger Mend My Pace.
> *(72–73, 76–79, 82–87)*

The first and last stanzas, on the other hand, provide an unindented left margin and lines of similar feet: firm poetic structures of order, solidity, reliability. The central lines on fear prepare a visual moment of stillness in which the problem and the answer lie clear: "There can be No Unworthyness but Feare."

But it is fear which dominates – or in fact undermines – the effort of the poem, its movement towards faith and sanctuary. By the middle of the poem, the frequent images of refuge and home have virtually disappeared, overwhelmed by the poet's list of sins and his urgent self-reminders of God's grace: "None Ever Fail'd of Help, That Thither Fled. / Then Why? / Lord! Why Should Others Come & yet not I?" (119–21); "Presumcon's Not So Sinfull as Despair. / With all my Guilt, / Ile Fly Unto The blood That Thou has Spilt, / Tho' No Assureance Does Appear" (148–51). Although the poem ends with that reassuring vision of heaven, the final two lines, presumably meant to be taken rhetorically, open up a small, disturbing fissure of doubt:

> There Thy Full Presence Ever shall Appeare,
> Heaven Were No Heaven, if Thou Wer't Not There.   *(213–14)*

The first confident declarative clause seems faintly shaken by the rhetorical negatives in the next. Furthermore, by the end of the poem the number of solid, unindented, evenmeasured lines is less than half those at the beginning. The hope of refuge and the attempt to construct it seem inadequate to secure it.

Throughout his life Defoe worked to construct his own "securer Towne" on every available front by investigating through his cultural projects and generic experiments the "modern" patterns and power of the intersections between spaces and structures. In his career(s) as a merchant he was quick to acquire the symbolic spatial security of a gentleman: a house in the City and a house in the country. He tried to extend his fortunes by initiating Barbonian building projects. He persistently sought royal and political patronage. And he quickly learned how his texts themselves could fortify those attempts at security, creating or even becoming sources of refuge.[19]

But in that "Fleeing For Refuge" ends on a faint note of doubt about the existence or reliability of genuine refuge, it would become a selffulfilling prophecy. Most of Defoe's attempts to build a foundation of security overextended themselves and failed – sometimes dramatically, sometimes shamefully. For the next twenty years he would slip in and out of bankruptcy, in and out of prison, in and out of hiding. Defoe's works would explore more and more deeply the private or hidden spaces of London. The structures of hideouts, of prisons, of repossessed houses come to haunt – psychologically and then metaphorically – the images of church, warehouse, and home. The dominant issue that surrounds particularly the private structures in Defoe's writings becomes whether a building is what it appears to be. John Bender argues that in his novels Defoe "showed how, in confinement, the internal forces of psychological motivation fuse dynamically with the physical details of perceptual experience. Here is the penitentiary imagined as the meeting point of the individual mind and material causes" (*Imagining the Penitentiary*, 43). This analysis can be widened: both long before and well after Defoe wrote novels, and well beyond prison walls, he imaginatively represented the fundamental intersection of physical details and perceptual experience in the cultural contexts of a rebuilt, redefined, expanding, and constantly changing city. The physical structures of Defoe's life and works offer a real and a symbolic space in which to find the contemporary issues structuring private space: reliability, security, openness, definition, and order – and betrayal, vulnerability, confinement, disguise, and chaos.

The spaces of houses

During the late seventeenth and early eighteenth centuries "the family became the focus of private life. For one thing, it occupied a space of its own" (Chartier, "Community, State, and Family," 401), with increasing emphasis on personal privacy.[20] The nature of domestic space changed: the architectural appearance of the closet, the corridor, the back stairs reallocated space *around the individual* first in the great country houses and later in urban upper- and middle-class houses.[21] But the London house of the rebuilding was not yet become the Victorian *home*; rarely if ever does Restoration and early eighteenth-century literature display a sense of possession or intimate habitation. This may be partly because even the houses of the wealthy were not in fact owned; churches and corporations owned most of the land and freeholds were comparatively rare. London was largely *tenanted* by all classes of citizens.[22] And the vast new tract of houses made available to middle-class Londoners by speculative builders such as Nicholas Barbon carried their own threats to secure occupancy: the new houses were as likely to collapse as the ruinous old ones because of the great demand for bricks and the consequent temptation by brickmakers "to mix the slop of the streets, ashes, scavenger's dirt and everything that will make the brick earth or clay go as far as possible."[23] Pepys's nightmares of collapsing houses after the Fire thus had a long legacy into the eighteenth century for more than just the poor of the City.

Defoe was early on textually preoccupied with the precariousness of houses. When a terrible storm swept the country in November 1703, damaging or destroying thousands of houses, churches, and public buildings, Defoe had lost the brick and pantile factory that would have profited enormously from the rebuilding.[24] He published a poem and a descriptive essay on the storm, and the essay *The Storm: Or, a Collection of the most Remarkable Casualties and Disasters Which happen'd in the Late Dreadful Tempest, Both by Sea and Land* (1704) in particular reveals his fascination with the details of structural devastation, economic implications for brickmakers, and their psychological implications for the spaces of daily life. The storm offered Defoe an event that begged for a personal as well as religious and public interpretation; interpreting Defoe's essay on the storm points to his deepening suspicion of the treacherous possibilities of private space.

Defoe's description of the devastation in London fastens immediately upon the tiles, where he dwells in torturous detail on the extent of the loss, the mistakes the tile merchants made in overcharging the people, and he concludes with the forlorn certainty "that all the Tiles which shall be made this whole Summer, will not repair the Damage in the covering of Houses within the Circumference of the City, and Ten Miles Round" (*Storm* 73).[25]

After considering the tiles, Defoe turns his attention to the dead. The most destruction was caused, he says, by "the Fall of Chimneys; and as the Chimneys in the City Buildings are built in large Stacks, the Houses being so high, the Fall of them had the more Power, by their own Weight, to demolish the Houses they fell upon" (*Storm* 73). He notes that twenty-one people were killed, but he spends most time and energy describing those who, had they *abandoned* the "security" of their homes, might have survived, as one example among many suggests:

> A Carpenter in *White-Cross-street* was kill'd almost in the same Manner, by a Stack of Chimneys of the *Swan* Tavern; which fell into his House: it was reported, That his Wife earnestly desir'd him not to go to Bed; and had prevailed upon him to sit up till near two a Clock, but then finding himself very heavy, he would go to Bed against all his Wife's Intreaties; after which . . . [he] was kill'd in his Bed: and his Wife, who would not go to Bed, escap'd. (*Storm* 75–76)

Defoe might have quoted from the Fire poems discussed in chapter one, or from his own "Fleeing For Refuge": "To Tarry Here / Is Certaine Death." The text is haunted by the grisly ways the storm (and by extension *any* disaster such as plague, fire, persecutors, creditors, financial ruin, and public disgrace) can penetrate the safest house. Unlike the Fire, through which many had safely slept that first night, the storm had terrifyingly invalidated the presumably universal comforting image of the security of Bed: those who relied on its refuge were indeed "fatally sleepy." People were crushed in the streets and their houses provided no refuge.

Two years earlier Defoe had remarked that "*Vertue*'s a Beauteous Building form'd on high, / *Vice* is Confusion and Deformity."[26] Within those two years he had once again seen his fortunes and his reputation destroyed, his family in need, his home invaded, and now his city once again violated. Literally as well as figuratively, all around Defoe buildings so hopefully built or rebuilt on high buckled under the incalculable weight of confusion and deformity.

In the summer of 1708, Defoe described his life as "a banish'd condition, a distracted, unsettled circumstance . . . for a series of 16 years [since his first bank-ruptcy] in a state of affliction, and yet without prospect of deliverance" (*Review* v:212). For the next ten years he slowly worked his way back to another shaky prosperity, but the brutal (if often self-generated) intersections of time and place in Defoe's life had pushed him firmly and finally outside all centers. As Backscheider says, Defoe would become "a man who largely worked and traveled alone, rather than one immersed in the vigorous community exchanges of the tight neighborhood of the ancient Corporation of the City of London" (*Daniel Defoe*, 135). He was no longer numbered among the comfortable City merchants; he lived in mutual distrust with London's Dissenting community for his ill-received *Shortest Way with the Dissenters* (1703); he moved out of the City to Newington Green; he devoted his writing energies to the *Review*; and he began in earnest a long career in secret service to the Crown. He had earlier declared that the Dissenter who conforms is "like a Workman that Builds with one Hand, and pulls down with t'other."[27] But Defoe himself, like his future fictional creations, had perfected the pattern of building a refuge as if in order to pull it down. If in every refuge there lurks implicit prison or close disaster, then the first response might well be, like Crusoe, "to throw down [our] Enclosures . . . that the Enemy might not find them."[28] The hope of sanctuary built into "Fleeing For Refuge" has been shaken by doubts: in the very structures designed to meet the most primitive human requirements of private space, "No Assureance Does Appear."

Defoe's fictional houses

Defoe was early on interested in the social, religious, and psychological spaces of the house. He claims in the introduction to *The Family Instructor* (1715) that "the Way . . . taken for this [work], is entirely *New*" (2), referring presumably to its dialogic form, its individualized characters, its sustained variety of different points of view, and its leisured, spacious, proto-novelistic narrative (see Backscheider, *Daniel Defoe*, 336). But *The Family Instructor* also prefigures Defoe's later fiction in its attention to physical space, to the differently charged significances of a father's chamber or a daughter's closet, an apprentice's refuge in a hayloft, a husband's grieving in a garden, and his wife's repentance downstairs. Domestic relations and spiritual revelations are plotted within well-defined domestic walls; we know when characters rush downstairs or out the door, when they lurk in the lime-walk, when the emblematic authority of a father calls his child "upstairs" for reckoning.

Between 1715 and 1724 Defoe found the time, the room, and the relative peace in which to develop novelistic space, which almost by definition publicizes eighteenth-century private life.[29] As Backscheider shows in detail, the decade before that had been spent covering astonishingly large geographical, political, and literary territories in the service of Harley and Godolphin, as an agent of the Union with Scotland, and as the author of the *Review* and hundreds of pamphlets. Much of what he saw, learned, and wrote during this period would be digested later into the novels. After his move to a larger house in Stoke Newington in 1714 and his serious illness in 1715, Defoe began to develop and define the contours of imaginative private space.

I have chosen to conclude this work with readings of *Robinson Crusoe* (1719) and *Roxana* (1724) – Defoe's first and last novels – because each offers a different but equally intensive study of the creation and occupation of private space in ways which would become paradigmatic for later novelistic representations of domestic habitation. I believe it is no generic accident that Defoe's novels are so preoccupied with the streets and houses of London. Crusoe, of course, lives so emphatically outside urban structures that he would seem to be an odd choice for this study, but just as some critics have identified his island as a metaphor for England, so his incessant preoccupation with the building, appearance, and signification of his island dwellings seems to me to be a virtual groundplan for the contemporary London housedweller's concerns for a reliable domestic refuge. *Robinson Crusoe* in his very isolation lays bare the cultural and novelistic requirements for private habitation of structural space. *Roxana*, on the other hand, picks up the threads of threat in domestic space – the vulnerability of exposure and hidden nastiness that characterizes Swift's dressing-room poems, the secret spaces of woodholes and closets and trapdoors in Restoration comedy, the real-life anxieties about insecure structures and the shifting unreliability of London's urban street signs and spaces. No one else of this period pays quite such attention to interior space as Defoe; he draws together the sweeping cultural concerns about the shifting meaning of contemporary London space in ways that will later be capitalized on by Richardson, Fielding, Sarah Scott, and many other eighteenth-century novelists of domestic space.

"Nothing Like a Habitation"

On his island, Crusoe wants above all things in this world domestic security – arguably as much as or more than he wants the grace of God. His narrative strategy combines with his literal efforts to produce the perfect architectural cipher: an invisible structure, a habitation looking nothing like a habitation, the perfectly reliable refuge. The texts and inset-texts of *Robinson Crusoe* thematically entwine with the self-covering hedge of Crusoe's outer wall. The amount of description that Crusoe devotes to the building process, to the periods of anxiety and refortification, to the imagined destruction, and to the final relinquishing of his Fortress, absorbs as much of his energy as the actual physical labor spent within the narrative sequence. Action is fortified by recollection, fortification itself is strengthened by narrative repetition. For Crusoe, the process of building and its final product are carefully replicated in the process of narration and the final text.

Yet the explicit architectural and topographical detail *of* the narrative would seem to thwart the secrecy and self-concealment that Crusoe worked so hard to achieve *within* his story, much as Goulemot argues that the intimacy of private narrative in the eighteenth-century novel creates "an impression of truth" precisely *because* it makes the private public; "the truth of what is said is grounded in the intimate and the private," in that which is hidden from public view. Thus "literature presents itself as a violation" (Goulemot, "Literary Practices," 386, 384). But Crusoe's story is written from the perspective of final repentance – after the Footprint, after his impulse to throw down his enclosures. Because of this imagined (but genuinely suffered) experience of exposure, destruction, and despair, Crusoe finally appears to understand – to his own satisfaction, at least – the nature and limitations of shelter, and he learns to move comfortably without as well as within his structures.[30] The narrator opens and offers the secrets of his private space first (in the narrative) to his readers and then (though prior in plot) to his successors on the island. Crusoe in the end fashions shelters that seem after all to work – to supply the security they promise. *Unlike* Roxana, Crusoe learns, like the complete English tradesman, to inhabit the paradoxes of his own constructions of private space.

Crusoe's first description of his dwelling on the island marks the enormous importance he attaches to the relationship between topographical and architectural appearance on the one hand and personal security and comfort on the other. After efficiently dismantling the obviously unsatisfactory shelter of the foundered ship, Crusoe devotes several pages to the location and construction of his future home. We are given not only exact measurements but also a firm visual picture:

> I found a little Plain on the Side of a rising Hill, whose Front towards this
> little Plain, was steep as a House-side, so that nothing could come down
> upon me from the Top; on the Side of this Rock there was a hollow Place
> worn a little way in like the Entrance or Door of a Cave . . . On the Flat of the
> Green, just before this hollow Place, I resolv'd to pitch my Tent: This Plain
> was not above an Hundred Yards broad, and about twice as long, and lay like
> a Green before my Door, and at the End of it descended irregularly every
> Way down into the Low-grounds by the Sea side. It was on the N.N.W. Side
> of the Hill, so that I was shelter'd from the Heat every Day, till it came to a W.
> and by S. Sun, or thereabouts, which in those Countries is near the Setting.
>
> (RC 44)

Crusoe recounts not only the size, the location, and the position, but also the colors, shapes, lines, and implicitly the shadows (from the evening sun). The way things look will measure the comfort and the security of his life. As Pat Rogers has noted, Crusoe's language transfers rapidly from an economic to a domestic vocabulary:[31] here, the adjectival "House-side" instantly confers a warm proprietal status on the "Green before my Door." The necessary conditions for both home and fortress pre-exist in the sense of the encompassable for the former: "little" plain repeated twice, a "little" hollow, "shelter" from heat, and the "Low-grounds" slipping gently down below him; and in the sense of the indomitable for the latter: the steep presence of rock, which in later descriptions will assume a fiercer aspect in contrast to the rest of the island. Crusoe's efforts may be, as Lennard J. Davis and others suggest, part of an ideologically grasping English imperialism,[32] but more immediately they indicate the basic human need to establish at least the *appearance* of a safe small order inside the larger living anarchy.

Comfort depends on security, and security involves structure as well as site:

> Before I set up my Tent, I drew a half Circle before the hollow Place, which took in about Ten Yards in its Semi/diameter from the Rock, and Twenty Yards in its Diameter, from its Beginning and Ending.
>
> In this half Circle I pitch'd two Rows of strong Stakes, driving them into the Ground till they stood very firm like Piles . . . and this Fence was so strong, that neither Man or Beast could get into it or over it . . . The Entrance to this Place I made to be not by a Door, but by a short Ladder to go over the Top, which Ladder, when I was in, I lifted over after me, and so I was compleatly fenc'd in, and fortify'd, as I thought, from all the World, and consequently slept secure in the Night. *(RC 44–45)*

Crusoe's first thought is to become first structurally and then visibly impenetrable. But a curious reversal in architectural signification occurs within the various building processes Crusoe sets up. Here, Crusoe constructs the fence to secure *himself* ("I was compleatly fenc'd in"). Gradually, however, the subject of protec⁄ tion and concealment becomes less Crusoe and more his home itself. One nor⁄ mally builds or occupies a house to shelter oneself, and on the manifest level this is of course what Crusoe does. But who constructs a shelter for the shelter?

In Defoe's experience, and thus for many of his characters, structures designed and built to offer protection *to* their occupants often seem to require pro⁄ tection *by* them. The collapse of the churches in the Fire has been discussed in chapter one. The Dissenting meeting⁄house, though a symbol of refuge, was also in need of sanctuary from fierce persecution; many of Defoe's religious pamphlets and his essays in the *Review* were designed to shield and protect the physical as well as religious structures of Dissent. Defoe had acquired a habit of offering shelter to shelters. Crusoe, like this authorial father, adds wall upon wall to his dwelling; his narrative builds description upon description as if to fortify the fortification.

Crusoe builds his second home – his "bower" – deeper within the warm spaces of the island, among the woods and hills, and fences it in with the high double hedge that figures most prominently in his general building strategies:

> The Circle of double Hedge that I had made, was not only firm and entire; but the Stakes which I had cut out of some Trees that grew thereabouts, were all shot out and grown with long Branches . . . I was surpriz'd, and yet very

well pleas'd, to see the young Trees grow; and I prun'd them, and led them to grow as much alike as I could; and it is scarce credible how beautiful a Figure they grew into in three Years; so that though the Hedge made a Circle of about twenty five Yards in Diameter, yet the Trees, for such I might now call them, soon cover'd it; and it was a compleat Shade, sufficient to lodge under all the dry Season. (RC 77)

The trees enchant Crusoe not only for their satisfactory combination of beauty and utility, but more especially for their unique possibilities for camouflage:

This made me resolve to cut some more Stakes, and make me a Hedge like this in a Semicircle round my Wall; I mean that of my first Dwelling, which I did; and placing the Trees or Stakes in a double Row, at about eight Yards distance from my first Fence, they grew presently, and were at first a fine Cover to my Habitation, and afterward serv'd for a Defence also. (RC 77)

As the hedge grows, so does its significance, until, in Crusoe's eleventh year on the island, he can say with no small satisfaction: "As for my Wall made, *as before*, with long Stakes or Piles, those Piles grew all like Trees, and were by this Time grown so big, and spread so very much, that there was not the least Appearance to any one's View of any Habitation behind them" (RC 110). The number and nature of Crusoe's walls, his descriptions of those walls, and the position of those descriptions within the narrative, all begin to entwine as thickly as the hedge itself, and to the same ends.

The full nature of Crusoe's fortification cannot be understood apart from its textual reinforcements.[33] Within his recollected narrative, Crusoe describes the site and construction of his first fortress and fence in great detail, several pages before he "must go back" to the other (spiritual) things occupying his mind at the time (RC 45). One might argue that he would not necessarily have had time to think of the state of his soul as he struggled to protect himself from his projections of wild beasts and cannibals. But given that his narrative is written from the safe perspective of the rescued and redeemed, the fact that the preoccupation with building a camouflaged shelter *still* takes narrative precedence over other probable alternatives (such as a brisk lesson at the start on solitude, despair, or the tricky business of interpreting Providence) measures the real extent of Crusoe's concern with structural shelter. (This recollected inversion of intuitive priorities recalls Defoe's longingly detailed discussion of tiles in *The Storm* that precedes the narra-tive of human deaths.) Crusoe's building projects almost always frame his narra-tive meditations.

After first describing his "Fence or Fortress," Crusoe promises he will "go back to some other Things which took up some of my Thoughts" (RC 45). But in much the way that H.F. constantly circles up to and shies away from the subject of closed houses, Crusoe needs to pad softly back to his cave before really venturing out into spiritual autobiography: he records the separation and preservation of his gunpowder, the arrangement of his "Kitchin," and the taming of goats before he repeats: "Having now fix'd my Habitation, found it absolutely necessary to provide a Place to make a Fire in . . . But I must first give some little Account of my self, and of my Thoughts about Living" (*RC* 46). He then offers an account of his internal soliloquies of despondency and hope, leading to the textual insertion of a spiritual and physical accounting-sheet (*RC* 49–50). The meditation over, Crusoe trots happily back to his building projects, repeating both his efforts and his descriptions:

> Having now brought my Mind a little to relish my Condition . . . I began to apply my self to accommodate my way of Living, and to make things as easy to me as I could.
>
> I have already describ'd my Habitation, which was a Tent under the Side of a Rock, surrounded with a strong Pale of Posts and Cables, but I might now rather call it a wall, for I rais'd a kind of Wall up against it of Turfs, about two Foot thick on the Out-side, and after some time . . . I rais'd the Rafters from it leaning to the Rock, and thatch'd or cover'd it with Bows of Trees. (*RC* 50)

Crusoe's building projects frame his narrative, but from another perspective his narrative frames as well as fortifies his building projects. The building of the primary dwelling is described four times: each description, like the gradually accumulating fences, adds a further sense of narrative-upon-physical security for the narrator. The first description appears in the main narrative, followed by the surprising *précis* quoted above. The third and fourth appear in that slippery textual object, Crusoe's journal.[34] The journal adds to this project what is missing in the straight narration: "I work'd excessive hard these three or four Months to get my Wall done; and the 14th of April I closed it up, contriving to go into it, not by a Door, but over the Wall by a Ladder, that there might be no Sign in the Out-side of my Habitation" (*RC* 59). The central narrative descriptions emphasize strength, durability, even beauty; the journal reinforces the growing secrecy, the successful deception. The journal *also* interpolates another description of the fortress exactly when it insists it will not:

> *N.B.* This Wall being describ'd before, I purposely omit what was said in the Journal; it is sufficient to observe, that I was no less Time than from the 3d of *January* to the 14th of *April*, working, finishing, and perfecting this Wall, tho' it was no more than about *24* Yards in Length, being a half Circle from one Place in the Rock to another Place about eight Yards from it, the Door of the Cave being in the Center behind it. (*RC* 56)

Figure 25 George Cruikshank's drawing of Crusoe's hut.

After duplicating the previous descriptions, the journal gives them a last hammering home: "When this Wall was finished, and the Out-side double fenc'd
with a Turf-Wall rais'd up close to it, I perswaded my self, that if any People were
to come on shore there, they would not perceive any Thing like a Habitation"
(*RC* 57). The journal fortifies the narrative, and both fortify for the narrator the
security and invisibility of the dwelling.

Virtually every illustrated edition of *Robinson Crusoe* includes an image of
Crusoe's dwelling; yet, as with George Cruikshank's drawing above (see Figure
25), most figure *huts*, ignoring the fact that for Crusoe the *most* necessary condition
of the house is that it appear nothing like a habitation.[35] Yet it is Crusoe's obsessive
camouflaging itself that renders his hidden hut so imaginatively, mythically pow-

erful, so immanent and visual, the secret demanding to be public. Two and a half centuries of illustrators' "errors" reveal the precise psychological power of Crusoe's narrative: his incessant descriptions open and offer to the reader the layered secrets of his self-enclosures.

The pattern of narrative fortifying shelter and shelter framing psychological events stands out most sharply around the apocryphal event of the Footprint. Crusoe spends several paragraphs updating the reader on his structural improvements in security and comfort, not bashful about reminding us of the stout success of his wall: "As for my Wall made, *as before*, with long Stakes or Piles, those Piles grew all like Trees, and were by this Time grown so big, and spread so very much, that there was not the least Appearance to any one's View of any Habitation behind them" (*RC* 110). He discusses the good repair of his bower, the enclosures for his goats, the proliferation of hedge-walls, and his general and constant habit of "perfecting [his] enclosures" (*RC* 111) – within the verbal context of the most reiterated security in all his descriptions: *not the least, any one's View, any Habitation*. Into this virtual fortress of descriptive comfort and asserted security appears "the Print of a Man's naked Foot on the Shore" (*RC* 112). Suddenly the conceptual fortress disintegrates into its primitive and inadequate elements:

> [L]ike a Man perfectly confus'd and out of my self, I came Home to my Fortification, not feeling, as we say, the Ground I went on, but terrify'd to the last Degree . . . When I came to my Castle, for so I think I call'd it ever after this, I fell into it like one pursued; whether I went over by the Ladder as first contriv'd, or went in at the Hold in the Rock, which I call'd a Door, I cannot remember; no, nor could I remember the next Morning, for never frighted Hare fled to Cover, or Fox to Earth, with more Terror of Mind than I to this Retreat.
> *(RC 112)*

"Fortification" and "Castle" are apparently supported but actually undermined by the repeated terms of retreat. The sense of safe entrance (the definition and distinction between Inside and Outside) vanishes even from his memory. His "Door" reverts to its status of linguistic metaphor: what was once "call'd" a door is really just a hole in the rock. The grandly named, painstakingly built structures of defense and disguise break down into mere dens of prey – the hare's cover, the fox's earth – in which Crusoe no longer *lives* but *cowers*.

Crusoe's psychological scattering of his enclosures and retreat follows the descriptive shattering of their terms:

> The first Thing I propos'd to my self, was, to throw down my Enclosures, and turn all my tame Cattle wild into the Woods, that the Enemy might not find them; and then . . . to demolish my Bower, and Tent, that they might not

see any Vestiges of Habitation, and still be prompted to look farther, in order
to find out the Persons inhabiting. *(RC 114)*

Then begins another long rebuilding and a collecting of even more secret spaces.
The cave has a doorway that has to be resealed, and Crusoe builds another wall,
fortifying the interior wall to the thickness of ten feet, and outside that, he plants
his self-concealing trees:

> Thus in two Years Time I had a thick Grove and in five or six Years Time I
> had a Wood before my Dwelling, growing so monstrous thick and strong,
> that it was indeed perfectly impassable; and no Men of what kind soever,
> would ever imagine that there was any Thing beyond it, much less a
> Habitation. *(RC 117)*

The language of denial, already strong in the moments before the narration of the
Footprint, becomes almost shrill: "*no Men* of what kind *soever* would *ever* imagine
that there was *any Thing* beyond it, *much less* a Habitation." He does not in fact
throw down his enclosures – that utterly primitive if utterly self-destructive
human response to emotional threat – but he divides his goats among the various
"Enclosure[s] by Nature" that he finds in the woods, and his recollection of scattered space finally leads him toward the psychologically telling cave of the goat,
which becomes a new favorite "Place of Security, and such a Retreat as I wanted"
(RC 130).

Crusoe learns, as Moll does, that "the Evil which in it self we seek most to
shun, and which when we are fallen into it, is the most dreadful to us, is oftentimes
the very Means or Door of our Deliverance, by which alone we can be rais'd again
from the Affliction we are fallen into" *(RC 131)*. All the doorways Crusoe so
carefully seals and conceals are flung open by Friday and the Spaniard, and
Crusoe emerges, an odd musty blinking figure, back into the world, symbolically
as well as literally leaving his complicated psychological and structural fastnesses
behind.

The second rebuilding, both literal and psychological, of his secret spaces
fortifies Crusoe himself in some important new ways. In the terrifying incident of
the dying goat he begins to understand that "there was nothing in this Cave that
was more frightful than my self" *(RC 128)*. How we inhabit a house largely
depends upon how we inhabit ourselves. Crusoe returns to the significance of this
last dark cave in *Serious Reflections* (1720), dwelling over and over again on the
ways he haunted his island spaces with the devils of his own mind. He recommends that melancholic people "should never look behind them, and over their
shoulders, as they go upstairs; or look into the corners and holes of rooms, with a
candle in their hands; or turn about, to see who may be behind them, in any walks,
or dark fields, lanes, or the like; for, let such know, they will see the Devil, whether

he be there or no."[36] As in *The Family Instructor*, one must position oneself in the world by looking *out* and looking *up*. Crusoe here learns and in later mental retravelling confirms that the better part of structural security lies in perceptual trust (the message of *The Storm* apparently notwithstanding).

After twenty-four years the organic space of Crusoe's island has worked some change in him. In a short meditation he comes to terms with the essential precariousness of his most determined efforts. Whatever security he had enjoyed he now realizes was illusory, and he most sincerely seems to shift his dependence onto God:

> I came to reflect seriously upon the real Danger I had been in, for so many
> Years, in this very Island; and how I had walk'd about in the greatest
> Security, and with all possible Tranquillity; even when perhaps nothing but
> a Brow of a Hill, a great Tree, or the casual Approach of Night, had been
> between me and the worst kind of Destruction. *(RC 142)*

The conscious, spiritual challenge to his security is followed by a dream of intrusion transformed into welcome:

> I dream'd . . . the Savage that [the cannibals] were going to kill, jumpt away,
> and ran for his Life; and I thought in my Sleep, that he came running into my
> little thick Grove, before my Fortification, to hide himself; and that I seeing
> him alone, and not perceiving that the other sought him that Way, show'd my
> self to him, and smiling upon him, encourag'd him . . . and carry'd him into
> my Cave. *(RC 144)*

Granted, even in his sleep Crusoe attaches strings to his hospitality (the refugee must be alone and unfollowed), even so this is for Crusoe a very different imaginative response to the existence of the Other: like the frightful dying goat, this image is *himself*, fleeing for refuge to the hope set before him – someone seeking fortification in which to lie concealed. Indeed, Friday and the Spaniard are both made most welcome (albeit in strictly subordinate positions) within Crusoe's compound. After this dream, Crusoe realizes: "I was not at first so careful to shun the sight of these Savages, and avoid being seen by them, as I was now eager to be upon them" (*RC* 145). Fear and self-enclosure have been absorbed and changed into a desire to move, to act, to make contact – even if his first conception of contact – slaughter – is simply the inverted equivalent of self-destruction.

In some ways, all of Defoe's novelistic characters are fighting to control (in order to trust) physical and psychological space. Crusoe achieves it not only in the fact that he finally allows himself to leave the island, but also because he fuses narrative and physical fortifications as well as his domestic spaces and strategies, and bequeaths them to the new inhabitants of the island:

> I gave them the whole History of the Place . . . shew'd them my Fortifications,
> the Way I made my Bread, planted my Corn, cured my Grapes; and in a
> Word, all that was necessary to make them easy . . . In a Word, I gave them
> every Part of my own Story. *(RC* 199*)*

He gives up his story; his narrative publicizes his private space. With uncharacter-
istic openness and generosity, Crusoe relinquishes his most cherished secret
spaces, his most deeply held secrets. He decodes and defines the mysteries for surviving domestic life; he reinvests spatial and cultural signs with meaning. Once
his ink had run out *(RC* 76), Crusoe had learned to read and interpret the
material culture of his physical world: the canoe, for example, served as a painful
self-reminder of premature and self-defeating escape *(RC* 92); now Crusoe
becomes a memento or emblem to himself and to the reader in his moment of
resolved doubt *(RC* 140) and delivers up his stories with all their psychological
and structural significance to the penitent mutineers. It is a true exchange, a reciprocity of texts and topographical contexts: when he returns at the end of volume
1 he notes: "[I] saw my Successors the *Spaniards*, [and] had the whole Story of
their Lives . . . Besides this, I shar'd the Island into Parts with 'em" *(RC* 220).
Crusoe is able to leave without abandoning his island, in that sense internalizing
enough of the structures of security to move easily again – or rather, for the first
time – into the world.[37] Though he regrets the lack of a cave in which to hide his
money *(RC* 206), he finds he can still depend upon his old captain and the widow
(RC 206, 219) to care for the wealth that his Brazilian partner had faithfully shep-
herded during his twenty-eight years' absence. In short, by the end of his narrative
the spaces of physical and psychological private world are no longer haunted by
devils, beasts, and cannibals, but rather are *peopled* with systems and structures of
trust.

Sexual space, haunted space

More than any other of Defoe's novels, the last, *Roxana*[38] (1724), occupies, manipulates, depends upon, and disintegrates within domestic space. Like Crusoe,
Moll, and H.F., Roxana determines to penetrate other people's shelters and fortify
her own, but unlike the others, she fails. She at first seems the most spatially canny
of Defoe's characters, and she alone consciously understands and capitalizes on
the sexual power implicit in social space. Her story pivots on the most socially
powerful arrangement and employment of contemporary London lodgings, but
it begins in an empty house and ends in a haunted one. The first and final spaces of
the novel invalidate her command of its center and punish her for the attempt. In
the end, all her inhabited space – psychological as well as architectural – becomes
haunted space. Her attempt to find and create a psychologically secure structure

within predetermined spaces backfires, and concludes Defoe's own imaginative search for a fictional refuge.

Roxana's psychological story begins when her first husband abandons her and she confronts the poverty of a naked room:

> I was in a Parlour, sitting on the Ground, with a great Heap of old Rags, Linnen, and other things about me, looking them over, to see if I had anything among them that would Sell or Pawn for a little Money, and had been crying ready to burst myself, to think what I should do next . . . [I was] in Rags and Dirt, who was but a little before riding in my Coach; thin, and looking almost like one Starv'd, who was before fat and beautiful: The House, that was before handsomely furnish'd with Pictures and Ornaments, Cabinets, Pier-Glasses, and everything suitable, was now stripp'd, and naked . . . in a word, all was Misery and Distress, the Face of Ruin was every where to be seen. *(R 17–18)*

This chilling interior emptiness breeds the fear, insecurity, and obsessive need for control that influence the rest of her actions. Roxana's body and her house are bound together by parallel clauses in an identity that she will learn to exploit. H.F. had also implicitly identified the body with architectural dwelling, but mostly as a sign to read, and if unreadable, to be feared. For the first half of her story, Roxana is by far the most spatially aggressive of Defoe's characters (inhabiting the London of Charles II, as the full title page announces), fiercely determined never to return to an empty house.

Within this house Roxana begins a series of invisible occupancies, secretly inhabiting (and learning to control) spaces that appear closed and empty to the rest of the world. Her maid Amy thrusts the five children onto their unwilling paternal relatives and spreads the story that Roxana has been turned out of doors, and the house shut up, although they actually continue to live there for several years (R 21–22). The landlord, who had before seized her goods and stripped her house, now discovers she is beautiful, and replenishes her domestic interiors in the hope of sex. Roxana quickly manipulates his desire to assume control of the actual and symbolic function of the rooms, of the whole house, by *appearing* to relinquish spatial control:

> [A]fter Dinner [the landlord] took me by the Hand, Come, now Madam, says he, you must show me your House, (for he had a-Mind to see every thing over again) No, sir, said I, but I'll go show you *your* House, if you please; so we went up thro' all the Rooms, and . . . the Room which *was appointed* for himself. *(R 33, my emphasis)*

Roxana presses the landlord to stay the night (in the room *she* appoints), and then with a great show of reluctance sleeps with him – after he has legally endowed her with a good share of his wealth. Through it all Roxana appears grateful, submissive, and flattered, but she manages to acquire a firmer possession, a finer control, a dominance that occasionally surfaces in startlingly brutal ways: one night she strips Amy, throws open the landlord's bed, and thrusts her in, then stands aside to watch (R 46). The landlord may pay the bills and give orders to the staff, but Roxana orders the space herself, determining and controlling sexual boundaries.

Roxana repeats this pattern of secret occupation and invisible control during her long affair with the prince in Paris. The prince is so taken with her lodgings ("having a Way out into Three Streets, and not overlook'd by any Neighbours, so that he could pass and repass, without Observation; for one of the Back-ways open'd into a narrow dark Alley, which Alley was a Thorowfare, or Passage, out of one Street into another" [R 66]), as well as with her person, that she offers: "I would be wholly within-Doors, and have it given out, that I was oblig'd to go to *England* . . . I made no Scruple of the Confinement . . . so I made the House be, as it were, shut up" (R 67). She again collapses generic living space into powerful sexual space ("I prepar'd not my Rooms only, but myself" [R 61]), manipulating its apparent master by exaggerating forms of obeisance within the contours of her room: "When he came into my Room, I fell down at his Feet, *before* he could come to salute me, and *refus'd* to rise till he would allow me the Honour to kiss his Hand" (R 61, my emphasis). The apparent acts of homage implicitly forestall and disobey the prince's commands.[39] Such maneuvers prove so successful that by the time the affair is ended Roxana is an exceedingly wealthy and increasingly confident woman, almost ready openly to occupy private space.

Roxana repeats her patterns of manipulating sexual space with her next lover, the Dutch merchant. He lodges in a room just across the hall from her (in Rotterdam), and Roxana stages the seduction so well that the merchant thinks he takes quite a dashing advantage of a rare opportunity:

> About One a-Clock in the Morning, for so long we sat-up together, I said, *Come, 'tis One a-Clock, I must go to-Bed*; *Well*, says he, *I'll go with you*; No, No, says I, *go to your own Chamber*; he said he wou'd go to Bed with me: *Nay*, says I, *if you will*, I don't know what to say; *If I can't help it, you must*: However, I got from him, left him, and went into my Chamber, but did not shut the Door; and as he cou'd easily see that I was undressing myself, he steps to his own Room, which was but on the same Floor, and in a few Minutes undresses himself also, and returns to my Door in his Gown and Slippers . . . I made a seeming resistance, but it was no more indeed; for, *as above*, I resolv'd from the Beginning, he shou'd Lye with me if he wou'd, and for the rest, I left it to come after. (R 142-43)

To the merchant's enormous surprise, Roxana refuses to marry him, resolving instead to travel to London and conquer wider spaces by herself. She wants neither husband nor lover because she is unwilling to occupy her living spaces as either wife or mistress. She had earlier distinguished the whore from the wife in terms of the *possession* of private space; the whore "sculks about in Lodgings," while the wife

> appears boldly and honourably with her Husband; lives at Home, and possesses his House, his Servants, his Equipages, and has a Right to them all, and to call them her own; entertains his Friends, owns his Children, and has the return of Duty and Affection from them, as they are here her own, and claims upon his Estate, by the Custom of *England*, if he dies, and leaves her a Widow.
>
> *(R 132)*

Her language emphasizes ownership both of space and its domestic occupants, but given her past experience with husbands, she determines to inhabit private space *as* a wife without the inconvenience of a husband or the insecurities of a lover.

The central scene of the novel, in terms of narrative, psychological, and spatial control, is Roxana's ball in London, where she dons her Turkish dress and dances for the assembled company. After acquiring impressive lodgings in Pall Mall (becoming one of the fictional wealthy *tenants* of rather than homeowner in the city), and marketing a dazzlingly remote self-image (walking with Amy in the Mall but at first deliberately making no acquaintances), she finally gives a ball for her admirers in which her attention to physical space and dramatic timing is exquisitely controlled. She anticipates what will become the most fashionable arrangements for upper-class entertainment:

> I had a large Dining-Room in my Apartments, with five other Rooms on the same Floor, all which I made Drawing-Rooms for the Occasion, having all the Beds taken down for the Day; in three of these I had Tables plac'd, cover'd with Wine and Sweet-Meats; the fourth had a green Table for Play, and the fifth was my own Room, where I sat, and where I receiv'd all the Company that came to pay their Compliments to me.
>
> *(R 173)*

Roxana entertains in truly magnificent apartments: most town houses in London, even those of the aristocracy, could rarely boast so many rooms on one floor. All rooms are equally hers. She aggressively defines her space by determining the function of each room and positioning herself in stately splendor at the center of the social ritual.

Although the rooms Roxana rents most probably follow the kind of floor plan introduced by Inigo Jones in the mid-seventeenth century, which continued

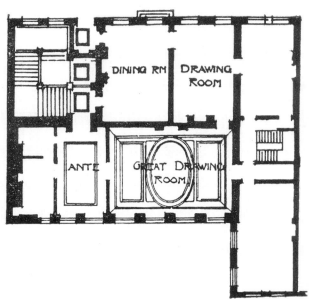

First Floor.

Figure 26 Roxana's rooms, after Inigo Jones.

to dominate upper-class town and country houses through the first quarter of the eighteenth century (see Figure 26), her method of occupying them anticipates social changes in entertainment, putting her in fashionable control of private life in private space. Roxana's series of rooms, with a different activity in each, breaks away from the tradition of all the guests moving together through the various events of the evening, and moves towards social diversity and independence.[40]

When Roxana learns that the king (Charles II) might appear at her ball in masquerade, she fortifies herself spatially: "I colour'd, as red as Blood itself cou'd make a face look, and express'd a great Surprize; however, there was no going back; so I kept my Station in my Drawing-Room, but with the Folding-Doors wide open" (*R* 173). The position and function of the room itself lend support and grandeur to her nervousness. And in a variation on Defoe's pattern of narrative reinforcement of novelistic action, Roxana decides to publicize her absolute ability to empower interior space. She slips upstairs to change into the Turkish costume and then reappears in the drawing room:

> I order'd the Folding-Doors to be shut for a Minute or two, till I had receiv'd the Compliments of the Ladies that were in the Room, and had given them a full View of my Dress . . . [T]he Folding-Doors were flung open, and [my dancing partner] led me into the Room: The Company were under the

> greatest Surprize imaginable; the very Musick stopp'd a while to gaze . . .
> [And when my partner] led me to the Drawing Room Door . . . I did not go
> in, as he thought I wou'd have done, but turn'd about, and show'd myself to
> the whole Rooms, and calling my Woman to me, gave her some Directions to
> the Musick, by which the Company presently understood that I would give
> them a Dance by myself.   (R 174–75)

No longer does Roxana invisibly inhabit the secret center of a house, manipulat
ing its spaces from behind a screen of gratitude; she has now moved firmly into the
center of fashionable London society, courting the *power* available in command
ing the gaze, the power of self-spectaclizing that determines the response of an
audience rather than being objectified by it. Roxana has apparently succeeded in
becoming a "*Man Woman*" (R 171) in assuming control of the social and spatial
centers of her life.

But the end of the novel subverts its middle, and undermines the faith we can
put here in the extent of Roxana's control of her interior spaces. Unknown to
Roxana (as well as to the reader), one of her domestics, watching from the
margins of this exotic scene, turns out to be her daughter Susan, one of the chil
dren whom Amy had pushed onto the unenthusiastic aunt (R 266). Susan does
not put the pieces together until much later in the novel, but the retroactive shadow
of her presence in this scene suggests that Roxana's past habits of invisible occu
pancy breed the very ghosts that come to haunt her. Her own narrative description
of personal strength and spatial power conceals the hidden weakness.

Roxana begins to disintegrate even before Susan actually confronts her. She
slips back rather suddenly into hidden darkness, sacrificing some of what she had
wanted (and at least temporarily achieved) as a "Man Woman" to become the
courtesan of (perhaps) an English prince. After a three year retirement, com
pressed secretly into a short paragraph ("with a Person, which Duty, and private
Vows, obliges her not to reveal, at least, not yet" [R 181]), Roxana emerges again
into the public eye, but notes: "I did not come Abroad again with the same
Lustre, or shine with so much Advantage as before . . . [I]t began to be publick,
that *Roxana* was . . . not that Woman of Honour and Virtue that was at first sup
pos'd" (R 181–82). After her personal and social triumph in the public spaces of
Pall Mall, she retreats into old patterns of secret habitations, but begins to find that
the darkness clings: "I seem'd like an old Piece of Plate that had been hoarded up
some Years, and comes out tarnish'd and discolour'd" (R 182). The conse
quences of self hoarding, of *secretly* occupying private space, are psychologically
and socially disfiguring.

Roxana tries to repolish her image, to make herself publicly presentable, but
she never acquires more than the *appearance* of respectability and wholesomeness,
and even that appearance is soon shaken by retribution for past secrecy with a sort

of psychological homelessness, a paralysis of agency. Moll Flanders had in some ways earned the full measure of the security and gentility she had long wanted: in declaring and sharing her full wealth with Jemy in the end, she finally fortified her original (deceptive) appearance of wealth with its reality. Crusoe's redemption also appears in his ultimate ability to share his real estate and his domestic secrets with the mutineers. Roxana, however, never really learns to *live* in her rooms; she occupies interiors in various roles, never truly comfortable when psychologically naked in a private space. Finally *no* rooms are hers.

Roxana's first defense against the threat of spatial penetration and disintegra-tion is (rather like Moll's) to change identity with a change of London address. With Amy's help, she can "transform [herself] into a new Shape, all in a Moment" (*R* 209). She lodges with a Quaker lady in the Minories, and gradually adopts the latter's style, dress, and apparent security, claiming triumphantly: "I was now in a perfect Retreat indeed; remote for the Eyes of all that ever had seen me" (*R* 211). But at precisely this point of complete disguise and protected enclo-sure, she begins to lose control of space more rapidly and to recover less easily. In some sense she has reverted to invisible occupancy, but this time *without* the sense of invisible agency. The success of the Dutch merchant's resumed courtship depends more on the discreet choreography of Roxana's landlady than on Roxana's own efforts:

> It was one Afternoon, about four a-Clock, my Friendly QUAKER and I sitting in her Chamber up-stairs, and very chearful, chatting together ... when somebody ringing hastily at the Door, and no Servant just then in the way, she ran down *herself*, to the Door ... She [brought the merchant] into a very handsome Parlour below-stairs ... I cou'd not speak one Word to her, nor stir off of my Chair, but sat as motionless as a Statue.   *(R 221–22)*

For Roxana, the parlor seems suddenly inaccessible — architecturally, physically, psychologically. The room for public reception and social intercourse has moved beyond her power.

Though Roxana does in time marry the merchant and become a countess, the habits of secret occupation and dark retreat steadily undermine her foundations of security. More and more often she finds herself paralyzed, trapped in a room, terrified by doors and windows and wide open streets. Nicole Castan argues that in the seventeenth and eighteenth centuries "the meaning of different spaces was subject to continual reinterpretation, and there was ambivalence about public and private roles ... The doorway and window, principal observation points, marked the boundary of the family's territory. The street was part public, part private, a place for meetings, exchange of news, and commentary on current events."[41] For Roxana, public and private space were spilling over into each other's territory much too dangerously; windows and doors admitted intruders; streets implied observation; the house was no longer a refuge but, in imagery recalling Defoe's *Storm*, conflated psychological and structural dangers: "*In a word*, it never Lightn'd or thunder'd, but I expected the next Flash wou'd penetrate my Vitals . . . it never blew a Storm of Wind, but I expected the Fall of some Stack of Chimneys, or some Part of the House wou'd bury me in its Ruins" (R 260). In a darkly logical extension of her earlier identification of building with body, Roxana now anticipates her psychological and social collapse in terms of structural disintegration.

In the end, no room, no arrangement of rooms, no prestigious or inconspicuous address, can supply Roxana with interior security or permit her spatial control. Susan doggedly tracks her down, invading her lodgings, demanding her recognition, haunting her daily thoughts and eroding her self-control until all her series of houses seem to entrap rather than empower her. Amy, so often the extreme manifestation of Roxana's most secret spaces,[42] acts out their shared sense of walled-in panic: thinking about Susan, she "starts up, runs about the Room like a distracted body; I'll put an End to it, that I will; I can't bear it; I must murther her . . . and then repeated it over three or four times, walking to-and-again in the Room" (R 272–73). Interior space crackles with frenetic, hostile, frustrated energy; the walls enclose and confine without protecting; the threat from without is met by a worse within. As with Crusoe in the cave of the dying goat, there is nothing more frightful than herself in Roxana's private spaces.

Finally Roxana loses even the semblance of spatial control, and her Quaker friend has to determine her actions, monitor her house, and direct her escape, finding release from the private through the spaces of private/public overlap:

> I was so confounded, I knew not what to do, or to say.
>
> My *happy Visitor* [the Quaker lady] had more Presence of Mind than I; *and ask'd me* . . . but hast *thou* no Way out backward to go to her? . . . Now it happen'd there was a back-Door in the Garden, by which we usually went and came to and from the House; so I told her of it: *Well, well*, says she, *Go out and make a Visit then, and leave the rest to me.* (R 318–19)

Susan has challenged Roxana's ability to control the spaces she inhabits, and her probable murder destroys it altogether: "As for the poor Girl herself, she was ever before my Eyes; I saw her by-Night, and by-Day; she haunted my Imagination, if she did not haunt the House; my Fancy show'd her me in a hundred Shapes and Postures; sleeping or waking, she was with me" (R 325). *All* Roxana's inhabited space is now haunted space. But in a sense, Susan's invisible presence had *already* haunted the apartments of Pall Mall, repeating Roxana's own habits of invisible occupancy, infiltrating spaces that had seemed most securely subordinated.

Roxana has forfeited whatever control she might have had over her interior spaces, both architectural and psychological. All her manipulations of space – her tricks with folding doors and drawing room entrances – prove only an illusion of control because she has inhabited her houses on false pretenses. She tried to make private space secret space; she could not come to terms with shifting boundaries. For such mishabitation, more than for sexual aggression (although the two are, of course, culturally linked) she is punished for presuming to command the centers of rooms.

Private space and novelistic narrative

I want to suggest that changing cultural perceptions of space in London after the Fire contributed to the production and power of the novel as a genre that visualizes and actively inhabits space. It seems to me to be no coincidence that architecture and the novel were simultaneously popularized and professionalized in the first quarter of the eighteenth century, when the rebuilt structures and spaces of the old City and the architectural and cultural development of the West End had settled on the one hand into basically stable and recognizable spatial territory but on the other produced new and often fluid cultural, economic, social, religious, and political practices. "Space *per se*, space as a contextual given,"[43] had been recovered, reperceived, redefined, and as I have argued in part I perhaps the whole range of London's inhabitants (in all social brackets, whether occupying City, Town, or Court) had been made forcibly aware of the *concept* of urban space – as presence rather than absence, as something with changeable and interpretable boundaries – through the conceptual and practical horrors of the Fire and the exigencies of rebuilding. *Space* was coming to be reperceived and redefined (explicitly in Defoe, implicitly in others) as *spatiality*, or "the created space of social organization and production... [or] the concrete expression of a combination of instances, an 'historical ensemble' of interacting material elements and influences" (Soja, *Postmodern Geographies*, 79, 84). As I have argued throughout this study, *many* forms of literary and cultural texts and projects in late seventeenth- and early eighteenth-century London (and later in Britain more generally) participated in a shared if diverse cultural attempt to define the boundaries and negotiate the patterns of the new London: newspapers, sermons, maps, plans, topographies, builders' manuals, architectural treatises, poems, plays, and novels, all offer literal or imaginative ways of constructing, conceptualizing, travelling, or inhabiting London in its newly signified public, private, and intermediary spaces.

There are at least three ways in which the changing configurations of space in London may have contributed to the emergence of the novel, and Defoe's urban narratives are some of the earliest and most varied (though by no means the first or only) explorations and expressions of imaginative habitation: the social (and

political) development of privacy and the emphasis on domestic space; the profes-
sionalism of architecture and the cultural awareness of the construction of domestic space; and the proliferation of London maps and topographies and the
widespread awareness of conceptualizing and travelling London streets. Each of
these three developments, themselves historically generated (or at least acceler-
ated) by the Fire and rebuilding, encouraged developments in what J. Paul
Hunter has called the narrative "conquest of space" through "the democratiza-
tion of travel and the proliferation of print" as "contemporary, interdependent
phenomena" involving a "sense of modernity" that was as conscious of "the
meanings of stasis as of motion."[44] Poetry and drama also, of course, played with
new forms and implications of space – I have discussed the public spaces of streets
in poetry (chapter four) and parks in drama (chapter five). But the novel in its
treatment of space is as different from poetry and drama as in its generic conventions; indeed, its treatment of space *requires* (produces?) its generic conventions.
Novelistic space is wider, its occupation longer, its visualization more detailed, its
spaces more intimately and privately known. A novel – and the experience of
reading a novel – *occupies* and *travels* space. The novel narratively visualized and
publicized the individual, subjective experience of changed space. As Hunter
argues: "In this tight atmosphere of everyday life, reading was an escape of a peculiarly spatial kind" (*Before Novels*, 127).

As critics and historians such as Watt, Stone, Hunter, McKeon, and
Armstrong have argued, the changing emphasis toward privacy in the middle-
and upper-class worlds of late seventeenth- and early eighteenth-century London
formed part of the cultural contexts of literacy and novel-reading. Valerie Pearl
argues that the post-Fire (and Fire-generated) move towards "a greater centralisa-
tion in London in the organisation of municipal services, that is, of paving, light-
ing, and the watch" in a direct sense reduced the individual citizen's role in civic
management.[45] That municipal centralization – which analogically parallels the
political centralization that would put poets and poetry out of the official, public
realm – eroded the milieu of the "wardmote" – the meetings or "inquests" of
ward officials (generally local residents) that micromanaged the moral and civic
affairs of the ward. The wardmote, precisely through its lack of privacy, its use of
all the semi-public spaces of windows and doorways and streets between houses
in communal self-surveillance, had "provided a close-knit and enduring society
with degrees of belonging, of neighbourliness, of recognition, and of security of
property" that now began to disintegrate (Pearl, "Change and Stability," 18).
Urban patterns shifted "from civic community to bourgeois privacy" (Manley,
Literature and Culture, 293), a privacy that included the concepts of individualism
and subjectivity as well as the experiences of aloneness and loneliness, of isolation
and strangeness.

Privacy was newly available both on the streets, in terms of urban anonymity (as Moll Flanders and Colonel Jack discover to their advantage), and in the houses, in terms of architectural space. Instead of interlocking suites of rooms, houses developed corridors and back stairs to keep the rooms themselves intact, and the development of the closet – a private room within a private room – marks the cultural interest in spatial interiority. Daily life was increasingly lived in the smaller rooms of the house.

Architecture and architectural space became matters of popular as well as polite interest, and in the eighteenth century architectural theory became explicitly interested in space as "a positive architectural quality . . . [possessing] as much, if not more architectural interest than the structure by which it was confined."[46] The early eighteenth-century architectural response to the changing perception of urban space as shifting, fluid, and abstract, was Palladianism, with its firm aesthetic prescriptions for stable perspectives and structural uniformity. Indeed, largely through Burlington's efforts Palladianism became for a time virtually the national architecture. Structural uniformity, as Simon Varey suggests, can be used to create or maintain social or political order.[47] Yet a sense of spatial solidity – even eternity – would have an inherent psychological appeal as well in a period of rapid political, economic, and social change. But by the 1730s, towards the end of Defoe's life, the interiors of upper- (and later middle-) class houses began to revolt against the demands of their symmetrical Palladian exteriors. Axial arrangements were gradually replaced by circular planning.[48] Instead of a series of box-like enclosures, divided by walls or colonnades, each view ending in a tidy terminal feature, rooms began to circle around magnificent staircases, or redistributed themselves in an asymmetrical disregard to the exterior announcements made by windows and rustications. The size and shape of rooms began to depend less on the need to balance form with function (for example, having rooms matching in size and importance at either end of the house and on every floor) and more on the requirements of function alone. Rooms could vary in shape and size simply for the visual excitement of it. And the same began to be true for buildings as a whole: "[People] liked to see buildings in a series and from a variety of constantly changing angles" (Girouard, *Life in the English Country House*, 211). Architectural space was deliberately *shaped*, fractured into multiple perspectives through these experiments with obliquity and parallax. Some of these effects were produced with large mirrors (recall Defoe's concern over the growing obsession with mirrors that spatially inflate structural interiors in *The Complete English Tradesman*), arranged so that the occupant of a room would see "not enclosing walls, but a series of open arcades through which architectural spaces extended in an infinite parallactic sequence beyond the confines of the room" (Collins, *Changing Ideals*, 27). The walls of the room became in some ways subordinate to the experience of its space, and that experience was intended to include successive changes in perspective. Architectural attention thus necessarily focuses on the occupant, the observer, the subject of the moment who sees and experiences such perspectival shifts.

These changes in architectural perception and structuring of space histori-cally coincide with the relative stabilization of building in London and its out-parts and with the exploration of individual and multiple, even contradictory, perspectives in the epistolary novel. The cultural and architectural attention to the experience of moving through the city or the house was matched by a narrative attention to the same experiences. The connection between novelistic space and the cartographic innovations and the increase in city maps and topographies after the Fire has been argued in chapters three and four.

What seems surprising, then, is the reputation that eighteenth-century novels have developed of being visually barren, with space rendered through direction or conception rather than through sensual experience. From Dorothy Van Ghent in 1953 to Simon Varey in 1990, Defoe scholars in particular (but also critics of later eighteenth-century novelists) have consistently characterized the spatial and struc-tural imagery of his novels, while rich in *things*, as decidedly blank in aspect. Van Ghent argues that the tangible material goods cluttering the pages of *Moll Flanders* are "not at all vivid in texture," that "to say Moll's world is made of *things* does not mean that it is a world rich in physical, sensuous textures – in images for the eye or for the tactile sense or for the tongue or the ear or for the sense of temperature or the sense of pressure. It is extraordinarily bare of such images."[49] Max Byrd agrees: Defoe's London "remains somehow two-dimensional, an abstract environment so to speak, without colors or smells or windows and doors."[50] George Starr points to "a paucity of visual detail."[51] J. Donald Crowley insists on the lack of sensuousness in Crusoe's experience.[52] And Simon Varey contrasts Defoe's vague, "generic" space with the "colourful similes and boisterous images of clutter and clatter" in Ned Ward and Thomas Brown (Varey, *Space*, 138).

I want to argue first, that we need to recognize a different cultural perception of space in the early eighteenth century as the source of its different textual repre-sentation – that we should not expect Defoe and other early novelists to furnish us with Dickensian detail. But neither should we *miss* the presence and resonance of the novelistic spatial detail that does exist simply because we might be expecting something else, something less "other." A different look at the cultural contexts of early novels, particularly but not exclusively Defoe's, can recover for us the charged fullness and weight of the kind of attention paid to space in imaginative and especially novelistic works – the richness within apparent spareness that also characterizes the visual and spatial detail of later eighteenth-century novels. What eighteenth-century readers expected – as well as what might have surprised and won them in Defoe – was a kind of visual detail different from what we typically expect from a post-Victorian-novel perspective, with a different emphasis, resonance, and effect.[53] The pictorial detail of Defoe's novels for contemporary readers captured a fledgling sense of place and recovered both a familiar and a strange past, clarifying his particular interests in spatial and structural relations in ways that later novelists would employ.[54]

Rachel Trickett argues that in fact for much of the eighteenth century many forms of specific visual detail were considered the province of poetry; the novel had to mark out its own spatial fields which began in human action and worked through the human psyche.[55] The kinds of spatial and structural detail that dominate nineteenth-century novels were neither available nor necessary to eighteenth-century novelists and readers:

> The lack of a descriptive rhetoric in eighteenth-century prose, at a time when so much of its development in verse was taking place, suggests that the writers of the period were peculiarly attentive to the function of the new genre, the novel, in contradistinction to that of poetry . . . Only when truth to human nature was not the first concern of the novelist, when writers of fiction could return to the freedom of romance rather than the veracity of history, when imagination more than observation was given priority, did a form of fiction develop in which some of the relationships between the figure and the landscape, the subject and the physical environment, could be attempted, however crudely. (Trickett, "'Curious Eye,'" 250)

Eighteenth-century novels, Trickett argues, developed their own idiosyncratic attention to space, highlighting human actions and relationships against a pictorially and spatially vague background that would not interfere with or unnecessarily color the moral movements of the text.

I have argued earlier in this chapter and in chapter four that Defoe's details of street names and street spaces in *Moll Flanders*, *Journal of the Plague Year*, and *Colonel Jack*, and the presentation and construction of private (domestic) space in *Robinson Crusoe* and *Roxana* supply their own vividness and structural detail of space to a contemporary London readership who had experienced first- or second-hand the destruction of familiar space and its public rearticulation and reconstruction. But I want to make a stronger argument, as my second point of criticism, for the *presence* of vivid, visual place detail in early novels. Some of that detail is not only spatially specific, it is in fact quite sensuous and textured. In Delarivier Manley's *The New Atalantis* (1709), for example, the scene where the Duchess comes upon the sleeping Germanicus is lushly, sensuously detailed:

> The Duchess softly entered the little chamber of repose. The weather violently hot, the umbrelloes were let down from behind the windows, the

sashes open, and the jessimine, that covered 'em, blew in with a gentle fragrancy. Tuberoses set in pretty gilt and china pots, were placed advantageously upon stands; the curtains of the bed drawn back to the canopy, made of yellow velvet, embroidered with white bugles, the panels of the chamber looking-glass. Upon the bed were strewed, with a lavish profuseness, plenty of orange and lemon flowers. And to complete the scene, the young Germanicus in a dress and posture not very decent to describe. It was he that was newly risen from the bath, and in a loose gown of carnation taffety, stained with Indian figures. His beautiful long flowing hair, for then 'twas the custom to wear their own tied back with a ribbon of the same colour; he had thrown himself upon the bed, pretending to sleep, with nothing on but his shirt and nightgown, which he had so indecently disposed, that slumbering as he appeared, his whole person stood confessed to the eyes of the amorous Duchess; his limbs were exactly formed, his skin shiningly white, and the pleasure the lady's graceful entrance gave him, diffused joy and desire throughout all his form.[56]

All the sensual details of interior private space are lavishly supplied, as if soft pornography anticipates the later novel's attention to the reader's desire to inhabit the textual space. But Defoe's novels themselves often have very rich, very warm, or very sensuous details. *Pace* Byrd and Van Ghent, Defoe's novels not only abound with windows and doors (think of the clattering open windows of *A Journal of the Plague Year* and the backdoor retreats of *Roxana*), they are also profuse in colors and textures. One of the caves on Crusoe's island was the most "glorious Sight seen in the Island . . . [T]he Walls reflected 100 thousand Lights to me from my two Candles; what it was in the Rock whether Diamonds, or any other precious Stones, or Gold . . . I knew not" (*RC* 140). Crusoe's description of his country bower and of his pleasure in his limes is even more luxurious:

> I found the Brook . . . and the Country became more woody than before; in this Part I found different Fruits, and particularly I found Mellons upon the Ground in great Abundance, and Grapes upon the Trees; the Vines had spread indeed over the Trees, and the Clusters of Grapes were just now in their Prime, very ripe and rich . . . [T]he Country appeared so fresh, so green, so flourishing, every thing being in a constant Verdure, or Flourish of *Spring*, that it looked like a planted Garden . . . [T]he green Limes that I gather'd, were not only pleasant to eat, but also very wholesome; and I mix'd their Juice afterwards with Water, which made it very wholesome, and very cool, and refreshing. (*RC* 79–80)

Crusoe is always enchanted by his raisins; we often experience with him the oppressive windless heat of the island.[57] Generally in Defoe's novels, we not only know *exactly* where we are, we also often experience the visual, aural, and physical conditions of our carefully specified place.

For Defoe's Londoners, the details of place names and street names, the patterns of urban housing, the arrangement of interior domestic space, the integrity of refuge and the semiotics of structural space, all charged the usually spare but occasionally rich visual details of his fiction with an imaginative and emotional appeal that has perhaps for us been buried under the more consistently elaborate detail of nineteenth-century novelists. Defoe's novels, shaped by the Fire and rebuilding of London, as well as by his own shaky occupation of urban space as a persecuted Dissenter, a shape-shifting spy, and an overly ambitious and often unlucky tradesman, captured and generated a new sense of spatial and structural detail – in the ways that human beings not only inhabited but also perceived and responded to their new urban and domestic spaces – that persisted within and profoundly influenced the narrative spaces and structures of the eighteenth-century novel.

Both Varey and Bender discuss the narrative strategies and structural imagery in Defoe's novels as designed to discover or create a social, moral, or political *order*. But as I have argued, Defoe's response to modern space is distinctly ambivalent – he sees in it as much the possibility for movement, expansion, profit, freedom, and power, as the threat of entrapment, misdirection, confinement, or exposure. That ambivalence informs his novels, suggesting possibilities for different novelistic approaches to and interpretations of space and structure. His urban novels elude as much as impose order; perhaps even more, they offer spatial as well as social negotiation. They map public and inhabit private space. Defoe's recovery and preservation of the losses of the past and the obscurities of the present, the elasticity of his texts in incorporating the old within the expanding lines of the new, all imply ways of engaging or exploiting (as well as controlling and containing) the possibilities of modern space. Defoe's ambiguous structures, born from the new/old, strange/known streets of London, recover the past, map the present, and anticipate the future. His narratives of London create novelistic spaces that later English writers – Richardson, Fielding, Burney, Austen, Dickens, Woolf – would inherit and occupy and alter and acknowledge. Over and over again "new Plans" of London would be narratively *lived and known.*

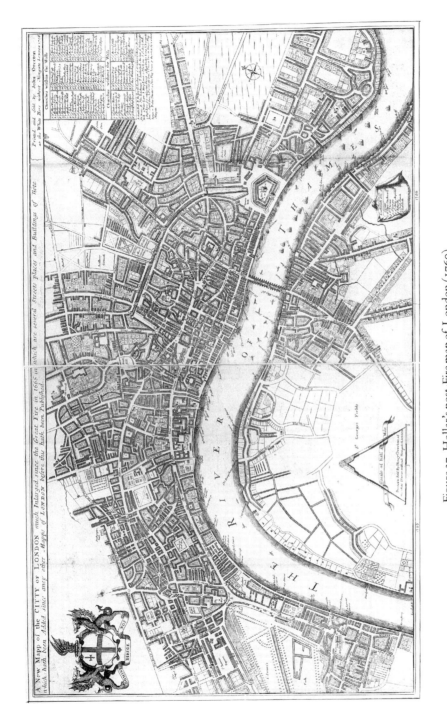

Figure 27 Hollar's post-Fire map of London (1760).

Figure 28 Strype's plan of London (1720).

Notes

I THE GREAT FIRE AND RHETORICS OF LOSS

1 John Evelyn, *The Diary of John Evelyn*, ed. E. S. De Beer, 6 vols. (Oxford: Clarendon Press, 1955), III:461.

2 [Simon Ford], *Londini quod Reliquum. Or, Londons Remains: In Latin and English* (1667), 2.

3 Elkanah Settle, *An Elegie On the late Fire And Ruines of London* (1667), 6.

4 John Stow, *A Survay of London. Contayning the Originall, Antiquity, Increase, Moderne estate, and description of that Citie, written in the yeare 1598. by Iohn Stow Citizen of London* (1598). (Further references will be cited *Survey*.)

5 J. Hillis Miller, *Topographies* (Stanford: Stanford University Press, 1995), 4.

6 See Christopher N. L. Brooke and Gillian Keir, *London 800–1216: The Shaping of a City* (Berkeley: University of California Press, 1975), 171–77; and Oskar Ekwall, *Street-Names of the City of London* (1954; Berkeley: University of California Press, 1965).

7 Maurice Merleau-Ponty, *The Phenomenology of Perception*, trans. Colin Smith (London: Routledge and Kegan Paul, 1962), 243.

8 See, for example, Maurice Merleau-Ponty, *The Primacy of Perception*, trans. James M. Edie (Evanston: Northwestern University Press, 1964); Henri Lefebvre, *The Production of Space*, trans. Donald Nicholson-Smith (Oxford: Blackwell, 1974, 1991); Michel de Certeau, *The Practice of Everyday Life*, trans. Steven Rendall (Berkeley and Los Angeles: University of California Press, 1984).

9 Edward W. Soja, *Postmodern Geographies: The Reassertion of Space in Critical Social Theory* (London: Verso, 1989), 120–21.

10 Spiro Kostof, *The City Shaped: Urban Patterns and Meanings Through History* (Boston: Little, Brown and Company, 1991), 13.

11 Lawrence Manley argues powerfully for an already urgent sense of urban change in the Tudor period, "when the mass disruptions attendant on socio-economic change, coinciding with the advent of a centralizing state, registered verbally in [textual] complaint as a decomposition and realignment of social myths and taxonomic structures and a recomposition of the effects of voice and address" (*Literature and Culture in Early Modern London* [Cambridge: Cambridge University Press, 1995], 71). Much of my argument for the topographical intensity of post-Fire literature will try to show the ways that literature both drew upon pre-existing traditions of textual and cultural urban attitudes, and how they shifted and transformed those traditions to address new anxieties.

12 Michel Foucault, *The Archaeology of Knowledge*, trans. A. M. Sheridan Smith (1969; New York: Pantheon, 1972), 138–39.

13 J. G. A. Pocock, *Virtue, Commerce, and History* (Cambridge: Cambridge University Press, 1985), 29.

14 Quoted in *London in Flames, London in Glory: Poems on the Fire and Rebuilding of London*

1666–1709, ed. Robert Arnold Aubin (New Brunswick: Rutgers University Press, 1943), ix.

15 The classic scholarly retellings are Walter George Bell, *The Great Fire of London in 1666* (London: John Lane, The Bodley Head, 1920), and T. F. Reddaway, *The Rebuilding of London after the Great Fire* (1940; London: Edward Arnold, 1951).

16 The *London Gazette* was first issued out of Oxford in November 1665, moving to London in 1666. See P. M. Handover, *Printing in London from 1476 to Modern Times* (London: George Allen and Unwin, 1960), 116–20.

17 Simon Ford, *The Conflagration of London Poetically delineated* (1667).

18 Robert Elborough, *London's Calamity by fire Bewailed and Improved, In a Sermon Preached at St. James Dukes' Place* (1666), 14.

19 Thomas Brooks, *London's Lamentations* (1670), 149. Brooks's title page continues the identification of St. Margaret's: "*New-Fish-street*, where that Fatal Fire first began that turned *London* into a ruinous Heap."

20 And in fact there *had* been a plot to burn London, kill the King and General Monck, and restore the Republic, in April of that year: John Rathbone and seven other officers and soldiers of the Parliamentary Army were arrested and executed. The date they had fixed on for their attempt was September 3, 1666 (Bell, *Great Fire*, 20).

21 *Extract uyt een Brief Van seeker particulier goede Vriendt, uyt London geschreven den 10–20 September, 1666* (quoted in Bell, *Great Fire*, 320).

22 Samuel Pepys, *The Diary of Samuel Pepys*, ed. Robert Latham and William Matthews (Berkeley: University of California Press, 1972), VII:277. (A relatively recent psychiatric stance calls it post-traumatic stress disorder and cites Pepys himself after the Fire as demonstrating "admirable coping skills" but then displaying signs of distress in memory impairment, bad dreams, displaced anger, and finally the common defense against survival guilt: "it was all predestined." See Wray Herbert, "Seventeenth-Century Stress," *Psychology Today* 17, no. 10 [October 1993]: 74. The caption under the illustration of the Great Fire reads: "London goes up in flames, Pepys comes down with PTSD.")

23 Anthony Wood, *The Life and Times of Anthony Wood, Antiquary, of Oxford, 1632–1695, Described by Himself*, ed. Andrew Clark (Oxford: Oxford Historical Society at the Clarendon Press, 1892), II:86.

24 Henry Griffith, London, September 18, 1666; quoted in Bell, *Great Fire*, 314.

25 William Stow, *Remarks on London* (1722), A4.

26 Royalist poetry often works to shore this up, almost as if proving by asserting, as in Simon Ford's trilogy of poems, *Londons Resurrection* (1669): "Thou [Charles], whose Command we Christians firmly trust, / Shall re-compose us out of crumbled Dust" (lines 81–82).

27 *A proclamation for a general fast through England and Wales* (October 10, 1666), 1.

28 Walter Scott, ed., *A Collection of Scarce and Valuable Tracts, On the Most Interesting and Entertaining Subjects: But Chiefly such as relate to the History and Constitution of These Kingdoms.* 2nd edn. (London: T. Cadell and W. Davies, 1812), VII:615. The inscription blaming the Catholics for the Fire ("But Popish frenzy, which wrought such horrors, is not yet quenched") was added to the Monument in 1681 and removed in 1831.

29 In 1679, however, these particular flames reignited in the fears surrounding the Popish

Plot. Another document was published in which it was "plainly proved, that the PAPISTS were the Contrivers and Actors in the Burning of that GREAT and NOBLE CITY" (*London's FLAMES: Being an Exact and Impartial Account of Divers Informations Given in to the Committee of Parliament... Concerning the Dreadful Fire of London in the Year 1666*). The document uses much of the same material of the 1667 account, including the topographical details for authority.

30 Karsten Harries, "Metaphor and Transcendence," *On Metaphor*, ed. Sheldon Sacks (Chicago: The University of Chicago Press, 1978, 1979), 82.

31 See Michel Foucault, "Space, Knowledge, and Power," *Diacritics* 16 (1986): 25, 27.

32 Most of the information comes from the *Dictionary of National Biography* (London: Smith Elder, 1885).

33 *A Journal of the Plague Year*, 1722, ed. Louis Landa (Oxford: Oxford University Press, 1990), 175.

34 Owen Stockton, *Counsel to the Afflicted: Or, Instruction and Consolation for such as have suffered Loss by Fire* (1667).

35 William Gearing, *No Abiding City in a Perishing World... Meditations occasioned by the late, sad, and lamentable Fire, in the City of London* (1667).

36 Nathaniel Hardy, *Lamentation, Mourning and Woe. Sighed forth in a Sermon Preached in the Parish-Church of St. Martin in the Fields, on the 9th Day of September. Being the next Lords-Day after the Dismal fire in the City of London* (1666), A2–A2v.

37 William Gearing, *God's Soveraignty Displayed... With an Application of the whole, to the distressed Citizens of London whose houses and goods were lately consumed by the FIRE: An excitation of them to look to the ends that God aims at in it, with directions how to behave themselves under their losses* [1667], 181.

38 William Thomas, *The Countries Sens of LONDONS Sufferings In the Late most Lamentable Fire* (1667), H4v.

39 Henry Hesketh, *A Sermon preached before the... Lord Mayor and aldermen of London, at Guild-hall Chappel upon the second of September, 1679* (1679). This sermon also points out that "our Temples were made Habitations for Owls" and "our Streets were made lurking places for Robbers."

40 Aubin, *London in Flames*, ix.

41 John Allison, *Upon the late Lamentable Fire in London. In an humble Imitation Of the most Incomparable Mr. Cowley his Pindarick Strain* (1667).

42 John Tabor, *Seasonable Thoughts in Sad Times, Being some Reflections on the Warre, the Pestilence, and the Burning of London* (1667).

43 Simon Ford, *Londons Resurrection, Poetically represented, and humbly presented to His Most Sacred Majesty* (1669).

44 J. G. [Joseph Guillim], *The Dreadful Burning of London: Described in a Poem* (1667), 2–3.

45 Simon Ford, *The Conflagration of London Poetically delineated* (1667), lines 321–24.

46 Daniel Defoe, *Colonel Jack* (1722), ed. Samuel Holt Monk (London: Oxford University Press, 1965), 43.

47 *London Undone; or, A Reflection upon the Late Disasterous Fire* (1666), in Aubin, *London in Flames*, 54.

48 The Fire was already shifting smaller as well as larger patterns of commercial structure, as the title page of Samuel Wiseman's *Londons' Fatal Fire* (1667) suggests: "Printed for

Peter Dring, at the Sign of the *Beaver* in the *Strand*, between *Ivy-bridge* and *Durham-Yard*, who formerly lived at the *Sun* in the *Poultrey* in *London*."

49 See Paul S. Seaver, *Wallington's World: A Puritan Artisan in Seventeenth-Century London* (London: Methuen, 1985), 51–66.

50 See, for example, Bell, *Great Fire*, 14; M. Dorothy George, *London Life in the Eighteenth Century* (1925; New York: Harper and Row, 1964).

51 See, for example, William Lithgow, *The present surveigh of London and Englands state* (1643).

52 Henry Griffith, September 18, 1666 (quoted in Bell, *Great Fire*, 315).

53 Wenceslaus Hollar, *A Map or Groundplot of the Citty of London, and the Suburbs thereof … by which is exactly demonstrated the present condition thereof, since the last sad accident of fire* (1666).

2 LONDINI RENASCENTI: THE SPACES OF REBUILDING

1 John Evelyn, *The Diary of John Evelyn*, ed. E. S. De Beer, 6 vols. (Oxford: Clarendon Press, 1955), III:462–63.

2 T. F. Reddaway, "London 1666: Fire and Rebuilding," Stevenson Lecture, University of London, November 4, 1965, 6–7.

3 *The Rebuilding of London*, Appendix A, "The 'Rejection' of Wren's Plan," 311–12.

4 Valentine Knight, *Proposals of a new Modell for Re-building the City of LONDON* (1666).

5 Wenceslaus Hollar, *A Plan of LONDON as in Q. Elizabeths Days* (1666).

6 John Evelyn, *A Character of England, As it was lately presented in a Letter, to a Noble Man of FRANCE*, 3rd edn. (1659), 9.

7 John Evelyn, *Fumifugium: Or, The Inconveniencie of the Aer and Smoak of London Dissipated* (1661), av.

8 John Evelyn, *A Panegyric to Charles the Second, Present to His Majestie the XXXIII. [sic] of April, being the Day of his CORONATION* (1661), 4, 8.

9 John Evelyn, *London Revived: Consideration for its Rebuilding in 1666*, ed. E. S. De Beer (Oxford: Clarendon Press, 1938).

10 Spiro Kostof, *The City Shaped: Urban Patterns and Meanings through History* (Boston: Little, Brown and Company, 1991), 215.

11 This part of Power's argument in part refutes J. E. Vance's claim that pre-capitalist London was characterized by spatial clusters of like occupations centered around respective guildhalls, which disintegrated under the pressures of capitalist commodification of real estate. Vance argues that occupational zoning was replaced by wealth zoning, keeping prosperous property-holders and tradesmen in London and forcing poorer craftsmen and workers into the poorer suburbs (J. E. Vance, "Land Assignment in Pre-capitalist, Capitalist, and Post-capitalist Cities," *Economic Geography* 47 [1971]: 101–120). Power argues that such a shift in the seventeenth century is not provable; and in fact uses the hearth tax assessments to show that not only in 1666 but late into the seventeenth century the City of London housed a traditional rather than a modern society, showing "little evidence of the rigid class segregations so common in the modern city" (M. J. Power, "The Social Topography of Restoration London," *London 1500–1700: The Making of the Metropolis*, ed. A. L. Beier and Roger Finlay [London: Longman, 1986], 221).

12 See Kostof, *The City Shaped*, 95, 112; and Lewis Mumford, *The City in History* (New York: Harcourt, Brace and World, 1961), 369–71.

13 Henry Fielding, *An Enquiry into the Late Increase of Robbers* (1751).

14 For discussions of the increasing interest of the middle and upper classes in seeing rooms, views, buildings in series and from a variety of constantly changing angles through parallax, see Peter Collins, *Changing Ideals in Modern Architecture 1750–1950* (London: Faber and Faber, 1965), 26–27; Mark Girouard, *Life in the English Country House* (New Haven: Yale University Press, 1978), 211–14; and Sir John Summerson, *Georgian London* (Harmondsworth: Penguin, 1945, 1962, 1969, 1978), 144–45.

15 For a fuller discussion of the evolution of the City boundaries, see Christopher N. L. Brooke and Gillian Keir, *London 800–1216: The Shaping of a City* (Berkeley: University of California Press, 1975), 133.

16 See Philippa Glanville, *London in Maps* (London: The Connoisseur, 1972), 26.

17 Richard Newcourt, *Three Mapps of London*, Guildhall MS 3441.

18 Newcourt also undertook *An Exact Delineation of the Cities of London and Westminster and the Suburbs thereof … Ichnographically described* (1598).

19 John Bender, *Imagining the Penitentiary: Fiction and the Architecture of Mind in Eighteenth-Century England* (Chicago: University of Chicago Press, 1987), 65.

20 Roger North, *Autobiography*, ed. A. Jessop (London: 1887), 54–55.

21 Edward Hyde, Earl of Clarendon, *Continuation of the Life of Edward Earl of Clarendon*, 3 vols. (Oxford, 1759), III:351.

22 Reddaway, "London 1666," 7.

23 Samuel Rolls, *Londons Resurrection or the Rebuilding of London Encouraged, Directed, and Improved, In Fifty Discourses* (1668), 125.

24 [James Ralph], *A Critical Review of the Publick Buildings, Statues and Ornaments In, and about London and Westminster* (1734), 3.

25 *English Architecture: Or, The Publick Buildings of London and Westminster* (1755), 102. See Reddaway, *The Rebuilding of London* for a discussion of the self-interested agenda shaping this diatribe (312).

26 Summerson, *Georgian London*, 56.

27 James Howell, *Instructions for Forreine Travell* (1642), "carefully edited by" Edward Arber (London: English Reprints, 1869), 73.

28 J. G. A. Pocock, *Virtue, Commerce, and History* (Cambridge: Cambridge University Press, 1985). See especially 92ff, which the following argument paraphrases.

29 First Rebuilding Act, Section IV (19 C.II II C.3).

30 Sir Roger Pratt, *The Architecture of Sir Roger Pratt*, ed. R. J. Gunther (Oxford: Oxford University Press, 1928), 12–13.

31 Samuel Pepys, *The Diary of Samuel Pepys*, ed. Robert Latham and William Matthews (Berkeley: University of California Press, 1972), VIII:87 (February 28, 1667). Quoted in Peter Mills and John Oliver, *The Survey of Building Sites in the City of London After the Great Fire of 1666*, ed. P. E. Jones and T. F. Reddaway (London: London Topographical Society, 1967), I:xiii. Much of the following summary of factual events comes from the introduction to this facsimile.

32 See Ralph Treswell, *The London Surveys of Ralph Treswell*, ed. John Schofield (London: London Topographical Society, 1987).

33 George Joye, *The Souper of the Lorde* (1533), quoted in Stephen Greenblatt, "Remnants of the Sacred in Early Modern England," *Subject and Object in Renaissance Culture*, ed. Margreta de Grazia, Maureen Quilligan, and Peter Stallybrass (Cambridge: Cambridge University Press, 1996), 340.

34 *The Fire Court: Calendar to the Judgments and Decrees of the Court of Judicature Appointed to Determine Differences Between Landlords and Tenants as to Rebuilding After the Great Fire*, ed. Philip E. Jones, 2 vols. (London: William Clowes and Sons Ltd., 1966), I:xviii.

35 The majority of cases were settled on the day they were called, with preference given to those in occupation (*Survey of Building Sites*, I:ii, xii, xv). If a disputant did not show up as scheduled, the Courts often proceeded without him or her, "so that the refractoriness of the defendants should not obstruct rebuilding" (I:xii; citing A.207, 351; B.681, 869, 878). The records show that "the disputes to be settled by the Court rarely gave rise to legal arguments and the proceedings of the Court were most often an exercise in arbitration. It endeavoured always to bring the parties to agreement and went to great lengths to avoid making a decree to which the parties had not consented or at least submitted" (I:xvi).

36 *The Fire Court*, I:xv [citing A.225, 243, 273; B.656].

37 Guildhall MS 5879.

38 Unless otherwise noted, all newspaper quotations will be from the *London Gazette*.

39 See Reddaway, *Rebuilding of London*, 75; and Power, "The Social Topography of Restoration London," 221–22.

40 Possibly *The Mercury*: "Publishing Advertisements of all sorts: as, Of Persons run away, lost, or spirited; Horses, or other Things lost or stoln, &c. For the prevention of Escaping, and discouragement of Evil-doers. And of Books to be sold; Lands or Houses to be lett. And the several Prices of both Foreign and English Commodities in *London*, and all other Places of Trade in all Parts of *England*, with all common Accidents. And an Office for the publishing Merchants Goods, where to be sold in *London* or the Out-ports [sic]; where Purchasers and Purchases are to be found, &c. As also all manner of Servants and Services, Apprentices, or Apprenticeships, Seamen, Souldiers, Nurses dry or wet, &c." (The quotation in the text comes from No. 21, August 15–19, 1667.)

41 Numbers 86 through 95 (September 10 to October 15, 1666) invariably broadcast fire, rebuilding, and relocation matters; after that, periodic advertisements and notices appear throughout the next few months (for example, for 1666, nos. 100, 103, 112–115, 118, 124, 125, 129, 130, 132, 135, 135, and 138).

42 Robert Hooke, *An Attempt to prove the motion of the earth from observations made by Robert Hooke Fellow of the Royal Society* (1674), 2–6 (my emphasis).

43 As the story goes, the Monument was originally planned by Wren to house some Royal Society experiments, but the vibrations from the local traffic disrupted those hopes. See Charles Welch, *The History of the Monument*, 6th edn. (London: City Lands Committee of the Corporation of London, 1921), 29.

3 REDRAWING LONDON: MAPS AND TEXTS

1 Daniel Defoe, *A Tour thro' the Whole Island of Great Britain*, 3 vols. (London, 1724–26), volume II, letter 2, pages 32–33. Subsequent citations of the *Tour* refer by number only to volume, letter, and page(s).

2 See Colin Nicholson, *Writing and the Rise of Finance: Capital Satires of the Early Eighteenth Century* (Cambridge: Cambridge University Press, 1994), 5, 14.

3 P. G. M. Dickson, *The Financial Revolution in England: A Study of the Development of Public Credit 1688–1756* (London: Macmillan, 1967), 15, 35. For a discussion of some postmodern ideological implications of the development of credit economies, see Patrick Brantlinger, *Fictions of State: Culture and Credit in Britain, 1694–1994* (Ithaca: Cornell University Press, 1996).

4 The mapping of England has a rather separate history from the mapping of London, coming into its own under Elizabeth with the combination of exploration, trade, conquest, and property redistribution. As Sarah Tyacke points out, the number of maps of England increased from 30 to perhaps 200 between 1500 and 1550. See Sarah Tyacke, ed., *English Map-Making 1500–1650* (London: British Library, 1983), Introduction, 15. For particularly useful summaries of London map histories, see Felix Barker and Peter Jackson, *The History of London in Maps* (London: Barrie and Jenkins, 1990); Ida Darlington and James Howgego, *Printed Maps of London, Circa 1553–1850* (1964; London: Dawson, 1978); John Fisher, ed., *A Collection of Early Maps of London 1553–1667* (London: Harry Margary and the Guildhall Library, 1981); Philippa Glanville, *London in Maps* (London: The Connoisseur, 1972); Carl Moreland and David Bannister, *Antique Maps*, 3rd edn. (1983; London: Phaidon Press, 1989, 1993); Helen M. Wallis, "Geographie is better than Divinitie; Maps, Globes, and Geography in the Days of Samuel Pepys," in *The Compleat Plattmaker*, ed. Norman J. W. Thrower (Berkeley: University of California Press, 1978); and David Woodward, "English Cartography, 1650–1750: A Summary," *The Compleat Plattmaker*.

5 The first surviving printed map of London, the "Copperplate," dates from about 1559; the other notable maps of London during this period are the "Agas" map (1545–1621); Braun and Hogenberg's map (Cologne, 1572); John Norden's *Speculum Britanniae* (1593); and the plan in John Speed's atlas *The Theatre of the Empire of Great Britaine* (1610–11). See Fisher, *Collection of Early Maps*; see also Barker and Jackson, *History of London in Maps*, 15. For an excellent discussion of the history, politics, and ideological implications of these maps and mapmakers, see Richard Helgerson, *Forms of Nationhood: The Writing of Elizabethan England* (Chicago: The University of Chicago Press, 1992). See also Henry B. Wheatley, "Notes upon Norden and His Map of London, 1593," *London Topographical Record*, 4th Annual Report, ed. T. Fairman Ordish (London: London Topographical Society, 1903), 42.

6 J. B. Harley, "Meaning and Ambiguity in Tudor Cartography", in *English Map-Making*, 22. See also Helgerson, *Forms of Nationhood*, chapter three.

7 Fisher works back from the Ogilby and Morgan groundplan, when London's population had swelled from 100,000 to 400,000, and which accurately records the number of houseplots. He estimates that the Copperplate Map shows one house for every three existing (*Collection of Early Maps*).

8 John Fitzherbert, *The Boke of Surueying, and Improuementes, newly corrected and amended, very necessarye for all men* (1587), 33v. The first edition was published in 1523, and is often misattributed to Sir Anthony Fitzherbert.

9 J. R. Hale, *Renaissance Europe 1480–1520*, 2nd edn. (Berkeley: University of California Press, 1977), 53–53.

10 See Moreland and Bannister, *Antique Maps*, 47; Peter Eden, "Three Elizabethan Estate Surveyors: Peter Kempe, Thomas Clerke and Thomas Langdon," in *English Map-Making*, 68.

11 See Peter Barber, "England II: Monarchs, Ministers and Maps, 1550–1625," in *Monarchs, Ministers and Maps: The Emergence of Cartography as a Tool of Government in Early Modern Europe*, ed. David Buisseret (Chicago: University of Chicago Press, 1992), 58; also Tyacke, Introduction, *English Map-Making*, 18.

12 Michel de Certeau, *The Practice of Everyday Life*, trans. Steven Rendall (Berkeley: University of California Press, 1984), 92.

13 This work is actually "a textbook on carrying out audits or valuations, with nothing about map-making or land measurement" (G. L'E. Turner, "Mathematical Instrument-making in London in the Sixteenth Century," *English Map-making*, 93).

14 John Holwell, *A Sure Guide to the Practical Surveyor* (1678), 190.

15 Wenceslaus Hollar and John Leake, *An exact svrveigh of the Streets, Lanes, and Chvrches, Contained within the rvines of the City of London* (1666, 1669).

16 David Woodward has characterized a "general mediocrity" in the cartographic advances and productions of England from 1650 to 1750. I do not mean to argue for vast technological *improvements* in post-Fire London maps, but for a distinctive cultural difference in strategy and quantity. See David Woodward, "English Cartography, 1650–1750: A Summary," in *The Compleat Plattmaker*, ed. Norman J. W. Thrower (Berkeley: University of California Press, 1978).

17 Ralph Hyde, ed., *The A to Z of Restoration London* (London: London Topographical Society, 1992), ix.

18 Well, mainly accurate. Ralph Hyde argues that "the number of buildings shown in the main streets . . . is likely to be correct. The outline ground plans of these buildings may also be correct. The information supplied in alleys and courts is less dependable and in some cases diagrammatic. Ogilby and Morgan's City of London map, the user must always bear in mind, is not a large-scale Ordnance Survey plan, and it should not be used as if it were" (Introduction, *A to Z*, xi).

19 Gregory King, part of the surveying team, noted that at first the map in progress "particularized nothing by only ye Streets Lanes etc. Whereupon Mr. King formed a New Project of that Survey at 100 feet per Inch [rather than 50], and expressed the groundplots of every individual house and Garden" (quoted in Hyde, Introduction, *A to Z*, vii).

20 William Leybourn, *The Compleat Surveyor: Containing the whole Art of Surveying of Land* (1674), 301. The first edition, published in 1657, did *not* include instructions for "taking the ICHNOGRAPHY or Ground-plot of *Cities*" (A3). The fact that a fifth edition of *The Compleat Surveyor* appeared in 1722 seems a measure of Leybourn's authority, as well as of the urgent interest in plotting the land.

21 Barker and Jackson note that on Morgan's map "subscribers could have their houses included for an extra ten shillings. Only eighteen did" (*History of London in Maps*, 43). While these numbers do not say much about the *actual* market for self-representation in maps, the gesture suggests that Morgan thought he *perceived* one; and my emphasis is weighted towards the textual and documentary figurations of the culture as much as towards the cultural figurations of texts.

22 Sarah Tyacke, "Map-Sellers and the London Map Trade c1650–1710," in *My Head is a Map*, ed. Helen Wallis and Sarah Tyacke (London: Francis Edwards and Carta Press, 1973), 65.

23 See *London Gazette* nos. 1139, 1168, 1172, 1189, 1267.

24 Advertisement for "Geographical Cards," *London Gazette*, No. 1063, January 24–27, 1675/6.

25 T. F. Reddaway, *The Rebuilding of London After the Great Fire* (London: Jonathan Cape, 1940), 300. See also Walter George Bell, *The Great Fire of London* (1923; London: Bracken Books, 1994), chapter sixteen.

26 See, for example, A. L. Beier and Roger Finlay, eds., *London 1500–1700: The Making of the Metropolis* (London: Longman, 1986); H. J. Dyos, "The Victorian City in Historical Perspective," *Exploring the Urban Past: Essays in Urban History by H. J. Dyos*, ed. David Cannadine and David Reeder (Cambridge: Cambridge University Press, 1982); Philippa Glanville, "The City of London," *Seventeenth-Century Britain: The Cambridge Cultural History*, ed. Boris Ford (Cambridge: Cambridge University Press, 1989, 1992); Sir John Summerson, *Georgian London* (1945; Harmondsworth: Penguin, 1978, 1986); E. Anthony Wrigley, "Urban Growth and Agricultural Change: England and the Continent in the Early Modern Period," *The Eighteenth-Century Town: A Reader in English Urban History 1688–1820*, ed. Peter Borsay (London: Longman, 1990).

27 George Rudé, *Hanoverian London 1714–1808* (Berkeley: University of California Press, 1971), 13. For a discussion in greater detail see Summerson, *Georgian London*, 39–42.

28 Lawrence Manley, *Literature and Culture in Early Modern London* (Cambridge: Cambridge University Press, 1995), 529.

29 See Patricia Crown, "British Rococo as Social and Political Style," *Eighteenth-Century Studies* 23, no. 3 (Spring 1990): 269–82; William A. Gibson, "Three Principles of Renaissance Architectural Theory in Pope's *Epistle to Burlington*," in *Pope: Recent Essays by Several Hands*, ed. Maynard Mack and James A. Winn (Brighton: The Harvester Press, 1980), 354; Summerson, *Georgian London*, 72–73; A. E. Richardson and C. Lovett Gill, *London Houses from 1660 to 1820: A Consideration of their Architecture and Detail* (London: B. T. Batsford, 1911), 41.

30 I have not found any evidence of women working in the building trades.

31 Samuel Rolls, *Londons Resurrection or the Rebuilding of London Encouraged, Directed, and Improved, in Fifty Discourses* (1668), 91–92.

32 Other examples include *Upon sight of London's stately new buildings* (1672); *Troia rediviva, or, the Glories of London* (1674); Thomas Jordan's *London in Luster* (1679), and William Gough's *Londinum triumphans* (1682).

33 *A Particular of the New-buildings within the Bills of Mortallity, and without the City of London, from the year 1656. to 1677 according to the account now taken by the Church-Wardens of the several Parishes. And the old account of New Houses from 1620 to 1656.*

34 *Arguments concerning the New-Buildings in the Parishes within the Weekly Bills of Mortality, without the City of* London [1680].

35 See also Sir William Petty, *Observations upon the Cities of London and Rome* (1687); *A Computation of the Increase of London* (1719).

36 For related discussions of the literary representations of size-anxiety, see Max Byrd,

London Transformed: Images of the City in the Eighteenth Century (New Haven: Yale University Press, 1978); W. B. Carnochan, *Confinement and Flight: An Essay on English Literature of the Eighteenth Century* (Berkeley: University of California Press, 1977); and Louis Landa, "London Observed: The Progress of a Simile," in *Essays in Eighteenth-Century English Literature* (Princeton: Princeton University Press, 1980).

37 For various perspectives on the earlier economic and social stability of London see, for example, Ian Archer, *The Pursuit of Stability: Social Relations in Elizabethan London* (Cambridge: Cambridge University Press, 1991); A. L. Beier and Roger Finlay, eds., *London 1500–1700: The Making of the Metropolis* (London: Longman, 1986); Jeremy Boulton, *Neighborhood and Society: A London Suburb in the Seventeenth Century* (Cambridge: Cambridge University Press, 1987); Christopher Brooke and Gillian Keir, *London 800–1216: The Shaping of a City* (Berkeley: University of California Press, 1975); Frank Freeman Foster, *The Politics of Stability: A Portrait of the Rulers in Elizabethan London* (London: Royal Historical Society, 1977); Valerie Pearl, "Change and Stability in Early Modern London," *London Journal* 5 (1979): 3–34; M. J. Power, "The Social Topography of Restoration London," in *London 1500–1700: The Making of the Metropolis*; Steven Rappaport, *Worlds within Worlds: Structures of Life in Sixteenth-Century London* (Cambridge: Cambridge University Press, 1989).

38 John Stow, *A Svrvay of London. Contayning the Originall, Antiquity, Increase, Moderne estate, and description of that Citie, written in the yeare 1598. by Iohn Stow Citizen of London* (1598). Further references will be cited *Survey*.

39 John Strype, *A Survey of the Cities of London and Westminster . . . Written at first in the Year* MDXCVIII, *By John Stow, Citizen and Native of London. Since Reprinted and Augmented by the Author; And afterwards by A.M. H.D. and others. Now lastly, Corrected, Improved, and very much Enlarged: And the Survey and History brought down from the Year 1633, (being near Fourscore Years since it was last printed) to the present Time* (1720).

40 See also *Literature and Culture*, 80–88, 315–20, 394, 422–27, etc.

41 Henri Lefebvre, *The Production of Space*, trans. Donald Nicholson-Smith (Oxford: Basil Blackwell, 1991), 53.

42 There are exceptions, of course: Drayton's *Poly-Olbion* (1613), for example, is also grounded in the growing urbanization and conspicuously active trade of Elizabethan London; John Leland gives an account of going round to monasteries to rescue old manuscripts, William Lambarde published a *Perambulation of Kent* (1570). These provide literary and historical contexts and traditions; but after the Fire comes a change in quantity as well as in kind. There are in fact many *more* "tours" and "perambulations" than before, in addition to the increasing numbers of "views"; it seems plausible that the increase in numbers contributes to changes in genre.

43 Part of the rhetorical strategies of these few early English descriptions of London may in fact have been directly or indirectly aimed at helping to control the unwieldy expansion of the city in Elizabethan and early Stuart times, and so would share to some extent in the literary and political agendas of the post-Fire topographies. But the rhetorical difference remains sharp, whether or not the actual post-Fire difference in urban instability is as great as it was perceived to be.

44 Howell acknowledges: "Concerning this present *Treatise*, although the trace, and form of the structure be mine own; yet, I am so much the Child of Modesty, as to

acknowledge to have fetch'd most of my *Materials* from others . . . as from Mr. *Stow*" (*Londinopolis*, BV). The *DNB* notes that *Londinopolis* was Howell's most popular publication, indicating, along with the Faithorne and Leybourn and the Hollar surveys, the pre-Restoration resurgence of interest in topographic London.

45 The value of detailed comprehensiveness of course has its own contextual history. William Lithgow's *The present Survegh of London and England's State* (1643), based on military interests, offers a very topographically specific "pedestriall march" of all the forts in a circuit which runs through Islington, "Holburne fields," Longfield, "S. Geilles fields," "Crabtree fields," and, like Defoe's *Tour*, offers its own surveyor's "circulary line" of the territory (B3–B3v).

46 This passage offers a lovely *literal* as well as symbolic connection between Defoe, who died "of a lethargy" in Ropemaker's Alley, and the not-so-proverbial Grub Street.

47 *Instances* of insistent topographic comprehensiveness occasionally appeared before and outside the rush of seventeenth- and eighteenth-century London guidebooks, but remained rare. See, for example, the title page of *A Book of the Names of all Parishes, Market Towns, Villages, Hamblets and Smallest Places, in England and Wales*, first published in 1643 and then in 1677 – presumably appealing to the newly larger market for such comprehensiveness.

48 At an oral presentation of a version of this section, Professor Herbert Tucker asked me whether there were any order to the presentation of all these King Streets. I've plotted them out on the map but haven't been able to find any; Stow not only reproduces but increases disorder – perhaps to elevate the critical importance of his own guide?

49 The guidebooks of the 1680s began to include accounts of the recently established penny post and lists of coaches, carriers, and governmental price regulations of public transport. See Harris, "London Guidebooks before 1800," *Maps and Prints: Aspects of the English Booktrade*, ed. Robin Meyers and Michael Harris (Oxford: Oxford Polytechnic Press, 1984), 35, 43.

50 The seventeenth-century artisan and diarist Nehemiah Wallington gives an account of his daughter Sarah virtually disappearing into a nearby parish, where she might have been lost forever if a passing servant hadn't recognized her. Much of London was more a collection of villages corporately tied together. See Paul S. Weaver, *Wallington's World: A Puritan Artisan in Seventeenth-Century London* (London: Methuen, 1985), 90.

51 For a related discussion of the political implications of the spatial and organization strategies of the letter, see Simon Varey, *Space and the Eighteenth-Century Novel* (Cambridge: Cambridge University Press, 1990), 205–6.

52 Pat Rogers, "Literary Art in Defoe's *Tour*," *Eighteenth-Century Studies* 6, no. 2 (Winter 1972–73): 153–85.

53 Geoffrey Sill, "Defoe's *Tour*: Literary Art or Moral Imperative?" *Eighteenth-Century Studies* 11, no. 1 (Fall 1977), 80.

54 Daniel Defoe, *Colonel Jack* (1722), ed. Samuel Holt Monk (Oxford: Oxford University Press, 1965), 43.

4 THE ART OF WRITING THE STREETS OF LONDON

1 T. S. Reddaway, *The Rebuilding of London after the Great Fire* (London: Jonathan Cape, 1940), 286.

2 M. J. Power, "The Social Topography of Restoration London," *London 1500–1700: The Making of the Metropolis*, ed. A. L. Beier and Roger Finlay (London and New York: Longman, 1986), 209.

3 See note 11 in chapter two for the context of Power's debate with J. E. Vance.

4 This point does require qualification. By 1695 most of the landed classes previously living in the City moved west into the new squares, while the merchants remained. But as Power points out, *within* the remaining groups, from wealthy merchant and aldermanic knight to artisan and worker, the social space was blurred by topographic proximity. See Lawrence Stone, "The Residential Development of the West End of London," *After the Reformation: Essays in Honor of J. H. Hexter*, ed. Barbara C. Malament (Philadelphia: University of Pennsylvania Press, 1980), 187.

5 J. Paul Hunter, *Before Novels: The Cultural Contexts of Eighteenth-Century English Fiction* (New York: Norton, 1990), 122.

6 Spiro Kostof, *The City Shaped: Urban Patterns and Meanings Through History* (Boston: Little, Brown and Company, 1991), 44.

7 Henry A. Harben, *A Dictionary of London* (London: Herbert Jenkins, 1918), xii.

8 See, for example, the 1631 Act of Common Council "for the reformation of sundry abuses practised by diuers persons vpon the common Markets, and streets of the City of London"; Henry Peachum's *Coach and Sedan* (1636); and the *Proclamation to Restrain the Abuses of Hackney Coaches in the Cities of London and Westminster* (October 18, 1660).

9 Richard Sennett, *Flesh and Stone: The Body and the City in Western Civilization* (New York: W. W. Norton, 1994), 256.

10 See M. Dorothy George, *London Life in the Eighteenth Century* (1925; New York: Harper and Row, 1964), 108; Reddaway, *Rebuilding of London*, 285; Christopher Hibbert and Ben Weinreb, *London Encyclopaedia* (1983; rev. edn., London: PaperMac, 1993), 864–66; F. G. Hilton Price, "Signs of Old London," *London Topographical Record*, 4th Annual Report, ed. T. Fairman Ordish (London: *London Topographical Society*, 1903), 70; and ibid., "Signs of Old London," *London Topographical Record*, 7th Annual Report (London: *LTS*, 1907), 28; Ronald Paulson, *Popular and Polite Art in the Age of Hogarth and Fielding* (Notre Dame: University of Notre Dame Press, 1979).

11 "That in all the Streets no Sign-posts shall hang cross, but the Signs shall be fixed against the Balconies, or some other convenient Part of the Side of the House" (*An Order made by the Lord Maior, Aldermen, and Common Council of the City of London, of the 29. of April last past* [1667]. Quoted in John Strype, *Survey of London* (1720), vol. 1, book 1, 237.

12 *The Spectator* No. 28 (April 2, 1711), in Richard Steele and Joseph Addison, *The Spectator*, ed. Donald F. Bond, 5 vols. (Oxford: Clarendon Press, 1965), 1: 116–17.

13 With many exceptions, of course; the old is never entirely swept away by the new, even in catastrophe. The Atlas and Hercules, for example, denoted Philip Lea's globe shop in 1688, and the Bishop's Head and Coffin, at the "Corner of Old Change, Near the Conduit, Next Door to Nag's Head Tavern," marked in 1692 the shop of Thomas Pursell, undertaker, who "sells all sorts of burial dresses and coffins" (Hilton Price, "London Street Signs," *LTR* 4:31).

14 Edward Copeland, "Remapping London: *Clarissa* and the Woman in the Window," in *Samuel Richardson: Tercentenary Essays*, ed. Margaret Anne Doody and Peter Sabor (Cambridge: Cambridge University Press, 1989), 57.

15 Lawrence Manley, *Literature and Culture in Early Modern London* (Cambridge: Cambridge University Press, 1995), 411.

16 John Heywood, "Seeking for a Dwelling-Place (1562)," *The Proverbs, Epigrams, and Miscellanies of John Heywood*, ed. John S. Farmer (London: Early English Drama Society, 1906; facsmile reprint New York: Barnes and Noble, 1966), 283–84.

17 Peter Earle, *A City Full of People: Men and Women of London 1650–1750* (London: Methuen, 1994), 4.

18 Pat Rogers, *Hacks and Dunces: Pope, Swift, and Grub Street* (London: Methuen, 1980), 2, 6.

19 Rogers quotes Jeffrey Hart, "Some Reflections on Johnson as Hero," *Johnsonian Studies*, ed. M. Wahba (Cairo, 1962), 28–29.

20 Peter Mills and John Oliver, *The Survey of Building Sites in the City of London after the Great Fire of 1666*, introduced by P. E. Jones and T. F. Reddaway, 5 vols. (London: London Topographical Society, 1967), 1:60.

21 See also Reddaway, *Rebuilding of London*, 288–94.

22 John Stow, *A Svrvay of London. Contaying the Originall, Antiquity, Increase, Moderne estate, and description of that Citie, writen in the yeare 1598. by Iohn Stow Citizen of London* (1598), 51–52. Further references will be cited *Survey*.

23 Dryden glosses this: "Augusta, *the old name of* London."

24 I focus on the 1729 *Variorum* here both because its textual "machinery" excavates its streets more thoroughly than the 1728 edition, and because the 1742 and 1743 editions, having moved geographically and conceptually almost entirely into the West End, belong to a markedly different – more *settled* – period of London's topographical history.

25 Alexander Pope, *The Poems of Alexander Pope*, Twickenham edition, ed. John Butt (New Haven: Yale University Press, 1963), 350. Further references will be cited in the text, abbreviated *DV*, followed by book and line number(s).

26 Pat Rogers's discussion (*Hacks and Dunces*, 144–62) of the historical and literary associations of Fleet Ditch is richly, invaluably detailed, and I do not aspire to match it.

27 See Aubrey Williams for a more specific discussion of the implications of the mayoral route in the *Dunciad*, particularly for the few divergences Pope makes (*Pope's Dunciad: A Study of its Meaning* [London: Methuen, 1955], 33–40).

28 Williams, however, sees the conceptual significance and rhetorical strategy of that stasis, arguing against earlier critics from John Dennis to Austin Warren (*Pope's Dunciad*, 29).

29 See, for example, Hunter, 106–109, 141, 161–63.

30 Further references will be cited in the text, abbreviated *T*, followed by book and line number(s).

31 (Or perhaps they just found a larger generic sack to hold it in?)

32 Richard Head, *The English Rogue, Described, In the LIFE of Meriton Latroon, A Witty Extravagant. Being a Compleat Discovery of the Most Eminent CHEATS of BOTH SEXES* (1672). 4 vols. Citations will be from the first volume of edition, abbreviated *ER*.

33 See Michael Shinagel, Introduction, *The English Rogue* (Boston: New Frontiers Press, 1961).

34 As discussed in chapter one, a number of clergymen took a dim view of Moorfields, attributing the Fire in part to the "sportings and wrestlings" there. A fine place to set up as beggar.

35 There is perhaps even more gender manipulation going on here, as street-reading suggests. Birchin Lane ("lane of the barbers") was primarily known for shops of *men's* ready-made clothes in the sixteenth and seventeenth centuries. Not that that would exclude shops for women's apparel, but would the contemporary expectations be different?

36 John Aubrey, *Brief Lives*, ed. Richard Barber (Woodbridge, Suffolk: The Boydell Press, 1975, 1982), 135.

37 The pagination gets peculiar in this first volume, running 1–288, 113–128, 267–282, 145–160, 1–129. The chapter numbers and tag words remain consistent. This quotation is from chapter 44.

38 Shinagel argues that Head wrote for and was read by "the sensation-seeking lower class reading public of the time" whose tastes he learned through his final career as a bookseller (Introduction, iii).

39 Edward Ward, *The London-Spy Compleat, In Eighteen-Parts* (1703). Further references will be from this edition, cited in the text and abbreviated *LS* followed by issue number and page(s).

40 *London Encyclopaedia*, 245. The entry cites Ward's allusion to "a fashionable promenade an hour before dinner time."

41 *Amusements Serious and Comical*, in In *The Works of Mr. Thomas Brown, In Prose and Verse, Serious, Moral, and Comical*, 4 vols. (1707), III:14.

42 Daniel Defoe, *Colonel Jack* (1722), ed. Samuel Holt Monk (London: Oxford University Press, 1965), 43, my emphasis.

43 See Homer O. Brown, "The Displaced Self in the Novels of Daniel Defoe," *ELH* 38, no. 4 (December 1971): 562–90.

44 George Starr, Introduction to *The Fortunes and Misfortunes of the Famous Moll Flanders* (Oxford: Oxford University Press, 1971), xx. Quotations will be from this edition, abbreviated *MF*.

45 Paul Alkon notes Defoe's technique for bridging past and present with a slightly different emphasis: "In order to understand the present or view the future by using the past as a guide and source of archetypes, distinctions between eras must often be collapsed or attention at least deflected from chronology" (*Defoe and Fictional Time* [Athens: University of Georgia Press, 1979], 40). But as Pocock points out, sometimes it's the continuity, the collapse of distinctions, that requires emphasis, and sometimes the discontinuity.

46 See, for example, *MF* 192, 200, 204, 214, 222, for the specter of Newgate.

47 Stuart Miller, *The Picaresque Novel* (Cleveland: Press of Case Western Reserve, 1967), 92. Quoted by Starr in the Oxford edition of *Moll Flanders*, 383. Starr qualifies this point – although not enough – by pointing out that "D. exploits but does not strictly speaking create the labyrinthine jumble of Moll's London surroundings."

5 NEW NARRATIVES OF PUBLIC SPACES: PARKS AND SHOPS

1 Lawrence Manley, *Literature and Culture in Early Modern London* (Cambridge: Cambridge University Press, 1995), 394.

2 Anne Barton, "London Comedy and the Ethos of the City," *The London Journal* 4, No. 2 (November 1978):158.

3 The tragedies of the Restoration lay elsewhere in time and space: ancient Rome, ancient Britain, Spain, Paris. As Barton demonstrates, tragedy has traditionally avoided the space of the city as a setting; or if the city does appear, it is usually as the backdrop for the isolated great house or palace, its presence mainly characterized by absence. "What Dickens later did for London, Dostoevsky for St Petersburg, and Balzac for Paris, neither Shakespeare nor any of his dramatic contemporaries wanted to do in tragic terms for the city in which they lived and worked" (Barton, "London Comedy," 159).

4 The *extent* to which the theaters were actually reopened (or rather, the extent to which they ever really closed), is still a matter of debate. Certainly private theater maintained itself through the Interregnum. But the licensing, building, and situating of the *public* theaters are distinctly Restoration matters.

5 See Emmet L. Avery and Arthur H. Scouten, *The London Stage: 1600–1800*, Part 1, ed. William Van Lennep (Carbondale, IL: Southern Illinois University Press, 1965), xxi–xxviii; Allardyce Nicoll, *A History of Restoration Drama 1660–1700*, 2nd edn. (Cambridge: Cambridge University Press, 1928), 268–303.

6 See also Donald J. Olsen, *Town Planning in London: The Eighteenth and Nineteenth Centuries* (New Haven: Yale University Press, 1964, 1982); Sir John Summerson, *Georgian London* (1945; Harmondsworth: Penguin, 1978, 1986); John Schofield, *The Building of London* (London: The British Museum, 1984).

7 Henri Lefebvre, *The Production of Space*, trans. Donald Nicholson-Smith (Oxford: Blackwell, 1991), 36.

8 As Avery and Scouten argue, "Pepys makes us aware that a greater diversity of persons by class, birth, and occupation attended occasionally and, apparently, year by year" (*The London Stage*, clxvi).

9 Douglas Bruster, *Drama and the Market in the Age of Shakespeare* (Cambridge: Cambridge University Press, 1992), 30.

10 References to plays generally will include act, scene, and page numbers.

11 For an excellent updated history and analysis of the London coffeehouse, see Steven Pincus, " 'Coffee Politicians Does Create': Coffeehouses and Restoration Political Culture," *The Journal of Modern History* 67 (December 1995): 807–834.

12 Thomas Sprat, *Observations on Monsieur de Sorbier's Voyage into England* (1665), 49.

13 See Ben Weinreb and Christopher Hibbert, eds., *The London Encyclopaedia* (London: Papermac, 1983); Susan Staves, *Married Women's Separate Property in England, 1660–1833* (Cambridge, MA: Harvard University Press, 1990).

14 Sometimes attributed to Dryden, though more likely by John Dover (1644?–1725).

15 There are exceptions, but most of the *City* city plays are by City writers such as Settle, or published in the City (rather than in the Fleet Street, Chancery Lane, or Covent Garden areas), such as Ravenscroft's *The London Cuckolds*: "Printed for *Jos. Hindmarsh* at the Sign of the Black-Bull near the Royal Exchange in *Cornhill*."

16 John Strype, *Survey of London* (1720), II.6.87.

17 See Olsen, *Town Planning*, 39–41; M. Dorothy George, *London Life in the Eighteenth Century* (1925; New York: Harper and Row, 1964), 74, 92–93; Summerson, *Georgian London*, 27–32; Strype; Schofield, *Building of London*, 168; *London Encyclopaedia*, 207–9.

18 I do not mean to lose sight of the fact that the parks had always been known for their underworld side. As Pat Gill argues, Corinna's promiscuity, in Rochester's "A Ramble

in St. James's Parke" is "both sexual and social, and in that doubled sense, an exemplary indication of the problem with all public thoroughfares: London streets, St. James's Park, and Corinna's vagina. All three not only indiscriminately allow all comers, as it were, but they also absorb or liquidate the comers' distinctions in the process" (" 'Filth of All Hues and Odors': Public Parks, City Showers, and Promiscuous Acquaintance in Rochester and Swift," *Genre* 27, No. 4 [Winter 1994], 337). I simply want to emphasize that the "darkness" became more visible to more kinds of people.

19 M. J. Power, "The Social Topography of Restoration London," *London 1500–1700: The Making of the Metropolis*, ed. A. L. Beier and Roger Finlay (London: Longman, 1986), 221. See also chapters two and four above.

20 *Examiner* No. 22 (December 21–28 1710).

21 See Colin Nicholson, *Writing and the Rise of Finance: Capital Satires of the Early Eighteenth Century* (Cambridge: Cambridge University Press, 1994); David Trotter, *Circulation: Defoe, Dickens, and the Economies of the Novel* (London: Macmillan, 1988). See also John F. O'Brien, "The Character of Credit: Defoe's 'Lady Credit,' *The Fortunate Mistress*, and the Resources of Inconsistency in Early Eighteenth-Century Britain," *ELH* 63 (1996), 604.

22 Much of this information comes from Betty R. Masters, *The Public Markets of the City of London Surveyed by William Leybourn in 1677* (London: London Topographical Society Publication no. 117, 1974).

23 *Time* had earlier been accorded its proper space and place; various Acts in the 1670s determined that "flesh markets were open on Mondays, Wednesdays and Fridays from 6 a.m. to 8 p.m. and on Saturdays from 6 a.m. to 10 p.m. . . . Fruit, vegetables, butter, eggs and all provisions other than meat or poultry, could be sold on every working day . . . Before 10 a.m. only the housekeepers of the city could buy in the public markets; and the market bell was rung three times during the day, at opening, at 10 a.m. to signal the hour when retailers might be admitted to buy, and at closing time" (Masters, *Public Markets*, 18).

24 Defoe, *An Essay upon Publick Credit* (1710), 6.

25 See Robert Mayer, *History and the Early English Novel* (Cambridge: Cambridge University Press, 1997); Everett Zimmerman, *Boundaries of Fiction* (Ithaca: Cornell University Press, 1997).

26 Since Defoe assumes that the tradesman almost always is, in fact, a man (although he notes exceptions), I will in general use his term and his masculine pronouns.

27 Defoe analyzes the gendering of commercial space, which I will discuss below. But it is worth noting here that, as contemporary texts and recent scholarship have pointed out, women occupied and tended commercial space in highly visible ways. In *Spectator* 454 (August 11, 1712), Steele wanders euphorically through the Royal Exchange, claiming: "It was not the least of the satisfactions in my survey to go upstairs, and pass the shops of agreeable females; to observe so many pretty hands busy in the foldings of ribands, and the utmost eagerness of agreeable faces in the sale of patches, pins, and wires, on each side of the counters". See also Paula McDowell's book on the women of Grub Street, forthcoming from Oxford University Press.

28 Quoted in Starr's notes to the Oxford edition (1971) of *Moll Flanders*, 388 (look at Strype).

29 Patricia Crown notes later French responses to the English innovations begun in Defoe's time: "Rouquet, in 1754, described a London merchant's shop: 'everything is clean and neat, enclosed in large glass show cases, whose frames are fresh painted, the signs are very large, well painted and richly gild, suspended from costly ironwork, illuminated with sconces' . . . Similar observations were made by . . . Pierre Grosely in 1765 who described the striking shops, enclosed with great glass doors, highly adorned, brilliant and gay, 'splendid show, greatly superior to anything of the kind in Paris'" ("British Rococo as Social and Political Style," *Eighteenth-Century Studies* 23, no. 3 [Spring 1990], 273). For other discussions of the appearance and evolution of the English shop, see Summerson, *Georgian London*; Jack Lindsay, *The Monster City: Defoe's London, 1688–1730* (London: Granada Publishing, 1978), 70–71; Alec Clifton-Taylor, *The Pattern of English Building* (London: Faber and Faber, 1972), 393–96; Rosamond Bayne-Powell, *Eighteenth-Century London Life* (New York: E. P. Dutton, 1938), 112–18.

30 The pagination of the first edition runs awry between pages 49 and 64 in volume one, so I will include signatures when a page number misleads the reference.

31 See especially *CET* 1:146, 159, 348–55.

32 See Leopold Damrosch, Jr., "Defoe as Ambiguous Impersonator," *Modern Philology* 71 (1973–74): 158; and William and Robert Chambers, editors of the 1839 edition (reprinted Gloucester: Alan Sutton Publishing, 1987), 70n.

33 See Paula Backscheider, *Daniel Defoe: His Life* (Baltimore: Johns Hopkins University Press, 1989), 102, 128, 198, 560–61n57; Michael Shinagel, *Daniel Defoe and Middle-Class Gentility* (Cambridge, MA: Harvard University Press, 1968).

34 Defoe's last major work, *The Compleat English Gentleman* (not published until the nineteenth century [ed. Karl Bülbring (London: David Nutt, 1890)]), argues from every possible angle the importance of admitting into the upper ranks the tradesman who has acquired – along with wealth – education, taste, virtue, sense, and cultivated manners. Boundaries of class in this new world of commercial wealth are not disappearing; they are simply expanding to accommodate the social implications of modern economic space.

35 Peter Earle, *The World of Defoe* (New York: Atheneum, 1977), 109.

36 Earle suggests that Defoe's optimism here about the smooth overlap of economic and social spheres is factually limited: "The labour market did not form a homogenous and competitive whole in which there was absolute occupational and geographic mobility. Instead it was composed of a series of heterogenous and for the most part non-competing categories, distinguished by location, sex, age, skill, education and a host of other different features" (Earle, *World of Defoe*, 111).

6 NARRATIVES OF PRIVATE SPACES: CHURCHES, HOUSES – AND NOVELS

1 Roger Chartier, "Community, State, and Family: Trajectories and Tensions," in *A History of Private Life*, ed. Philippe Ariès and George Duby, trans. Arthur Goldhammer (Cambridge, MA: Harvard University Press, 1989), III:400.

2 See, for example, Nancy Armstrong, *Desire and Domestic Fiction* (Oxford: Oxford University Press, 1987); Rosalind Ballaster, *Seductive Forms: Women's Amatory Fiction from 1684 to 1740* (Oxford: Clarendon Press, 1992); John Bender, *Imagining the Penitentiary: Fiction and the Architecture of Mind in the Eighteenth Century* (Chicago:

University of Chicago Press, 1987); J. Paul Hunter, *Before Novels: The Cultural Contexts of Eighteenth-Century English Fiction* (New York: W. W. Norton, 1990) and "The World as Stage and Closet," *British Theatre and Other Arts*, ed. Shirley Strum Kenny (Washington: Folger Shakespeare Library, 1984); Ian Watt, *The Rise of the Novel: Studies in Defoe, Richardson, and Fielding* (Berkeley: University of California Press, 1957).

3 See especially Hunter, *Before Novels*, and Watt, *The Rise of the Novel*.

4 Madeleine Foisil, "The Literature of Intimacy," *A History of Private Life*, III:384.

5 Wren, *Parentalia: Or, Memoirs of the Family of the Wrens*, 1750.

6 Spiro Kostof, *The City Shaped: Urban Patterns and Meanings Through History* (Boston: Little, Brown and Co., 1991), 293.

7 Lawrence Manley, *Literature and Culture in Early Modern London* (Cambridge: Cambridge University Press, 1995), 283.

8 Andor Gomme, "Architecture," *Seventeenth-Century Britain*, ed. Boris Ford (Cambridge: Cambridge University Press, 1989, 1992), 92.

9 See, for example, J. Paul Hunter, *The Reluctant Pilgrim: Defoe's Emblematic Method and Quest for Form in Robinson Crusoe* (Baltimore: Johns Hopkins University Press, 1966); Michael McKeon, *Origins of the English Novel 1600–1740* (Baltimore: Johns Hopkins University Press, 1987); G. A. Starr, *Defoe and Spiritual Autobiography* (Princeton: Princeton University Press, 1965).

10 Such as subscribing to the Thirty-Nine Articles, using the Book of Common Prayer, and becoming ordained by a bishop. See Paula Backscheider, *Daniel Defoe: His Life* (Baltimore: Johns Hopkins University Press, 1989); Gerald Cragg, *Puritanism in the Period of the Great Persecution 1660–1688* (Cambridge: Cambridge University Press, 1957); Donald Davie, *A Gathered Church: The Literature of the English Dissenting Interest, 1700–1930* (New York: Oxford University Press, 1978); Andrew Drummond, *The Church Architecture of Protestantism: An Historical and Constructive Study* (Edinburgh: T. and T. Clark, 1934); C. E. Whiting, *Studies in English Puritanism from the Restoration to the Revolution, 1660–1688* (London: Society for Promoting Christian Knowledge, 1931); Walter Wilson, *The History and Antiquities of Dissenting Churches and Meeting Houses, in London, Westminster, and Southwark*, 4 vols. (London, 1808); Elizabeth and Wayland Young, *Old London Churches* (London: Faber and Faber, 1956).

11 *A Proclamation Prohibiting all Unlawful and Seditious Meetings and Conventicles under Pretence of Religious Worship*, 1661.

12 Sermon XI, in *A Collection of Farewel-Sermons Preached by Mr Calamy, Mr Watson, Mr Sclater, Dr. Jacomb, Mr. Case, Mr. Baxter, Mr. Jenkins, Mr. Lye, Dr. Manton. To their respective Congregations at their departure from them* (1662), 36.

13 See Drummond, *Church Architecture*, 41–42; Whiting, *Studies in English Puritanism*, 448; Young and Young, *Old London Churches*, 4–5.

14 See also Drummond, *Church Architecture*.

15 Backscheider summarizes the years of worst persecution as 1662–64, 1670, and 1681–85 (*Daniel Defoe*, 7–10).

16 Whether the Foes remained in the city or fled to the countryside, and even though James Foe's house and tallow-chandler's shop numbered among the very few buildings spared in all of Broad Street Ward, and the rebuilding seems to have secured the fortunes of the

Foe family (Backscheider, *Daniel Defoe*, 4; James Sutherland, *Defoe* [London: Methuen, 1937] 13), I am taking what I believe to be a common-sense position – shared by most of Defoe's biographers – that as a child he could not have escaped witnessing the scenes of panic, terror, and grief, the evidence of destruction and loss, that dominated the city.

17 Daniel Defoe, *The Meditations of Daniel Defoe*, ed. George Harris Healey (Cummington, MA: The Cummington Press, 1946).

18 Numbers 35, Deuteronomy 19, Joshua 20. See F. Bastian, *Defoe's Early Life* (Totowa, NJ: Barnes and Noble, 1981), 81.

19 Defoe's earliest important work, *An Essay upon Projects* (1697), seizes the opportunity for a little revisionist self-history as it makes a bid for public favor and government sponsorship; many of his *Review* essays attempt to promote the tradesman's status as a gentleman, indirectly authorizing his own aspirations to gentility. And writing itself would more and more frequently become Defoe's quickest way to rebuilding the financial stability that periodically collapsed under other projects – the tile factory, the civet-cat farm.

20 See Lawrence Stone, *The Family, Sex, and Marriage in England 1500–1800* (abridged edition; New York: Harper and Row, 1977, 1979), 169.

21 See Stone, *Family, Sex, and Marriage*, 169; also Mark Girouard, *Life in the English Country House* (New Haven: Yale University Press, 1978); Hunter, *Before Novels*; Sir John Summerson, *Georgian London* (1945; Harmondsworth: Penguin, 1986).

22 Christopher Simon Sykes, *Private Palaces: Life in the Great London Houses* (London: Chatto and Windus, 1985), 21.

23 *London Chronicle*, June 2, 1764, quoted in M. Dorothy George, *London Life in the Eighteenth Century* (1925; New York: Harper and Row, 1964), 84. This newspaper account documents nearly one hundred years of brickmaking chicanery, and George notes that finally the persistent governmental attempts to regulate brickmaking were abandoned (*London Life*, 84).

24 See Michael Shinagel, *Daniel Defoe and Middle-Class Gentility* (Cambridge, MA: Harvard University Press, 1968), 61.

25 J. Paul Hunter suggests that Defoe's main purpose in *The Storm* is to interpret it as God's judgment on the sins of England (*The Reluctant Pilgrim* [Baltimore: Johns Hopkins University Press, 1966], 73). But Defoe still finds tiles of very absorbing personal interest.

26 Defoe, *Reformation of Manners* (1702), 88.

27 Defoe, *An Inquiry into the Occasional Conformity of Dissenters* (1698), 142.

28 Defoe, *The Life and Strange Surprizing Adventures of Robinson Crusoe of York, Mariner* (1719), ed. Michael Shinagel, 2nd edn. (New York: W. W. Norton, 1994), 116. Further references will be cited in the text, abbreviated *RC*.

29 Jean Marie Goulemot, "Literary Practices: Publicizing the Private," *The History of Private Life*, III:384.

30 In a slightly different context, Michael McKeon notes: "Robinson's imaginative enclosures are more treacherous than his physical ones because they cannot be held accountable to a standard that is clearly distinct from their own" (*Origins of the English Novel*, 327).

31 Pat Rogers, "Crusoe's Home," *Essays in Criticism* 24 (1974): 375–90.

32 Lennard J. Davis, " 'Known Unknown Locations': Ideology of Novelistic Landscape in *Robinson Crusoe*," *Sociocriticism* 4–5 (1986–87): 87–113. See also McKeon, *Origins of the English Novel*, 326–28; Simon Varey, *Space and the Eighteenth-Century English Novel* (Cambridge: Cambridge University Press, 1990), 154–55.

33 David Trotter offers a different account of Crusoe's use of textuality whereby "Crusoe lifts himself out of his absorption in materiality by exercising a technique of the self, a substitution of text for world" (*Circulation: Defoe, Dickens, and the Economies of the Novel* [London: Macmillan, 1988], 34. In Crusoe's economy of conversion, I would agree. But in his economy of domestic security, he employs text to *confirm* (the materiality of) the world. But both arguments converge: Crusoe finds in both cases how quickly a text can divorce itself from the world, or a journal from its larger narrative.

34 For different discussions about the function, appearance, chronology, and reliability of the journal, see Homer O. Brown, "The Displaced Self in the Novels of Daniel Defoe," *ELH* 38, no. 4 (December 1971): 562–90; Hunter, *The Reluctant Pilgrim*, 143–47; McKeon, *Origins of the English Novel*, 316–38.

35 In the fall of 1989 the Newberry Library in Chicago housed an exhibit of children's literature that featured editions of *Robinson Crusoe*; French editions seem particularly fascinated with Crusoe's hut, but German, Italian, Norwegian, Japanese, American, and English editions in the nineteenth and twentieth centuries also rarely failed to include some visualization of the invisible fortress.

36 Defoe, *Serious Reflections of Robinson Crusoe, with his Vision of the Angelic World* (London, 1790, III:267).

37 Michael Seidel argues, in a different context, that "Crusoe loses his fear of having his island penetrated when Defoe has him lose the desire to protect that which is no longer allegorically or historically primed for his holding of it" ("Crusoe in Exile," *PMLA* 96, no. 3 [May 1981], 370). Seidel makes symbolic temporal connections between Crusoe's exile and return and the troubled events of Stuart reign, but the events in Defoe's own life at this point equally mark the (temporarily) diminishing need for Defoe to protect what is no longer psychologically "primed for his holding of it." As Crusoe "progresses metaphorically as adventurer from the merchant class to the settled landed classes" (371), Defoe too moved comfortably into the suburbs – only to move imaginatively out again in the texts of the next few years.

38 Defoe, *Roxana; The Fortunate Mistress*, ed. Jane Jack (Oxford: Oxford University Press, 1964, 1986). Further references will be cited in the text, abbreviated *R*.

39 For additional examples of Roxana manipulating the prince through and within interior space, see 62, 63, 71, 77, 78–79, 96–97, 100.

40 See, for example, Maurice Barley, *Houses and History* (London: Faber and Faber, 1986); Hugh Braun, *Old English Houses* (London: Faber and Faber, 1962); Girouard, *Life in the English Country House*; A. E. Richardson and C. Lovett Gill, *London Houses from 1660 to 1820* (London: B. T. Batsford, [1911]); Sykes, *Private Palaces*.

41 Nicole Castan, "The Public and the Private," *A History of Private Life*, III:403, 402.

42 See Terry Castle, " 'Amy, Who Knew My Disease': A Psychosexual Pattern in Defoe's *Roxana*," *ELH* 46 (1979): 81–96.

43 Edward Soja, *Postmodern Geographies: The Reassertion of Space in Critical Social Theory* (London: Verso, 1989), 79.

44 Hunter, *Occasional Form: Henry Fielding and the Chains of Circumstance* (Baltimore: Johns Hopkins University Press, 1975), 146, 151.

45 Valerie Pearl, "Change and Stability in Seventeenth-century London," *The London Journal* 5, no. 1 (May 1979), 18.

46 Peter Collins, *Changing Ideals in Modern Architecture 1750–1950* (London: Faber and Faber, 1965), 22. He adds tentatively (although the bulk of his own argument supports this): "There are even some theorists who contend that this new attitude towards space constitutes the basic principle which distinguishes the style of the modern [twentieth century] age" (26).

47 See Simon Varey, *Space and the Eighteenth-Century English Novel* (Cambridge: Cambridge University Press, 1990), 37, 40.

48 For more extensive discussions of these changes, see, for example, Collins, *Changing Ideals*, 26–27; Girouard, *Life in the English Country House*, 211–14; Summerson, *Georgian London*, 144–45.

49 Dorothy Van Ghent, *The English Novel: Form and Function* (New York: Harper and Row, 1953), 34–35.

50 Max Byrd, *London Transform'd: Images of the City in the Eighteenth Century* (New Haven: Yale University Press, 1978), 13.

51 Introduction to *Moll Flanders* (Oxford: Oxford University Press, 1971), xx.

52 Introduction to *Robinson Crusoe* (Oxford: Oxford University Press, 1972), xv.

53 For analyses of the kinds of readers Defoe could have expected, see Backscheider, *Defoe*, 446–47; Hunter, " 'The Young, the Ignorant, and the Idle': Some Notes on Readers and the Beginnings of the English Novel," *Anticipations of the Enlightenment in England, France, and Germany*, ed. Alan Charles Kors and Paul J. Korshin (Philadelphia: University of Pennsylvania Press, 1982): 259–82, and chapter three in *Before Novels*; McKeon, *Origins of the Novel*, 52; Shinagel, *Defoe and Middle-Class Gentility*, 107–21.

54 I have argued elsewhere about the visual and spatial detail of private space in the novels of Defoe, Richardson, and Austen; see "Gendering Rooms: Domestic Architecture and Literary Acts," *Eighteenth-Century Fiction* 5, no. 4 (July 1993): 349–72, and my unpublished dissertation, "Housing Defoe's Projects: The Rebuilding of London and Modern Literary Space," The University of Chicago, 1992. For corresponding arguments about the architectural and visual vagueness of Austen's novels, see Nikolas Pevsner, "The Architectural Setting of Jane Austen's Novels," *Journal of the Warburg and Courtauld Institutes* 31 (1968): 404–42; Alastair Duckworth, *The Improvement of the Estate: A Study of Jane Austen's Novels* (Baltimore: Johns Hopkins University Press, 1971); John Dixon Hunt, "Architecture/Buildings," *The Jane Austen Handbook*, ed. J. David Grey (London: Athlone Press, 1986), 5–6.

55 Rachel Trickett, " 'Curious Eye': Some Aspects of Visual Description in Eighteenth-Century Literature," *Augustan Studies: Essays in Honor of Irvin Ehrenpreis*, ed. Douglas Lane Patey and Timothy Keegan (Newark: University of Delaware Press, 1985), 239–52. See also Jean Hagstrum, "Pictures to the Heart: The Psychological Picturesque in Ann Radcliffe's *The Mysteries of Udolpho*," *Greene Centennial Studies*, ed. Paul J.

Korshin and Robert R. Allen (Charlottesville: University Press of Virginia, 1984), 434–41, in which he argues that "the sensuous in Mrs. Radcliffe is also the sensual, or at least anticipates the sensual" (441), supporting the idea of changed value in novelistic detail.

56 Delarivier Manley, *The New Atalantis*, ed. Rosalind Ballaster (Harmondsworth: Penguin, 1992), 20–21. See John Richetti, *Popular Fiction Before Richardson* (Oxford: Clarendon Press, 1969, 1992); Rosalind Ballaster, *Seductive Forms: Women's Amatory Fiction from 1684 to 1740* (Oxford: Clarendon Press, 1992); and for a good discussion of the reversal of gender roles in the construction of the gaze, see Toni Bowers, "Sex, Lies, and Invisibility: Amatory Fiction from the Restoration to Mid-Century," *The Columbia History of the British Novel*, ed. John Richetti (New York: Columbia University Press, 1994), 50–72.

57 For example: "Dec. 28, 29, 30. Great Heats and no Breeze; so that there was no Stirring abroad, except in the Evening for Food . . . [January 1] Very hot still, but I went abroad early and late with my Gun" (*RC* 56); "the Weather prov'd hazey for three or four Days . . . and not being able to see the Sun, I wander'd about very uncomfortably . . . the Weather being exceeding hot, and my Gun, Ammunition, Hatchet, and other Things very heavy" (*RC* 81).

Bibliography

PRIMARY SOURCES

(Unless otherwise noted, place of publication is London for early editions.)

An Account of a Great & Famous Scolding-Match between Four Remarkable Scolding Fish-Women of Rosemary-lane, and the like Number of Basket-Women of Golden-lane. 1699.

An Account of the Names of the immediate Tenants, now inhabiting the severall Houses and Grounds, in brick-Lane, Old-streete, Blew-Boar Court, Blew-Anchor-Ally, &c. 1671. Guildhall MS 17,254.

"An Act for Rebuilding the City of London." 1667. *The Statutes at Large.* 1770. III:304.

Adams, John. *Index Villaris.* 1680 and 1690.

[Adamus, Johannes.] *Londinum Heroico Carmine Perlustratum; The Renowned City of LONDON Surveyed, and Illustrated In a Latine Poem By J. Adamus a Transylvanian. And translated into English By W. F. of Grays-Inn J. C.* 1670.

Addison, Joseph, and Richard Steele. *The Spectator.* Ed. Donald F. Bond. 5 vols. Oxford: Clarendon Press, 1965.

[Allison, John.] *Upon the Late Lamentable Fire in London.* 1667.

Anglia Rediviva: A Poem on His Majesties Most Joyfull Reception into Enland [sic]. 1660.

Arguments Concerning the New-Buildings in the Parishes within the Weekly Bills of Mortality, without the City of London. [1680.]

Ashmole, Elias. *The Antiquities of Berkshire.* 1719.

Aubrey, John. *Brief Lives.* Ed. Richard Barber. Woodbridge, Suffolk: The Boydell Press, 1975, 1982.

Barbon, Nicholas. *An Apology for the Builder: Or, A Discourse Shewing the Cause and Effects of the Increase of Building.* 1685.

Behn, Aphra. *The City-Heiress.* 1698.

Bell, William. *City Security Stated.* 1661.

[Blackmore, Sir Richard.] *A Satyr Against Wit.* 1700.

Blondel, Pierre. *Plan de Paris.* Paris, 1710.

A Book of the Names of All Parishes, Market Towns, Villages, Hamblets and Smallest Places, in England and Wales. Alphabetically set down, as they be in every Shire. 1643, 1677.

Boyle, Robert. *Certain Physiological Essays, Written at distant Times, and on several Occasions.* 1661.
The Works of the Honourable Robert Boyle, Esq. Epitomiz'd. By Richard Boulton, of Brazen-Nose College in Oxford. 4 vols. 1699.

Bramston, James. *The Art of Politicks.* 1729.
The Man of Taste. 1733.

Brome, Alexander. *The Poems of Horace, Rendred in English and Paraphrased by Several Persons.* 3rd edn. 1680.

Brome, Richard. *A Joviall Crew.* 1661.

Brooks, Thomas. *London's Lamentations*. 1670.

Brown, Thomas. *Amusements Serious & Comical*. 1700.

    A Description of Mr. D—n's Funeral. A Poem. 1700.

    The Town Display'd. 1701.

    The Works of Mr. Thomas Brown, In Prose and Verse, Serious, Moral, and Comical. 4 vols. 1707.

Brydall, John. *Camera Regis, Or, A Short View of London*. 1676.

Burton, Robert [i.e. Nathaniel Crouch]. *Admirable Curiosities, Rarities and Wonders in England, Scotland, and Ireland*. 1718.

    Historical Remarques and Observations of the Ancient and Present State of London. 1681.

    A New View of London ... Continued by an Able Hand. 1730.

Camden, William. *Britain, or A Chorographicall Description of the Most flourishing Kingdomes, England, Scotland, and Ireland*. 1637.

Campbell, Colen. *Vitruvius Britannicus*. 2 vols. 1715.

Campbell, Robert. *The London Tradesman*. 1747.

[Caryll, John.] *The English Princess*. 1667.

[Chamberlayne, Edward.] *Angliae Notitia*. 1667–71.

    England's Wants. 1667.

The Charter: A Comical Satyr. [1682.]

Chippendale, Thomas. *The Gentleman and Cabinet Maker's Director*. 1754.

Clarendon, Edward Hyde, Earl of. *Continuation of the Life of Edward Earl of Clarendon*. 3 vols. Oxford, 1759.

Clavell, Robert. *A General catalog of books since ... 1666*. 1680.

A Collection of Farewel-Sermons Preached by Mr Calamy ... To Their Respective Congregations at Their Departure from Them. 1662.

A Collection of Scarce and Valuable Tracts, On the Most Interesting and Entertaining Subjects: But Chiefly such as relate to the History and Constitution of These Kingdoms. Ed. Sir Walter Scott. 2nd edn. 1812.

A Collection of the Names of Merchants. 1677.

A Comical New Dialogue between Mr. G——ff, A Pious Dissenting Parson, and a Female Quaker (A Goldsmith's Wife) near Cheapside. [n.d.]

A Computation of the Increase of London, And Parts Adjacent; with some Causes thereof and Remarks thereon. 1719.

The Court of Neptune Burlesqu'd. A Satyr upon the City. [1700.]

Cowley, Abraham. *Cutter of Coleman-Street*. 1658.

[Crane, Richard.] *A Lamentation over Thee, O London*. 1665.

[Crook, John.] *Compassion to All*. 1665.

[Crouch, John.] *Londinenses Lacrymae. Londons Second Tears mingled with her Ashes. A Poem*. 1666.

    A Mixt poem, partly historicall, partly panegyricall, upon the happy return of his sacred majesty Charles the Second. 1660.

The Cupulo. A Poem. Occasion'd By the Vote of the House of Commons for Covering that of St. PAUL's with British Copper. 1708.

D., J. *The Mall: Or the Modish Lovers*. 1674.

Davenant, Sir William. *Two Excellent Plays*. 1665.

Davies, Sir John. *Epigrams*. 1590.

Defoe, Daniel. *An Appeal to Honour and Justice*. 1715.

Atlas Maritimus & Commercialis. 1728.

Augusta Triumphans. 1728.

A Brief Historical Account of the Lives of the Six Notorious Street-Robbers, Executed at Kingston. 1726. *Romances and Narratives by Daniel Defoe*. Ed. George A. Aitken. Vol. XVI. London: Dent, 1905.

The Compleat English Gentleman. 1730. Ed. Karl D. Bülbring. London: David Nutt, 1927.

The Complete English Tradesman. 2 vols. 1725.

The Complete English Tradesman. Ed. William and Robert Chambers. 1839. Gloucester: Alan Sutton, 1987.

Conjugal Lewdness. 1727. Ed. Maximilian Novak. Gainesville: Scholars' Facsimiles & Reprints, 1967.

The Consolidator: Or, Memoirs of Sundry Transactions from the World in the Moon. Translated from the Lunar Language, By the Author of The True-born Englishman. 1705.

Due Preparations for the Plague as Well for Soul as Body. 1722.

An Effectual Scheme for the Immediate Preventing of Street Robberies. 1731.

An Essay at Removing National Prejudices against a Union with Scotland. Parts I–V. Edinburgh, 1706.

Essay on the History and Reality of Apparitions. 1727.

An Essay upon Projects. 1697.

An Essay upon Publick Credit. 1710.

Every Body's Business, is No Body's Business. 1725.

The Family Instructor, in Three Parts. Newcastle, 1715.

The Farther Adventures of Robinson Crusoe. 1719. London: Chatto and Windus, 1904.

The Fortunes and Misfortunes of the Famous Moll Flanders. 1722. Ed. G. A. Starr. Oxford: Oxford University Press, 1971.

A General History of Discoveries and Improvements. 1725–27.

The History and Remarkable Life of the Truly Honourable Col. Jacque, Commonly Call'd Col. Jack. 1722. Ed. Samuel Holt Monk. Oxford: Oxford University Press, 1965.

History of the Plague in London, 1665. In *The Novels and Miscellaneous Works of Daniel De Foe*. Ed. Sir Walter Scott. Vol. V. London: George Bell, 1888.

Hymn to the Pillory. 1703.

An Inquiry into the Occasional Conformity of Dissenters. 1698.

A Journal of the Plague Year. 1722. Ed. Louis Landa. Oxford: Oxford University Press, 1990.

The Letters of Daniel Defoe. Ed. George Harris Healey. Oxford: Clarendon Press, 1955.

The Libraries of Daniel Defoe and Phillips Farewell. Ed. Helmut Heidenreich. Berlin: W. Hildebrand, 1970.

The Life, Adventures, and Pyracies, of the Famous Captain Singleton. 1720. Ed. Shiv K. Kumar. Oxford: Oxford University Press, 1973.

The Life and Strange Surprizing Adventures of Robinson Crusoe. 1719. Ed. J. Donald Crowley. Oxford: Oxford University Press, 1972.

The Life and Strange Surprizing Adventures of Robinson Crusoe. Ed. Michael Shinagel. 2nd edn. New York: W. W. Norton, 1994.

The Life and Surprising Adventures of Robinson Crusoe. Illustrated by George Cruikshank. London: David Bogue, 1853.

The Life of Jonathan Wild. 1725.

The Manufacturer. October 13, 1719, to February 17, 1720. Introduced by Robert M. Gosselink. Delmar, NY: Scholars' Facsimiles and Reprints, 1978.

The Meditations of Daniel Defoe. Ed. George Harris Healey. Cummington, MA: The Cummington Press, 1946.

Memoirs of a Cavalier. 1720. London: Constable and Co., 1926.

A New Family Instructor. 1727.

The Protestant Monastery. 1727.

Reformation of Manners. 1702.

The Review. 1704–13.

Roxana, Or, The Fortunate Mistress. 1724. Ed. Jane Jack. Oxford: Oxford University Press, 1964, 1986.

Serious Reflections during the Life and Surprising Adventures of Robinson Crusoe, with His Vision of the Angelic World. 1720, 1790. *The Works of Daniel Defoe*. Ed. G. H. Maynadier. Vol. III. New York: Crowell, 1903.

The Shortest Way with the Dissenters. 1702.

The Storm: Or, a Collection of the most Remarkable Casualties and Disasters Which happen'd in the Late Dreadful Tempest, Both by Sea and Land. 1704.

Street-Robberies, Consider'd. 1728.

A Tour thro' the whole Island of Great Britain. 3 vols. 1724–26.

A Tour thro' the whole Island of Great Britain. Ed. Pat Rogers. Harmondsworth: Penguin, 1971.

The Versatile Defoe: An Anthology of Uncollected Writings. Ed. Laura A. Curtis. Totowa, NJ: Rowman and Littlefield, 1979.

Dekker, Thomas. *The Gvls Horne-booke: Stultorum plena sunt omnias*. 1609.

DeLaune, Thomas. *The Present State of London: Or, Memorials comprehending a Full and Succinct Account of the Ancient and Modern State thereof*. London, 1681.

[Dewsbury, William.] *This for Dear Friends in London*. 1665.

A Dialogue Betwixt Tom and Dick, the Former a Country-man, the Other a Citizen, Presented to His Excellency and the Council of State, at Drapers Hall in London, March 28. 1660.

Discourse Shewing the Great Advantages that New-Buildings, And the Enlarging of Town and Cities Do bring to a Nation. 1678.

Dryden, John. *Annus Mirabilis*. 1666.

　Mac Flecknoe. 1682.

Dugdale, William. *The Antiquities of Warwickshire*. 1656.

　The History of St. Paul's Cathedral. 1658.

Durfey, Thomas. *Collin's Walk through London and Westminster*. 1690.

　Madam Fickle; or, The Witty False One. 1677.

Earle, John. *Micro-cosmographie, or, A Peece of the World Discovered; in Essayes and Characters. Newly Composed for the Northerne parts of this Kingdome*. 3rd edn. 1628.

　The World Display'd: Or, Several Essays; Consisting of the various Characters and Passions of its principal Inhabitants. 1740.

Elborough, Robert. *London's Calamity by Fire Bewailed and Improved, In a Sermon Preached at St. James Dukes Place*. 1666.

Elderton, William. "A New Merry Newes." 1606.

England's Joy, for London's Loyalty. 1664.

English Architecture: Or, The Publick Buildings of London and Westminster. [1756.]

Etherege, Sir George. *The Comical Revenge; or, Love in a Tub*. 1664.

  The Man of Mode; or, Sir Fopling Flutter. 1676.

[Evans, David Morier.] *The City; or, The Physiology of London Business, with Sketches on 'Change and at the Coffee Houses*. London: Baily Brothers, 1845.

Evelyn, John. *A Character of England, As it was Lately Presented in a Letter, to a Noble Man of FRANCE*. 1659.

  The Diary of John Evelyn. 6 vols. Ed. E. S. De Beer. Oxford: Clarendon Press, 1955.

  Fumifugium: Or, The Inconveniencie of the Aer and Smoak of London Dissipated. 1661.

  London Revived; Consideration for its Rebuilding in 1666. Ed. E. S. De Beer. Oxford: Clarendon Press, 1938.

  Navigation and Commerce, Their Original and Progress. 1674.

  A Panegyric to Charles the Second, Preached to His Majestie the XXXIII. *[sic] of April, Being the Day of His CORONATION*. 1661.

Falkland, Henry. *The Mariage [sic] Night*. 1664.

Farquhar, George. *Sir Harry Wildair*. 1701.

Fielding, Henry. *Enquiry into the Causes of the Late Increase of Robbers*. 1751.

Fiennes, Celia. *The Journeys of Celia Fiennes*. Ed. Christopher Morris, foreword by G. M. Trevelyan. London: Cresset Press, 1949.

  Through England on a Side Saddle. London: Field and Tuer, 1888.

The Fire Court: Calendar to the Judgments and Decrees of the Court of Judicature appointed to determine differences between landlords and tenants as to rebuilding after the Great Fire. 2 vols. Ed. Philip E. Jones. London: William Clowes and Sons, 1966.

Fitzherbert, John. *The Boke of Surueying, and Improvements, newly corrected and amended, very necessarye for all men*. [Attributed to Sir Anthony Fitzherbert.] 1537. [1587.]

Flecknoe, Richard. *The Damoiselles*. 1667.

Ford, Simon. *The Conflagration of London Poetically delineated*. 1667.

  Londini quod Reliquum. Or, Londons Remains: In Latin and English. 1667.

  Londons Resurrection, Poetically represented. 1669.

The Foreigner's Guide: Or, a necessary and instructive Companion Both for the Foreigner and Native, In Their Tour through the Cities of London and Westminster. 1729.

Gay, John. *The Beggar's Opera*. 1728. Ed. Bryan Loughrey and T. O. Treadwell. Harmondsworth: Penguin, 1986.

  Trivia; or, The Art of Walking the Streets of London. 1716.

Gearing, William. *No Abiding City in a Perishing World. Meditations occasioned by the late sad, and lamentable fire, in the City of London*. 1667.

  God's Soveraignty Displayed. [1667].

Gerbier, Sir Balthazar. *Counsel and Advice to All Builders*. 1663.

Gough, R[ichard.] *Anecdotes of British Topography; Or, An Historical Account of What has been done for illustrating the Topographical Antiquities of Great Britain and Ireland*. 2 vols. 1758.

Gough, William. *Londinum Triumphans, Or, An Historical Account of the Grand Influence the Actions of the City of London have had upon the Affairs of the Nation*. 1682.

Gt. Brit. Parliament. House of Commons. *London's Flames Being an Exact Account . . .* 1679.
    A True and Faithful Account of . . . the Late Dreadful Burning . . . 1667.

Gt. Brit. Sovereigns, etc., 1660–1685 (Charles II). *His Majesties declaration to his city of London upon occasion of the late Calamity by the lamentable fire.* September 13, 1666.
    His Majesties Most Gracious Speech to Both Houses of Parliament. September 21, 1666.
    A Proclamation for a General Fast through England and Wales. October 10, 1666.
    A Proclamation for Restoring Goods Imbezzll'd during the Late Fire and Since. September 19, 1666.
    A Proclamation for the Suppressing of Disorderly and Unseasonable Meetings, in Taverns and Tipling-houses, and also Forbidding Footmen to Wear Swords, and Other Weapons, within London and Westminster. September 29, 1660.
    A Proclamation Prohibiting All Unlawful and Seditious Meetings and Conventicles under Pretence of Religious Worship. January 10, 1660/1.
    A Proclamation Prohibiting the Seizing of Any Persons, or Searching Houses without Warrant, except in Time of Actuall Insurrections. January 17, 1660/1.
    A Proclamation to Restrain the Abuses of Hackney Coaches in the Cities of London, and Westminster, and the Suburbs thereof. October 18, 1660.
    A Proclamation Touching the Charitable Collections for Relief of the Poor Distressed. 1668.

Greene, Robert. *Life and Complete Works.* 15 vols. Ed. A. B. Grosart. London: Huth Library, 1881–83.

Grose, Francis. *Antiquities of England and Wales.* 1773.

[Guillim, Joseph.] *Akamaton Pyr, Or The Dreadful Burning of London: Described in a Poem.* 1667.

Guilpin, Edward. *Skialetheia.* 1598.

Gwynn, John. *London and Westminster Improved.* [With an introduction by Samuel Johnson.] 1766.

Halfpenny, William. *Magnum in Parvo: or, The Marrow of Architecture.* 1728. New York: Benjamin Blom, 1968.
    Practical Architecture, or a Sure Guide to the True Working According to the Rules of that Science. 5th edn. 1730. New York: Benjamin Blom, 1968.

Hardy, Nathaniel. *Lamentation, Mourning and Woe. Sighed forth in a Sermon Preached in the Parish-Church of St. Martin in the Fields, on the 9th Day of September.* 1666.

Harvey, Gideon. *A Discourse of the Plague.* 1665.

Hatton, [Edward.] *A New View of London; Or, an Ample Account of that City.* 1708.

Haywood, Eliza. *The Masquerade Novels of Eliza Haywood.* Ed. Mary Anne Schofield. Delmar: Scholar's Facsimiles and Reprints, 1986.

Head, Richard. *The English Rogue Described in the Life of Meriton Latroon.* 4 vols. 1672.
    The English Rogue. Ed. Michael Shinagel. Boston: New Frontiers Press, 1961.

Heath, John. *Two Centuries of Epigrammes.* 1610.
    Witts Recreations. 1640.

Hesketh, Henry. *A Sermon Preached before the . . . Lord Mayor and Aldermen of London, at Guild-hall Chappel upon the Second of September, 1679.*

Heylyn, Peter. *Cosmographie.* 1666.

Heywood, John. *Three Hundred Epigrammes, upon Three Hundred Prouerbes,* in *The Proverbs, Epigrams, and Miscellanies of John Heywood.* Ed. J. S. Farmer. London: EEDS, 1906.

Hicks, William. *London Drollery: Or, the Wits Academy.* 1673.

Hogarth, William. *The Analysis of Beauty.* Ed. Joseph Burke. Oxford: Clarendon Press, 1955.

Hollar, Wenceslaus. *A Map or Groundplot of the City of London, and the Suburbs thereof . . . by which is exactly demonstrated the present condition thereof, since the last sad accident of fire.* 1666.

Another Plan of London After the Fire, Showing the Part Demolished. 1666.

Bird's-eye Plan of London Before the Fire with the Arms of the City Companies. 1667.

Bird's-eye Plan of the West Central District of London. [1658].

An Exact Surveigh of the Streets, Lanes, and Churches Contained Within the Ruines of the City of London (by John Leake). 1666, 1669.

The Kingdome of England & Principality of Wales Exactly Described with Every Sheere. & the small town in euery one of them in Six Mappes, Portable for euery Mans Pocket. 1644.

A New Map of the Citties of London, Westminster and ye Borough of Southwarke. 1675.

Plan of London after the Fire, Showing the Part Demolished. 1666.

A Plan of LONDON as in Q. Elizabeths Days. 1666.

Holwell, John. *A Sure Guide to the Practical Surveyor.* 1678.

Hooke, Robert. *An Attempt to prove the motion of the earth from observations made by Robert Hooke Fellow of the Royal Society.* 1674.

Howell, James. *Instructions for Forreine Travell.* 1642.

Londinopolis, an Historicall Discourse or Perlustration of the City of London. 1657.

Hume, David. *The History of England from the Time of Julius Caesar to the Revolution in 1688.* 1778. 6 vols. Indianapolis: Liberty Classics, 1983.

Jacob, Giles. *The Poetical Register: Or, the Lives and Characters of the English Dramatick Poets.* 1729.

Jordan, Thomas. *London in Luster: Projecting Many Bright Beams of Triumph Disposed into Several Representations of Scenes and Pageants.* 1679.

King, William. *Art of Cookery.* 1708.

A Journey to London. 1698.

Knavery in all trades; or, The Coffee-house. 1664.

Knavery Unmask'd. [1709.]

Knight, Valentine. *Proposals of a new Modell for Re-building the City of LONDON.* 1666.

[Langley, Batty]. *An Accurate Description of Newgate.* 2nd edn. 1729.

Langley, Batty. *The Builder's Chest-book; or, A Complete Key to the Five Orders of Columns in Architecture.* 1727. Farnborough: Gregg International Publishers, 1971.

The City and Country Builder's and Workman's Treasury of Design. 1740.

The Lawyer Turn'd Butcher, and the Physician, Cook: Or, Hungry Dogs will Eat Dirty Pudding. 1702.

LeBlanc, J.-B. *Lettres Concernant le Gouvernement, la Politique, et les Mœurs des Anglois et des François.* Paris, 1745.

Lediard, Thomas. *Some Observations on the Scheme, Offered by Messrs. Cotton and Lediard for Opening the Streets and Passages to and from the Intended Bridge at Westminster.* 1738.

Leigh, Valentine. *The Moste Profitable and Commendable Sciences, of Surueying of Landes, Tenements, and Hereditamentes.* 1577.

Leybourn, William. *The Compleat Surveyor: Containing the whole Art of Surveying of Land.* 5th edn. 1722.

The Public Markets of the City of London Surveyed by William Leybourn in 1677. Ed. Betty R. Masters. London: London Topographical Society, Publication no. 117, 1974.

Lithgow, William. *The Present Survegh of London and England's State.* 1643.

London Gazette. 1666–1745.

London Undone; or, A Reflection upon the Late Disasterous Fire. 1666.

Mackworth, Sir Humphrey. *England's Glory, or, The Great Improvement of Trade in General, by a Royal Bank or Office of Credit, to be Erected in London.* 1694.

Macky, John. *A Journey through England. In Familiar Letters from a Gentleman Here, To His Friend Abroad.* 2nd edn. 1722.

Maitland, William. *The History of London from its Foundation by the Romans to the Present Time.* 1739.

Mandery, Venterus. *Mellificium Mensionis: or, The Marrow of Measuring.* 1682, 1727.

Manley, Delarivier. *The New Atalantis.* 1709. Ed. Rosalind Ballaster. Harmondsworth: Penguin, 1992.

[Mayne, Jasper.] *The City Match.* 1659.

Mills, Peter, and John Oliver. *The Survey of Building Sites in the City of London after the Great Fire of 1666.* Ed. P. E. Jones and T. F. Reddaway. 5 vols. London: London Topographical Society, 1967.

Morden, Robert. *A Prospect of London; A Book of the Prospects of the Remarkable Places in and about the City of London.* [1690.]

Morgan, William. *London &c. Actually Survey'd By Wm. Morgan, His Maties. Cosmo^gr. 1681/2.* London: London Topographical Society, 1904.

Morris, Robert. *An Essay in Defence of Ancient Architecture.* 1728. Westmead: Gregg International Publishing, 1971.

  Rural Architecture. 1750.

Moxon, Joseph. *Mechanick Dyalling.* 1668.

  A Tutor to Astronomy and Geography. 1665.

N., E. *London's Sins Reproved.* 1665.

New Remarks of London: Or, A Survey of the Cities of London and Westminster ... Collected by the Company of Parish-Clerks. 1732.

A New-thing, of Nothing. 1664.

Newcourt, Richard. *Three Mapps of London.* 1666. Guildhall MS 3441.

Norden, John. *Speculum Britanniae.* 1593.

North, Roger. *Autobiography of Roger North.* Ed. A. Jessop. London, 1887.

Ogilby, John. *The Relation of His Majestie's Entertainment Passing through the City of London.* 1661.

Ogilby, John, and William Morgan. *London Survey'd or, an Explanation of the Large Map of London.* 1677.

Oldham, John. "The Thirteenth Satire of Juvenal Imitated." *Works.* 1682.

Oldys, William. *A Dissertation upon Pamphlets, and the Undertaking of Phoenix Britannicus, to Revive the Most Excellent Among Them.* 1731.

Oxenbridge, John. *A Double Watch-word, or the Duty of Watching; and Watching to Duty.* 1661.

Palladio, Andrea. *The First Book of Architecture.* 1663.

  The Four Books of Architecture. Trans. Isaac Ware. 1737. Reprinted with an introduction by Adolf K. Placzek. New York: Dover, 1965.

The Parish Complaint against Mr Lindsay & Mr Hawkins upon an encroachment made upon the Parish ground. Guildhall MS 20,388.

A Particular of the New-buildings within the Bills of Mortallity, and without the City of London, from the year 1656. to 1677. 1680.

Payne, Neville. *The Morning Ramble.* 1673.

Peachum, Henry. *Coach and Sedan.* 1636.

    The Compleat Gentleman. 1661.

Pennant, Thomas. *The Antiquities of London.* 2nd edn. 1818.

Pepys, Samuel. *The Diary of Samuel Pepys.* Ed. Robert Latham and William Matthews. Berkeley: University of California Press, 1972.

Petty, Sir William. *Observations upon the Cities of London and Rome.* 1687.

[Philalethes, Theophilus.] *Great Britains Glory, or, A Brief Description of the present State, Splendor, and Magnificence of the Royal Exchange.* 1672.

A Plan of the City and Suburbs of London as Fortified by Order of Parliament in the Years 1642 & 1643.

Pope, Alexander. *The Poems of Alexander Pope.* Twickenham Edition. Ed. John Butt. New Haven: Yale University Press, 1963.

Porter, Thomas. *The Carnival.* 1664.

Pratt, Sir Roger. *The Architecture of Sir Roger Pratt.* Ed. R J. Gunther. Oxford: Oxford University Press, 1928.

[Ralph, James.] *A Critical Review of the Publick Buildings, Statues and Ornaments In, and about London and Westminster.* 1734.

Ravenscroft, Edward. *The Citizen Turn'd Gentleman.* 1672.

    The English Lawyer. 1678.

    The London Cuckolds. 1683.

[Rawlinson, Richard.] *The English Topographer.* 1720.

Revet, Edward. *The Town-Shifts, or, the Suburb-Justice.* 1671.

Reynell, Carew. *The True English Interest: Or an Account of the Chief National Improvements.* 1674.

[Robinson, William.] *Proportional Architecture; or, the Five Orders regulated by Equal Parts.* 1733. Farnborough: Gregg International Publishers, 1971.

Rocque, John. *John Rocque's Map: The A to Z of Georgian London.* 1746. Ed. Ralph Hyde. Kent: Harry Margary, 1981.

[Roe, Daniel.] *God's Judgments.* [1666.]

Rolls, Samuel. *Londons Resurrection or the Rebuilding of London Encouraged, Directed, and Improved, in Fifty Discourses.* 1668.

Rouquet, André. *The Present State of the Arts in England.* 1753–54.

Royal Society. *Philosophical Transactions.* 1665–1745.

St. Benet Gracechurch. *An Account of the inhabetants which are howse-keapers in the presint of St Bennit Grace Church and what time they came in after the dredful fyer. In London taken the 14th of December 1670.* Guildhall MS 4056.

St. Bride Fleet Street. *List of Householders 1666.* Guildhall MS 14,819.

Sancroft, William. *Lex Ignea.* 1666.

Settle, Elkanah. *An Elegie on the Late Fire and Ruines of London.* 1667.

Shadwell, Thomas. *Epsom-Wells.* 1673.

    The Libertine. 1676.

The Miser. 1672.

The Sullen Lovers. 1668.

A Short Account of the Proceedings of the College of Physicians, London, in relation to the Sick Poor of the said City, and Suburbs thereof. 1697.

A Short and Serious Narrative of Londons Fatal Fire. 1667.

A Short Answer to a Late Book, entituled, Tentamen Medicinale. 1705.

Smith, John. *England's Improvement Reviv'd: In a Treatise of all Manner of Husbandry and Trade by Land and Sea.* 1673.

Smith, William. *De Urbis Londini Incendio Elegiea.* 1667.

Sorbiere, Samuel. *Relation d'un Voyage en Angleterre.* 1664.

Speed, John. *Speed's Maps Epitomiz'd or the Maps of the Counties of England alphabetically placed.* 1681.

The Theatre of the Empire of Great Britaine. 1611.

Sprat, Thomas. *History of the Royal Society.* 1667.

Observations on M. de Sorbier's Voyage. 1665.

[Stapleton, Sir Robert.] *The Step-mother.* 1664.

Stent, Peter. *A Catalogue of Books, Pictures, Maps.* 1662.

Stockton, Owen. *Counsel to the Afflicted: or, Instruction and Consolation for such as have suffered Loss by Fire.* 1667.

Stow, John. *A Svrvay of London. Contayning the Originall, Antiquity, Increase, Moderne Estate, and Description of that Citie.* 1598.

The Survey of London. Ed. H. B. Wheatley. Intro. Valerie Pearl. London: Dent, 1987.

Stow, William. *Remarks on London.* 1722.

Strype, John. *A Survey of the Cities of London and Westminster . . . Corrected, Improved, and very much Enlarged.* 2 vols. 1720.

Swift, Jonathan. "A Description of a City Shower." 1710.

The Examiner No. 22. December 21–28, 1710.

Tabor, John. *Seasonable Thoughts in Sad Times, Being Some Reflections on the Warre, the Pestilence, and the Burning of London.* 1667.

Taylor, John. *Travels and Circular Perambulation.* 1636.

Taylor, Thomas. *England exactly Described or a Guide to Travellers In a Compleat Sett of Mapps of all the County's of England.* [1715.]

Thomas, William. *The Countries Sens of LONDONS Suffering In the Late most Lamentable Fire.* 1667.

The Town-Rakes: Or, The Frolicks of the Mohocks or Hawkubites. 1712.

Treswell, Ralph. *The London Surveys of Ralph Treswell.* Ed. John Schofield. London: London Topographical Society, 1987.

Troia Rediviva, or, the Glories of London. 1674.

A True and Faithful Account of the Several Informations . . . [concerning] the late Dreadful Burning . . . of London. 1667.

A Collection of Scarce and Valuable Tracts. Ed. Sir Walter Scott. 1812.

[Tuke, Sir Samuel.] *The Adventures of Five Hours.* 1664.

Uffenbach, Zacharias Conrad von. *London in 1710: From the Travels of Zacharias Conrad von Uffenbach.* Trans. and ed. W. H. Quarrell and Margaret Mare. London: Faber and Faber, 1934.

Upon Sight of London's Stately New Buildings. 1672.

A View of London and Westminster. 1725.

A View of the Town. [1732.]

Vitruvius. *The Ten Books of Architecture.* Trans. M. H. Morgan. Cambridge, MA: Harvard University Press, 1916.

Waller, Edmund. *Poems, &c.* 1664.

  Upon Her Majesties New Buildings. 1665.

Ward, Edward. *Hudibras Redivivus.* 1708.

  The London Spy. 1698–1700, 1703.

  Vade Mecum for Malt-Worms: Or, a Guide to Good Fellows. 1720.

  A Walk to Islington: With a Description of New Tunbridge-Wells, and Sadlers Musick-house. 1695.

Ware, Isaac. *A Complete Body of Architecture.* 1756.

Waterhouse, Edward. *A Short Narrative of the Late Dreadful Fire in London.* 1667.

[Wilson, John.] *Andronicus Commenius.* 1664.

  The Cheats. 1664.

  The Projectors. 1665.

Wilson, Walter. *The History and Antiquities of Dissenting Churches and Meeting Houses in London, Westminster, and Southwark.* 4 vols. 1808.

Wiseman, Samuel. *Londons' Fatal Fire.* 1667.

Wood, Anthony. *The Life and Times of Anthony Wood, Antiquary, of Oxford, 1632–1695, described by Himself.* Ed. Andrew Clark. Oxford: Oxford Historical Society at the Clarendon Press, 1892.

[Worcester, Edward Somerset]. *A Century of Names.* 1663.

Wotton, Sir Henry. *The Elements of Architecture.* 1624.

Wren, Christopher. *Parentalia: Or, Memoirs of the Family of the Wrens.* 1750.

Wycherley, William. *The Country Wife.* 1675.

  The Gentleman Dancing-Master. 1673.

  Love in a Wood. 1670.

[Yolkney, Walter.] *The Entertainment of the Lady Monk, at Fishers-Folly.* 1660.

SECONDARY SOURCES

Adams, Bernard. *London Illustrated 1604–1851.* London: Oryx Press, 1983.

Alkon, Paul. *Defoe and Fictional Time.* Athens: University of Georgia Press, 1979.

Allen, Beverly Sprague. *Tides in English Taste.* 2 vols. Cambridge, MA: Harvard University Press, 1937.

Altick, Richard. *The Shows of London.* Cambridge, MA: Belknap Press of Harvard University Press, 1978.

Archer, Ian W. "John Stow's *A Survey of London.*" *The Theatrical City.* Ed. David Smith, Richard Strier, and David Bevington. Cambridge: Cambridge University Press, 1995.

  The Pursuit of Stability: Social Relations in Elizabethan London. Cambridge: Cambridge University Press, 1991.

Archer, John. "Character in English Architectural Design." *Eighteenth-Century Studies* 12, no. 3 (Spring 1979): 339–71.

Armstrong, Nancy. *Desire and Domestic Fiction.* Oxford: Oxford University Press, 1987.

Aubin, Robert Arnold. *London in Flames, London in Glory: Poems on the Fire and Rebuilding of London 1666–1709*. New Brunswick: Rutgers University Press, 1943.

Avery, Emmet L. and Arthur H. Scouten. *The London Stage: 1660–1800*. Part 1. Ed. William Van Lennep. Carbondale, IL: Southern Illinois University Press, 1965.

Bachelard, Gaston. *The Poetics of Space*. Trans. Maria Jolas. Paris: Presses Universitaires de France, 1958; Boston: Beacon Press, 1969.

Backscheider, Paula. *Daniel Defoe: Ambition and Innovation*. Lexington: The University Press of Kentucky, 1986.

    Daniel Defoe: His Life. Baltimore: Johns Hopkins University Press, 1989.

    "Defoe and the Geography of the Mind." *The First English Novelists: Essays in Understanding*. Ed. J. M. Armistead. Knoxville: The University of Tennessee Press, 1985.

Bagrow, Leo. *History of Cartography*. Revised and enlarged by R. A. Skelton. London: C. A. Watts and Co. Ltd., 1964.

Baker, Ernest A. *The History of the English Novel*. Vol. III. London: H. F. and G. Witherby, 1929.

Ballaster, Rosalind. *Seductive Forms: Women's Amatory Fiction from 1684 to 1740*. Oxford: Clarendon Press, 1992.

Barber, Peter. "England II: Monarchs, Ministers and Maps, 1550–1625." *Monarchs, Ministers and Maps: The Emergence of Cartography as a Tool of Government in Early Modern Europe*. Ed. David Buisseret. Chicago: University of Chicago Press, 1992.

Barker, Felix, and Peter Jackson. *The History of London in Maps*. London: Barrie and Jenkins, 1990.

Barley, Maurice. *Houses and History*. London: Faber and Faber, 1986.

Bartel, Roland. *Johnson's London*. Boston: D. C. Heath and Company, 1956.

Barton, Anne. "London Comedy and the Ethos of the City." *The London Journal* 4:2 (1978): 158–80.

Bastian, F. *Defoe's Early Life*. Totowa, NJ: Barnes and Noble, 1981.

    "Defoe's *Journal of the Plague Year* Reconsidered." *Review of English Studies* 16 (1965): 151–73.

Battestin, Martin, with Ruthe Battestin. *Henry Fielding: A Life*. London: Routledge, 1989.

    The Providence of Wit: Aspects of Form in Augustan Literature and the Arts. Oxford: Clarendon Press, 1974.

Bayne-Powell, Rosamond. *Eighteenth-Century London Life*. New York: E. P. Dutton, 1938.

Bedford, John. *London's Burning*. New York: Abelard-Schuman, 1966.

Beier, A. L., and Roger Finlay, eds. *London 1500–1700: The Making of the Metropolis*. London: Longman, 1986.

Bell, Ian A. *Literature and Crime in Augustan England*. London: Routledge, 1991.

Bell, Walter George. *The Great Fire of London in 1666*. London: John Lane, The Bodley Head, 1920.

Bender, John. *Imagining the Penitentiary: Fiction and the Architecture of Mind in Eighteenth-Century England*. Chicago: University of Chicago Press, 1987.

Berne, Eric. "The Psychological Structure of Space with Some Remarks on *Robinson Crusoe*." *Psychoanalytic Quarterly* 25 (1956): 549–67.

Besant, Sir Walter. *London in the Eighteenth Century*. London: Black, 1903.

    London in the Time of the Stuarts. London: Black, 1903.

Birdsall, Virginia Ogden. *Defoe's Perpetual Seekers: A Study of the Major Fiction*. Lewisburg: Bucknell University Press, 1985.

Blewett, David. *Defoe's Art of Fiction*. Toronto: University of Toronto Press, 1979.

Blunt, Anthony. *Art and Architecture in France 1500–1700*. 4th edn. Harmondsworth: Penguin, 1983.

Boardman, Michael. *Defoe and the Uses of Narrative*. New Brunswick: Rutgers University Press, 1983.

Bogorod, Samuel N. "Milton's 'Paradise Lost' and Gay's 'Trivia': A Borrowing." *Notes and Queries* 195, no. 5 (March 4, 1950): 98–99.

Borsay, Peter, ed. *The Eighteenth-Century Town: A Reader in English Urban History 1688–1820*. London: Longman, 1990.

Boulton, Jeremy. *Neighbourhood and Society: A London Suburb in the Seventeenth Century*. Cambridge: Cambridge University Press, 1987.

Bowers, Terence. "The Nation Imagined: Defoe's *Tour thro' the Whole Island of Great Britain*." Unpublished conference paper, Kansas City, MWASECS 1991.

Bowers, Toni O'Shaughnessy. "Sex, Lies, and Invisibility: Amatory Fiction from the Restoration to Mid-Century." *The Columbia History of the British Novel*. Ed. John Richetti. New York: Columbia University Press, 1994.

Bradbrook, Muriel. "The Politics of Pageantry: Social Implications in Jacobean London." *Poetry and Drama 1570–1700: Essays in Honour of Harold F. Brooks*. Ed. Anthony Coleman and Anthony Hammond. London: Methuen, 1981.

Brantlinger, Patrick. *Fictions of State: Culture and Credit in Britain, 1694–1994*. Ithaca: Cornell University Press, 1996.

Braudel, Fernand. *Capitalism and Material Life 1400–1800*. Trans. Miriam Kochan. London: Collins, 1981.

The Structures of Everyday Life. New York: Harper and Row, 1985.

Braudy, Leo. "Daniel Defoe and the Anxieties of Autobiography." *Genre* 6 (1973): 76–97.

Braun, Hugh. *Old English Houses*. London: Faber and Faber, 1962.

Braunfels, Wolfgang. *Urban Design in Western Europe*. Chicago: University of Chicago Press, 1988.

Brett-James, Norman G. *The Growth of Stuart London*. London: London and Middlesex Archaeological Society, 1935.

"London Traffic in the Seventeenth Century." *Nineteenth Century and After*. November 1925.

Brooke, Christopher N. L. and Gillian Keir. *London 800–1216: The Shaping of a City*. Berkeley: University of California Press, 1975.

Brown, Homer O. "The Displaced Self in the Novels of Daniel Defoe." *English Language and History* 38, no. 4 (1971): 562–90.

Brown, Laura. *Alexander Pope*. Oxford: Basil Blackwell, 1985.

Brownell, Morris R. *Alexander Pope and the Arts of Georgian England*. Oxford: Clarendon Press, 1978.

Bruster, Douglas. *Drama and the Market in the Age of Shakespeare*. Cambridge: Cambridge University Press, 1992.

Buck-Morss, Susan. *The Dialectics of Seeing: Walter Benjamin and the Arcades Project*. Cambridge, MA: MIT Press, 1989.

Burgess, C. F. "The Ambivalent Point of View in John Gay's *Trivia*." *Cithara* 4 (1964): 53–65.

Burke, Thomas. *The Streets of London through the Centuries*. London: B. T. Batsford, 1940.

Butt, John. *The Augustan Age*. New York: W. W. Norton, 1965.

Byrd, Max. *London Transformed: Images of the City in the Eighteenth Century*. New Haven: Yale University Press, 1978.

Carnochan, W. B. *Confinement and Flight: An Essay on English Literature of the Eighteenth Century*. Berkeley: University of California Press, 1977.

Carr, David. *Time, Narrative, and History*. Bloomington: Indiana University Press, 1986.

Carter, Harold. *The Study of Urban Geography*. 3rd edn. London: Edward Arnold, 1981.

Castagnoli, F. *Orthogonal Town-Planning in Antiquity*. Cambridge, MA: MIT Press, 1971.

Castan, Nicole. "The Public and the Private." *A History of Private Life*. Ed. Philippe Ariès and Georges Duby. Trans. Arthur Goldhammer. 5 vols. Cambridge, MA: Belknap Press of Harvard University Press, 1989. III: 402–45.

Castle, Terry. " 'Amy, Who Knew My Disease': A Psychosexual Pattern in Defoe's *Roxana*." *English Literature and History* 46 (1979): 81–96.

Masquerade and Civilization. Stanford: Stanford University Press, 1986.

Certeau, Michel de. *The Practice of Everyday Life*. Trans. Steven Rendall. Berkeley: University of California Press, 1984.

Chandler, Eric V. "Pope's Emetic: Bodies, Books, and Filth." *Genre* 27, No. 4 (Winter 1994): 351–76.

Chartier, Roger. "Community, State, and Family: Trajectories and Tensions." *A History of Private Life*. Ed. Philippe Ariès and Georges Duby. Trans. Arthur Goldhammer. 5 vols. Cambridge, MA: Belknap Press of Harvard University Press, 1989. III: 399–401.

Chatterton, Frederick, ed. *Shop Fronts: A Selection of English, American, and Continental Examples*. London: Architectural Press, 1927.

Clifton-Taylor, Alec. *The Pattern of English Building*. London, Faber and Faber, 1972.

Cohen, Murray. *Sensible Words: Linguistic Practice in England 1640–1785*. Baltimore: Johns Hopkins University Press, 1977.

Colley, Linda. *Britons: Forging the Nation 1707–1837*. New Haven: Yale University Press, 1992.

Collins, Peter. *Changing Ideals in Modern Architecture 1750–1950*. London: Faber and Faber, 1965.

Colomb, Gregory. *Designs on Truth: The Poetics of the Augustan Mock-Epic*. University Park, PA: Penn State University Press, 1992.

Colvin, H. M. *A Biographical Dictionary of English Architects 1660–1840*. London: John Murray, 1954.

English Architectural History: A Guide to Sources. London: Pinhorns, 1967, 1976.

Copeland, Edward. "Remapping London: *Clarissa* and the Woman in the Window." *Samuel Richardson: Tercentenary Essays*. Ed. Margaret Anne Doody and Peter Sabor. Cambridge: Cambridge University Press, 1989.

Copley, Stephen. *Literature and the Social Order in Eighteenth-Century England*. London: Croom Helm, 1984.

Cragg, Gerald. *Puritanism in the Period of the Great Persecution 1660–1668*. Cambridge: Cambridge University Press, 1957.

Crown, Patricia. "British Rococo as Social and Political Style." *Eighteenth-Century Studies* 23, no. 3 (Spring 1990): 269–82.

Damrosch, Leopold, Jr. "Defoe as Ambiguous Impersonator." *Modern Philology* 71 (1973–74): 153–59.

Darby, H. C., ed. *An Historical Geography of England before A.D. 1800: Fourteen Studies.* Cambridge: Cambridge University Press, 1936.

Darlington, Ida, and James Howgego. *Printed Maps of London, Circa 1553–1850.* 2nd edn. Folkestone, Eng.: Dawson, 1978.

Darnton, Robert. "A Bourgeois Puts His World in Order: The City as a Text." *The Great Cat Massacre and Other Episodes in French Cultural History.* 1984; rpt. New York: Vintage Books, 1985.

Davie, Donald. *A Gathered Church: The Literature of the English Dissenting Interest, 1700–1930.* New York: Oxford University Press, 1978.

Davis, Lennard. *Factual Fictions: The Origins of the English Novel.* New York: Columbia University Press, 1983.

"'Known Unknown' Locations: Ideology of Novelistic Landscape in *Robinson Crusoe*." *Sociocriticism* 4–5 (1986–87): 87–113.

Resisting Novels: Ideology and Fiction. New York: Methuen, 1987.

Dickson, P. G. M. *The Financial Revolution in England: A Study of the Development of Public Credit 1688–1756.* London: Macmillan, 1967.

Doody, Margaret. *The Daring Muse: Augustan Poetry Reconsidered.* Cambridge: Cambridge University Press, 1985.

Drake, Nathan. *Shakespeare and His Times: Including the Biography of the Poet.* 2 vols. London: T. Cadell and W. Davies, 1817.

Drummond, Andrew. *The Church Architecture of Protestantism: An Historical and Constructive Study.* Edinburgh: T. and T. Clark, 1934.

Duckworth, Alastair. *The Improvement of the Estate: A Study of Jane Austen's Novels.* Baltimore: Johns Hopkins University Press, 1971.

"Jane Austen's Accommodations." *The First English Novelists: Essays in Understanding.* Ed J. M. Armistead. Knoxville: The University of Tennessee Press, 1985.

Dutton, Ralph. *London Homes.* London: Allan Wingate, 1952.

Dyos, H. J. "The Victorian City in Historical Perspective." *Exploring the Urban Past: Essays in Urban History by H. J. Dyos.* Ed. David Cannadine and David Reeder. Cambridge: Cambridge University Press, 1982.

Earle, Peter, *A City Full of People: Men and Women of London 1650–1750.* London: Methuen, 1994.

The World of Defoe. New York: Atheneum, 1977.

Eaves, T. C. Duncan and Ben D. Kimpel. *Samuel Richardson, A Biography.* Oxford: Clarendon Press, 1971.

Eden, Peter. "Three Elizabethan Estate Surveyors: Peter Kempe, Thomas Clerke and Thomas Langdon." *English Map-Making 1500–1650.* Ed. Sarah Tyacke. London: British Library, 1983.

Ekwall, Oskar Eilert. *Street-Names of the City of London.* 1954. Berkeley: University of California Press, 1965.

Ellis, Stewart Marsh. "John Gay and London." *Mainly Victorian.* London: Hutchinson, c.1924.

Evans, Robin. *The Fabrication of Virtue: English Prison Architecture, 1750–1840*. Cambridge: Cambridge University Press, 1982.

Fabricant, Carole. *Swift's Landscapes*. Baltimore: Johns Hopkins University Press, 1982.

Fairfield, Sheila. *The Streets of London: A Dictionary of the Names and their Origins*. London: Macmillan, 1983.

Fastnedge, Ralph. *English Furniture Styles from 1500 to 1830*. Harmondsworth: Penguin, 1955, 1967.

Fisher, John, ed. *A Collection of Early Maps of London 1553–1667*. London: Harry Margary and the Guildhall Library, 1981.

Fisher, Lois H. *A Literary Gazetteer of England*. New York: McGraw-Hill, 1980.

Flanders, W. Austin. "Defoe's *Journal of the Plague Year* and the Modern Urban Experience." *Centennial Review* 16 (1972): 328–48.

Flynn, Carol Houlihan. *The Body in Swift and Defoe*. Cambridge: Cambridge University Press, 1990.

Foisil, Madeleine. "The Literature of Intimacy." *A History of Private Life*. Ed. Roger Chartier. Trans. Arthur Goldhammer. 5 vols. Cambridge, MA: Belknap Press of Harvard University Press, 1989. III: 327–61.

Fordham, Sir Herbert George. *Some Notable Surveyors and Map-Makers of the Sixteenth, Seventeenth, and Eighteenth Centuries and their Work*. Cambridge: Cambridge University Press, 1929.

Foster, Frank Freeman. *The Politics of Stability: A Portrait of the Rulers in Elizabethan London*. London: Royal Historical Society, 1977.

Foucault, Michel. *The Archaeology of Knowledge and the Discourse on Language*. Trans. A. M. Sheridan Smith. 1969. New York: Pantheon Books, 1972.

Discipline and Punish: The Birth of the Prison. Trans. Alan Sheridan. 1975. New York: Vintage Books, 1979.

Madness and Civilization: A History of Insanity in the Age of Reason. Trans. Richard Howard. 1961. New York: Vintage Books, 1965.

The Order of Things: An Archaeology of the Human Sciences. 1966. New York: Vintage Books, 1970.

Power/Knowledge: Selected Interviews and Other Writings 1972–1977. Ed. Colin Gordon. New York: Pantheon Books, 1980.

"Of Other Spaces." *Diacritics* 16, no. 1 (1986): 22–27.

Fowler, Alastair. *The Country House Poem: A Cabinet of Seventeenth-Century Estate Poems and Related Items*. Edinburgh: Edinburgh University Press, 1994.

Kinds of Literature: An Introduction to the Theory of Genres and Modes. Cambridge, MA: Harvard University Press, 1982.

Frank, Ellen Eve. *Literary Architecture*. Berkeley: University of California Press, 1979.

Fuller, Thomas. *The History of the Worthies of England*. Ed. P. Austin Nuttall. 3 vols. London: T. Tegg, 1840.

Furbank, P. N. and W. R. Owens. *The Canonisation of Daniel Defoe*. New Haven: Yale University Press, 1988.

Fussell, Paul. *The Rhetorical World of Augustan Humanism*. Oxford: Clarendon Press, 1965.

George, M. Dorothy. *London Life in the Eighteenth Century*. 1925. New York: Harper and Row, 1964.

Gibson, William A. "Three Principles of Renaissance Architectural Theory in Pope's *Epistle to Burlington*." *Pope: Recent Essays by Several Hands.* Ed. Maynard Mack, James A. Winn. Brighton: The Harvester Press, 1980.

Gibson-Jarvie, Robert. *The City of London: A Financial and Commercial History.* Cambridge: Woodhead-Faulkner, 1979.

Giedion, Sigfried. *Space, Time, and Architecture: The Growth of a New Tradition.* 5th edn. Cambridge, MA: Harvard University Press, 1977.

Gill, Pat. " 'Filth of All Hues and Odors': Public Parks, City Showers, and Promiscuous Acquaintance in Rochester and Swift." *Genre* 27, No. 4 (Winter 1994):333–50.

Gillis, Christina Marsden. *The Paradox of Privacy: Epistolary Form in* Clarissa. Gainesville: University Presses of Florida, 1984.

Girouard, Mark. *Cities and People: A Social and Architectural History.* New Haven: Yale University Press, 1985.

   Life in the English Country House. New Haven: Yale University Press, 1978.

Glanville, Philippa. "The City of London." *Seventeenth-Century Britain: The Cambridge Cultural History.* Ed. Boris Ford. Cambridge: Cambridge University Press, 1989, 1992.

   London in Maps. London: The Connoisseur, 1972.

Godfrey, Walter H. *A History of Architecture in and around London.* London: Phoenix House: 1962.

Gombrich, E. H. *The Sense of Order.* Ithaca: Cornell University Press, 1984.

Gomme, Andor. "Architecture." *Seventeenth-Century Britain: The Cambridge Cultural History.* Ed. Boris Ford. Cambridge: Cambridge University Press, 1989, 1992.

Goulemot, Jean Marie. "Literary Practices: Publicizing the Private." *A History of Private Life.* Ed. Roger Chartier. Trans. Arthur Goldhammer. 5 vols. Cambridge, MA: Belknap Press of Harvard University Press, 1989. III: 363–95.

Grandsen, Antonia. *Historical Writing in England* II: *c. 1307 to the Early Sixteenth Century.* Ithaca: Cornell University Press, 1982.

Gutkind, Erwin Anton. *International History of City Development.* New York: Free Press of Glencoe, 1964.

Habermas, Jürgen. *The Structural Transformation of the Public Sphere: An Inquiry into a Category of Bourgeois Society.* Trans. Thomas Burger. 1961. Cambridge, MA: MIT Press, 1991.

Hagstrum, Jean. *The Sister Arts: The Tradition of Literary Pictorialism and English Poetry from Dryden to Gray.* Chicago: The University of Chicago Press, 1958.

   "Pictures to the Heart: The Psychological Picturesque in Ann Radcliffe's *The Mysteries of Udolpho*." *Greene Centennial Studies.* Ed. Paul J. Korshin and Robert R. Allen. Charlottesville: University Press of Virginia, 1984.

Hale, J. R. *Renaissance Europe 1480–1520.* 2nd edn. Berkeley: University of California Press, 1977.

Handover, P. M. *Printing in London from 1476 to Modern Times.* London: George Allen and Unwin, 1960.

Harben, Henry A. *A Dictionary of London.* London: Herbert Jenkins, 1918.

Harley, J. B. "Meaning and Ambiguity in Tudor Cartography." *English Map-Making 1500–1650.* Ed. Sarah Tyacke. London: British Library, 1983.

Harries, Karsten. "Metaphor and Transcendence." *On Metaphor.* Ed. Sheldon Sacks. Chicago: The University of Chicago Press, 1978, 1979.

Harris, John. *The Palladians*. New York: Rizzoli, 1982.

Harris, Michael. "London Guidebooks before 1800." *Maps and Prints: Aspects of the English Booktrade*. Ed. Robin Meyers and Michael Harris. Oxford: Oxford Polytechnic Press, 1984.

Harris, Tim. *London Crowds in the Reign of Charles II: Propaganda and Politics from the Restoration until the Exclusion Crisis*. Cambridge: Cambridge University Press, 1987.

Harvey, P. D. A. *The History of Topographical Maps: Symbols, Pictures and Surveys*. London: Thames and Hudson, 1980.

Heal, Sir Ambrose. *The Signboards of Old London Shops*. London: Batsford, 1942.

Hearsey, John E. N. *London and the Great Fire*. London: John Murray, 1965.

Heawood, Edward. "John Adams and his Map of England." *The Geographical Journal* 79, no. 1 (January 1932): 37–44.

Hecht, Anthony. "Houses as Metaphors: The Poetry of Architecture." *Obbligati: Essays in Criticism*. New York: Atheneum, 1986.

Heidegger, Martin. "Building Dwelling Thinking." *Basic Writings*. Ed. David Farrell Krell. New York: Harper and Row, 1977.

Helgerson, Richard. *Forms of Nationhood: The Elizabethan Writing of England*. Chicago: University of Chicago Press, 1992.

Herbert, Wray. "Seventeenth-Century Stress." *Psychology Today* 17, no. 10 (October 1983): 4.

Hibbert, Christopher, and Ben Weinreb. *The London Encyclopaedia*. 1983. Rev. edn. London: Papermac, 1993.

Hind, Arthur M. *Wenceslaus Hollar and His Views of London and Windsor in the Seventeenth Century*. London: John Lane, 1922.

Howgego, James. *Printed Maps of London Circa 1553–1850*. 1964. London: Dawson, 1978.

Hunter, J. Paul. *Before Novels: The Cultural Contexts of Eighteenth-Century English Fiction*. New York: W. W. Norton, 1990.

"'News, and New Things': Contemporaneity and the Early English Novel." *Critical Inquiry* 14 (Spring 1988): 493–515.

Occasional Form: Henry Fielding and the Chains of Circumstance. Baltimore: Johns Hopkins University Press, 1975.

The Reluctant Pilgrim: Defoe's Emblematic Method and Quest for Form in Robinson Crusoe. Baltimore: Johns Hopkins University Press, 1966.

"The World as Stage and Closet." *British Theatre and Other Arts*. Ed. Shirley Strum Kenny. Washington: Folger Shakespeare Library, 1984.

"'The Young, the Ignorant, and the Idle': Some Notes on Readers and the Beginnings of the English Novel." *Anticipations of the Enlightenment in England, France, and Germany*. Ed. Alan Charles Kors and Paul J. Korshin. Philadelphia: University of Pennsylvania Press, 1947.

Hyde, J. K. "Medieval Descriptions of Cities." *Bulletin of the John Rylands Library* 48 (1966): 308–40.

Hyde, Ralph, ed. *The A to Z of Restoration London*. London: London Topographical Society, 1992.

Irving, William Henry. *John Gay's London*. Cambridge: Harvard University Press, 1928.

Jameson, Fredric. *The Political Unconscious: Narrative as a Socially Symbolic Act*. Ithaca: Cornell University Press, 1981.

Jesse, J. Heneage. *London: Its Celebrated Characters and Remarkable Places*. London: Richard Bentley, New Burlington Street, 1871–1873. [14] vols.

Jones, Eric. "The Fashion Manipulators: Consumer Tastes and British Industries, 1660–1800." *Business Enterprise and Economic Change*. Ed. Louis P. Cain and Paul J. Uselding. Kent: Kent State University Press, 1973.

Jones, William Powell. *The Rhetoric of Science: A Study of Scientific Ideas and Imagery in Eighteenth-Century English Poetry*. London: Routledge and Kegan Paul, 1966.

Jourdain, Margaret. *English Interior Decoration 1500 to 1830: A Study in the Development of Design*. London: B. T. Batsford, 1950.

   English Interiors in Smaller Houses from the Restoration to the Regency 1660–1830. New York; Charles Scribners, [1923].

Judges, A. V., ed. *The Elizabethan Underworld*. London: George Routledge and Sons, 1930.

Kaufmann, Emil. *Architecture in the Age of Reason: Baroque and Post-Baroque in England, Italy, and France*. 1955. New York: Dover, 1968.

Kent, William, ed. *An Encyclopaedia of London*. London: J. M. Dent and Sons, 1937.

Kernan, Alvin B. *The Plot of Satire*. New Haven: Yale University Press, 1965, 1974.

Kinkead-Weekes, Mark. "Defoe and Richardson: Novelists of the City." *Dryden to Johnson*. Ed. Roger Lonsdale. New York: Peter Bedrick, 1987.

Knapp, Bettina. *Archetype, Architecture, and the Writer*. Bloomington: Indiana University Press, 1986.

Kostof, Spiro. *The City Shaped: Urban Patterns and Meanings Through History*. Boston: Little, Brown and Co., 1991.

Kroll, Richard W. F. *The Material Word: Literate Culture in the Restoration and Early Eighteenth Century*. Baltimore: Johns Hopkins University Press, 1991.

Landa, Louis. "London Observed: The Progress of a Simile." *Essays in Eighteenth-Century English Literature*. Princeton: Princeton University Press, 1980.

Lean, V. S. *Collectanea*. 4 vols. Bristol: J. W. Arrowsmith, 1904.

Lee, William. *Daniel Defoe: His Life, and Recently Discovered Writings*. London: John Camden Hotten, 1869.

Lefebvre, Henri. *The Production of Space*. Trans. Donald Nicholson-Smith. Oxford: Blackwell, 1991.

Lethaby, W. R. "Hollar's Map." *London Topographical Record*. 4th Annual Report. Ed. T. Fairman Ordish. London: London Topographical Society, 1903.

Lillywhite, Bryant. *London Signs*. London: George Allen and Unwin, 1972.

Lindsay, Jack. *The Monster City: Defoe's London, 1688–1730*. London: Hart-Davis, MacGibbon, 1978.

Lipking, Lawrence. *The Ordering of the Arts in Eighteenth-Century England*. Princeton: Princeton University Press, 1970.

London History and Topography. London: Greater London Council History Library, 1939.

Lynch, Kevin. *A Theory of Good City Form*. Cambridge, MA: MIT Press, 1981.

McClung, William A. *The Country House in English Renaissance Poetry*. Berkeley: University of California Press, 1977.

McCorquodale, Charles. *History of the Interior*. New York: Vendome Press, 1983.

McKeon, Michael. *The Origins of the English Novel 1600–1740*. Baltimore: Johns Hopkins University Press, 1987.

McKillop, Alan Dugald. *The Early Masters of English Fiction*. Lawrence: University of Kansas Press, 1956.

McNeil, David. "*A Journal of the Plague Year*: Defoe and Claustrophobia." *Southern Review* 16, no. 3 (November 1983): 374–85.

McVeagh, John. *Tradefull Merchants: The Portrayal of the Capitalist in Literature*. London: Routledge and Kegan Paul, 1981.

Manley, Lawrence. *Literature and Culture in Early Modern London*. Cambridge: Cambridge University Press, 1995.

Mayer, Robert. *History and the Early English Novel*. Cambridge: Cambridge University Press, 1997.

Merleau-Ponty, Maurice. *The Phenomenology of Perception*. Trans. Colin Smith. London: Routledge and Kegan Paul, 1962.

    The Primacy of Perception. Ed. James M. Edie. Evanston: Northwestern University Press, 1964.

    The Prose of the World. Trans. John O'Neill. Ed. Claude Lefort. Evanston: Northwestern University Press, 1973.

Miller, J. Hillis. *Topographies*. Stanford: Stanford University Press, 1995.

Miller, Stuart. *The Picaresque Novel*. Cleveland: Press of Case Western Reserve, 1967.

Moore, John Robert. *Daniel Defoe: Citizen of the Modern World*. Chicago: The University of Chicago Press, 1958.

Moreland, Carl, and David Bannister. *Antique Maps*. 3rd edn. London: Longman, 1983; Phaidon Press, 1989, 1993.

Morris, A. E. J. *History of Urban Form: Before the Industrial Revolution*. 2nd edn. New York: Wiley, 1979.

Mumford, Lewis. *The City in History: Its Origins, Its Transformations, and Its Prospects*. New York: Harcourt, Brace, and Jovanovich, 1961.

Nicholson, Colin. *Writing and the Rise of Finance: Capital Satires of the Early Eighteenth Century*. Cambridge: Cambridge University Press, 1994.

Nicoll, Allardyce. *A History of Restoration Drama 1660–1700*. 2nd edn. Cambridge: Cambridge University Press, 1928.

Norman, Philip. *London Signs and Inscriptions*. London: Elliot Stock, 1893.

Novak, Maximilian. "Defoe and the Disordered City." *PMLA* 92, no. 2 (March 1977): 241–52.

    Defoe and the Nature of Man. Oxford: Oxford University Press, 1963.

    "Defoe's Use of Irony." *The Uses of Irony: Papers on Defoe and Swift*. Los Angeles: William Andrews Clark Memorial Library, 1966.

Novak, Maxmilian, ed. *English Literature in the Age of Disguise*. Berkeley: University of California Press, 1977.

    Realism, Myth, and History in Defoe's Fiction. Lincoln: University of Nebraska Press, 1983.

    "Shaping the Augustan Myth: John Dryden and the Politics of Restoration Augustanism." *Greene Centennial Studies: Essays Presented to Donald Greene in the Centennial Year of the University of Southern California*. Ed. Paul J. Korshin and Robert R. Allen. Charlottesville: University Press of Virginia, 1984.

O'Brien, John F. "The Character of Credit: Defoe's 'Lady Credit,' *The Fortunate Mistress*, and the Resources of Inconsistency in Early Eighteenth-Century Britain." *ELH* 63, no. 3 (1996): 603–31.

Olsen, Donald J. *Town Planning in London: The Eighteenth and Nineteenth Centuries.* 1964. 2nd edn. New Haven: Yale University Press, 1982.

Passingham, William J. *London's Markets: Their Origin and History.* London: Samson Low, Marston, 1935.

Paulson, Ronald. *Popular and Polite Art in the Age of Hogarth and Fielding.* Notre Dame, IN: University of Notre Dame Press, 1979.

Pearl, Valerie. "Change and Stability in Seventeenth-Century London," *The London Journal* 5 (1979).

Peterson, Richard S. *Imitation and Praise in the Poems of Ben Jonson.* New Haven: Yale University Press, 1981.

Peterson, Spiro. "Defoe and Westminster 1696–1706." *Eighteenth-Century Studies* 12, no. 3 (Spring 1979): 306–38.

Pevsner, Nicholas. "The Architectural Setting of Jane Austen's Novels." *Journal of the Warburg and Courtauld Institutes.* Vol. 31. London: The Warburg Institute, 1968.

Pincus, Steven. "'Coffee Politicians Does Create': Coffeehouses and Restoration Political Culture." *The Journal of Modern History* 67 (December 1995): 807–834.

Pinkus, Philip. *Grub Street Stripped Bare.* London: Constable, 1968.

Pocock, J. G. A. *Virtue, Commerce, and History.* Cambridge: Cambridge University Press, 1985.

Porter, Roy. *London: A Social History.* Cambridge, MA: Harvard University Press, 1995.

Power, M. J. "The Social Topography of Restoration London." *London 1500–1700: The Making of the Metropolis.* Ed. A. L. Beier and Roger Finlay. London: Longman, 1986: 199–223.

Price, F. G. Hilton. "Signs of Old London." *London Topographical Record.* Vol. 4. London: London Topographical Society, 1903.

"Signs of Old London." *London Topographical Record.* Vol. 7. London: London Topographical Society, 1907.

Price, Martin. *To the Palace of Wisdom: Studies in Order and Energy from Dryden to Blake.* Garden City, NY: Doubleday, 1964.

Priestley, Harold. *London: The Years of Change.* London: Frederick Muller, 1966.

Pritchett, V. S. and Evelyn Hofer. *London Perceived.* London: Chatto and Windus, 1962.

Quennell, Marjorie and C. H. B. Quennell. *A History of Everyday Things in England, 1066–1799.* London: B. T. Batsford, 1957.

Rappaport, Steven. "Social Structure and Mobility in Sixteenth-Century London: Part 1." *The London Journal* 9 (1983).

Rasmussen, Steen. *London: The Unique City.* London: Jonathan Cape, 1937.

Reddaway, T. F. "London 1666: Fire and Rebuilding." Stevenson Lecture. London: Bedford College, 1965.

The Rebuilding of London after the Great Fire. 1940. London: Edward Arnold, 1951.

Rice, Matthew. *Traditional Houses of Rural Britain.* New York: Cross River Press, 1991.

Richardson, A. E. *Introduction to Georgian Architecture.* London: Art and Technics, 1949.

Richardson, A. E., and C. Lovett Gill. *London Houses from 1660 to 1820: A Consideration of their Architecture and Detail.* London: B. T. Batsford, 1911.

Richetti, John. *Defoe's Narratives: Situations and Structures*. Oxford: Clarendon Press, 1975.
  Popular Fiction Before Richardson. Oxford: Clarendon Press, 1969, 1992.

Ricoeur, Paul. *Time and Narrative*. Vol. III. 1985. Trans. Kathleen Blamey and David
  Pellauer. Chicago: The University of Chicago Press, 1988.

Riley, H. T., ed. *The White Book of the City of London*. London: Camden Society, 1862.

Robinson, A. H. and B. B. Petchenik. *The Nature of Maps: Essays toward Understanding Maps
  and Mapping*. Chicago: University of Chicago Press, 1976.

Rogers, Pat. "Crusoe's Home." *Essays in Criticism* 24 (1974): 375–90.

Rogers, Pat, ed. *Defoe: The Critical Heritage*. London: Routledge and Kegan Paul, 1972.
  Grub Street: Studies in a Subculture. London: Methuen, 1972.
  Hacks and Dunces: Pope, Swift, and Grub Street. London: Methuen, 1980.
  "Literary Art in Defoe's *Tour*: The Rhetoric of Growth and Decay." *Eighteenth-Century
  Studies* 6, no. 2 (Winter 1972–73): 153–85.
  Literature and Popular Culture in Eighteenth-Century England. Sussex: Harvester Press, 1985.
  Robinson Crusoe. London: George Allen and Unwin, 1979.

Rubinstein, Stanley. *Historians of London: An account of the many Surveys, Histories, Perambulations,
  Maps and Engravings made about the City and its Environs, and of the dedicated Londoners who made
  them*. Hamden, CT: Archon Books, 1968.

Rudé, George. *Hanoverian London 1714–1808*. Berkeley: University of California Press, 1971.
  Paris and London in the Eighteenth Century: Studies in Popular Protest. London: Collins, 1970.

Sack, Robert. *Human Territoriality*. Cambridge: Cambridge University Press, 1986.

Said, Edward. *Culture and Imperialism*. New York: Vintage, 1993.

Saisselin, R. G. "Neo-Classicism: Images of Public Virtue and Realities of Private
  Luxury." *Art History* 4 (March 1981): 14–36.

Sale, William M., Jr. *Samuel Richardson: A Bibliographical Record of His Literary Career with
  Historical Notes*. New Haven: Yale University Press, 1936.
  Samuel Richardson, Master Printer. Ithaca: Cornell University Press, 1950.

Schofield, John. *The Building of London from the Conquest to the Great Fire*. London: British
  Museum Publications and Museum of London, 1984.
  "Ralph Treswell's Surveys of London Houses c.1612." *English Map-Making 1500–1650*.
  Ed. Sarah Tyacke. London: British Library, 1983.

Schonhorn, Manuel. "Defoe's *Journal of the Plague Year*: Topography and Intention." *Review
  of English Studies* 19 (1968): 387–402.

Scott, Geoffrey. *The Architecture of Humanism: A Study in the History of Taste*. 2nd edn. New
  York: Charles Scribner's Sons, 1969.

Secord, Arthur. "Defoe in Stoke Newington." *PMLA* 66, no. 2 (March 1951): 211–25.

Seidel, Michael. "Crusoe in Exile." *PMLA* 96, no. 3 (May 1981): 363–74.

Sennett, Richard, ed. *Classic Essays on the Culture of Cities*. New York: Appleton-Century-
  Crofts, 1969.
  Flesh and Stone: The Body and the City in Western Civilization. New York: W. W. Norton, 1994.

Shapiro, Barbara. *Probability and Certainty in Seventeenth-Century England: A Study of the
  Relationships between Natural Science, Religion, History, Law, and Literature*. Princeton:
  Princeton University Press, 1983.

Sharpe, Kevin, and Steven N. Zwicker, eds. *Politics of Discourse: The Literature and History of
  Seventeenth-Century England*. Berkeley: University of California Press, 1987.

Sherbo, Arthur. "Virgil, Dryden, Gay, and Matters Trivial." *PMLA* 85 (October 1970), 1063–71.

Shinagel, Michael. *Daniel Defoe and Middle-Class Gentility*. Cambridge, MA: Harvard University Press, 1968.

Sill, Geoffrey M. "Defoe's *Tour*: Literary Art or Moral Imperative?" *Eighteenth-Century Studies* 11, no. 1 (Fall 1977): 79–83.

Skelton, R. A. *Maps: A Historical Survey of their Study and Collecting*. Chicago: University of Chicago Press, 1972.

Slack, Paul. "Metropolitan Government in Crisis: The Response to the Plague." *London 1500–1700: The Making of the Metropolis*. Ed. A. L. Beier and Roger Finlay. London: Longman, 1986.

English Towns in Transition. Oxford: Oxford University Press, 1976.

Smith, David. *Antique Maps of the British Isles*. London: B. T. Batsford, 1982.

Soja, Edward. *Postmodern Geographies: The Reassertion of Space in Critical Social Theory*. London: Verso, 1989.

Spacks, Patricia Meyer. *Desire and Truth: Functions of Plot in Eighteenth-Century English Novels*. Chicago: The University of Chicago Press, 1990.

John Gay. New York: Twayne Publishers, 1965.

Stallybrass, Peter, and Allon White. *The Politics and Poetics of Transgression*. Ithaca: Cornell University Press, 1986.

Starr, George A. *Defoe and Spiritual Autobiography*. Princeton: Princeton University Press, 1965.

Staves, Susan. *Married Women's Separate Property in England, 1660–1833*. Cambridge, MA: Harvard University Press, 1990.

Steinberg, S. H. *Five Hundred Years of Printing*. Harmondsworth: Penguin, 1955, 1961.

Stone, Lawrence. *The Crisis of the Aristocracy, 1588–1641*. Oxford: Clarendon Press, 1965.

The Family, Sex, and Marriage in England 1500–1800. London: Weidenfeld and Nicolson, 1977.

The Family, Sex, and Marriage in England 1500–1800. Abridged edition. New York: Harper and Row, 1977, 1979.

"The Residential Development of the West End of London in the Seventeenth Century." *After the Reformation: Essays in Honor of J. H. Hexter*. Ed. Barbara C. Malament. Philadelphia: University of Pennsylvania Press, 1980.

Summerson, Sir John. *Architecture in Britain, 1530–1830*. London: Penguin, 1953.

The Architecture of the Eighteenth Century. London: Thames and Hudson, 1969, 1986.

Georgian London. 1945. Harmondsworth: Penguin, 1978, 1986.

"The Tyranny of Intellect: A Study of the Mind of Sir Christopher Wren." *RIBA Journal*, February 20, 1937.

Sutherland, James. *Daniel Defoe: A Critical Study*. Cambridge, MA: Harvard University Press, 1971.

Defoe. Philadelphia: J. B. Lippincott, 1938.

"Some Early Troubles of Daniel Defoe." *Review of English Studies* 9 (1933): 275–90.

Sykes, Christopher Simon. *Private Palaces: Life in the Great London Houses*. London: Chatto and Windus, 1985.

Tames, Richard. *A Traveller's History of London*. Gloucestershire: The Windrush Press, 1992.

Thornton, Peter. *Authentic Decor: The Domestic Interior 1620–1920*. New York: Viking, 1984.

Tilley, M. P. *A Dictionary of the Proverbs in England in the Sixteenth and Seventeenth Centuries*. Ann Arbor: University of Michigan Press, 1950.

Trickett, Rachel. "'Curious Eye': Some Aspects of Visual Description in Eighteenth-Century Literature." *Augustan Studies: Essays in Honor of Irvin Ehrenpreis*. Ed. Douglas Lane Patey and Timothy Keegan. Newark: University of Delaware Press, 1985.

Tristram, Philippa. *Living Space in Fact and Fiction*. London: Routledge, 1989.

Trotter, David. *Circulation: Defoe, Dickens, and the Economies of the Novel*. London: Macmillan, 1988.

Tuan, Yi-Fu. *Topophilia: A Study of Environmental Perception, Attitudes, and Values*. Englewood Cliffs, NJ: Prentice-Hall, 1974.

Turner, G. L' E. "Mathematical Instrument-making in London in the Sixteenth Century." *English Map-Making 1500–1650*. Ed. Sarah Tyacke. London: British Library, 1983.

Turnor, Reginald. *The Smaller English House 1500–1939*. London: B. T. Batsford, 1952.

Tyacke, Sarah. "Introduction." *English Map-Making 1500–1650*. Ed. Sarah Tyacke. London: British Library, 1983.

"Map-sellers and the London Map Trade c. 1650–1710." *My Head is a Map*. Ed. Helen Wallis and Sarah Tyacke. London: Francis Edwards and Carta Press, 1973.

Van Ghent, Dorothy. *The English Novel: Form and Function*. New York: Harper and Row, 1953.

Vance, J. E., Jr. "Land Assignment in the Pre-capitalist, Capitalist, and Post-capitalist City." *Economic Geography* 47, no. 2 (April 1971): 101–20.

Varey, Simon. *Space and the Eighteenth-Century English Novel*. Cambridge: Cambridge University Press, 1990.

Vernay, Arthur Stannard. *Decorations and English Interiors*. New York: William Helburn, 1927.

Vidler, Anthony. *The Writing of the Walls: Architectural Theory in the Late Enlightenment*. Princeton: Princeton Architectural Press, 1987.

Wall, Cynthia. "Gendering Rooms: Domestic Architecture and Literary Acts." *Eighteenth-Century Fiction* 5, no. 4 (July 1992): 349–72.

"Housing Defoe's Projects: The Rebuilding of London and Modern Literary Space." Unpublished dissertation. The University of Chicago, 1992.

Wallace, Anne D. *Walking, Literature, and English Culture: The Origins and Uses of Peripatetic in the Nineteenth Century*. Oxford: Clarendon Press, 1993.

Wallis, Helen M. "Geographie is Better than Divinitie. Maps, Globes, and Geography in the Days of Samuel Pepys." *The Compleat Plattmaker: Essays on Chart, Map, and Globe Making in England in the Seventeenth and Eighteenth Centuries*. Ed. Norman J. W. Thrower. Berkeley: University of California Press, 1978.

Watkin, David. *English Architecture: A Concise History*. London: Thames and Hudson, 1987.

The English Vision: The Picturesque in Architecture, Landscape, and Garden Design. New York: Harper and Row, 1982.

The Rise of Architectural History. Chicago: The University of Chicago Press, 1983.

Watt, Ian. *The Rise of the Novel: Studies in Defoe, Richardson, and Fielding*. Berkeley: University of California Press, 1957.

Wayne, Don E. *Penshurst: The Semiotics of Place and the Poetics of History*. Madison: University of Wisconsin Press, 1984.

Weaver, Paul S. *Wallington's World: A Puritan Artisan in Seventeenth-Century London*. London: Methuen, 1985.

Weinreb, Ben, and Christopher Hibbert, eds. *The London Encyclopaedia*. London: Papermac, 1983.

Welch, Charles. *The History of the Monument*. 6th edn. London: City Lands Committee of the Corporation of London, 1921.

Wells, Susan. "Jacobean City Comedy and the Ideology of the City." *ELH* 48:1 (1981): 37–60.

Wheatley, Henry B. "Notes upon Norden and His Map of London, 1593." *London Topographical Record*. Vol. 4. London: London Topographical Society, 1903.

Whiting, C. E. *Studies in English Puritanism from the Restoration to the Revolution, 1660–1688*. London: Society for Promoting Christian Knowledge, 1931.

Wilford, John Noble. *The Mapmakers*. New York: Vintage Books, 1981, 1982.

Williams, Aubrey. *Pope's Dunciad: A Study of its Meaning*. London: Methuen, 1955.

Williams, Raymond. *The Country and the City*. London: Chatto and Windus, 1973.

Wilson, A. N., ed. *The Norton Book of London*. New York: W. W. Norton, 1993.

Wilson, Walter. *The History and Antiquities of Dissenting Churches and Meeting Houses, in London, Westminster, and Southwark*. 4 vols. (London, 1808).

Wittkower, Rudolf. *Palladio and Palladianism*. New York; George Braziller, 1974.

Woodward, David A. "English Cartography, 1650–1750: A Summary." *The Compleat Plattmaker: Essays on Chart, Map, and Globe Making in England in the Seventeenth and Eighteenth Centuries*. Ed. Norman J. W. Thrower. Berkeley: University of California Press, 1978.

Wrigley, E. Anthony. "A Simple Model of London's Importance in Changing English Society and Economy 1650–1750." *Towns in Societies: Essays in Economic History and Historical Sociology*. Ed. Philip Abrams and E. A. Wrigley. Cambridge: Cambridge University Press, 1978.

"Urban Growth and Agricultural Change." *The Eighteenth-Century Town: A Reader in English Urban History 1688–1820*. Ed. Peter Borsay. London: Longman, 1990.

Young, Elizabeth and Wayland. *Old London Churches*. London: Faber and Faber, 1956.

Zimmerman, Everett. *Boundaries of Fiction*. Ithaca: Cornell University Press, 1996.

Defoe and the Novel. Berkeley: University of California Press, 1975.

Index

London, (cont.)
110; Ratcliffe, 174; Redriff, 174; Shadwell, 14; Shooter's Hill, 154; Stoke Newington, 194; Wapping, 174; theaters: history of, 151–2, 235n4; Covent Garden, 127; Dorset Garden, 152; Gibbon's Tennis Court, 151; Haymarket, 127; Lincoln's Inn Fields, 127, 151–2, 151, 163; Theatre Royal, 152; wards: Castle Baynard, 105; Cheap, 99; Cripplegate, 101; Farringdon, 99, 105; Queenhithe, 105

London, rebuilding, 39–63; committees overseeing, 53; economics of, 39; legal issues of, 56–9, 65; poems of, 71–3, see also genre; practicalities of, 39; plans of, 40; progress of, 53

London, streets (etc.): Acton Road, 91; Addle Street, 101; Aldermanbury, 12, 101, 105; Aldersgate, 12, 47, 136; Aldersgate Street, 8; Aldgate, 36, 47, 137; "Anniseed Cleer" [Agnes St. Clare?], 24, 110, 142; Arundel Street, 133; Ave Maria Lane, 99, 122; Barbican, 125, 126; Bartholomew Close, 144, 145; Bartholomew Lane, 12; Basinghall Street, 8, 12, 56; Baynard's Castle, 12, 101; Beech Lane, 100; Billingsgate Street, 12, 115, 140, 144, 174; Birchin Lane, 135, 234n35; Bishopsgate, 47, 138, 188; Bishopsgate Street, 12, 36, 110, 187; Blackfriars, 12, 158; Blackwall, 158; Bloomsbury, 66, 91; Bow Lane, 136; Bow Street, 157; Bread Street, 12, 57, 101,

121, 124; Brentford Road, 91; Bridges Street, 151, 157; Broad Street, 36, 68, 154, 187; Bucklersbury, 100; Budge Row, 89; Burchover Lane [Birchin?], 101; Bunhill Fields, 126; Cannon Street, 8, 12, 34; Chancery Lane, 128; Charing Cross, 158; Charterhouse Lane, 144; Charterhouse Yard, 144, 145; Cheapside, 5, 12, 42, 51, 56, 99, 120, 133, 135, 137, 154, 168, 174; Chick Lane, 14, 145; Clare Market, 151; Clerkenwell, 142; Coldharbour, 12; Coleman Street, 8, 12; Cornhill, 12, 51, 67, 89, 138, 174; Covent Garden, 14, 52, 136, 140, 151, 157, 159–61, 160, 163, 164, 165; Crabtree Fields, 231n45; Creed Lane, 122; Cripplegate, 12, 100; Crutched Friars, 36, 68; Deptford, 110; Doctors' Commons, 12, 140; Dog Row, 110; Drapers' Gardens, 138, 139; Drury Lane, 133, 157, 159; Dunghill Lane, 125; Eastcheap, 9, 12, 135, 174; Exchange Alley, 89; Farthing Pye House Field, 24, 110, 142; Fenchurch Street, 8, 12, 110, 115, 143; Field Lane, 145; Fish Street, 98–9, 103, 118, 154, 155; Fish Street Hill, 9, 12; Fleet Ditch, 55, 125, 128; Fleet Street, 11, 26, 34, 35, 69, 118, 128, 133, 138, 163; Foster Lane, 12, 99, 105, 136, 175, 177; Friday Street, 12, 125; Golden Lane, 100; Gracechurch Street, 8, 12, 141, 168, 174; Gray's Inn Walks, 157; Great Wild Street, 157; Grub Street,

100, 105, 127, 231n46; Gutherons Lane (Gutter Lane), 100; Hand Alley, 187; Haymarket, 166; Highgate, 11; Hog Lane, 24, 110, 142; Holborn Bridge, 8, 35, 68, 84, 145; Holborn Fields, 231n45; Holborn Street, 8, 14, 136; Holloway Lane, 24, 110, 142; Hyde Park Corner, 91; Ivy Lane, 3, 56, 66, 99; King's Square, see Soho Square; King Streets (15 of them), 106; Lad Lane, 101; Lamb's Conduit Fields, 157; Leadenhall Street, 36, 110, 168; Lime Street, 12, 84, 110; Lincoln's Inn Fields, 19, 135, 138, 140, 163; Little Britain, 144; Little St. Helen's, 188; Lombard Street, 12, 34, 36, 67, 68, 137, 138, 139, 164; London Bridge, 63, 100, 121; London Wall, 10, 110, 138; Long Alley, 24, 110, 142; Long Lane, 138, 144, 158; Longacre, 157; Lothbury, 12; Love Lane, 3, 68, 101, 105, 118; Ludgate, 28, 35, 47, 67, 128, 129, 136, 158, 164, 174; Ludgate Hill, 11, 26, 34; Mark Lane, 8, 12, 67, 69; Marylebone Road, 91; Middle Row, 118, 119; Mile End, 110; Milk Street, 12, 101; Mincing Lane, 8, 12; Monmouth Street, 132; the Monument, 73, 74, 75, 86, 126, 222n28, 226n43; Moorfields, 6, 9, 10, 12, 19, 30, 31–2, 105, 110, 132, 135, 138, 154, 164, 233n34; Moorgate, 12, 47, 158; Mugwell Street, 105, 187; Mustard Alley, 164; New Canal, 86; New Fish Street, 8, 222n19; Newgate Street, 11, 26, 34, 35, 144, 168; Oat